MASS ATROCITIES AND THE POLICE

MASS ATROCITIES AND THE POLICE

A New History of Ethnic Cleansing in Bosnia and Herzegovina

Christian Axboe Nielsen

BLOOMSBURY ACADEMIC
LONDON • NEW YORK • OXFORD • NEW DELHI • SYDNEY

BLOOMSBURY ACADEMIC
Bloomsbury Publishing Plc
50 Bedford Square, London, WC1B 3DP, UK
1385 Broadway, New York, NY 10018, USA
29 Earlsfort Terrace, Dublin 2, Ireland

BLOOMSBURY, BLOOMSBURY ACADEMIC and the Diana logo are trademarks of
Bloomsbury Publishing Plc

First published in Great Britain 2024

Copyright © Christian Axboe Nielsen, 2022

Christian Axboe Nielsen has asserted his right under the Copyright,
Designs and Patents Act, 1988, to be identified as Author of this work.

Cover design by Adriana Brioso
Cover background © Maxim Gertsen / Alamy Stock Vector

All rights reserved. No part of this publication may be reproduced or transmitted
in any form or by any means, electronic or mechanical, including photocopying,
recording, or any information storage or retrieval system, without prior
permission in writing from the publishers.

Bloomsbury Publishing Plc does not have any control over, or responsibility for,
any third-party websites referred to or in this book. All internet addresses given
in this book were correct at the time of going to press. The author and publisher
regret any inconvenience caused if addresses have changed or sites have ceased
to exist, but can accept no responsibility for any such changes.

A catalogue record for this book is available from the British Library.

A catalog record for this book is available from the Library of Congress.

ISBN:	HB:	978-1-7883-1525-8
	PB:	978-1-3502-0455-3
	ePDF:	978-1-3502-0456-0
	eBook:	978-1-3502-0457-7

Typeset by Integra Software Services Pvt. Ltd.

To find out more about our authors and books visit www.bloomsbury.com
and sign up for our newsletters.

CONTENTS

List of Acronyms	vi
Preface	viii
Introduction	1

Chapter 1
FROM ELECTIONS TO WAR: THE POLICE AND THE PURPOSEFUL
DESTRUCTION OF BOSNIA (NOVEMBER 1990–MARCH 1992)   11

Chapter 2
THE POLICE AND THE FORCIBLE SEIZURE OF POWER
(APRIL AND MAY 1992)   51

Chapter 3
SEARCH, DETAIN, DESTROY: ETHNIC CLEANSING, EXPULSIONS
AND POLICE CONCENTRATION CAMPS (APRIL–DECEMBER 1992)   73

Chapter 4
OF RED BERETS AND PLAUSIBLE DENIABILITY: SERBIA'S SUPPORT
FOR THE RS MUP   117

Chapter 5
THE BOSNIAN SERB POLICE, ONGOING ETHNIC CLEANSING
AND GENOCIDE IN SREBRENICA, 1993–5   135

Epilogue and Conclusion
THE BOSNIAN SERB POLICE AND NEGATIVE PEACE IN DAYTON BOSNIA   149

Notes	162
Bibliography	222
Index	228

ACRONYMS

ABiH	*Armija Bosne i Hercegovine* (Army of Bosnia and Herzegovina)
AOR	Area of Responsibility
ARK	*Autonomna regija Krajina* (Autonomous Region of Krajina)
BCS	Bosnian/Croatian/Serbian
BiH	*Bosna i Hercegovina* (Bosnia and Herzegovina)
CSB	*Centar službi bezbjednosti* (Security Services Centre)
DPA	Dayton Peace Agreement
DSZ	*Društvena samozaštita* (Social Self-Protection)
EC	European Community
HDZ	*Hrvatska demokratska zajednica* (Croat Democratic Union)
HOS	*Hrvatske oružane snage* (Croatian Armed Forces)
HRB	*Hrvatsko revolucionarno bratstvo* (Croatian Revolutionary Brotherhood)
HVO	*Hrvatsko vijeće obrane* (Croatian Defence Council)
ICTY	International Criminal Tribunal for the Former Yugoslavia
JATD	*Jedinica za antiteroristička dejstva* (Unit for Anti-Terrorist Actions)
JNA	*Jugoslovenska narodna armija* (Yugoslav People's Army)
JPN	*Jedinica za specijalne nam[j]ene* (Unit for Special Purposes)
JSO	*Jedinica za specijalne operacije* (Unit for Special Operations)
KOS	*Kontraobaveštajna služba* (Counterintelligence Service)
KPJ	*Komunistička partija Jugoslavije* (Communist Party of Yugoslavia)
LRT	Leadership Research Team
MUP	*Ministarstvo unutrašnjih poslova* (Ministry of Internal Affairs)
ONO	*Opštenarodna odbrana* (All People's Defence)
OSUP	*Opštinski sekretarijati za unutrašnje poslove* (Municipal Secretariats of Internal Affairs)
OTP	Office of the Prosecutor
PSUP	*Pokrajinski sekretarijat za unutrašnje poslove* (Provincial Secretariat for Internal Affairs)
RDB	*Resor državne bezbednosti* (Division of State Security)
RH	*Republika Hrvatska* (Republic of Croatia)
RS	*Republika Srpska*
RSK	*Republika Srpska Krajina*

SČP	*Srpski četnički pokret* (Serb Chetnik Movement)
SDA	*Stranka demokratske akcije* (Party of Democratic Action)
SDB	*Služba državne bezb(j)ednosti* (State Security Service)
SDS	*Srpska demokratska stranka* (Serb Democratic Party)
SFRJ	*Socijalistička Federativna Republika Jugoslavija* (Socialist Federal Republic of Yugoslavia)
SJB	*Služba javne bezb(j)ednosti* (Public Security Service)
SJS	*Služba javne sigurnosti* (Public Security Service – Croatia)
SKBiH	*Savez komunista Bosne i Hercegovine* (League of Communists of Bosnia and Herzegovina)
SKH	*Savez komunista Hrvatske* (League of Communists of Croatia)
SKJ	*Savez komunista Jugoslavije* (League of Communists of Yugoslavia)
SNB	*Služba nacionalne bezbjednosti* (National Security Service)
SNSD	*Stranka nezavisnih socijaldemokrata* (Party of Independent Social Democrats)
SOS	*Srpske odbrambene snage* (Serb Defence Forces)
SPO	*Srpski pokret obnove* (Serb Movement of Renewal)
SRBiH	*Socijalistička Republika Bosna i Hercegovina* (Socialist Republic of Bosnia and Herzegovina)
SRH	*Socijalistička Republika Hrvatska* (Socialist Republic of Croatia)
SRS	*Srpska Radikalna Stranka* (Serb Radical Party)
SSNO	*Savezni sekretarijat za narodnu odbranu* (Federal Secretariat for People's Defence)
SSUP	*Savezni sekretarijat za unutrašnje poslove* (Federal Secretariat for Internal Affairs)
SUP	*Sekretarijat za unutrašnje poslove* (Secretariat for Internal Affairs)
TO	*Teritorijalna odbrana* (Territorial Defence)
UB	*Uprava bezbednosti* (Security Administration)
UDB-a	*Uprava državne bezbednosti* (State Security Administration)
VRS	*Vojska Republike Srpske* (Army of Republika Srpske)

PREFACE

This book has been a long time coming. In a way, it started nearly twenty years ago, when I as a freshly minted history PhD from Columbia University walked into the 'playpen' – the large common room of the Leadership Research Team (LRT) at the UN's International Criminal Tribunal for the Former Yugoslavia (ICTY) in The Hague. I had had the good fortune of meeting several LRT analysts while doing archival research in Croatia. Given that my own research involved a lot of police documentation from interwar Yugoslavia, one of the analysts had during a coffee break suggested that I might one day be interested in coming to work at the ICTY. I had of course heard of the ICTY, but up until that moment I had never for a moment thought that I could work there. That seemed more like a job for lawyers and police. But the analyst put me in touch with Patrick Treanor, the head of the LRT, and he explained that his team consisted in part of historians who spoke Bosnian/Croatian/Serbian (BCS) fluently and who had strong track records doing archival research. Indeed, Treanor himself had for years worked as a historian at the US Department of Justice's Office of Special Investigations, which investigated historical mass atrocities, in particular those committed by Nazi Germany and its allies during the Second World War.

Treanor explained to me that they badly needed an analyst who could conduct research on the Bosnian Serb police and on other Serb-controlled police forces in the former Yugoslavia. By the end of my first day at work, several binders of documentation lay on my desk, and Treanor had given me clear marching orders: read the existing internal analytical reports and these primary sources, and then when you are done, we will talk about how you can produce a report on the Bosnian Serb police. The desired report was supposed to complement the recently completed 'Bosnian Serb leadership report' which Treanor had drafted along with several of his analysts.

A few weeks later, I started tentatively drafting the document that grew into several subsequent reports on the Bosnian Serb police, and which ultimately led to my expert testimony in five trials at the ICTY as well as two trials in Canada. These reports in turn form the basis of the current book, where I attempt to present my findings and analysis in, I hope, a more accessible and digestible format.

I want to thank Patrick Treanor above all for giving young and in many aspects naïve historian the opportunity of a lifetime. Never during my archival research as a graduate student had it occurred to me that I might one day be sitting in a courtroom and responding to questions posed during cross-examination by none other than Radovan Karadžić, or that trial chambers at the ICTY would extensively cite my reports and testimony in convicting perpetrators of war crimes, crimes against humanity and genocide. It has truly been an incredible and incredibly fulfilling journey, and that journey continues to this day.

I am also profoundly grateful to my analyst colleagues at the LRT, whom I doubtlessly annoyed and exasperated with my recurring need to exuberantly show them yet another 'fascinating' document which I had just unearthed. Our conversations and collaboration made me a better historian and analyst, and I am honoured to count many of them as both friends and colleagues. My gratitude also extends – and this I mean very sincerely – to most of the defence lawyers who subjected me and my reports to challenging levels of scrutiny during their cross-examinations of me. I absolutely believe that all those accused of atrocity crimes must and should have very competent legal counsel, and the best defence lawyers who cross-examined me in many ways contributed to improving my understanding of the Bosnian Serb police.

I extend my thanks to Vladimir Petrović, Mark Biondich and the anonymous reviewer for their comments on the first draft of this book. As always, any flaws and mistakes are my own responsibility. I am grateful to Thomas Stottor, Tomasz Hoskins and Nayiri Kendir at I.B. Tauris and Bloomsbury for their support for the book.

As readers of my previous books will know, I rely heavily on primary sources and have an abiding passion for archives. As Kirsten Weld has shown in her fascinating and compassionate book on the police archives of Guatemala, *Paper Cadavers*, archives are so much more than a repository of historical documentation. Among other things, they are also the professional abode of archivists, a group of very idiosyncratic individuals, the best of whom share the historian's love of documents but also a healthy suspicion towards the historian's intentions. In my own case, it was I who was insufficiently aware of a certain archivist's extracurricular intentions towards me. Today, over twenty years after I stepped into the Croatian State Archives, I remain bound by the spell cast by Dorotea Smešnjak. Her companionship has proved invaluable as always as I worked on this book, and for this I owe her deep gratitude.

INTRODUCTION

Between April 1992 and December 1995, approximately 100,000 people were killed in the war in Bosnia and Herzegovina. Many of the war's mass atrocities have since been prosecuted as crimes against humanity, war crimes and genocide at the United Nations' International Criminal Tribunal for the Former Yugoslavia (ICTY), as well as in courts in the former Yugoslavia and several other national jurisdictions. A truly massive number of publications exist about the war.[1] However, these focus overwhelmingly on the political disintegration of Yugoslavia, and the subsequent role of the various militaries engaged in the conflict, including the Bosnian Serb Army, the Army of Bosnia and Herzegovina and the Croatian Defence Council, as well as the protracted intervention and assistance of the militaries of Croatia and Serbia.

While it is true that these armies conducted the brunt of the major military offensives, cases at the ICTY have demonstrated that the police and a motley array of associated paramilitary forces perpetrated a very high proportion of the violations of international humanitarian law. Indeed, the malicious actions of the police often preceded and triggered actual armed conflict during a time when they were charged with protecting public security. Later, during the war, police officers committed many of the most notorious crimes far away from actual combat zones. In several notorious cases, the atrocities committed by police and paramilitary forces were so extreme that they even earned the criticism and opprobrium of the armies with which these forces were aligned. By focusing on the key role of the police in initiating and implementing the practice of 'ethnic cleansing', this book will provide an incisive and analytical account of a crucial dimension of the Bosnian war that has hitherto been neglected outside the voluminous but technical judgements issued by the ICTY. And even at the ICTY, recognition of the real extent of police involvement in the perpetration of atrocities came relatively gradually.

It is the primary and original thesis of this book that the war in Bosnia and Herzegovina began with the police, and that the issues of policing and crimes committed by the police are crucial to understanding not only the essence of the war but also key shortcomings in the subsequent peace. During socialist Yugoslavia (1945–91), police officers were sworn to protect and serve the ethnically heterogeneous Yugoslav population in the name of communism and 'brotherhood and unity'. Tragically, as the country splintered at the beginning of the 1990s, many of those same police officers became instrumental in the destruction of the state and began moving down a path leading to the establishment of the first police-run concentration camps in Europe since the Second World War. Segments of the formerly multi-ethnic Yugoslav police first ethnically cleansed their own ranks and then began searching for and exterminating those civilians whose existence imperilled or challenged the establishment of ethnically pure states. In an analogy with Nazi German war crimes committed in the Second World War, it was the police and not the army that led the way, even if the regular armed forces later became just as heavily involved in the commission of war crimes. Moreover, looking beyond the war, I argue that the failure of the international community to create a unified Bosnian police force after the war is one of the main inhibitors preventing the integration of the Bosnian state.

By the time of the outbreak of armed conflict in Bosnia and Herzegovina, the police had disintegrated along ethnic lines, meaning that there were essentially three forces dominated by the Bosnian Muslims, the Bosnian Serbs and the Bosnian Croats, respectively. This study will focus primarily on the activities of the Bosnian Serbs and their successful efforts to create and operate their own police force in Bosnia and Herzegovina. Based on a model pioneered by Serbs in Croatia, and supported by Serbs in Serbia, the Bosnian Serbs were the prime movers between 1990 and 1992 in pushing for the ethnically based division of the police. The strategy of the Bosnian Serbs was in turn later emulated to a considerable extent by Bosnian Croat nationalists who wished to establish an ethnically Croat entity in Bosnia. As with their erstwhile colleagues, the Croats implemented this plan with the ambition of eventually merging their entity with the ethnic 'fatherland'. Although politicians of all three ethnicities contributed to the politicization and militarization of the police, it is the status of the Bosnian Serbs as prime – and ultimately crucial – movers that informs the choice of this study.

My focus on the Bosnian Serbs in this book is also a product of my own professional experience working as a research officer at the ICTY. Upon my arrival at the ICTY in the summer of 2002, I was assigned within the Leadership Research Team (LRT) of the Office of the Prosecutor (OTP) to analyse the workings of the Bosnian Serb police. My ambit of analysis expanded rapidly and eventually resulted in a number of expert reports on the basis of which I testified in five trials at the ICTY: *Krajišnik, Stanišić and Župljanin, Karadžić, Hadžić* and *Stanišić and Simatović* (retrial). Of particular note here is the second trial, in which Mićo Stanišić, the first Bosnian Serb minister of internal affairs, was one of the defendants. I also testified based on versions of these reports in civil and criminal trials in Canada and Bosnia. As such, a significant portion of the research presented here has been subjected to – and has withstood – extensive cross-examination, which one could well call a particularly thorough type of peer review. Several of the aforementioned trial chambers have relied to a considerable extent on these reports in reaching their findings regarding the role of the Bosnian Serb police force and its leaders, as is evident in the footnotes of these trial chambers' judgements.[2] To a very considerable extent, this book will rely upon documentation obtained by the ICTY regarding policing in Bosnia. I was intimately involved in the collection and analysis of such documentation during the years in which I worked full-time for the ICTY, and I subsequently continued to consult and testify at the ICTY as an external consultant until its closing in 2017.

The desire for ethnically pure police forces in large part emerged out of a desperate perceived need for security in a disintegrating state troubled by past historical incidents of mass violence.³ The key question became 'why should I be a minority in your country if you can be a minority in mine?'⁴ In Croatia and later in Bosnia and Herzegovina, the leaders of the Serb minority in 1990 and 1991 convinced themselves and their followers that an imminent genocide – a recurrence of the Second World War – awaited Serbs if they did not fight to remain in Yugoslavia.⁵ The strategy adopted was one of offensive creative destruction: by decentralizing the police and forcing the creation of Serb Autonomous Districts (*Srpske autonomne oblasti*, SAOs), Radovan Karadžić and his associates undermined the viability and territorial integrity of independent Croatian and Bosnian states in which they feared political marginalization and, at worst, extermination. As RS Assembly Deputy Jovo Mijatović noted after the war started, 'at the moment when we had to destroy a unitary Bosnia, the SAO regions, the districts … were the best solution'.⁶ Yet, in doing so, the Bosnian Serbs ended up inflicting upon their erstwhile neighbours many of the horrors which the Bosnian Serbs themselves hoped to avoid, as former member of the Bosnian Serb Presidency Biljana Plavšić and a number of other accused admitted in their guilty pleas before the ICTY.⁷

Many Serb leaders, including Radovan Karadžić in Bosnia, felt that they could not trust the Yugoslav People's Army, which still served as a powerful guardian of the multi-ethnic Yugoslav state and regarded nationalism with suspicion. Bosnian Serb police officers worked hand in glove with Karadžić's Serb Democratic Party to decentralize Bosnia to the point of collapse. The frequently profane conversations in which Karadžić conferred with Bosnian Serb police officers in 1991 and 1992 were intercepted and provide detailed insight into their plans and deeds. The police covertly and illegally distributed arms and ammunition to Bosnian Serb villagers throughout Bosnia and initiated the training of paramilitary forces who later stood primed to attack their Bosnian Muslim and Bosnian Croat neighbours. The Bosnian Serb police would later brag about and reward those police officers who had purged Croats and Muslims from the ranks of the police months before armed conflict commenced. The leadership of Serbia secretly provided vital material and financial assistance, including the deployment of paramilitary units linked to the Serbian Ministry of Internal Affairs to Croatia in 1991 and to Bosnia in the spring of 1992.

Hence, in the crucial first months of the war, Karadžić and the rest of the Bosnian Serb leadership rightly viewed the forces of the Bosnian Serb Ministry of Internal Affairs (*Ministarstvo unutrašnjih poslova*, MUP) as the only truly loyal armed force at their disposal. Cooperating with other Serb-controlled forces, the Bosnian Serb police spearheaded the takeover of municipalities throughout Bosnia. Using the pretence of ultimatums for the handing over of weapons, the Bosnian Serb police on behalf of the Serb Democratic Party launched a systematic campaign of persecution against the non-Serb civilian population. Those who were not immediately killed were either expelled or, in thousands of cases, detained for long periods of time in makeshift concentration camps in which they were beaten and abused, and in some cases tortured and killed. Sexual assault and rape were frequently deployed against women in these facilities, but also against men as a weapon of intimidation and humiliation.[8] By the end of 1992, the Bosnian Serbs had asserted their control over approximately two-thirds of Bosnian territory. In the following two years, even as the frontlines ebbed and swayed, the Bosnian Serb police collaborated with the Army of Republika Srpska (*Vojska Republike Srpske*, VRS) in the continuing implementation of ethnic cleansing. The war in Bosnia in some sense culminated with the genocide in Srebrenica, in which the Bosnian Serb police participated. After the genocide, the police worked with their colleagues in the army to ensure that mass graves would remain hidden from international investigators.

Yet even after the war concluded at the end of 1995, the reliance of the Bosnian Serb leadership upon the police did not end. After the signing of the Dayton Accords, the Bosnian Serb police worked for years to thwart at every step the Accords' successful implementation. By assisting fugitives suspected of war crimes – including many in their own ranks – and by working every day to prevent the return of refugees and displaced persons, the Bosnian Serb police ensured that the negative peace characterized by the absence of armed conflict could not flower into a positive peace of reconciliation and inter-ethnic cooperation.

Although the international community succeeded in disbanding the Army of Republika Srpska and establishing the ethnically integrated Armed Forces of Bosnia and Herzegovina in 2006, Republika Srpska successfully opposed the creation of a multi-ethnic unitary police force in Bosnia. The protracted obstruction orchestrated by the Bosnian Serb leadership clearly reveals an understanding that a dominantly Serb police force is necessary for the consolidation of ethnic cleansing in the largely ethnically homogeneous Serbian entity. This policy and the reliance for the maintenance and exercise of power on the police are visible today in the rule of Milorad Dodik who for years has controlled the reins of power in Republika Srpska and today serves as the Bosnian Serb member of Bosnia's collective presidency. However, far from obstructing Dayton, Dodik has come to view the peace agreement as the main protection for Republika Srpska and as a vehicle for perpetuating his hold on power and impunity against investigation and possible prosecution. At the same time, he never tires of provoking by raising the prospect of Republika Srpska's secession from Bosnia, and in doing so implicitly rattles the sabre of the Bosnian Serb police force, the only armed force under his control. In doing so, Dodik dangerously channels Mićo Stanišić. The first of his two books opens by citing Radovan Karadžić's praise of the Bosnian Serb police for securing the establishment of Republika Srpska.[9]

On police as perpetrators

I have written this book out of a frustration that most of the countless available histories of the war in Bosnia tend to say so little about the role of the police in Bosnia's disintegration and war. Indeed, even at the ICTY, it took a number of years before adequate attention began to be devoted to the investigation and prosecution of police perpetrators. I am well aware that, like most books written to address the omissions of others, this book conversely risks overemphasizing the role of the police. Some might say that a historian who has also spent the better part of two decades working for various courts and tribunals as an analyst and expert witness on the police, I suffer from a kind of chronic version of what is in the region known as *profesionalna deformacija* (professional deformation). This condition could theoretically lead to a book that ignores and/or belittles existing scholarship and exaggerates the role of the police and claims about their significance. Having already recently written a survey of the collapse of Yugoslavia and the wars of Yugoslav succession, I believe that risk to be slight, however, and more than outweighed by the additional nuances that a proper understanding of this topic will provide.

Another possible reason for potentially regarding this book as superfluous is that there is nothing novel about the claim that police officers can be perpetrators of crimes, including mass atrocities. The most obvious example is the voluminous literature on the crimes of the SS in Nazi Germany, as well as in particular Christopher Browning's seminal book on Reserve Police Battalion 101.[10] Moving beyond the Holocaust, books have been written about police as perpetrators in 'death squads' in many different countries around the world.[11] Moreover, in a more general context taking into consideration peacetime human rights abuses, abundant research has shown how police forces have maintained the apartheid regime in South Africa, and police brutality in the United States, particularly against Blacks and other minorities, has for obvious reasons in recent years received significant scholarly attention.[12] Yet while such studies are worth keeping in mind and have influenced the present book, I would argue that there are very specific elements including state disintegration and regional history that lend a particular dimension to the case of policing in Bosnia during the war.

It has been observed about the historiography of Nazi crimes during the Second World War that the Wehrmacht tended to emerge relatively unscathed because the lion's share of the focus was on the crimes committed by the SS. By contrast, at the ICTY, with a few notable exceptions, the vast majority of prosecutors and investigators for years devoted most attention to the conduct of the various regular armed forces that had emerged during the collapse of Yugoslavia and the concomitant disintegration of the Yugoslav People's Army. Some attention was also paid to particularly notorious paramilitary actors and, of course, to the civilian leaders who played major roles in the various armed conflicts that erupted and had legal responsibility as commanders-in-chief. The police and their role in ethnic cleansing were relatively ignored.

Moreover, despite the abundant literature on the Bosnian war, there remains a paucity of scholarly focus on the Bosnian Serb leadership, particularly though not only in English. Robert Donia's book on Radovan Karadžić of course interlocks with this book and likewise emerges from an expert report prepared for the ICTY.[13] Adis Maksić has produced a solid and nuanced analysis of the Serb Democratic Party's ideology and role.[14] It should also be noted that Marko Attila

Hoare has treated the complementary topic of the prewar (para)military evolution of Bosnian Muslim police and military forces.[15]

This book focuses predominantly on the role of the Bosnian Serb police, particularly what became the Republika Srpska Ministry of Internal Affairs (*Ministarstvo unutrašnjih poslova Republike Srpske*, RS MUP). There are several reasons for this focus. First, as the analyst who was primarily responsible at the ICTY for researching these matters, I believe that there can be no doubt that the Bosnian Serbs were the primary movers in terms of the destruction of the socialist Bosnian Ministry of Internal Affairs. I also share and agree with the conclusion of multiple cases at the ICTY that the Bosnian Serb leadership could not reasonably expect to achieve its strategic goals without engaging in the commission of widespread and systematic atrocities, crimes which were ultimately shown at the ICTY to have encompassed war crimes, crimes against humanity and genocide.

In choosing to focus on the Bosnian Serbs and their approach to policing, I therefore concentrate on the prime movers and base myself on well over a decade of research on this topic. However, it is important and necessary for me to stress that in maintaining this focus, I do not in any way claim that the Bosnian Serbs were the sole adherents of ethnically based policing in Bosnia, nor do I assert that only the Bosnian Serb police forces committed crimes during the war. The police forces formed by the Bosnian Croats and the Bosnian Muslims also committed crimes. However, the latter in particular, formed in special and more reactive circumstances, committed far fewer crimes than their Bosnian Serb counterparts. I make this statement not as an aspersion or dismissal of the suffering of any of the victims of the war. Indeed, I have elsewhere argued strongly against the scourge of competitive collective victimhood which still afflicts the former Yugoslavia, and for the confirmation of the essential humanity of the war's victims in the face of ethnic or nationalist reductionism.[16] Yet we must also keep in mind the undeniable fact that the Bosnian war claimed far more Bosnian Muslim (Bosniak) victims than Serb or Croat victims. According to ICTY OTP demographers, in a conflict where 65 per cent of the fatalities were combatants and 35 per cent were civilians, 'some 65% [of fatalities] were Muslims, 22% Serbs, 9% Croats and about 5% were Others'.[17]

That having been said, the very complicated events which transpired between the November 1990 multi-party election and the subsequent horrific course of the war show that there is enough blame to go around – or to put it differently – that none of the three 'sides' in Bosnia is without blame. This book therefore also takes into account the manoeuvrings of Muslims and Croats, including their own illegal prewar actions contributing to the destabilization of Bosnia and Yugoslavia. During the war, former members of the Bosnian police became both victims and perpetrators, and in some cases both. Very many professional police officers found themselves pushed into a war that they did not want and acquitted themselves to the best of their abilities in an excruciatingly tragic and difficult situation. This also without doubt applies to many Bosnian Serb police officers, and I have personally on many occasions had the opportunity of meeting and speaking with many of them. My conversations with them have left me with no doubt that many of them feel a deep sense of regret and shame regarding the crimes that were committed in their name. I know for a fact that some of these men processed their feelings by assisting the ICTY in investigating and prosecuting these crimes and in facilitating the apprehension of fugitives from international criminal justice. In any case, the point of this book is not to assign blame but to provide a source-driven analytical account of the role of the police in state disintegration, armed conflict and the commission of atrocities, and ultimately to highlight why neglecting the police leads to a flawed understanding.

Like my previous book on political assassinations perpetratred by the Yugoslav State Security Service, the present book builds on my previous expert reports, in this case those I prepared for various cases at the ICTY. Therefore, it is important and necessary for me to state that this book draws extremely extensively on documentation from the ICTY's archives, as well as on ICTY judgements and witness testimony. However, it is neither my desire nor intent to comment on the judgements or jurisprudence of the ICTY. The main purpose of this book is to provide an accessible overview and analysis of the police as perpetrators in the Bosnian war.

The structure of the book

Armed conflict did not break out in Bosnia overnight, and the process of creating ethnically based police forces also took place over a protracted period. The first chapter of the book examines the path from elections and tentative democratization to war. In November 1990, a coalition of three nationalist parties (Bosnian Muslim, Serb and Croat) defeated the reformed communist party at the first multi-party elections in Bosnia and Herzegovina since the Second World War. Emulating the communist-era system of spoils and clientelism, the victorious coalition divided power, but their internal differences quickly came to the fore as they struggled for control of the Bosnian police force. By the summer of 1991, the Bosnian Serbs, who wished to prevent the secession of Bosnia from Yugoslavia at any price, began to develop detailed plans to destroy the multi-ethnic Bosnian Ministry of Internal Affairs from within and replace it with an ethnically Serb police force loyal primarily to Radovan Karadžić's Serb Democratic Party (*Srpska demokratska stranka*, SDS).

The second chapter focuses on the Bosnian Serb police and the forcible seizure of power. At the very outset of the war in April 1992, the Bosnian Serb leadership relied heavily on the Bosnian Serb police, the only armed force exclusively under their control. While the Yugoslav People's Army and the Territorial Defence forces provided the heavy weaponry necessary to assert military control over territory, the Bosnian Serb police in cooperation with nationalist paramilitaries followed the precise instructions of the SDS and took over civilian power in a large number of municipalities, using lethal force as a tool of intimidation against Bosnian Muslims and Croats.

Following the takeover of areas designated by the SDS as being 'Serbian municipalities', the Bosnian Serb police set about implementing the set of measures that came to be known euphemistically as 'ethnic cleansing'. Based on material from ICTY trials, the third chapter will carefully analyse how, in conjunction with the political and military leadership, the police conducted 'disarmament' campaigns which served as a pretext for the detention of tens of thousands of civilians, including children, the elderly and women. In detention facilities such as Omarska, Keraterm, Luka, Kula and others, the police over a period of months committed crimes including murder, rape and torture against those unlawfully detained based primarily on their ethnicity. At the same time, the Bosnian Serb police paradoxically increasingly had to confront their erstwhile paramilitary partners, whose particularly extreme and often chaotic violence challenged the establishment and stability of Republika Srpska. By the end of 1992, the Bosnian Serbs controlled approximately 70 per cent of the country's territory.

Throughout the period examined in this book, Serbia's leadership under President Slobodan Milošević supported the Bosnian Serbs and their strategic objectives. The fourth chapter provides an overview of the origins of this assistance in the establishment of training centres for Serb police units in Croatia. Using covert means, the State Security Service of the Ministry of Internal Affairs of Serbia provided material and financial assistance as well as expert trainers. While maintaining plausible deniability, these instructors not only trained police officers who would sow chaos in both Croatia and Bosnia, but also gave birth to the Unit for Special Operations, a unit so potent that it would years later go on to assassinate the prime minister of Serbia.

With the frontlines stabilized for much of the next two years, the Bosnian Serb police concentrated on consolidating the gains and segregation achieved in the first year of the war. Ethnic cleansing proceeded throughout this period. The book's fifth chapter covers this period of the war, which is in many ways the least understood but includes a mysterious uprising against the Bosnian Serb leadership by disgruntled veterans disgusted by corruption and abuses of power. Although the Bosnian Serb Army led by General Ratko Mladić instigated and planned the genocide, they relied to a considerable extent on the Bosnian Serb police to detain and implement the mass killings which took place after the surrender of the 'safe haven'. Later, as NATO began its bombardment of Republika Srpska, the Bosnian Serb police and paramilitaries acted as enforcers as their self-proclaimed state risked complete collapse.

The book's final chapter starts by describing how the Bosnian Serb political leadership again used the police as an enforcement mechanism, but this time as the main instrument of resistance against the Dayton Peace Accords. The Bosnian Serbs despised this agreement, and they were initially determined to undermine it by further militarizing the police and by using the police to prevent Bosnian Muslims and Croats from returning to those areas whence they had been forcibly removed during the war. Even after the SDS was removed from power and replaced by an ostensibly pliable and pro-Western leader, Milorad Dodik, the structural framework of Dayton and Dodik's own ambitions ensured that the police remained the main obstacle to lasting peace in Bosnia. With the forced dissolution of the Bosnian Serb Army, the Bosnian Serb police once again became the only armed force in Bosnia exclusively under Bosnian Serb control. Over a quarter of a century after the end of the Bosnian war, Dodik relies on the police to secure his power base, to prevent investigations of corruption and organized crime and to 'weaponize' his repeated threats to call for a referendum on the secession of Republika Srpska from Bosnia and Herzegovina.

Sources and terminology

This book, like the expert reports on which it is based, relies overwhelmingly on primary sources from the police and other official sources. In particular, the intent is to let the Bosnian Serb police and their political masters speak with their own words. As noted in my expert testimony at the ICTY, this methodology has the advantage of depicting events from the point of view of the perpetrators, reflecting their ideological framework and self-justifications for their actions. It also allows the reader to see the often shockingly bold and self-congratulatory expressions of pride from the perpetrators of crimes during the halcyon days of their 'success'. Conversely, numerous documents also reveal the qualms and concerns which actors in the police and the army had about the atrocities committed in the course of constructing an ethnically homogeneous police force and Serb republic.

Unless otherwise noted, the primary source documents cited in this book stem from the document collections of the ICTY, collections which arose in the course of over twenty years of investigations and prosecutions. As an analyst employed by the OTP at the ICTY, I was personally involved in the process of document collection, particularly of documents pertaining to Serb police forces in Serbia, Montenegro, Croatia and Bosnia and Herzegovina. Most, but not all, of the sources cited and obtained by the ICTY are available through the UN International Residual Mechanism for Criminal Tribunals' Unified Court Records database.[18] Also, unless otherwise noted, all translations from these documents are my own. The major exception to this applies to quotes from witnesses in the transcripts of the ICTY. Unfortunately – and very disappointingly – the ICTY has maintained transcripts only in English and French, and only rarely in Bosnian/Croatian/Serbian (BCS), and I therefore must rely on these transcripts when quoting witness testimony. While the audio-video recordings of the original testimony exist in the ICTY's archive, these recordings are generally speaking not accessible.

Primary sources stemming from the ICTY are listed in the relevant footnotes alongside the electronic record number (ERN) used to identify each document at the Tribunal. While a considerable majority of the documents cited in this book were introduced as exhibits in court cases at the ICTY, a very substantial portion are not publicly available but were cited in expert reports written by myself and others. For the sake of consistency, and because I cite documentation used in a number of cases, I have therefore chosen to provide the ERNs for all documents instead of exhibit numbers. As I have done in the past, I will be happy to assist any researchers who might later need assistance locating relevant ICTY sources in the online Unified Court Records of the United Nations International Residual Mechanism for Criminal Tribunals, and I issue a sincere invitation to such researchers to contact me.

One potential objection regarding the role of the police in the Bosnian conflict deserves particular mention. Since the time of Yugoslavia's dissolution until the present day, rumours and allegations have thrived regarding the alleged role of the Yugoslav People's Army's counterintelligence service, known as the *Kontraobavještajna služba*, KOS. While speculation on this topic is largely confined to journalistic or publicistic accounts, and to interviews with various participants in various popular talk shows in the former Yugoslavia, a few scholars have also chosen to make mention of such allegations in their publications.[19]

There can certainly be no doubt that the KOS played a considerable role in Yugoslavia's demise. Nor can there be any doubt that the influence of the KOS extended beyond the military and included informants or agents in both the political and police structures of the country. This book will on occasion make brief reference to allegations related to the KOS. However, as I noted in my previous book on the operations of the Yugoslav State Security Service, such allegations, even where they merit mention, are to be viewed with considerable scepticism and caution. Until such time as the relevant archives of the Yugoslav military become accessible – and that time remains very distant, if it indeed ever comes – it would be foolhardy and misguided to make any definitive statements about the role of the KOS. In the meantime, a great many things can be explained in detail and very convincingly without resorting to rumour and innuendo.

A brief note on terminology: this book generally follows the terminology used by the actors encompassed by this history. Hence, the term 'Bosnian Muslims' or 'Muslims' is used to refer to the population currently known as Bosniaks. I also follow convention in referring to Bosnia as shorthand for Bosnia and Herzegovina. As Catherine Baker, Rogers Brubaker and others have noted, it is fiendishly difficult to write a book on this and similar topics without employing reductionist language claiming that 'the Croats did this and the Serbs did that'. Suffice it to say that while I too occasionally stumble in this manner, I have tried my best to make it clear that concrete actions were the result of specific actors in positions of power and not nations as a whole.[20]

Unless otherwise noted, all translations from BCS are my own. The main exception regards quoted testimony by BCS-speaking witnesses at the ICTY, which was translated in the courtroom, and where I have been obliged to use the English-language transcripts.

Chapter 1

FROM ELECTIONS TO WAR: THE POLICE AND THE PURPOSEFUL DESTRUCTION OF BOSNIA (NOVEMBER 1990–MARCH 1992)

A proper understanding of the importance of policing for the breakup of Yugoslavia requires first taking into account the centrality of policing for communist rule. For most of the period from 1945 until the beginning of 1990, Socialist Yugoslavia was a party-state in which the League of Communists (originally known as the Communist Party of Yugoslavia) enjoyed a political monopoly. The death of president for life Josip Broz Tito in May 1980 combined with a protracted economic crisis and rioting in Kosovo to raise serious questions about the country's viability, but during the following decade the communists showed no sign of voluntarily relinquishing power. However, with the fall of the Berlin Wall in November 1989 and the rapid toppling of communist party-states throughout Eastern Europe, all but the most conservative Yugoslav communists began to realize that change was in the air.

Structured federally, socialist Yugoslavia encompassed six republics: Slovenia, Croatia, Bosnia and Herzegovina, Serbia, Montenegro and Macedonia. In five of the six republics, a clear connection existed between the largest ethnicity and the republic: between Slovenia and Slovenes, Croatia and Croats, Serbia and Serbs, and so forth. Bosnia and Herzegovina with its ethnic patchwork dominated by Bosnian Muslims, Serbs and Croats, was hence unique. To use the words of the later leader of the reformed Bosnian communists, Nijaz Duraković, 'Bosnia-Herzegovina, as a Yugoslavia in miniature, was always a kind of a seismograph for all pressing questions in the field of inter-ethnic relations in our country'.[1] In part owing to past episodes of ethnically motivated mass violence – above all during the Second World War, when Bosnia had been a part of the fascist so-called Independent State of Croatia – and in part because of the never completely extinguished irredentist aspirations of politicians in Croatia and Serbia, Bosnia's communist leadership also had a well-earned reputation for being the most conservative and staid in the country.

Policing in Yugoslavia

As in other communist party-states in Eastern Europe, the party – known since November 1952 as the League of Communists of Yugoslavia (*Savez komunista Jugoslavije*, SKJ) – legally and constitutionally controlled the state. From the very outset of communist rule, the Ministry of Internal Affairs, in whose purview policing was located, served as a linchpin of state power.[2] Together with the military, the police constituted the second element of the state's monopoly on armed force. Yet on a daily basis the average citizen of the country was much more likely to encounter members of the 'People's Police' (*Narodna milicija*) than soldiers. In this sense, police officers personified the state's power both to maintain order and to repress anti-state action if necessary. And the 'secret police' in the form of the Yugoslav State Security Service, also part of the Ministry of Internal Affairs, symbolized the invisible but (allegedly) omnipresent and omniscient eye of the party-state.[3]

For the first twenty years of the country's existence, the federal authorities very strictly controlled all matters pertaining to policing. The key person responsible for this structure was Aleksandar Ranković, one of Tito's closest associates and the first head of the Ministry of Internal Affairs in socialist Yugoslavia. In 1966, however, Ranković was purged for allegedly trying to use the state security service to usurp power.[4] Thereafter, the SKJ cautiously accelerated the decentralization of the Yugoslav state.

A further milestone, in the history of both the socialist Yugoslav state and the police, was the promulgation in 1974 of what turned out to be the final federal constitution. The republics as well as the two autonomous provinces, Kosovo and Vojvodina, received very considerable powers and, in many fields, could act quite autonomously of the federal Yugoslav state. Only defence and foreign policy remained almost exclusively in the purview of the federal authorities. While communists in Slovenia and Croatia in particular hailed the 1974 constitution as a progressive step in the right direction, many in Serbia regarded the constitution as an emasculation of state power and as a further attack on Serbia's role in the Yugoslav state.

In practice, the decentralization meant that the six republics and two autonomous provinces had broad discretion in devising and implementing policing policies. Notwithstanding the criticism emanating from Serb communists, there was relatively little detectable policy divergence, not least because the 1974 constitution, like all previous Yugoslav constitutions, made it clear that the SKJ was the sole holder of power. Behind the scenes, the republican and provincial leagues of communists wielded significant power because they controlled personnel decisions.

As long as Tito acted as the ultimate arbiter of all decisions in the state, the system functioned quite well, but immortality proved elusive even for the great leader. After his death in May 1980, the slogan 'after Tito, Tito' (*posle/poslije Tita, Tito*) expressed the principled desire to continue to steer his course, including upholding the official ideology of 'brotherhood and unity'.[5] Yet such a slogan had more to do with political necrophilia than any constructive agenda, and in the years ahead various Yugoslav communist functionaries proved perfectly capable of adopting mutually contradictory positions while claiming to wear the Titoist mantle.

Particularly in the ethnically diverse context of Bosnia and Herzegovina, the personnel question would come to occupy a central place in the discussions leading to the breakup of the country. It is important to remember that ethnicity had always been a prominent factor regarding personnel decisions in socialist Yugoslavia, particularly so in Bosnia. Practically speaking, this resulted in the 'key' (*ključ*) system which aspired to manage and maintain staffing in the police proportional to the country's ethnic demography. For reasons going back to the communist-led uprisings against the fascist Croat regime occupying Bosnia during the Second World War, Serbs had historically been overrepresented in military and police structures in Bosnia, as well as in the League of Communists of Bosnia and Herzegovina (*Savez komunista Bosne i Hercegovine*, SKBiH).[6]

Neven Anđelić usefully notes that the apportioning of posts in socialist Bosnia along ethnic lines should not be conflated with the notion that a Bosnian Croat represented only Bosnian Croat interests, a Bosnian Muslim represented only Bosnian Muslim interests, etc. Anđelić describes a delicately maintained system in which 'unwritten rules … were always respected', and where those appointed on an ethnic basis pledged to govern and work in the spirit of 'brotherhood and unity' and Bosnia as a whole, being cognizant of but transcending particularistic ethnic interests.[7] This system, which proved difficult to sustain after the death of Tito, faced total demise once multi-party democracy came to Bosnia.

The collapse of communism and the November 1990 elections in Bosnia and Herzegovina

During the decade following the death of Tito, amidst a chronic economic crisis informed by Yugoslavia's bankruptcy, mounting inflation and unemployment, the SKBiH remained stubbornly conservative and resistant to reforms.[8] However, in September 1987 a young communist named Slobodan Milošević carried out an internal putsch in the Central Committee of the League of Communists of Serbia.[9] Although initially regarded by some as a relatively liberal and reformist politician, Milošević by late 1988 revealed his plans to undo central tenets of the 1974 constitution by recentralizing power in Belgrade.

Milošević increasingly seemed to be positioning himself as the new Tito. But while Milošević had initially like all other communists parroted the virtues of the great leader, Marxism–Leninism and 'brotherhood and unity', there were signs that he could proffer himself as first and foremost a leader of Serbs. Indeed, Milošević literally stumbled over the power of nationalism on a visit to Kosovo in April 1987 when he famously proclaimed that he would protect local Serbs.[10]

As a product of the SKJ, Milošević knew very well that the key to power resided in personnel questions. Therefore, this quintessential apparatchik devised a clever strategy to expand Serbia's – and by extension his own – power. By organizing 'antibureaucratic revolutions', Milošević had the ability to purge those who opposed him and to stack party committees with his own supporters, all in the name of progress and reforms. The first 'antibureaucratic revolution' was carried out in the summer of 1988 in Vojvodina.[11] The so-called Yoghurt Revolution, which earned its moniker because of the cups of yoghurt thrown at Vojvodina's communists, ended with the resignation of the province's communist leadership in October 1988. They were replaced with loyal allies of Milošević. The strategy was repeated in Montenegro, where the old leadership resigned in January 1989. In Kosovo, Azem Vllasi, the ethnic Albanian communist leader, was jailed the following month. Milošević's willingness to opportunistically wrap himself in the cloak of Serbian nationalism became evident when he in June 1989 organized a gigantic jubilee celebration of the 600th anniversary of the Battle of Kosovo at Gazimestan. These two elements – the opportunistic appropriation and nationalism and the recalibration of party-state politics for a post-communist period – would soon also be evident in Bosnia and Herzegovina.

Meanwhile, in March 1989, Serbia annulled Kosovo and Vojvodina's autonomy. Many Serbs who despised the 1974 constitution greeted this step euphorically. With this move, Milošević through his allies now controlled the votes of Serbia, Kosovo, Vojvodina and Montenegro in the rotating Yugoslav Presidency, nearly a majority. This development greatly alarmed the republican leaderships in Slovenia and Croatia, which feared that the next logical step in Milošević's campaign would be to strengthen the federal authorities, recentralizing Yugoslavia with Serb communists occupying key positions and with all of the most important decisions being taken in Belgrade. Seen from the vantage point of Ljubljana and Zagreb, this potentially implied a return to the rigid authoritarian centralism that had existed from 1945 until the purge of Ranković in 1966. And although Ranković had kept a very low profile since his ouster, massive crowds attended his funeral in 1983, signalling an uncritical and factually problematic rehabilitation of him as a paragon of Serbian nationalism.[12]

The combination of Milošević's power grab and his embrace of nationalism provoked a counterreaction in the two northwestern republics. By the end of 1989, the authorities in Slovenia were blocking pro-Milošević 'meetings for the truth' and Serbia countered with a boycott against Slovenian products. At the 14th SKJ Congress in January 1990 in Belgrade, the Slovenian communists attempted to resist Milošević's centralization attempts. When this failed, the delegations from both Slovenia and Croatia left the meeting, an act that symbolized the collapse of communism in Yugoslavia. In any case, any increased tension between Croatia and Serbia was also bound to have enormous ramifications for Bosnia and Herzegovina.

In the course of 1990, the first multi-party elections since the Second World War were held, first in Croatia and Slovenia in the spring, in Macedonia and Bosnia and Herzegovina in November, and finally in Serbia and Montenegro in December. In the months before the Bosnian elections, new political parties began to crystallize. Initially, a ban on ethnically defined political parties remained in effect, with the result that what would become the dominant Bosnian Muslim party was established as the Party of Democratic Action (*Stranka demokratske akcije*, SDA). However, nationalists challenged this ban, and on 11 June 1990, the SRBiH Constitutional Court ruled against it.[13] As a result, the Bosnian Serbs in the following month formed the Serb Democratic Party (SDS BiH) as a sister party of the eponymous main party of the Croatian Serbs. Likewise, the Bosnian

Croats established the Croat Democratic Union of Bosnia and Herzegovina (*Hrvatska demokratska zajednica Bosne i Hercegovine*, HDZ BiH) as a sister party of the HDZ in Croatia. These three nationalist parties crafted a coalition against the erstwhile communists who were split between the League of Communists of Bosnia and Herzegovina and the pan-Yugoslav Federation of Reform Forces of Yugoslavia (*Savez reformskih snaga Jugoslavije*). The slogan of the nationalist coalition was 'in our Bosnia and Herzegovina, in Yugoslavia, we were and will remain together'.[14]

In light of the catastrophic enmity among the three parties and the later armed conflict, it is perhaps not surprising that many in Bosnia, including most present-day nationalists, have essentially wilfully erased most memories of the mutually existing comity that caused these parties to campaign together in 1990 against the reformed communists. Bosnians today of all ethnicities are for example often shocked to hear that the leader of the SDA, Alija Izetbegović, was a guest of honour at the founding assembly of the SDS in July 1990.[15] Bosnian Serbs, in particular, are much fonder of recounting Izetbegović's role as a defendant in a 1983 Sarajevo show trial in which he was accused of Muslim nationalism and Islamic fundamentalism.[16] At this stage, as evidenced by the SDS's statute, the parties emphasized coexistence and mutual respect for others even as they also reserved the right to advance the interests of their own respective ethnic community.[17]

The first Bosnian multi-party elections proved to be a resounding success for the nationalist coalition. Of the 240 places in the two houses of the Bosnian Assembly (parliament), the nationalists took 202. In the elections, the SDS won absolute victories in thirty-seven municipalities and shared power in many others.[18] Henceforth, the SDA, the SDS and the HDZ increased their voluble and regular proclamations to be the exclusive legitimate voices of the Bosnian Muslims, the Bosnian Serbs and the Bosnian Croats, respectively.

The political annihilation of the reformed communists and the massive victory of the nationalists ensured that all political conflicts and energy would now be focused on the division of power among the victors. And in this competition, all three parties took a zero-sum approach and fully emulated the communist approach to party-state control. Armina Galijaš has scathingly and correctly observed that 'after the prostration of the one-party system the inhabitants of Bosnia-Herzegovina received three parallel one-party systems'.[19] Or as Adis Maksić puts it, 'the principle could be seen as an "ethno-party key" rather than an "ethnic key."'[20] Immediately after the elections, negotiations began with a view to apportioning government and civil service posts in accordance with the election results. Momčilo Krajišnik of the SDS became the speaker of the Bosnian Assembly, and Jure Pelivan of the HDZ became prime minister. In the Bosnian Presidency, Alija Izetbegović of the SDA took the primary spot, with one other member of the SDA (Fikret Abdić), and two members of the SDS (Biljana Plavšić and Nikola Koljević) and the HDZ (Stjepan Kljuić and Franjo Boras), supplemented by one self-declared Yugoslav, Ejup Ganić (who belonged to the SDA), respectively, constituting the rest of the presidency.[21] Yet it should also be noted that the formation of the first multi-party government took nearly three months, with problematic consequences for Bosnia and its citizens as there was no functioning government in a time of economic crisis.[22]

Given that the Yugoslav People's Army (*Jugoslovenska narodna armija*, JNA), and by extension the Territorial Defence (*Teritorijalna odbrana*, TO) remained under the control of federal Yugoslav organs, the police were the only component of the state's monopoly of armed force that was up for grabs immediately after the elections.[23] This situation, including the powers and authority vested in the police, ensured that the division of posts in the Ministry of Internal Affairs would be particularly fraught. By 22 December, a specific triparty agreement emerged on the apportioning of municipal posts in the police.[24] Within the SRBiH Ministry of Internal Affairs (*Ministarstvo unutrašnjih poslova*, MUP), the leading positions were divided as follows:

Minister of Internal Affairs: Alija Delimustafić (SDA)
Deputy Minister: Vitomir Žepinić (SDS)
Undersecretary for the State Security Service (SDB): Branko Kvesić (HDZ)
Deputy Undersecretary for the SDB: Boro Sušić (SDS)[25]
Assistant Minister for Police Affairs: Avdo Hebib (SDA)[26]
Assistant Minister for the Prevention and Detection of Crime:
Momčilo Mandić (SDS)

The SRBiH Assembly confirmed the appointments of Delimustafić and Žepinić at a session in February 1991.[27] Not all the leading jobs in the ministry were initially filled by a specific person, but the allocation of the posts among the three parties was the guiding principle. As an important distinction, the parties nominated people whom they believed would represent the respective party's interests in the ministry, but the persons nominated were not necessarily party members.[28] In this manner, the three parties initially appointed many career MUP officials who had significant experience.

Over time, as we shall see, however, loyalty to party-political interests came to be even more important than ethnic identity. This resulted in the filling of a number of important posts with political appointees who lacked any relevant experience.[29] As noted, ethnicity had also played a significant role in personnel decisions prior to 1990, but with the advent of a tripartite party-state, with each party claiming to speak for one ethnicity, matters became much more tense. Decisions to promote, demote or dismiss personnel increasingly risked being exploited as alleged evidence that one ethnicity was favoured or faced unfair discrimination. It must be stressed that none of the three victorious parties distinguished themselves by their behaviour, aspiring for complete control if they had majorities at the municipal level and showing no interest in governing by consensus.[30] The result was 'administrative paralysis'.[31]

Exacerbating the ethnic stratification and politicization of the police, a number of older veteran employees of the ministry availed themselves of the regime change to retire or were pushed out. This meant that a number of important posts were left or made vacant and would have to be filled as part of the horse-trading that the new parties were engaged in. In the words of one mid-level Bosnian Serb who had been employed in the SRBiH MUP since 1977, 'the ministry started breaking up at the seams along national lines or ethnic lines'.[32] Many police officers deplored what they saw as a new preference for political loyalty over professional experience and ability.

In principle, tripartite agreement existed that posts should be allocated in a manner proportional to the election results. Once the census was conducted in March 1991, there was also some consensus that the uniformed police in particular should reflect the ethnic composition of the country, on a municipality-by-municipality basis.[33] During this process, the SRBiH MUP consulted with the executive organs of the municipal assemblies in order to achieve agreement regarding police appointments. The final decision on the hiring or reassignment of employees in the MUP rested in the hands of the minister, who was of course an SDA appointee and who had to manage the demands of the two other parties. It is not difficult to see how this created an atmosphere of interparty tension and distrust.

Though there were some issues affecting the overall accuracy of the available data and hence statistics, as of 24 June 1991, excepting the SDB, the SRBiH MUP counted 8,958 employees. Of these 39 per cent were Serbs, 33 per cent Muslims, 14 per cent Croats and 14 per cent of other ethnicities (including self-declared Yugoslavs).[34] When compared to the results of the 1991 census, which according to the SRBiH MUP counted 43.7 per cent Muslims, 31.3 per cent Serbs and 17.3 per cent Croats, the Serbs were clearly disproportionately represented in the police. As for the SDB, the proportions among its 547 employees were 35 per cent Serbs, 34 per cent Muslims, 19 per cent Croats and 12 per cent other ethnicities, meaning that Serbs and Croats were overrepresented. In addition, there were nine persons in the SSUP in Belgrade representing Bosnia and Herzegovina, and all of them were Serbs. In the uniformed police, Serbs were even more overrepresented: 44 per cent Serbs, 34 per cent Muslims, 11 per cent Croats and 11 per cent others.

However, there were also accusations on the part of the Bosnian Serbs that the Bosnian Muslims had artificially inflated their numbers in the 1991 census by counting a large number of Muslims who actually stemmed from the Sandžak.[35] This was an area, straddling southern Serbia and northern Montenegro, with a majority Muslim population. The Bosnian Serbs alleged that the SDA was hiring Sandžak Muslims in the active and in particular the reserve staff of the uniformed police as a way of increasing Muslim dominance.[36] According to the political scientist Neven Anđelić, the SDA's mobilization among the Muslims of the Sandžak showed that 'the character of the SDA was similar to that of the SDS and the HDZ. They did not respect republican borders and were in the process of marking their ethnic territory'.[37] Indications are that the SDA, the SDS and the HDZ all engaged in the practice of inflating the police reserve forces in the period between the November 1990 elections and the outbreak of armed conflict, and at least some of these reserve police officers lacked proper qualifications and, in some cases, actually had criminal records.[38] Moreover, they tended to receive only perfunctory training. In practice, therefore, the normally strict regulations set for the recruitment of police were undermined and circumvented.

By the end of June 1991, the SRBiH MUP complained that national parties, i.e. the three victorious parties, were in the municipalities acting as exclusive bearers of personnel decisions.[39] Without properly consulting with the MUP, these parties were nominating and appointing individuals, in some cases unqualified individuals or even persons with criminal records.[40] Sometimes these appointments also violated previously existing interparty agreements, as well as an agreement that those candidates already employed in the MUP should receive preference. The MUP noted that the SDS had criticized the ministry's slow pace of appointments but argued that the SDS itself had not in a timely manner provided appropriate nominations for police posts in a number of the municipalities which it controlled. Rising tensions between the MUP and individual municipalities resulted in the issuance of unilateral ultimatums with which the nationalist parties tried to force the appointments of their preferred candidates. Such ultimatums included calls to boycotts or the takeover of police facilities, which in some cases apparently did occur. Former officials of the SRBiH MUP who testified at the ICTY indicated that in those municipalities where one party – and hence one ethnicity – came to dominate, police officers of other ethnicities found themselves marginalized and assigned to less important tasks.[41] Such situations could all too easily cause a further deterioration of inter-ethnic relations.

Hence, there were several disagreements among the three parties: about appointments to leadership positions, the ethnic distribution within the uniformed police force and the overall size of the active and reserve staff of the uniformed police. These disagreements trickled down to the regional and municipal levels. Directly below the seat of the ministry in the hierarchy came nine security services centres (*Centri službi bezbjednosti*, CSBs). The plural form, 'services', connoted the combination of the public and the state security services in these centres, located in Bihać, Banja Luka, Doboj, Goražde, Livno, Mostar, Sarajevo, Tuzla and Zenica. Accordingly, there were three top posts in each of the CSBs: the chief of the CSB itself, and the heads of the public security and state security sectors, respectively. The SDS received three CSBs (Banja Luka, Doboj and Goražde), four public security sectors (Goražde, Mostar, Sarajevo and Tuzla) and three state security sectors (Banja Luka, Bihać and Livno). Zenica was the only CSB without any SDS representative at the top. In addition to these posts at the CSBs, the SDS was also allotted the post of chief of the city Secretariat of Internal Affairs (*Sekretarijat unutrašnjih poslova*, SUP) for Sarajevo, which coordinated policing in the city's ten municipalities.

Each of the regional CSBs in turn stood above a number of subordinate municipal public security stations (*Stanice javne bezbjednosti*, SJBs). In the SJBs, the two most important posts were the chief and the commander of the station, respectively. At the bottom of the hierarchy were local police stations which located in villages or in suburbs of larger towns.

Even when agreement was attained between the SRBiH MUP and the municipalities regarding appointments to police posts, problems ensued. According to the ministry, quite a number of those appointed since the multi-party elections displayed primary allegiance to the political party which had appointed them, ignoring directives and instructions received from the ministry. Instead these officials tended to coordinate closely with the municipal assemblies, which were usurping the ministry's jurisdiction. Some new municipal police officials ignored the hierarchy of the ministry by leapfrogging the CSBs to appeal directly to the seat of the ministry.

Likewise, police officers of various ethnicities also saw fit to address their own grievances directly to the new political parties. In July 1991, Goran Zečević, a Bosnian Serb and a former employee of the SRBiH MUP, sent a letter to the SDS Council in Sarajevo.[42] Zečević claimed that the SDS was losing positions in the MUP to which it was entitled 'without a shot being fired', though several of the positions he mentioned as being occupied by the SDA and the HDZ had in fact been allotted to these parties by tripartite agreement. Zečević stated that the position of deputy minister occupied by Vitomir Žepinić was essentially powerless, and that the position of undersecretary for public security had been deliberately abandoned because it necessitated the appointment of a Serb who would hold real authority over the whole of the public security service. Meanwhile, the uniformed police rested under the control of Avdo Hebib, a Muslim. Zečević's proposed remedies hinted at policies that the SDS came to adopt towards the SRBiH MUP. He noted with approval that barricades had been formed in some areas. He then offered a specific recommendation on personnel policy.

> It is necessary to hire people who do not personally have any professional or political stains, regardless of whether they have formally joined the SDS. In my opinion, insofar as it is desirable to parry the aggressive policy of domination of the SDA and the HDZ in the MUP, it is necessary to also hire people who until recently led the service of the organs of internal affairs and are of Serb nationality, regardless under which circumstances they left the service. They have valuable experience and knowledge, have information of inestimable value [and] possess the right experience in the organization and operationalization of the service.[43]

The SDA and the HDZ, Zečević averred, had succeeded in marginalizing Serbs in the ministry through a mixture of new appointments and reorganization of responsibilities. Of particular concern was the 'loss' of SUP Sarajevo and control over the police, which was now in the hands of Avdo Hebib of the SDA. Zečević suggested that for the SDS it was of greatest importance to have Serbs – if possible, qualified Serbs – as employees in the SRBiH MUP, regardless of whether they were actually members of the SDS. Zečević thought that a large intake of Serbs was urgently needed to counter the alleged formation of a covert Muslim police force composed of 1,000 men from Sandžak.

Only a few days after Goran Zečević sent his letter to the SDS Council, Stojan Župljanin, the head of CSB Banja Luka, wrote to Biljana Plavšić, the Bosnian Serb member of the SRBiH Presidency, in her capacity as the president of the Council for the Preservation of the Constitutional Order of SRBiH.[44] Župljanin claimed that Avdo Hebib, Assistant Minister for the Police, and Hilmija Selimović, assistant minister for Legal and Administrative Affairs and Foreigners, were conspiring to form a purely Muslim 'army' out of the police. Župljanin wrote that he and his Serb colleagues had suggested that the SRBiH MUP hire either former (Serb) members of the Croatian MUP or former (Serb) employees of the SRBiH MUP who had allegedly been driven out of the service with the use of 'perfidious methods'. These persons would be hired instead of training new recruits, thereby saving the ministry money. Yet Župljanin claimed that Hebib and Selimović instead insisted on 400 new candidates, of whom 80 per cent stemmed from the Sandžak. Župljanin attached a statement by the brother of a Muslim police officer who claimed that, exacerbating the situation, Muslims were being sent to receive training in Croatia.[45] It should, however, be noted that many Bosnian Serb police officers had received training in Serbia at some point in their careers.

Indications also exist that quite a number of Serbs in the SRBiH MUP identified with the SDS and with Karadžić and shared his frustration with the personnel situation. On 9 September 1991, a group of 'leading employees of Serb nationality in SRBiH MUP' issued a public statement criticizing the ministry's reaction to a recent *Oslobođenje* commentary on Radovan Karadžić.[46] The MUP was reacting to comments made by Karadžić at a 5 September press conference in Sarajevo. According to the article, entitled 'Incitement to War', Karadžić had accused the SRBiH MUP of constituting the 'core' of a new armed force in Bosnia and Herzegovina and of engaging in 'anti-army matters' (*antiarmijski poslovi*), i.e. working against the JNA. Karadžić had also alleged that the Serbs in some areas no longer trusted the SRBiH MUP. Around the same time, Karadžić told both Nikola Koljević and Serbian President Slobodan Milošević that the Serbs were being pushed into a corner and would have to react by forming their own police.[47] In a conversation with leading SDS member Miodrag Simović, Karadžić also stated that he was going to tell Žepinić that the Serbs in the MUP should go into 'opposition'. 'We are going to break … to break up everything and then we will make our own SUP [sic] separately and with other people and we will separately make a government, we will make everything separately.'[48] In the context of this latter conversation, which took place on 16 September, Karadžić claimed that the removal of Neđo Vlaški, who should have on behalf of the SDS been serving as undersecretary for the SDB, was 'the drop that made the cup flow over'.

The published SRBiH MUP statement pleaded with Karadžić, as the leader of one of the main parties in Bosnia and Herzegovina, to be more responsible in his public statements. By contrast, the Serbs in the SRBiH MUP reacting to this statement claimed that the Steering Council of the SRBiH MUP had not been properly consulted regarding this matter. Taking the opportunity to list other grievances, the drafters of the statement argued that the Deputy Minister Žepinić was being circumvented regarding important personnel decisions. The appointment and rotation of personnel in the State Security Service were a particularly sore point. The Serbs complained that the position of deputy undersecretary of SDB, which the inter-party agreement had allocated to the Serbs, had been eliminated, leading to a situation in which, according to the subsequent summary of one Bosnian Serb, 'absolute control of the work and all the activities of that service was in the hands of the Muslims'.⁴⁹ Moreover, whereas the SDS claimed to be the sole arbiter of personnel decisions related to Serbs in the SRBiH MUP, the statement alleged that 'servile Serbs' (*poslušni Srbi*) were being appointed without consultation with the SDS.⁵⁰ Other complaints regarded the allegedly improper use of the SRBiH MUP special police unit, the aforementioned 'anti-army' sentiments and the allegedly illegal issuance of SRBiH MUP identification cards. The statement concluded that 'such one-sided and irregular moves damaging the Serb nation lead to divisions in the ministry. This can only have incalculable consequences, and the Serb cadres cannot bear responsibility for that'.

These tensions regarding personnel appointments in the SRBiH MUP were apparent on the regional and the municipal level. On 19 September 1991, the chief of CSB Banja Luka, Stojan Župljanin, wrote to the chief of SJB Prijedor regarding recent personnel appointments at that SJB.⁵¹ Župljanin protested against the recent appointment of employees by the SJB without prior consultation and approval from CSB Banja Luka. Župljanin reminded the chief of the SJB that personnel policy was controlled by the chief of the CSB. Of the five employees (four Bosnian Muslims and one Bosnian Serb) mentioned in the dispatch, Župljanin stated that he would only allow the latter to be retained, as the proper checks had been conducted for that employee.

In the late summer and autumn of 1991, the comments of the Bosnian Serb leadership and leading Bosnian Serb officials in the SRBiH MUP continued to be characterized by complaints about cadre issues.⁵² Senior Serb officials in the SRBiH MUP also reported on alleged Muslim and Croatian terrorist activities aimed against the safety and well-being of the Serb people.⁵³ Simultaneously, in some areas, such as in the Prijedor region, non-Serb police officials reported on 'problematic' and tense relations with military (JNA and TO) authorities.⁵⁴ Tensions rose still further when Milan Martić, the Minister of Internal Affairs of the Croatian Serbs, was arrested on a Croatian arrest warrant by the police in Bosnia and Herzegovina on 9 September 1991.⁵⁵ Already months earlier, SRBiH Presidency member Ganić had accused Martić's police of engaging in acts tantamount to armed aggression against Bosnia.⁵⁶ Martić was released shortly thereafter. At the beginning of October 1991, a dispute broke out in Srebrenica over the allocation of police posts.⁵⁷

Meanwhile, given the party-political nature of the disagreement about staffing in the SRBiH MUP, it comes as no surprise that senior party officials intervened constantly and directly in personnel issues. On the Bosnian Serb side, conversations intercepted in 1991 and 1992 by the SRBiH MUP SDB demonstrate that Radovan Karadžić as leader of the SDS took a particular keen interest in such matters.⁵⁸ He spoke frequently with SDS appointees in the ministry, his most important interlocutors being Deputy Minister Vitomir Žepinić and Assistant Minister Momčilo Mandić.⁵⁹ Karadžić's interventions demonstrated detailed knowledge of specific personnel decisions in the ministry, including at the regional and municipal levels. By the end of May 1991 at the latest, Karadžić had decided that personnel decisions affecting Serbs in the SRBiH MUP had to be taken by the SDS's leadership.⁶⁰ Župljanin pleaded with Plavšić to put an end to this 'perfidious game' in which 'Serb cadres and the Serb people' were the victims. Several phone calls made between Radovan Karadžić and Biljana Plavšić confirm that Plavšić raised the matter at a meeting of the Council for the Protection of the Constitutional Order on 26 July 1991, and that Karadžić was also aware of the matter.[61]

In the course of discussions regarding personnel issues, Karadžić told Žepinić that the SDS should be allowed to nominate 35.65 per cent of the posts in the SRBiH MUP.[62] This was the percentage of Serbs that Karadžić believed lived in Bosnia and Herzegovina. Karadžić was particularly worried about the allotment of posts within the SDB, most likely because Karadžić suspected or had perhaps become alerted to the electronic surveillance of leading SDS members by the SDB. On 17 June 1991, Mandić told Karadžić that the issue of posts in the SDB had to be resolved soon. 'Otherwise we will be ruined.'[63] On 8 July, Karadžić asked Žepinić to ensure that the leading Serbs of the ministry meet every morning to discuss events, 'so that no one is appointed without the full approval of all the Serbs there.'[64] Using obscenities, Karadžić made it clear that there would be 'horrible' consequences if the SDS did not get its way. Karadžić stated that he had met the previous evening with Izetbegović and Zulfikarpašić. According to Karadžić,

> I told them to their faces that we will form a parallel government, we will form a parallel police force. We will pull out our people and the government will have to pay them. We will pull out all our men under arms. We will completely form a parallel state, if you continue to fuck around. And they only watched and blinked, because we will do that. God our father cannot prevent us from doing that, because they have started against us in a way that they are fucking us and fucking us over. And there is no question, we will do this in a week. Well, let there be war, yes let there be war, but we will finish the job once and for all.

In the same conversation, Karadžić made it absolutely clear that the only acceptable Serbs in the SRBiH MUP were those who had been directly approved by the SDS and by the other Serbs in the SRBiH MUP. Karadžić told Žepinić to instruct Dragan Devedlaka, a Serb SRBiH MUP SDB operative, not to nominate anyone for any posts without prior approval from the SDS. In a separate conversation on the same day, Karadžić made the same point to Devedlaka directly.[65]

On 18 September 1991, Karadžić told Žepinić that Karadžić had finally realized that even if 90 per cent of the employees in the SRBiH MUP were Serbs, it would not make much of a difference. Karadžić argued that the Serbs followed the Law on Internal Affairs and the internal regulations of the ministry too much for their own good.[66] Karadžić further demanded that the leading Serbs in the SRBiH MUP meet for coffee every morning to discuss personnel decisions, and Žepinić agreed. Karadžić reiterated this stance repeatedly in subsequent conversations. Karadžić also insisted that those Serbs who were appointed hold important positions.[67]

Although Žepinić was the most senior Serb in the SRBiH MUP, and therefore logically the principal interlocutor for Karadžić, conversations during the summer and autumn of 1991 showed Žepinić losing the confidence of Karadžić.[68] On

2 September 1991, Karadžić rebuked Žepinić with reference to a controversial personnel appointment that had finally been resolved. 'Vito, you have told me hundreds of times that this is so, and then it wasn't.' Karadžić accused Žepinić of letting Avdo Hebib and the other Muslims make a Muslim army out of the SRBiH MUP behind the Serbs' backs. Žepinić countered by accusing Karadžić of listening to others instead. Žepinić also told Karadžić to appoint someone else if Karadžić was dissatisfied with Žepinić's performance.

As a result of such disagreements, Karadžić turned instead to Momčilo Mandić, who as assistant minister for the Prevention and Detection of Crime was subordinate to Žepinić. Žepinić also on several occasions tried in vain to resign his post, testifying later that he 'had realized that my concept and my political views and thinking, as well as the way I managed the Ministry of Interior, were all in conflict with the policies and intentions of the ethnically-based parties which were then in power'.[69] Nevertheless, at least until the end of the autumn of 1991, Karadžić continued to treat Žepinić publicly as the top Bosnian Serb in the SRBiH MUP.

The impact of the war in Croatia

The increased tensions and frayed nerves within the SRBiH MUP and the tripartite nationalist coalition in Bosnia must be situated within the context of the war in Croatia. Together with Slovenia, Croatia declared its independence from Yugoslavia on 25 June 1991. Fighting between Croatia's nascent armed forces on the one hand and the JNA and rebellious Croatian Serbs on the other erupted almost immediately. Though large-scale combat did not occur until the late summer, the effects of the outbreak of war in Croatia on Bosnia were profound. Geographically and ethnically speaking, Bosnia was surrounded by parties to the conflict, and the conflict of course pitted Croats and Serbs – two of Bosnia's three largest ethnic groups – against each other. The support of the SDA and most Bosnian Muslims for Croatia's independence, bearing with it the corollary the desire for Bosnian independence, created the clear impression among Serbs in Bosnia that the Bosnian Muslims were siding with Croats against Serbs.

Both political and military spillover into Bosnia were guaranteed, as northwestern Bosnia in particular became a military staging ground and essential supply route for the JNA.[70] Adding to the tensions, a significant number of Serbs working in the Croatian MUP faced dismissal during 1991, and a number of them came to Bosnia looking for employment. Simultaneously, Croatian Serbs fleeing from the conflict came in large numbers to Bosnia, where their need for housing and employment placed additional pressure on an already-acute situation. And many Bosnian Croats meanwhile headed to Croatia to support Croatia's war for independence, even as the Bosnian Croats also organized politically in the nascent entity 'Herceg-Bosna' which the HDZ-BiH unilaterally proclaimed on 18 November 1991.

Perhaps the most dramatic example of the consequences of the Croatian war for Bosnia came from the apparent direct involvement of some Bosnian reserve police units in the war. A much later official draft report from the Bosnian Serb police noted:

> It is necessary to emphasise that already in October 1991 all SJBs from the territory of Eastern Herzegovina put more than half of their police reserve forces at the disposal of the JNA without the approval of the then SRBiH MUP. A special police unit of SAO Herzegovina was sent to the Dubrovnik battlefield. It later took part in actions in Čapljina and Mostar municipalities.

All of this contributed to the 'preparation for the final division' of the SRBiH MUP.[71]

For the SRBiH MUP, the immediate impact of the Croatian war made itself felt on issues regarding the mobilization of the reserve police force and the training and increase in the size of this force. The reality of the Croatian war had a very real impact upon these discussions, particularly in municipalities bordering Croatia.[72] Top SRBiH officials visited some of the affected municipalities only weeks after the start of the war in Croatia, noting the drastically heightened tension and the self-organization of worried citizens into improvised armed groups, as well as the arrival of thousands of Serb 'refugees' from Croatia.[73] Much of the population in the area was reported to feel neglected or even 'revolted' by the alleged lack of response by the republican authorities in Sarajevo. The republican officials assessed the risk of an outbreak of armed conflict between self-organized groups of Serbs and Muslims as considerable, and asked for the SJBs in the area to be fully staffed and for a mobilization of the reserve staff of the police to be considered. CSB Banja Luka had already undertaken a 'test mobilization' of the reserve police force after allegedly not having received any response from the SRBiH MUP regarding the implementation of reserve mobilization. At the same time, the officials also acknowledged the reality that some HDZ and SDA municipal officials were encouraging Croats and Muslims to boycott the call-up of reserves being undertaken by the JNA.

Already on 10 July 1991, Delimustafić sent a warning to all SJBs and CSBs warning against the illegal engagement of reserve police forces and providing a copy of legal provisions regulating the circumstances permitting the engagement of reserve police forces. According to those regulations, the SRBiH MUP deployed reserve police forces in a state of emergency.[74] Delimustafić and other members of the ministry's steering council had received quite a lot information revealing that local and regional officials were making decisions on the staffing of the reserve police staff that were not in accordance with regulations, in particular as concerned the ethnic composition of the staff and the requirement that members be properly qualified and without criminal records.[75] On 16 September, Deputy Minister Žepinić insisted that the composition of the reserve staff of the police had to be in harmony with the population's ethnic composition, noting that some municipalities had been given permission by the MUP to activate their reserve staffs.[76]

The issue of the mobilization of police reserve forces continued to be hotly debated throughout the summer and autumn of 1991. In September, an agreement was reached between the SSUP and the SRBiH MUP on the formation of a working group whose task it would be to monitor the staffing levels of the active and reserve police forces, their ethnic distribution and the deployment of mixed military and police patrols throughout Bosnia.[77] All three sides contributed to the swelling of the reserve police force, drawing recruits from their party membership and arming them.[78] In the case of the Bosnian Muslims and the SDA, some reserve police recruits went to Croatia for training.[79] On 11 July, the SDA, referring to an agreement between SRBiH MUP and the MUP of Croatia, sent the MUP of Croatia over 200 names of candidates for police training in the latter's training centre.[80] This fact combined with allegations of an influx of Sandžak Muslims into the SRBiH MUP to greatly agitate the SDS.

On 23 September Delimustafić attended the 10th Session of the Council for the Protection of Constitutional Order.[81] The first topic discussed was the security situation in the republic, which had particularly been influenced by events in Croatia and the presence of JNA reservists from Montenegro on the territory of Herzegovina. The Council supported the efforts of the SRBiH MUP to maintain peace and decided to continue to support the SRBiH MUP. A proposal was made that during the mobilization of the reserve police attention should be paid to the national composition of the reserve units, and that in the course of patrols by regular and reserve police the multi-national composition of patrols should be ensured in order to reassure the population. The Council also agreed to propose to the political parties that they intensify their activity to reduce inter-ethnic tension and mistrust. Furthermore, the Council discussed incidents in Čapljina involving the SJB in that municipality and the distribution of weapons. Another topic was information about activities at home and abroad aimed at violent changes to the constitutional order. The Council proposed that the SDB increase its work in this area and cooperate with the JNA's security service. Finally, the organization and assignment of the Detachment for Special Purposes, the sole existing special police unit in the MUP, was debated. Delimustafić did not participate in this discussion.[82] According to the discussion the Detachment for Special Purposes should only be used by decision of the Minister of Internal Affairs. The Council did instruct that account should be taken of the national composition of MUP organs, especially management staff.

On 26 September 1991 Delimustafić issued instructions to the SRBiH MUP concerning the mobilization of the reserve police. This had been ordered by the presidency. The reserve would be considered as accredited police while carrying out duties. Delimustafić added that reservists sometimes did not act in accordance with the law or regulations, for example, in uniforms or handling of weapons, and also in reporting on activities. As a consequence, Delimustafić ordered that all branches of the MUP ensure that the reserve police act in accordance with regulations and that proper command and control of the reserve police was exercised.[83]

In a dispatch sent to all SDS municipal boards a few days before Delimustafić's instructions, the party's President, Radovan Karadžić, expressed concern about the purpose of the mobilization of the reserve police force in Bosnia and Herzegovina.[84] Nevertheless, he instructed all municipal boards to ensure that Serbs reported for mobilization.

Delimustafić claimed later that the mobilization was not fully successful because the republic lacked the money with which to pay its reserve police.[85] According to an undated order by Delimustafić, the MUP stressed that the reserve police force 'must not be used and engaged in ways and situations that are not stipulated by the law'. Failure to respect these provisions would carry legal sanctions against persons responsible. Subordinate entities were instructed that reserve forces could be engaged in professional training programmes. In addition, these forces could, with the prior consent of the SRBiH MUP, be used to carry out special security jobs and tasks and to provide necessary help in cases of natural disasters. In exceptional circumstances the SRBiH MUP could engage the reserve forces in accordance with the Law on All People's Defence.[86]

Another indication of the splintering of the MUP came on 20 September 1991 when Delimustafić sent instructions to all branches of the CSB and SJB noting that they were obliged to report to the ministry all important security events and measures undertaken as a consequence. This apparently had not been done in certain cases.[87]

The impact of the war in Croatia of course also had implications for the cooperation of the JNA and the SRBiH MUP. Joint police and army patrols have already been mentioned. In late October 1991, the SRBiH MUP cooperated with JNA Military Security, the Federal Secretariat for Internal Affairs (SSUP) and the JNA in a joint action entitled '*Punkt* '91' (Point '91). This action aimed to control all traffic in and out of the Socialist Republic of Bosnia and Herzegovina in order to prevent the illegal trade of goods and weapons, and the movements of armed individuals and paramilitary groups.[88] At the same time, however, the SRBiH MUP SDB was receiving reports that certain Serbs in the SRBiH MUP – such as those at SJB Pale – were engaged in covert attempts to acquire arms and assist the formation of Serb Autonomous Districts (*Srpske autonomne oblasti*, SAOs) in Bosnia and Herzegovina, which will be discussed subsequently.[89] And at a session of the SRBiH Presidency in October 1991, Alija Izetbegović voiced concerns that the distribution of weapons to TO units was taking place unevenly, with certain units and regions favoured, and that some units were ignoring the chain of command and were therefore de facto becoming paramilitary formations.[90]

The fragmentation of the police: The Croatian backdrop

Before proceeding to discuss further developments in Bosnia and Herzegovina, it is essential to review the establishment of ethnically Serb 'autonomous districts' and police forces in neighbouring Croatia. Much of what later transpired in Bosnia, particularly the actions of the Bosnian Serbs, followed a template first invented by the Serbs of Croatia, namely the strategic use of regionalization or decentralization in order to achieve an ethnically separate police force and, with it, ethnic separation from other ethnic groups.[91] Conversely, the Bosnian Muslims and Bosnian Croats to some extent emulated the strategy adopted by the Croatian state in converting existing republican organs including the police into organs of newly independent states.

In Croatia, the nationalist Croat Democratic Union (*Hrvatska demokratska zajednica*, HDZ) led by the controversial historian and former Partisan general Franjo Tuđman was established in June 1989. Partly in reaction to the HDZ, and in particular to the perceived threat against them, many Croatian Serbs rallied around the Serb Democratic Party (*Srpska demokratska stranka*, SDS), which was founded in February 1990 by Jovan Rašković and other Croatian Serbs. The declared goal of the SDS was to represent and defend the interests of Serbs in Croatia. Yet approximately two-thirds of Croatian Serbs actually supported the reformed communists in the elections.[92] Only in the municipalities of Donji Lapac, Gračac and Knin did the SDS attain majorities. However, the HDZ and the SDS subsequently implicitly cooperated in radicalizing the political climate, another ominous harbinger for Bosnia. The political developments in Croatia and, in particular, the rapidly rising tensions between Croats and Serbs had very real implications for policing and for the security situation in Bosnia.

The SDS wanted to remain within a Yugoslavia led strongly from Belgrade, and the party counteracted Croatian nationalist currents towards independence with a campaign of decentralization within Croatia. In its own words, the goals and tasks of the SDS were amongst others

> the dismantling of the party-state ... the creation of conditions for the full affirmation of the spiritual and cultural identity of every Yugoslav nation by itself, regardless of which federal unit it is located in; ensuring the constitutional possibility of establishing territorial autonomy in the framework of federal units, insofar as the population on the territory with a particular ethnic composition or cultural-historical identity decides this by referendum ... [and] the taking of constant care regarding the state of all diasporas of the Serb nation in Yugoslavia, and particularly in Croatia.[93]

Although the HDZ obtained 41.5 per cent of the votes in the first democratic multi-party elections, this gave them a two-thirds majority in the Croatian parliament, the Sabor.[94] At the end of May 1990, Tuđman won election as president. The victory of the HDZ heightened the already considerable anxiety among the Serb minority, where many felt that Serbs would be subject to discrimination and the loss of political rights.

Croatia was in 1991 predominantly inhabited by ethnic Croats but had a sizable Serb minority. According to the last census conducted in Yugoslavia in 1991, the Socialist Republic of Croatia had a population of 4,784,265 people, of which 3,736,356 (78.1 per cent) were Croats and 581,663 (12.2 per cent) were Serbs.[95] The fears of the Serb minority were frequently manipulated by politicians and the media by alluding to mass atrocities during the Second World War. From 1941 until 1945 the fascist Independent State of Croatia (*Nezavisna Država Hrvatska*, or NDH) had implemented extremely discriminatory policies against Serbs and other minorities and perpetrated a genocide against the Serbs of the NDH, the territory of which included all of Bosnia and Herzegovina and parts of Serbia.[96]

Subsequent events in Croatia have significantly distorted analysis of the Croatian Serbs. In particular, maps showing a large concentration of the Serbs in those areas which later attempted to secede from Croatia distort the actual demographic distribution of the Serbs in Croatia before the war. It is certainly true that the area historically known as the Krajina – the old Austro-Hungarian military frontier – as well as certain areas of in particular Eastern Slavonia, Baranja and Syrmia had very sizable and in some cases overwhelmingly majority Serb populations. However, particularly the Krajina was very sparsely populated. Thus, even though there were numerous municipalities in this featuring almost exclusively Serb populations, the majority of Serbs in Croatia actually lived in larger cities such as Zagreb, Karlovac, Osijek, Rijeka, Split, etc. where they had for decades or even centuries cohabited with Croats and many others.

Nonetheless, in the context of the political transformations and increasing tension between Serbs and Croats in Croatia, the SDS began to contemplate the establishment of self-rule for areas inhabited predominately by Serbs. On 27 June 1990, the municipalities of Knin, Benkovac, Gračac, Donji Lapac, Obrovac and Titova Korenica – all of them sparsely populated – founded the Association of Municipalities of Northern Dalmatia and Lika.[97] Milan Babić, a dentist, was the 'president' of this association. On 25 July, Croatian Serbs held a mass political gathering at Srb and issued a 'Declaration on the Sovereignty and Autonomy of the Serb Nation'.[98] The Declaration called for the formation of a Serb National Congress (*Srpsko nacionalno vijeće*), which would be charged with holding a referendum on the position of the Serb nation in Croatia.[99] On 31 July, the Serb National Congress chose Babić as its president and called again for a referendum to be held. The referendum, in which only Serbs were permitted to vote, was held between 19 August and 2 September 1990, resulting in an overwhelming vote for the autonomy of Serbs in Croatia.[100]

Shortly before the referendum began, the authorities of the Republic of Croatia stated that the referendum was illegal, and Croatian police deployed to police stations in areas populated by a Serb majority in an unsuccessful attempt to disarm the police there.[101] The chief of the Secretariat for Internal Affairs (*Sekretarijat za unutrašnje poslove*, or SUP) in Šibenik also suspended several employees of the Public Security Station in Knin, including its chief, Milan Martić.[102]

Martić proved to be a charismatic but also polarizing figure among the Croatian Serbs. Starting with Serbs in the police in his own municipality, Martić began to form a police force that acted increasingly independently of the Croatian Ministry of Internal Affairs. Martić's key role in this process was underlined by the fact that both Serbs and Croats began to refer to the police in the area as *Martićevci*, i.e. Martić's men.[103]

In order to prevent the Croatian police from exercising their authority on the territory where the referendum was being carried out, Serbs in the affected area erected a variety of improvised brigades. In many cases, logs were placed across roads, effectively blocking them, whereby this episode of Yugoslavia's disintegration came to be known as the 'Log Revolution' (*Balvan revolucija*). Nearly two years later, in July 1992, the government of what had come to be known as Republika Srpska Krajina retroactively proclaimed 17 August 1990 to have been the beginning of the war 'on the territory of Republika Srpska Krajina'.[104]

As these developments occurred, the Croatian government under the control of the HDZ moved deliberately to strengthen and militarize the Croatian police force in preparation for the foundation of a future Croatian army.[105] In order to counter the ongoing attempts by the JNA to disarm the TO in Croatia, the Croatian government and some Croats in the JNA such as General Martin Špegelj organized the illegal importation of weapons from neighbouring Hungary.[106] The result was that as of 15 January 1991, there were approximately 30,000 armed police officers under the control of the Croatian government, which was more than the number of JNA soldiers stationed in Croatia.[107] However, Špegelj in his memoirs recalls that as of December 1990, there was widespread opposition in the Croatian MUP to its transformation into a military force.[108] In addition, the government commenced the establishment of an auxiliary formation known as the National Protection (*Narodna zaštita*, NZ). On 5 May 1991, President Tuđman issued a decision on the establishment of a new Croatian National Guard (*Zbor narodne garde*, ZNG), specifying that the ZNG was being established 'for the purposes of defending the constitutional order, the unity and territorial integrity of the Republic of Croatia'.[109] In late May 1991 in the stadium of the football club Zagreb, a review of the ZNG took place. Hence, considerably before the beginning of the war in Croatia, both Croats and Serbs perceived the police as being crucial to their future plans.

Considerably earlier, in September 1990, tensions rose as the Croatian MUP demanded that Serbs hand in 'illegal' weapons and ammunition, a demand viewed by Serbs as an attempt to disarm the police in areas inhabited predominantly by Serbs.[110] The Serbs feared that such a disarmament would, at best, presage the widespread discrimination and harassment of Serbs or, at worst, a campaign of persecution and extermination of the type seen during the Second World War.

In November 1990, the Croatian Sabor promulgated a new law on internal affairs. Among the features of the new law was a change in terminology. The municipal public security stations (SJS) were henceforth to be known as police stations (PS), and in some cases more 'Croatian' words were to be used (e.g. '*unutarnji poslovi*' instead of '*unutrašnji poslovi*' for 'internal affairs'). Particularly contentious was the choice of the word '*redarstvenik*' instead of the previously existing '*milicionar*' for 'police officer'. Recognizing that the new term carried with it echoes of the Ustasha police, it was quickly dropped in favour of the more international term '*policajac*'.[111] In addition, the insistence of the Croatian authorities on Croatian symbols for police uniforms was strongly opposed by many Serbs.[112]

On 20 December 1990, the municipal assembly in Knin, whose president was Milan Babić, adopted a decision on the implementation of a statute for a Serb Autonomous District of Krajina (*Srpska Autonomna Oblast Krajine*, or SAO Krajina).[113] According to Article 1 of the Statute, the SAO Krajina was 'established in order to realize the national equality, as well as cultural and historical characteristics of the Serb people residing on the territory of the Dalmatian and Military Krajina, which is located in the structure of the Republic of Croatia in the frame of federal Yugoslavia'.[114] Article 9 of the Statute provided for the 'autonomy of the judicial and police organs which operate in the District'. Although the SAO Krajina was the first and by far the most important SAO in Croatia, the Serbs also established SAOs in Western Slavonia and for Eastern Slavonia, Baranja and Western Syrmia.

Only a few days later, the Croatian Sabor promulgated a new constitution. It controversially defined the Republic of Croatia as 'the national state of the Croat nation and the state of members of other nations and minorities who are citizens'.[115] Many Serbs in Croatia interpreted this wording as a harbinger of their second-class status in a future independent Croatia. The political scientist Mila Dragojević writes that 'the issue of naming ethnic minorities in the new constitution ... became part of the symbolic repertoire of the public discourse before the eruption of violence. ... The symbolism of this constitutional amendment was heightened by the evidence of actual discrimination against Serbs'.[116] In addition, as the Croatian authorities began to adopt a series of symbols and insignia designed to nurture Croatian national identity and statehood, the Serbs objected to a number of these because of both real and alleged associations with those symbols and insignia which had been used by the NDH in the 1940s. The exaggerated and emotional rhetoric of both HDZ and SDS leaders contributed throughout 1990 and 1991 to a deterioration of the relationship between Croats and Croatian Serbs. This worsening also pushed a number of Serbs who had in the 1990 elections voted for or been elected for the SDP to join the SDS instead.

On 4 January 1991, the SAO Krajina Executive Council transformed the Knin police station into a 'regional SUP' covering the territory of the SAO Krajina.[117] According to Article 2 of the decision, 'this Secretariat alone is responsible for and authorized to carry out all affairs from the area of internal affairs and public security on the territory of the Serb Autonomous District of Krajina'.[118] On the same day, Milan Martić was appointed as the head of this SUP, which encompassed the police stations of Knin, Obrovac, Benkovac, Gračac, Titova Korenica, Donji Lapac, Dvor na Uni, Glina, Kostajnica and Vojnić.[119] The SAO Krajina was growing. The SUP was tasked to take care of all matters relating to internal affairs, ensuring 'all human and civil rights without regard to the religious, racial and national affiliation of the population'.[120] Coordination with the MUP of Croatia was to occur as needed, but the jurisdiction of the MUP of Croatia and its orders were pronounced null and void for the area of the SAO Krajina. Notification of this change was sent to internal affairs organs in Croatia, Serbia and Bosnia and Herzegovina, as well as to the president of the Presidency of the SFRJ.[121]

Article 7 of the SAO Krajina Executive Council decision on the establishment of the SUP for the SAO Krajina dictated that the Executive Council would be responsible for elaborating the structure of the SUP and the manner of its work.¹²² On this basis, the Executive Council on 19 January 1991 issued a decree on the internal organization and work of the Secretariat of Internal Affairs.¹²³ It should be noted that the actual text of the decree referred to a *Ministry* of Internal Affairs, a shift in terminology that mirrored developments elsewhere in Yugoslavia. Likewise, the organs of internal affairs henceforth adopted the term 'public security stations' at the municipal level, in accordance with a contemporary shift in methodology in Bosnia and Herzegovina.

Since winning the elections in April and May 1990, the HDZ-controlled government and President Franjo Tuđman had pushed increasingly for the establishment of an independent Croatia. In the first months of 1991, Croatia continued to move towards independence. On 21 February, the Croatian Sabor passed a resolution initiating Croatia's disassociation from the SFRJ, though this resolution still contemplated the possibility of a loose federation of sovereign republics.¹²⁴ On 19 May, Croatia held a referendum on independence, resulting in a positive vote, though the referendum was not held in areas controlled by the SAO Krajina.¹²⁵ Croatia declared its independence from the SFRJ on 25 June.¹²⁶

Meanwhile, on 1 April 1991, the Executive Council of the Assembly of the SAO Krajina decided to unite the SAO Krajina with the Republic of Serbia, a decision that was, however, not reciprocated.¹²⁷ On 30 April, the SAO Krajina Assembly announced a referendum on joining the SAO Krajina to the Republic of Serbia, and on staying in Yugoslavia with 'Serbia, Montenegro and others who wish to preserve Yugoslavia.'¹²⁸ On that date, the Assembly also elected Milan Babić as the president of the Executive Council of the SAO Krajina.¹²⁹ The referendum, which was held on 12 May, resulted in a large majority favouring remaining in Yugoslavia.¹³⁰

Two incidents occurring during this period underline the importance of policing on the road to war in Croatia. On 31 March 1991, an armed altercation took place in Plitvice National Park in Croatia between the police of the Croatian MUP and the police of the SUP of the SAO Krajina.¹³¹ The national park occupied a strategic location on the main road connecting Zagreb and Dalmatia, and it was hence crucial not only to maintaining the Croatian government's control over a major region of the country but also for the very significant tourist industry. The Croatian leadership therefore decided to dispatch police to the park to disperse the blockades which local Serbs had erected there. Two people, one Serb and one Croat, were killed and nearly two dozen people were injured during the armed altercation, which came to be referred to as the Plitvice Bloody Easter (*Plitvički krvavi Uskrs*). Together with Benkovac police officer Goran Alivanja, who had been killed in November 1990, they became the first fatalities of the coming Croatian war.¹³² During the incident at Plitvice, the Croatian authorities arrested several persons, including Goran Hadžić, who would go on to become the president of the RSK in 1992.¹³³ Hadžić sustained a beating at the hands of the Croatian authorities.

According to a contemporaneous Yugoslav military report, the incident at Plitvice resulted from the 'gradual unification' of predominantly Serb municipalities and the preparation of the armed defence of the SAO Krajina in reaction to Croatian moves towards independence.[134] According to the JNA, 'the immediate cause for the armed conflict at Plitvice [was] the decision of the municipal assembly of Titova Korenica to proclaim the Plitvice lakes a public enterprise of the so-called SAO Krajina, and the expressed readiness to defend this territory even at the price of armed conflict'.[135] On the Croatian side, forces of MUP Croatia were dispatched with the goal of reasserting control over the area, and arguably preparing for a direct armed confrontation with Knin.[136] The military report concluded that, despite pressure from the JNA for both parties to cease and desist, there was a significant danger of a full-scale 'civil war of broader measures which would result in numerous human victims and migrations of people accompanied by the creation of ethnically pure areas'.[137] After the altercation, the JNA set up a buffer zone between the Croatian police and the Croatian Serbs, which had the effect of de facto recognizing the autonomy of the Croatian Serbs.

On the day of the incident at Plitvice, in a dispatch sent to the SFRJ Presidency, Milan Martić characterized the incident as an act of 'armed aggression' by MUP Croatia.[138] Martić reiterated this view on 25 April in a dispatch sent to the SFRJ Presidency, SSUP, the Federal Secretariat for People's Defence (*Savezni sekretarijat za narodnu odbranu*, SSNO) and the MUPs of Croatia and Serbia.[139] Meanwhile, on 1 April, Babić ordered the mobilization of the TO of the SAO Krajina and of volunteer units.[140]

A second noteworthy incident prior to the outbreak of the Croatian war occurred on 2 May 1991 in the village of Borovo Selo near Vukovar.[141] As was the case at Plitvice, the Croatian police had attempted to reassert their control over an area when fighting erupted.[142] At Borovo Selo this had been done in a highly provocative way by firing rockets into the village.[143] Together with earlier incidents at Plitvice and Pakrac, the clash at Borovo Selo contributed significantly to a deterioration of the relations between Croats and Serbs in Croatia.[144] After the incident at Borovo Selo, the Serb National Council announced that there was no alternative to the formation of armed volunteer formations and the arming of the Serb nation in the area.[145] This was viewed as an unfortunate contingency for the case that the JNA could not or would not be able or willing to protect the Serbs.

The *Balvan revolucija* of August 1990 together with the Plitvice, Pakrac and Borovo Selo incidents in the spring of 1991 together marked the most significant flare-ups in Croatia before the actual war commenced in the summer of 1991. Of course, in addition to these episodes, an increasing number of sporadic and isolated violent attacks against both Serbs and Croats occurred in villages and towns across Croatia. The fact that all the most significant incidents prior to June 1991 involved primarily police and paramilitary forces, and not the military, supports the contention that the issue of policing played a key, driving role in the events leading to eventual full-scaled armed conflict. The much more heavily armed JNA was, by contrast, still confined to a largely reactive role, even though it certainly over time increasingly sided implicitly and then finally explicitly with the cause of the Croatian Serbs.[146]

The ethnically driven regionalization implemented by the Serbs in Croatia and the reliance upon the police force proved to be successful strategies which would later be adopted by the Bosnian Serbs. With the SAOs, the Serbs in effect established control over territory which they intended to preserve in Yugoslavia in the case of Croatia's secession. Although the Serbs in Croatia undoubtedly also looked to the JNA to protect and assist them, at the local level the police afforded the Croatian Serbs the maximum amount of control. Whereas the army was tightly controlled in Belgrade and had a broader and in principle Yugoslav agenda, the local police commanders in the SAOs could be counted upon to prioritize the interests of the Serbs in Croatia.

The second aspect of developments in and conversion of policing in Croatia that proved attractive to the Croatian Serbs was the militarization of the police. It followed from the reliance upon the local police and their presumed loyalty to the Serbian national cause that it would be beneficial to the Croatian Serbs if these police forces were not only placed under the control of the SAOs but also strengthened in terms of manpower and firepower. In the case of the SAO Krajina, this evolution into an armed (para)military force was symbolized by Milan Martić's appointment in May 1991 as the SAO Krajina minister of defence.[147]

Serb Autonomous Districts in Bosnia and the decentralization of Policing

Two processes – ethnicization and politicization – informed policing in both Croatia and Bosnia and Herzegovina in the relatively brief period between the multi-party elections and the outbreak of armed conflict. In the context of the increasingly dysfunctional Yugoslav state these combined into a combustible third process that would emerge as the necessary catalyst for state collapse and disintegration: ethnically based regionalization. It is essential to understand that neither of the first two processes was completely new compared to the preceding decades of policing in socialist Yugoslavia, nor did they solely affect the police. Policing was by definition politicized in the party-state, though this was most keenly felt in the Yugoslav State Security Service, whose very mandate required defending not only the state but also the party's leading role as enshrined in the constitution. Likewise, as noted, the authorities in socialist Yugoslavia had always very precisely kept track of the ethnic composition of the police (and the public sector in general).

The focus on ethnicization and politicization after the first multi-party elections, however, took place in a much more tense atmosphere in which parties founded specifically on the basis of narrow ethnically defined interest jockeyed for position and power.

For the SDS and for Serb cadres in the SRBiH MUP, the autumn of 1991 was marked by cautious steps in the direction of a consolidation of their position within MUP. The SDS and leading Serbs in the SRBiH MUP demanded 'professionalism' in the police.¹⁴⁸ As we have seen, among the grievances aired by Serb police officers in 1991 were deficiencies in training, understaffing and, most importantly, an imbalance in the ethnic structure of police cadres in Bosnia. As a result of these grievances and contemporary political developments, the SDS and leading Serbs in the SRBiH MUP at some point in the late summer or early autumn of 1991 began to contemplate a decentralization of internal affairs.

These thoughts about decentralization of policing went hand in hand with a process of political regionalization pursued by the Bosnian Serbs. In theory, decentralization would allow the Bosnian Serbs more discretion in terms of how they implemented decisions of the republican authorities in Sarajevo with which they disagreed. At the same time, decentralization would provide a platform for a variety of foundational activities, which could – and in actual fact did – lead to the establishment of a separate ethnically defined political entity.¹⁴⁹

The move towards decentralization manifested itself as the Bosnian Serbs began to establish Serb Autonomous Districts (*Srpske autonomne oblasti*, or SAOs) in September 1991.¹⁵⁰ SAO Herzegovina was formed on 12 September, followed by the proclamation of the Autonomous Region of Krajina (*Autonomna regija Krajina*, ARK) in Banja Luka on 16 September.¹⁵¹ Three days later, an SAO North-eastern Bosnia was established; SAO Romanija was also formed in mid-September. Finally, in early November an SAO Northern Bosnia Assembly met for the first time and SAO Birač was formed as well. The SAOs drew on the model previously used by the Serbs of Croatia.

While camouflaged somewhat as a purely administrative exercise which would yield significant economic benefits for the municipalities involved, the experience of SAO Krajina revealed that the SAOs were intricately linked to security. On 9 September 1991, Karadžić in a phone conversation with Serbian President Slobodan Milošević stated that the policy of regionalization was intended to thwart the SDA's drive towards Bosnian independence.¹⁵² In the words of Slobodan Popović, who served as a reformed communist in the Banja Luka city assembly, the ARK

> was formed in order to fulfil military-police functions. All the people involved in this agreement spoke in the assembly only about the organization of the police and the military, and not about the economy. The police, the military, that is also important, but there are also more important things, like education, economic and employment policy, culture, etc. This was not raised at all. This was the continuation of the policy which had already taken hold in Croatia.¹⁵³

In the SRBiH Presidency, Ejup Ganić worried about 'possible secession', stating that the SAOs 'smell of the creation of federal units in the framework of Yugoslavia'.¹⁵⁴ Approximately a year later, at the twentieth session of the Bosnian Serb Assembly in September 1992, SDS member Jovo Mijatović stated that the SDS had pursued regionalization in order 'to destroy a unitary Bosnia'.¹⁵⁵

A working paper prepared within the SRBiH MUP SDB in September 1991 discussed the possibility of decentralizing internal affairs in Bosnia and

Herzegovina.[156] Decentralization was seen as having negative consequences for the Bosnian Serbs. According to this working paper, decentralizing internal affairs 'in conditions of civil war in the country' was 'illusory'. In this context, the decentralization of internal affairs would lead to negative consequences, including the formation of ethnically segregated police forces and their involvement in armed conflicts. These forces would 'very quickly and easily be transformed into paramilitary units and formations, and that means the road to fratricidal war in these areas'.

The author(s) accused the Muslims and Croats of already pursuing the formation of ethnically based police forces. The Serbs therefore had to take appropriate steps. This involved, *inter alia*, cooperating closely with the JNA. The more nationalist Bosnian Serb leaders harboured doubts about the extent to which they could rely on support from communist JNA officers indoctrinated and sworn to defend 'brotherhood and unity'. At a minimum, the armed might of the JNA had to remain neutral with respect to the Bosnian Serbs' ambitions, and there was an affinity between the JNA and the Bosnian Serbs' goal of keeping Bosnia and Herzegovina in Yugoslavia. Therefore, 'the current state of security of the Serb nation will to a great extent continue to depend on successful cooperation between the MUP and the JNA, and especially in those municipalities where the Serb nation is a minority'.

In order to protect Bosnian Serb interests, the author(s) believed that new CSBs could be formed to correspond with the SAOs. 'With the establishment of CSBs for the territory of the SAOs, ministries of internal affairs of those regions would be created de facto.' In other words, if certain municipalities with significant Serb populations were currently subordinated to a CSB located in a region in which Serbs were a minority, then a new CSB should be created around a gerrymandered Serb majority area. This would essentially harmonize the structure of policing in Bosnia and Herzegovina with the political structures being unilaterally established by the Bosnian Serbs. Existing or new CSBs could be established covering the territory of the SAOs, and thereby creating an explicit connection between political decentralization and decentralization of the police. Any other kind of decentralization was not in the interest of the Bosnian Serbs, because such a decentralization 'assumes the establishment of organs of internal affairs only in the municipalities with a majority Serbian population'. In other words, the Bosnian Serbs did not accept that a portion of the Serb population of Bosnia and Herzegovina might be 'stranded' in municipalities in which they would constitute an ethnic minority and would be policed mainly by Croats or Bosnian Muslims.

Next, the author(s) posed a rhetorical question. 'How and in what manner can the full security of the Serb population be secured in those municipalities in which the Serbs are in a minority?' The answer given was that 'only an expert body at the level of the Republic' could perform such a function. This meant the creation of a 'Serbian MUP'. This, in turn, begged the question of the relationship between a 'Serbian MUP' and the existing SRBiH MUP. In addition, any new MUP would need to be financed from some source. This was hardly a minor issue, since internal affairs consumed huge financial resources – 60 per cent of the SRBiH budget, in the case of the SRBiH MUP.

Given that the political situation, the security situation and the financial prerequisites for decentralizing internal affairs did not obtain, the working paper proposed four steps, all in the context of the maximum use of federal institutions:

1. the continuation of cooperation with the JNA and SSUP, and the support of this cooperation by the SAOs;
2. the active engagement of Serbian deputies in the SRBiH Assembly regarding the proposed law on changes and amendments to the Law on Internal Affairs, especially with an eye towards the establishment of CSBs that would meet the needs of the SAOs;
3. the active engagement of Serbs in the SRBiH Government regarding the drafting of a new rulebook (*pravilnik*) on the internal organization of the SRBiH MUP, the emphasis being on the establishment of police stations and posts in areas of majority Serbian settlement within municipalities with Serb minorities; and
4. the active engagement of Serbs in both the SRBiH Government and Assembly regarding the passage of a new SRBiH MUP rulebook on wartime organization, with the emphasis on an increase of reserve police officers in police stations in areas with a Serb majority.[157]

Should these four steps be blocked or prove impossible to implement, the working paper proposed an alternative, more drastic path of action:

- establish municipal secretariats of internal affairs (*opštinski sekretarijati za unutrašnje poslove*, OSUPs) or, respectively, transform the SJBs into OSUPs;
- for the areas of the SAOs, establish CSBs which would have a State Security and Public Security Sector, and which could carry out the most complicated operational tasks and coordinate the work of the OSUPs in the municipalities; and
- establish a Serbian MUP at the republican level.

As is evident from the foregoing options, the Bosnian Serbs resented the abolition of the OSUPs, a step that had been an integral part of the pre-1990 SRBiH Law on Internal Affairs. Yet even the authors of this paper admitted that the OSUPs had been abolished because the municipalities proved unable to finance them from the municipal budgets. This, and not any attempt to centralize control of internal affairs in Sarajevo, had been the primary factor underlying this reform.

If the second, more drastic path were taken, the author(s) of the working paper expected vociferous opposition from the Bosnian Muslims and Bosnian Croats. In fact, a worsening of the security situation in Bosnia and Herzegovina would likely result. 'In these conditions, the assistance of federal institutions, and above all from the JNA and SSUP, as well as the MUP of Serbia and Montenegro will be necessary for the Serbian security service' in Bosnia and Herzegovina. 'It is therefore necessary that we establish contact with those organs regarding this question and that they contemplate concrete measures and possibilities for their assistance regarding personnel and equipment.'[158] In order to staff any new CSBs or indeed a new ministry, the author(s) suggested relying upon both reliable active Bosnian Serb SRBiH MUP employees and on retired employees.

A further illustration of the prominence of the strategy of decentralization appeared with the production, in October 1991, of a 'strictly confidential' position paper entitled 'Possibilities of Organising a Serbian Ministry for Internal Affairs'.[159] The document envisioned four alternative ways of pursuing this strategy.

First, the Assembly of the Serb People and the 'Serbian government' (not yet established by the Assembly) would name a Serbian minister and assistants, who would then appoint Serb personnel to all other key positions in the ministry; the Serbian MUP would then work in cooperation with the existing MUP on questions of mutual interest, such as the use of office space, vehicles and funds; this alternative was described as *not* dividing the existing MUP organizationally and amounted to creating a 'shadow' Serbian MUP within the SRBiH MUP.

The second alternative was similar to the first but involved the physical separation of the two organizations, which would have their own premises, vehicles, equipment and financing; they would still have contact with respect to 'disputed issues' and joint operations.

The third alternative was the organizational separation of certain components of MUP, such as the CSBs in Banja Luka, Doboj and Goražde, into independent units by decision of the Serbian assembly and government; these CSBs would then have to secure a source of financing; the paper noted that over 3,000 employees would work in these three CSBs plus a new one in Trebinje, a bill for the creation of which was then before the SRBiH Assembly.

Finally, the Serbian assembly and government could declare void the 1989 amendments to the Law on Internal Affairs; this would restore the old municipal secretariats of internal affairs, which had been much more independent from the republican MUP and were responsible to the municipal assemblies rather than the ministry.

It should be noted that the first two alternatives presumed the cooperation of the existing SRBiH MUP, while the last two were based on totally independent initiatives of the Serbian assembly and 'government'. Therefore, it is crucial to step back and briefly summarize the formation of those self-proclaimed Serbian organs that would, within the next months, rapidly involve into the nascent 'Republic of the Serb People of Bosnia and Herzegovina'. It should be kept in mind that while these organs pretended to be ethnically defined and speak for all Bosnian Serbs, the SDS almost exclusively directed and controlled the entire approach and the resulting organs. For example, Patrick J. Treanor calls the Bosnian Serb Assembly, whose establishment we will now examine, 'not only the creation but also the creature of the SDS'.[160]

These papers on the possibility of decentralization of internal affairs in Bosnia and Herzegovina provided a virtual template for subsequent events. Importantly, the reasoning underlying them, and in particular the suggestion that different courses of action would need to be taken depending on whether a municipality had a minority or majority Serb population, anticipated later SDS instructions.

Notwithstanding the aforementioned establishment of the SAOs, the Bosnian Serbs largely worked within the existing republication institutions of the Socialist Republic of Bosnia and Herzegovina until October 1991. However, in the middle of that month, the simmering political tensions between the SDS on the one hand and the SDA and the HDZ on the other boiled over. It is a matter of interpretation as to how regretfully – if at all – the SDS regarded this meltdown. Patrick J. Treanor in his analysis wrote that 'it is plain that at least a temporary break with the legitimate Bosnian Assembly was already foreseen, and possibilities [were] discussed to force the SDA and the HDZ parties to "bring the Assembly down"'.[161]

On 10, 11 and 14 October 1991, the SRBiH Assembly held its eighth joint session. The polemical rhetoric and unreconcilable parties' positions regarding Bosnia's possible secession from Yugoslavia culminated in a speech by Radovan Karadžić in which he implicitly threatened the Bosnian Muslim nation with extermination, even while claiming that he was not deploying threatening rhetoric.

> I ask you to please realize seriously, this is not good what you are doing. This is the road on which you wish to put Bosnia and Herzegovina, the same highway of hell and suffering which Slovenia and Croatia have travelled. Do not think that you will not lead Bosnia and Herzegovina into hell, and the Muslim nation maybe into extinction. Because the Muslim nation cannot defend itself if there is war here![162]

In the ensuing furore, the SDS and a number of other Serb deputies walked out of the Assembly, with Krajišnik suspending the session.[163] However, the Bosnian Muslim and Bosnian Croat deputies remained and voted in favour of a platform that pointed Bosnia towards independent statehood. As Robert J. Donia notes,

> the votes taken in the absence of SDS delegates ended any hope of interparty consensus in the Bosnian Parliament … nullified the veto power that Serb leaders had counted upon, and ended the last real prospect that Bosnia would remain in Yugoslavia. And for the first time in public, Karadžić predicted the physical annihilation of the Bosniak people if their leaders did not yield to his demands.[164]

After this debacle, the SDS Deputies' Club led the establishment of a new 'Assembly of the Serb People', which convened for the first time on 24 October in the SRBiH Assembly's building, with Momčilo Krajišnik, the speaker of the SRBiH Assembly, now acting as the speaker of the new self-proclaimed assembly.[165] At the constitutive session, speakers competed to describe the alleged oppression of the Serbs as a 'constitutive nation' in Bosnia. Deputy Slobodan Bijelić noted that Serbs had been the victim of genocide earlier in the century and now risked the same or similar threat.[166] Krajišnik spoke about the danger of the Serbs being systematically outvoted in the republican Assembly, claiming that Serbs were being subjected to laws and regulations that subverted their vital interests. Krajišnik specifically cited the SRBiH MUP, which he alleged was 'in the hands of the SDA–HDZ coalition, and there exist indications that the enormous increase of the reserve staff of the police[, its] feverish technical equipping and arming serving the creation of a particular army in Bosnia and Herzegovina'.[167] Simultaneously, they also declared that they wished to remain in 'the joint state of Yugoslavia, with Serbia, Montenegro, SAO Krajina, SAO Slavonia, Baranja and Western Syrmia, as well as with others who declare that they wish to stay'.[168]

As the legislative organ of the Bosnian Serbs, the newly self-proclaimed assembly set about creating laws and regulations and establishing those institutions that would together become Republika Srpska. These codified documents were eventually published in a new *Official Gazette of the Serb People in Bosnia and Herzegovina* (*Službeni glasnik srpskog naroda u Bosni i Hercegovini*). In order to illustrate the widespread popular support for its policies, first and foremost the policy of remaining in Yugoslavia, the Bosnian Serb Assembly on 9–10 November 1991 organized a 'plebiscite of the Serb people'.[169] As noted in the title, this referendum was ethnically defined, and not surprisingly, the overwhelming majority of the Serbs who participated in it voted to remain in Yugoslavia.[170]

The Bosnian Serb Assembly used the results of the plebiscite as the basis of a 'Decision on the Territories of Municipalities, Local Communities and Populated Places in BH Which Are Considered Territory of the Federal State of Yugoslavia'.[171] Issued on 21 November 1991, the decision essentially considered all those areas in which the majority of Serbs had voted 'yes' as part of the Yugoslav state – i.e. regardless of what the SRBiH Assembly or non-participants in the referendum might decide. On 11 December, the Bosnian Serb Assembly asked the JNA to defend the aforementioned territory.[172]

Having formed what was in effect a parallel legislative body, the Bosnian Serb Assembly in December proceeded to establish a parallel government. On 21 December, the Assembly proclaimed a Council of Ministers in which Mićo Stanišić, who headed the SUP in Sarajevo and was also a special advisor to the minister or the SRBiH MUP, figured as minister of internal affairs.[173] Vitomir Žepinić, who as deputy minister in the SRBiH MUP was the more senior official, was only appointed as a minister without portfolio. These two appointments underlined Žepinić's de facto demotion. Stanišić's appointment resulted from the objections of two delegates to Žepinić. These delegates were dissatisfied with the work of Žepinić as SRBiH MUP deputy minister.[174] One of the delegates, a certain Bjelošević, advocated removing Žepinić from his post in the SRBiH MUP and also expressed the wish that a Serbian police force would soon be established in Bosnia and Herzegovina. Bjelošević nominated Stanišić instead. At that point, Momčilo Krajišnik, as president of the Assembly, suggested that both Žepinić and Stanišić be appointed.

What was the relationship between Mićo Stanišić and the SDS? In his later trial at the ICTY, Stanišić consistently tried to dissociate himself from the SDS and claimed that he had not been a member of the party. According to his final trial brief, 'contrary to the allegation made by the OTP, Stanišić was not a member of the

SDS party. He was never nominated or elected to any position within the SDS. ... There is no evidence that Stanišić was a member of the SDS'.[175] It is therefore rather astonishing that Stanišić in the first of his two books about the war in Bosnia placed much emphasis on his role in establishing the SDS – which he at times referred to as 'our party' – and working closely together with it. Stanišić wrote that 'we worked diligently and hard. We completed all tasks on time. Each person from the party's initiative committee, whose member I was as well, had his tasks'.[176] With respect to the Main Board, the highest body of the SDS, Stanišić stated that 'from the most active members, forty names were selected for the Main Board of the party. I was also nominated'.[177] Based on Stanišić's own words, there can be little doubt that he was not only a founding SDS member but also a prominent one. Stanišić's analysis of the political situation in prewar Bosnia depicts a situation in which the SDA as the SDS's chief rival allegedly worked 'in a planned and organized manner ... from outvoting and legal violence [*majorizacija i pravno nasilje*] to a prepared strategy on how to destroy Serbs in BiH by using a Muslim army and members of the Muslim part of the MUP, so that Serbs disappear from this area'.[178] Such an interpretation of prewar events shows Stanišić to be in complete alignment with the SDS party line.

However, it does seem to be the case that certain members of the SDS harboured suspicions towards Stanišić because he had in the 1980s participated in investigations into financial malfeasance by Karadžić and Krajišnik.[179] Not coincidentally, while Stanišić in his first book bemoaned the emergence of nationalist politics in Bosnia at the beginning of the 1990s, he very subjectively treated Muslim and Croat nationalism as problematic, while regarding Serbian nationalism and the SDS as a purely defensive and necessary phenomenon.[180]

Before proceeding further, it bears noting that, already by February 1991, the SDS had clearly begun to contemplate what might occur were the SRBiH to cease functioning. A 23 February SDS confidential position paper, 'Modus Operandi of Municipalities in the Conditions that Republican Organs Cease to Function', argued that power would devolve to municipal agencies which would cooperate with federal agencies if republican organs ceased to function.[181] The same document also foresaw the use of the JNA and security forces in this situation. Another document from the same month claimed that the SDS organs would not 'impair the work of already organised services', but would rather increase the 'efficiency of legal organs'.[182] In socialist Yugoslavia, the authorities had extensively developed provisional measures for extraordinary or crisis situations through federal, republican and municipal committees for 'all-people's defence and social self-protection' (*opštenarodna odbrana i društvena samozaštita*, ONO and DSZ).[183]

As the crisis in Bosnia deepened during the autumn of 1991, the SDS further developed these ideas. The key document embodying this strategy was entitled 'Instructions for the Organization and Activity of Organs of the Serbian People in Bosnia and Herzegovina in Extraordinary Circumstances'.[184] These instructions set forth the establishment and operation of municipal crisis staffs under SDS control, though it should be noted that indications exist that in at least some municipalities, such crisis staffs had been established significantly earlier.[185] A significant feature of the instructions was a two-tiered and two-phase approach. Those municipalities in which the SDS had majority control were referred to as Variant A municipalities. These municipalities would gradually cease abiding by SRBiH laws and would also ignore other parties and their representatives, and heeding only the orders of parallel Serbian authorities. In each municipality, the SDS would immediately form a 'crisis staff', the membership of which would include the local chief of the SJB or SM. The police were therefore part and parcel of the municipal crisis staffs from their inception.

In the municipalities where Serbs constituted a minority, referred to as Variant B municipalities, they would strive to establish Serbian institutions and thus split the existing municipalities. The crisis staffs established in these municipalities would include the SDS candidates for chief of SJB or SM. Importantly, this meant that there would be SDS-controlled crisis staffs essentially wherever Serbs resided.

Even more significantly, given the zero-sum nature of this strategy, it was logically speaking impossible to see how the establishment of these crisis staffs would avoid contributing to the ongoing political conflict in the densely interwoven interethnic context of Bosnia. All of the institutions contemplated in the Instructions would be completely controlled by the Bosnian Serbs, and in particular by the SDS, which was establishing (parallel) political structures at the local, municipal, regional and republican level. Yet the Instructions assumed that an actual order for implementation would not be issued until later. Such implementation would involve mobilization of the police and the TO and JNA.

During the first phase the crisis staffs were supposed to prepare for the takeover of essential municipal organs, which were broadly defined. The crisis staffs were to prepare an estimate of the manpower of the security forces and to work towards raising those to full strength. The crisis staffs were to be manned by duty officers and to communicate as needed amongst themselves and with the SDS leadership.

During the second phase, the starting date for which was not set out in the instructions, the police and other security forces in the municipalities would be mobilized in coordination with the JNA. The takeover of essential municipal organs would then be implemented in Variant A municipalities, including buildings belonging to the police. Meanwhile, in Variant B municipalities the Serb population would take up a more defensive posture, awaiting the possibility of breaking out and forming new, Serb-majority municipalities in those portions of the municipality in which they could feasibly control. Variant B included token phrases regarding the representation of non-Serbs who declared their loyalty to Yugoslavia.

In the meantime, the security situation in Bosnia had continued to deteriorate throughout the autumn of 1991, particularly the case in areas bordering conflict zones in Croatia. On 23 September 1991, CSB Banja Luka began issuing a weekly report every Monday compiling information of significant crimes and security-related incidents occurring on the territory of CSB Banja Luka.[186] The steering council of the CSB issued these reports on the basis of Article 124 of the Rulebook on the Internal Organization of the SRBiH MUP. The first report included information on the spillover of the conflict in Croatia into northwestern

Bosnia and Herzegovina. It also included details on increasingly violent attacks on businesses, places of worship, public infrastructure and private individuals, using firearms and explosive devices. The chief of CSB Banja Luka, Stojan Župljanin, concluded that 'the increased activity of the ever more numerous paramilitary groups in uniforms and in civilian clothing is particularly worrying. Through their illegal activities they seriously menace the security situation, with dangers for the outbreak of armed conflicts with the reserve and active staffs of the police and with citizens'.

It is particularly worth noting that the report referred to negative activities of Veljko Milanković, 'who is, on his assertion, the commander of a detachment of the police of SAO Krajina'. On 23 September 1991, Župljanin also sent a detailed report about the activities of armed groups, including that of Milanković, in northwestern Bosnia to Biljana Plavšić, Momčilo Krajišnik, Miodrag Simović, Vitomir Žepinić and General Lieutenant Colonel Nikola Uzelac.[187] Župljanin wrote a subsequent report about Milanković in December 1991.[188] As will be seen, subsequently, numerous paramilitary groups whose members stemmed entirely or in part from Serbia were active in the war in Bosnia and Herzegovina.[189]

In December 1991, the SRBiH MUP produced an analytical report entitled 'Information on Activities in the Country and Abroad Directed at the Violent Change or Endangerment of the Constitutionally Confirmed Order'.[190] At the outset, this report identified ethnically based organizations as the main threats to law and order in Bosnia and Herzegovina. These organizations manifested themselves as 'civilian guards', 'volunteer groups' and other types of formations. Whereas such organizations had existed earlier, they had in the second half of 1991 become increasingly sophisticated and were now engaged in the formation of 'parallel (national) authorities'. The use of illegal weapons was widespread and on the rise.[191] As had been seen already in Srebrenica, in some municipalities, the ethnic distribution of posts in the police stations contributed to a rise in tensions.[192] The report argued that the activities of armed Serb groups were closely coordinated with political attempts by the Serbs to regionalize and ethnically homogenize power in Bosnia and Herzegovina.

The monthly report of CSB Banja Luka covering the period from 30 December 1991 to 30 January 1992 spoke of increased tensions, and frequent but small-scale incidents involving firearms in nearly every municipality in the jurisdiction of that CSB.[193] Many of these incidents involved JNA reservists.

The Republic of the Serb Nation in Bosnia and Herzegovina

On 9 January 1992, the SDS proclaimed the Republic of the Serb Nation in Bosnia and Herzegovina – later simply renamed as Republika Srpska – while also calling for a peaceful agreement that would allow the constituent nations of Bosnia to coexist.[194] This moved the political process of self-proclaimed Serbian institutions forward, with the promulgation of a constitution for the Serbian Republic coming at the end of February. Notably, the Bosnian Serbs not only laid claim to the territory covered by the SAOs which they had unilaterally established the previous autumn, but also includes those areas in which Serbs had constituted a majority prior to the genocide committed against them by the fascist Croatian regime during the Second World War.[195] Those persons of other ethnicities inhabiting these areas were not consulted or asked for their consent in the establishment of the Serbian Republic.

On the following day, the SRBiH Presidency by a majority vote pronounced the establishment of the new Republic of the Serb Nation to be unconstitutional. Nikola Koljević and Biljana Plavšić, the two Serb members of the presidency, predictably voted against this pronouncement.[196] Significantly, in the context of policing, the finding that the new political formation was unconstitutional meant that everything related to it fell under the purview of the SRBiH MUP State Security Service (SDB).

At the beginning of February 1992, Radovan Karadžić wrote a long complaint about the position of Serbs in the SRBiH MUP.[197] He circulated his letter, dated 6 February 1992, to a broad group of recipients, including the SRBiH Presidency, the SRBiH Government, the SRBiH Assembly, the SRBiH MUP, Tanjug and RTV Sarajevo. Among the long list of grievances Karadžić cited were the absence of a CSB in Trebinje, the tapping of phone lines by Munir ('Munja') Alibabić of the SRBiH MUP SDB and the lack of Serbian cadres in a host of positions that were allegedly reserved for Serbs. Significantly, Karadžić authorized Assistant SRBiH MUP Minister Momčilo Mandić to 'participate, in the name of the Serbian Democratic Party, in the resolution of cadre and organizational questions in Bosnia and Herzegovina MUP'. This announcement merely confirmed an accomplished fact, as Karadžić had consulted regularly with Mandić on MUP personnel issues since at least the summer of 1991.

After the formation of the Serbian Republic on 9 January 1992, the next milestone from the perspective of the Serbs in the SRBiH MUP arrived a month later, at a meeting in Banja Luka held on 11 February.[198] Stojan Župljanin opened the meeting, which was attended by both Mandić and Stanišić. Almost all of the remaining participants later came to possess important functions in the RS MUP: Čedo Kljajić, Slavko Drašković, Stanko Stojanović, Andrija Bjelošević, Nenad Radović, Vladimir Tutuš, Krsto Savić, Goran Žugić, Dragan Devedlaka, Goran Radović, Milan Krnjajić, Neđo Vlaški, Malko Koroman, Predrag Ješurić, Neđeljko Kesić, Igor Velašević and Vaso Škondrić.

As the host of the event, Stojan Župljanin emphasized the need to provide employment within MUP for an estimated 600 Serbian police officers from Croatia. Stanišić then told the participants that the Council of Ministers wanted 'Serbian power' to be felt in those parts of Bosnia and Herzegovina that were under Serbian control, complained of Muslim domination of the SRBiH MUP and said that it was necessary to establish a Serbian MUP going from municipal and regional organizations all the way up to a Serbian ministry. Tellingly, Stanišić and several other speakers insisted that the Muslims, not the Serbs, were spearheading the attempt to split the SRBiH MUP. Allegations were made of Muslim involvement in illegal arms deals.

Čedo Kljajić, another leading official in the SRBiH MUP, complained that there had been appointments of inspectors and the deployment of these inspectors in the field without his knowledge.[199] Kljajić thought that it should be publicly announced that the SRBiH MUP was not united. He believed that only the Serbs were obeying the law. He thought that the SDA and the SDS could not work together with respect to the SRBiH MUP and threatened to resign unless a Serbian MUP was established within a week. Another participant, Nenad Radović, informed the meeting that the Assembly of the Serb People had already taken a decision on the formation of a Serbian MUP. Furthermore, Goran Žugić, who worked in the State Security Service in Tuzla, told those present that 'before adopting the Law on Internal Affairs people working in the field should be consulted first. Laws should be drafted as if we were in wartime and they should be applied to war conditions'.[200] Predrag Ješurić from Bijeljina noted that he had been in contact with the MUP of Serbia with respect to 'material assistance'.

The key conclusions from the 11 February meeting in Banja Luka related to the creation of a 'Serbian Steering Council' (*kolegij*) within the SRBiH MUP under the direction of Mandić. In the words of the minutes of the meeting, 'it is incumbent upon the Serbian Steering Council of the SRBiH MUP to carry out all preparations necessary for the functioning of the Serbian MUP after the adoption of the constitution of the Serbian Republic of BiH'.[201] Symptomatic of his declining status and role, Deputy Minister Vitomir Žepinić did not attend this meeting, nor was he represented in the new Steering Council. Andrija Bjelošević from Doboj criticized Žepinić at the meeting for allegedly favouring Muslims. Clearly, Žepinić's position was insecure.[202]

At the end of the meeting on 11 February, a long list of points was adopted. These included naming Mandić as the head of the Serbian Steering Council in the SRBiH MUP and several proposals geared towards the establishment of a Serbian Ministry of Internal Affairs in Bosnia and Herzegovina. Further confirming their drive towards their own ministry, the participants at the meeting referred to the 'activities and decisions of the Serbian MUP', although it had not yet been formally established. They also discussed specific details such as emblems and insignia for the future police force of this Serbian MUP.

Two days after the meeting in Banja Luka, Mandić sent a dispatch to Župljanin (Banja Luka), Bjelošević (Doboj), Stojanović (Goražde), Savić (Nevesinje/Trebinje), Cvjetić (Sokolac), Ješurić (Bijeljina) and Stanišić (SUP Sarajevo) asking them to arrange meetings with leading personnel in their areas.[203] The purpose of the meetings was to implement the conclusions reached at the 11 February meeting. On 14 February, Karadžić apparently gave the long-anticipated signal to SDS members to initiate the second stage of preparations in the 19 December 1991 Instructions.[204] Further indicating that plans were proceeding apace, in early March 1992 Župljanin delivered a report on the security situation in his AOR to the (SDS-dominated) Assembly of the Autonomous Region of Krajina (ARK).[205] SRBiH MUP regulations did not provide for reporting to these self-declared regional assemblies.

At the end of February 1992, the SRBiH authorities in Sarajevo held a referendum on the independence of Bosnia and Herzegovina. The referendum, which was boycotted by the Bosnian Serbs, resulted in a vote for independence. The vote contrasted with the plebiscite that the Bosnian Serbs had held in November 1991 on remaining in Yugoslavia, underlying the growing and seemingly inseparable gulf between the Bosnian Serbs on the one hand, and the Bosnian Muslims and Bosnian Croats on the other.

The SDS Crisis Staff also gave voice to discontent surrounding personnel policy in the SRBiH MUP. Indeed, the crisis staff appeared to view the disputes in the SRBiH MUP as a prominent cause of problems in Bosnia and Herzegovina as a whole. On 2 March 1992, the SDS Crisis Staff issued a list of 'conditions for negotiations', which included a demand for a 'cadre transformation' within twenty-four hours.[206]

This followed a crisis which had erupted when a guest at a Serbian wedding in the old town of Sarajevo had been shot dead. According to the Serbs, the shooting was political in character, and the assailants were criminals who allegedly enjoyed support from Bosnian Muslims in the SRBiH MUP.[207] The Serbs responded by erecting barricades around Sarajevo. The men manning these barricades were armed, in some cases with heavy weapons such as machine guns and rocket launchers. In some cases, the men at the barricades had a criminal background. Motorists encountering the barricades were subjected to searches.[208] On 2 March 1992, the SDS Crisis Staff issued a list of 'conditions for negotiations', which included a demand for a 'cadre transformation' in the Ministry of Internal Affairs within twenty-four hours.[209] Meanwhile, similar obstructions were erected in some other parts of Bosnia. The crisis was eventually peacefully resolved, with the barricades being removed by 4 March 1992. Nonetheless, the episode highlighted the brittle nature of the security situation in Bosnia and Herzegovina.

On 6 March 1992, the SRBiH MUP SDB presented an analysis of the events in Sarajevo of 1–4 March to the SRBiH Presidency, Assembly, Government and to the Council for the Protection of the Constitutional Order.[210] The first barricades had been erected by 'persons of Serb nationality', which provoked 'persons of Muslim nationality' to react by establishing their own barricades. Taking into consideration the high degree of coordination visible in the establishment of the barricades, and the fact that those Serbs guarding the barricades were equipped with weapons, communications equipment and food, the report concluded that the barricades were not spontaneous in nature. The report found that the leadership of the SDS Crisis Staff had played a significant and guiding role in the barricades episode. These included Rajko Dukić, Danilo Veselinović, Jovan Tintor, Dragan Vučetić, Jovo Jovanović, Ratko Adžić and others. 'In addition, much available information indicates that a number of active and reserve employees of Serb nationality of the SRBiH MUP were directly involved in the organising of the barricades and other activities.' A subsequent internal SRBiH MUP study of the barricades incident concluded that twenty-four employees of the SRBiH MUP had participated directly in the incident. Mandić and Stanišić were among those named.[211]

Biljana Plavšić told Rajko Dukić on 2 March 1992 that the Muslims had agreed to the demands related to the SRBiH MUP.[212] These included that the distribution of positions in the SRBiH MUP be in accordance 'with agreements reached immediately following the [November 1990] elections'. In addition, the SDS demanded that no actions be taken by the SRBiH MUP against the persons manning the barricades that had been set up or against any other Serbs in Bosnia and Herzegovina.[213]

A hasty meeting of the presidency and representatives of the JNA and the SRBiH MUP convened on 3 March to resolve the crisis. One of the practical consequences that flowed from this (short-lived) defusing of tensions was the formation of patrols composed of a mixture of Serbs and Muslims and drawn from both the police and the army in the Sarajevo area.[214] On 12 March, the Council for the Protection of the Constitutional Order convened and agreed to undertake urgently to place the paramilitary groups existing 'in all three peoples' of Bosnia and Herzegovina under the joint control of SRBiH MUP and the JNA. These groups would then be dissolved.[215] The Council highlighted the need for continued cooperation between the SRBiH MUP and the JNA and called for all important decisions in the SRBiH MUP to be reached by consensus among the representatives of Serbs, Croats and Muslims. The Council also noted that the 'depoliticisation' of all government organs was essential if the state were to function properly.

Documents published in *Slobodna Bosna* on 12 March alleged that Dragan Kijac and Momčilo Mandić were the main SRBiH MUP figures involved in the barricades, and that Kijac had regularly called the SDS at the Holiday Inn to report on the situation.[216] In an article entitled 'Why Is Delimustafić Protecting Žepinić?' the authors (identified only under the collective title of the magazine) accused 'high-ranking police officials' of Serb nationality, including Momčilo Mandić and Dragan Kijac (the head of police in Sarajevo) of organizing the blockade of Sarajevo at the beginning of the month. The centrepiece of the article was a photocopy of a document purported to be a list of phone calls received by Rajko Dukić at the Holiday Inn during the blockade. The authors accused Delimustafić of providing Žepinić (and other Serbs in the SRBiH MUP) with protection. Ridiculing the concept that Žepinić and Delimustafić represented the 'Boro and Ramiz' tandem holding the SRBiH MUP – and, by extension Bosnia and Herzegovina – together, the authors forthrightly blamed these two for impending disaster.[217] In an accompanying article, the authors further accused Momčilo Mandić of masterminding the 5 March letter of grievances of Serbian employees in SJB Stari Grad.[218] The same article stated that Delimustafić had formed a three-member commission to investigate the reasons underlying the complaints of Serbs in the SRBiH MUP.

In the meantime, on 3 March 1992, the Banja Luka newspaper *Glas* had reported that the chief of CSB Banja Luka, Stojan Župljanin, stated that 'we are afraid of uncontrolled processes which could arise in Bosnia and Herzegovina.[219] For now we are in control of the situation on the territory of the region. However, in the case of a destruction of peace and security, it would be very difficult to re-establish order'. Župljanin further stated that 'our strategic goal is to preserve peace'. On the following day, Župljanin reiterated that the goal of the residents of Bosnian Krajina was to preserve peace 'at any cost'. He demonstrated his familiarity with the goals of the Assembly of the Serb People. 'Asked by journalists whether the CSB in Banja Luka would in the future carry out the orders of MUP BiH, Župljanin answered that the Centre in his jurisdiction would not carry out any kinds of orders of MUP BiH which might eventually be directed against the interests of the Serb nation.'[220]

Tensions continued to rise within the SRBiH MUP as well. On 12 March 1992, Delimustafić ordered all CSBs and SJBs to update their statistics on personnel.[221] This included ensuring that the ethnic composition of the police force matched the ethnic distribution of the population in the respective area of operation. It should be noted that these instructions were accompanied by the observation that numerous irregularities had been observed in recent SRBiH MUP personnel policies. However, in the meantime Serbian police at SJB Stari Grad in Sarajevo continued to express dissatisfaction with their situation.[222] In reaction to the dispute at SJB Stari Grad, the Serbian police officials at SJB Pale and SJB Sokolac demanded on 23 March that all Muslim police officers return their weapons and uniforms and cease to work at these stations. According to the complaint filed by the Muslims, the Serbs took these steps in concert with the crisis staffs of the 'Serbian District of Pale' and SAO Romanija. As a result of the incidents at Pale and Sokolac, the SRBiH MUP formed a commission to investigate.[223]

A strictly confidential paper prepared in March 1992 by Serbs in the SRBiH MUP SDB gave articulation to their grievances.[224] The paper argued that Serbs were being systematically marginalized in the State Security Service. Reiterating the type of discourse that had been heard in earlier grievances in September 1991, the authors argued that non-Serbs and 'servile Serbs' advanced in the ministry while Serbs favoured by the SDS languished or were pushed out of the SDB. Investigations on anti-state activities were allegedly overwhelmingly focused on activities by Serbs, and in particular by the SDS. 'The activity of extremists from non-Serbian ethnic groups is presented only as a reaction to Serbian extremism.' The Serbs also claimed that the alleged Serbian extremist activities were not well-documented and that inappropriate conclusions were reached. Interestingly, after enumerating a long list of other grievances, the authors of the paper concluded that the 'most directly responsible' individual for these problems and illegalities was the Deputy Minister of SRBiH MUP, Vitomir Žepinić, a Serb and an appointee of the SDS.

In its conclusions, the March 1992 paper sought the use of well-trained Serbs in SDB who would 'struggle without compromise for the interests of the Serb nation within constitutional and other legal restrictions'. This had to be taken into consideration when the SDS made recommendations for appointments for MUP and SDB. Reliable Serbs already in SDB should be consulted when SDB appointments were made.

Amidst this intensely ethnicized and politicized atmosphere, Minister Delimustafić took some attempts to clamp down on the most egregious abuses.[225] His efforts were apparently in vain, as the SRBiH MUP continued to fragment.

Increasingly, individuals at all levels of the ministry transferred their loyalty to specific parties and even persons. Information was unevenly shared and distributed, both among government organs and the MUP or within the MUP itself.[226] Similarly, the MUP found itself accused of not following well-established legal guidelines for cooperation with other republican and federal government organs.[227]

Meanwhile, the (self-proclaimed) legal foundation of the Serbian Republic of Bosnia and Herzegovina took shape. At the end of February 1992, the Bosnian Serb Assembly promulgated a constitution and a number of laws such as the Law on Internal Affairs. Debates regarding policing and the future of the SRBiH MUP also continued in the Assembly. At the tenth session of the Bosnian Serb Assembly held on 11 March, the Assembly unanimously called for the implementation of the new Law on Internal Affairs by the Council of Ministers.[228] A week later, at the eleventh session, Momčilo Krajišnik, the president of the Assembly, referred specifically to the need for 'ethnic separation on the ground'.[229] Miroslav Vještica, an SDS delegate from Bosanska Krupa, referred to the need for the establishment of a Serb police force and a 'Serbian MUP' so that the Serbs could seize control of 'their territories'. Significantly, Vještica noted that the Bosnian Serbs of Bosanska Krupa had to some degree already de facto established control over their territory during the past half year.[230]

At the end of the eleventh session of the Bosnian Serb Assembly, Karadžić alluded to the fact that the Bosnian Serbs would soon announce that they were withdrawing from the SRBiH MUP. Indeed, he made it clear that the appropriate insignia for a new MUP had already been ordered. According to Karadžić, 'our police will have to behave legally. No one will be allowed to have a hair missing, regardless of religious faith, nation. Everyone must feel completely safe'.[231] Krajišnik asked the deputies to think seriously before the next Assembly session about the best candidates in their regions for a Serbian MUP.

On 23 March, Radovan Karadžić, in his capacity as the president of the SDS, sent a dispatch out to all SDS municipal presidents.[232] Karadžić noted that an operations centre had been established at the republican level. At the municipal level, he ordered that the SDS duty officer's desks cooperate with their relevant SJBs twenty-four hours a day, seven days a week.

During the twelfth session of the Bosnian Serb Assembly held on 24 March, several speakers, including Radovan Karadžić, made a number of statements related to the nascent Bosnian Serb Ministry of Internal Affairs. According to Karadžić, the police force was of great interest. He pointed out that no international agreement limited the size of a regular and reserve police force. Referring to the new RS Law on Internal Affairs, Karadžić stated that

> we have a legal basis in the Law on Internal Affairs, we also have badges and at in that moment to come – and this will be very soon – we can form what we wish to. There are reasons why this will come in two-three days, such are the estimates, I cannot give you the reasons now. At that moment, all the Serbian municipalities, both the old ones and the newly established ones, would literally assume control

over the entire territory of the municipality concerned. Zvornik municipality put under [its] control everything that constitutes the Serbian municipality of Zvornik. Then, at that moment, for the next three-four days, there will be a unique methodology and you will be able to apply it in the municipalities you represent. This includes the things that must be done as well as the method of work: How to separate the police force, take the funds that belong to the Serb people and establish control.

At the end of his comments, Karadžić made one final, but crucial point: 'The police must be under the control of the civilian authority, it must obey it; there is no discussion about that – that is the way it must be.'[233] In other words, the SDS and the nascent political organs of the Bosnian Serb republic, presided over by Karadžić, would exercise command and control over the police. The desire for control over the police also revealed lingering doubts and suspicions among the Bosnian Serb leaders about the extent to which they could rely on the TO and JNA for support in the event of armed hostilities.

Earlier in the day, Karadžić had strongly hinted that the establishment of a Bosnian Serb police force was imminent. Miroslav Vještica complained that the formation of the police force of the Serbian Republic of Bosnia and Herzegovina had already been agreed for that day. He saw no reason why this had to be postponed once again. Vještica insisted that the Assembly should work all night if necessary to achieve the formation of a Serb police force and the appointment of a Minister of Internal Affairs. 'We could then go home with homework: to take over power in our Serbian Republic of Bosnia and Herzegovina.' Krajišnik confirmed that the formation of a Serb police force had indeed been on the agenda.

The thirteenth session of the Bosnian Serb Assembly was held on the same day as the twelfth session, 24 March 1992.[234] Mićo Stanišić was nominated as the minister of internal affairs, and accepted. The Assembly accepted him with only one dissenting vote. In his speech accepting his nomination, Stanišić repeated all of the standard Bosnian Serb grievances about the SRBiH MUP. He also alleged that the SRBiH MUP had been used to distribute weapons to a new Army of Bosnia and Herzegovina, but that the Serbs had not received any ammunition or weapons at all. Stanišić asserted that he would head a professional police force, 'an organ of the state administration that will in fact protect property, life, body and other riches which it will be of interest to protect'.[235]

On 9 March 1992, the SRBiH Presidency's Council for the Protection of the Constitutional Order had stated that 'all decisions, means and activities of the MUP need to be the result of agreements by the most responsible officials in the MUP, especially the representatives of all three nations'.[236] Yet those officials were by early March at loggerheads, and were extensively engaged in exacerbating a profound security dilemma.[237] As the security and political crisis in Bosnia deepened, and as the fear increased that Bosnia would go hurtling off the edge of a cliff into armed conflict, ordinary people as well as rank-and-file police officers found themselves increasingly boxed in, compelled to choose one of the mutually antagonistic sides. Yet choosing a side may have had more to do with the sense of being stuck in a zero-sum game of opportunistic nationalist rivalry than in actually preferring nationalism per se. That is, for many police officers and ordinary citizens, the choice to go along with the developments was a negative choice. Unfortunately, as other scholars have shown, reformist, progressive and multi-ethnic voices were not as 'loud' or effective as the nationalists.[238] In the ethnonationalist clientelist structure that subsumed the old communist clientelist structure, only those whom the new nationalist parties viewed as being sufficiently nationalist could count on protection and promotion.

The activation of the Serbian MUP did not take place until after the ceremonial promulgation of the Bosnian Serb constitution on 27 March. Meanwhile, Serbs such as Vitomir Žepinić and Biljana Plavšić continued to participate in Bosnian republican decision-making. For example, they attended the 13th Session of the Council for the Protection of Constitutional Order of the SRBiH Presidency, where the principles of professionalism in the work of the SRBiH MUP were further endorsed.

Chapter 2

THE POLICE AND THE FORCIBLE SEIZURE OF POWER (APRIL AND MAY 1992)

Three days later, in Sokolac, Stanišić inspected a parade of Bosnian Serb police affiliated with SAO Romanija. According to Stanišić,

> From today, the Serbian Republic of Bosnia and Herzegovina has its own police. The legal basis of our existence is the Constitution of the Serbian Republic of Bosnia and Herzegovina and the Law on Internal Affairs which the Assembly has recently adopted at its session. In addition, our existence has legality on the basis of the negotiations of the three national communities under the auspices of the European Community. From today we will act as the police of the Serbian Republic of Bosnia and Herzegovina which will professionally and not politically, the way the MUP of the old Bosnia and Herzegovina did, carry out its work and tasks with the goal of protecting property, life, bodies and the remaining security of all citizens equally on the territory of the Serbian Republic of Bosnia and Herzegovina.[1]

Meanwhile, the situation in the Bosnian Krajina was still deteriorating, and relations between the ministry in Sarajevo and CSB Banja Luka had become severely strained. On 31 March 1992, *Glas* reported that Stojan Župljanin had announced 'energetic measures' against those destabilizing the situation in northwestern Bosnia. Župljanin stated that he was 'sorry that the Ministry of Internal Affairs in BiH has turned into a political organization and that because of [its] negative relationship towards the Bosnian Krajina does not permit that the material, personnel and technical problems in our centre are solved'.[2] In the interval between the passage of the law on the new Serbian MUP and its entry into force on 31 March, the SDS withdrew Vitomir Žepinić from the SRBiH MUP after the Serbian Assembly selected Stanišić as the first actual minister of internal affairs.[3]

The final death knell for the SRBiH MUP came on the same day, when Assistant Secretary Momčilo Mandić issued a circular informing all parts of the MUP that pursuant to the action of the Assembly of the Serb People four days earlier, the new Law on Internal Affairs would be applied as of 1 April and that Mićo Stanišić had been named minister.[4] Although Vitomir Žepinić had been offered a position as 'coordinator' in the new ministry, he did not accept this. He therefore held no position in the new 'Serbian Ministry of Internal Affairs'.[5] On 4 April, Žepinić wrote a resignation letter to the president of the Bosnian Serb Assembly.[6]

In his first book, Mićo Stanišić described a meeting of the SRBiH MUP Steering Council on 1 April 1992 which Stanišić claimed to have convened.[7] Minister Delimustafić was present at the outset, but Deputy Minister Žepinić chaired most of the meeting. According to Stanišić, he claimed that his appointment as minister of the new RS MUP was merely in accordance with negotiations for the peaceful division of Bosnia. Stanišić recalled that he spoke for an hour after which his SRBiH MUP colleagues 'congratulated me on the establishment and beginning of the work of the MUP of the Serbian Republic of BiH'.[8] Stanišić then noted that, on the same day the Steering Council of the SRBiH MUP issued a dispatch regarding an agreement that had been reached regarding 'the possible future state organization of BiH', which would involve a now initiated 'reorganization of the organs of internal affairs and their security services'.[9] This dispatch mentioned the establishment of the RS MUP but also noted that there should be no unilateral seizures of buildings or equipment by the police of one ethnicity, nor should the dismissal of police officers of any ethnicity take place. Though belied by later events, this dispatch in Stanišić's account proves that the Bosnian Serbs were merely peacefully implementing a tripartite agreement.

Žepinić also provided his own first-hand account of the collapse of the SRBiH MUP to interrogators from the RS National Security Service (SNB) – the RS MUP's state security service – albeit at the end of August 1992.[10] Žepinić's refusal to support the new RS MUP made him appear as both a fool and a traitor in the eyes of Stanišić and others. Indeed, when Žepinić finally left Sarajevo, he made his way to Belgrade in an attempt to emigrate, but he was abducted in front of the Canadian Embassy.[11]

During his interrogations in August 1992, Žepinić told the SNB about a meeting on 5 April 1992. Momčilo Krajišnik, the president of the Assembly of the Serb People, called the meeting at his office, and Radovan Karadžić, Nikola Koljević, Aleksa Buha, Branko Đerić, Miodrag Simović, Momčilo Mandić, Mićo Stanišić and Milenko Karišik were all in attendance. At the meeting, Žepinić was attacked for having agreed to pay a visit to the base of the SRBiH MUP special police unit together with Alija Delimustafić. Žepinić argued that the special police unit could not be split along ethnic lines. He offered his resignation.[12] The rest of the persons present then asked Žepinić to call the top Bosnian Serbs in the special police unit and get them to agree to the formation of a Bosnian Serb special police unit. Žepinić agreed to this. A second meeting took place at Krajišnik's office on the same day. Žepinić was informed that the seat of the SDS would be moving to Pale 'for security reasons', but that the SDS would be in touch regarding Žepinić's move to an advisory post in the SSUP.

Even after Mandić sent his dispatch, the new self-proclaimed ministry did not immediately take shape in all areas that it claimed as its jurisdiction, nor did the disintegration of the ministry take place overnight. Upon reading Mandić's telex of 31 March 1992, Delimustafić reacted by dispatching a note to all offices of the SRBiH MUP. Delimustafić called Mandić's move illegal and regrettable.

Delimustafić asked all offices to continue to obey only the SRBiH MUP.¹³ On 1 April, the SRBiH MUP sent out a dispatch in the name of the ministry's Steering Council – including Žepinić, Mandić and Stanišić's names – calling for managing staff in the entire ministry to secure 'normal conditions for work', including the return of all employees to their appointed posts.¹⁴

Mandić did not manage to persuade all Serbs to join the new Bosnian Serb MUP. At SJB Zvornik, for example, the employees called for calm and professionalism. They professed not to want any ethnic division of the police.¹⁵ On 3 April, the RS Minister of Internal Affairs, Mićo Stanišić, wrote to all CSBs and SJBs on the territory of the 'Serbian Republic' to remind them that they were to obey only the orders issued by the RS MUP.¹⁶ On the other hand, some municipalities such as Pale, Sokolac and Ilidža had already expelled all non-Serbs from their police forces. Similar action was undertaken at SJB Ilijaš on 31 March.¹⁷ Dragan Vikić, a Bosnian Croat and the head of the SRBiH MUP special forces, refused to comment publicly on the dissolution of the SRBiH MUP. The same position was taken by the two senior Croats in SRBiH MUP, Bruno Stojić and Branko Kvesić.¹⁸

The SRBiH MUP and the Bosnian government desperately tried to resist the formation of the Bosnian Serb MUP. At the beginning of April 1992, Ejup Ganić, a member of the SRBiH Presidency, warned that any employees who left the SRBiH MUP should consider themselves permanently fired.¹⁹ On 5 April, the SRBiH MUP formally fired Momčilo Mandić.²⁰ The same day, the RS MUP issued an announcement in which it accused the Bosnian Muslims of the 'former Ministry of Internal Affairs' of trying to take control of the ministry and the Krtelji building in which the SRBiH MUP special unit was based.²¹ The Muslim 'Green Berets' had allegedly expelled all Serbian police officers from the ministry and launched an armed attack on Krtelji.²² The Muslims, led by Jusuf Pušina, then allegedly seized the weapons and equipment of the special unit. The RS MUP announcement concluded by asking 'the Serb nation and all well-intentioned citizens of Sarajevo' not to surrender their weapons or believe the 'propaganda' spread by the SDA about the Serbs.

Yet the measures taken by the SRBiH MUP to prevent the formation of a Bosnian Serb Ministry of Internal Affairs were in vain. On 3 April 1992, Mićo Stanišić derisively referred to Delimustafić's call for all SRBiH MUP employees to return to their previous places of employment and heed the instructions of the ministry as 'disinformation and the conduct of psychological warfare [*vođenje specijalnog rata*]'.²³ Three days later, Momčilo Mandić, the new deputy minister of RS MUP, organized the armed takeover of the police academy at Vraca.²⁴ This building became the first seat of the RS MUP.²⁵ Milenko Karišik, a Serb who had until recently served as the second-in-command in Dragan Vikić's special police unit, led and coordinated this operation.²⁶ Stanišić later claimed that the Muslims had violated an agreement according to which the academy's facilities would be allocated to the new Serb MUP, and in his first book he disingenuously claims that Mandić was merely implementing an agreement between him and Delimustafić to take over the facility at Vraca.²⁷ But in retrospect, Mandić stated:

When we set out for Vraca to take the police academy, we knew that we would be shot dead as terrorists if we failed. We knew that Bosnia and Herzegovina would be recognised on 7 [sic] April. If I and Karišik's special police had not raided, we would certainly have been proclaimed terrorists and the state of Bosnia and Herzegovina would have executed us.[28]

Mandić was very eager to keep weapons from falling into the hands of Vikić's unit and called General Kukanjac and Colonel Vukota Vukotić regarding this matter.[29] The 6 April assault on Vraca came to be seen by Bosnian Serbs as the birth of the RS MUP, and was celebrated as such later. For the first months of the war, the headquarters of the RS MUP was divided between Vraca and Pale.[30]

The RS Law on Internal Affairs was essentially a slightly rewritten version of the 1990 SRBiH MUP law.[31] The new ministry continued to maintain ties to federal institutions and the Yugoslav state. The new law also marked a change in terminology from the standard Yugoslav '*milicija*' to the more international '*policija*'. The very fact that the Bosnian Serbs changed so little in the law made it quite apparent that the root cause of their dissatisfaction with the previous system had little to do with legal principles and that their objections instead were rooted in ethnically based political views.

The demise of the SRBiH MUP and the Cutileiro negotiations

Could this deteriorating situation have been rescued through concerted negotiations sponsored by the 'international community'? Clearly, by the end of March 1992, the prospects for maintaining a unified and multi-ethnic SRBiH MUP – and hence maintaining peace in a united Bosnia – had been diminishing for some time. The few well-intentioned attempts to keep the MUP from splitting proved futile.[32] On the diplomatic front, the European Community and the United States both worked to achieve a peaceful, political solution to the crisis in Bosnia and Herzegovina. Although negotiations continued until the very end of March, with further rounds of talks planned for April, no diplomatic solution was achieved.

At the ICTY in those trials in which Bosnian Serbs were defendants, the defence consistently argued that the Bosnian Serbs had done nothing improper in establishing their own political entity in 1992, and that the formation of the Bosnian Serb police should hence be seen as part of this process. According to the defence, an agreement brokered by international mediators provided the legal basis for the establishment of three police forces in Bosnia, with the imprimatur of the European Community. The trial chamber in *Stanišić & Župljanin* observed that 'Stanišić was of the view that, having created the Council of Ministers as a centrally organised authority for the RS, the Serbs had met the conditions for the International Commission in Lisbon to consider a solution to the problem in BiH'.[33] And Mićo Stanišić himself devoted a significant portion of his own first book to claims that the Bosnian Serbs established the RS MUP not only in good faith but based on a tripartite agreement brokered by the international community.[34]

There were indeed serious negotiations in the late winter and early spring of 1992 chaired by the Portuguese diplomat José Cutileiro, who took over as the coordinator of the EC's Conference on Yugoslavia in January 1992. These negotiations, which the EC launched in August–September 1991, aimed at a peaceful solution of the crisis. On 23 February Cutileiro succeeded in having the leaders of the three nationalist parties agree to a 'Statement of Principles for New Constitutional Arrangements for Bosnia and Herzegovina'. The first of these principles stated that Bosnia would 'be a state composed of three constituent units, based on national principles and taking into account economic, geographic and other criteria'.[35] The legislatures and governments of the constituent units would have the ability to decide upon a wide array of matters, including policing. At a meeting of SDS delegates on 28 February, Karadžić said that the Bosnian Serbs were looking forward to having their own police force based on the negotiations in Lisbon.[36] In principle, negotiations were set to continue in Sarajevo, but Izetbegović and Karadžić were involved in a high-stakes confrontation over the Bosnian independence referendum, which was held on 29 February and 1 March. The referendum backed independence, but the Serbs boycotted it. Cutileiro brought Izetbegović and Karadžić to the negotiating table in mid-March in Sarajevo, and on 18 March Izetbegović agreed to Cutileiro's principles. Negotiations were then set to continue, but by the end of the month Izetbegović reversed course and withdrew his signature, and a final legally binding agreement never came into being. In the words of the US diplomat Herbert Okun, testifying at the ICTY,

> one has to bear in mind that the Cutileiro plan died aborning. It never was completed. ... Indeed, if you look at the last page over the date Sarajevo, 18 March, the last sentence reads, and I quote from the Cutileiro plan paper: 'This paper is the basis of further negotiations.' So it was clear that this was a discussion paper. It was not a complete and formal plan.[37]

Contemporaneous observers also saw a gap between the Bosnian Serbs' understanding of the negotiations and what Cutileiro was offering. US Ambassador Warren Zimmermann told Nikola Koljević that Cutileiro was 'trying to preserve the territorial integrity of Bosnia. What you're describing is partition'.[38]

From the Bosnian Serb perspective, the logical outcome of the EC negotiations led by Cutileiro was the legalization of the Serbian Republic and, by extension, the establishment of an ethnically Serb police force in that republic. And that was certainly a possible outcome. Indeed, several historians have essentially accused Cutileiro of adopting a stance close to that of the SDS.[39] Be that as it may, Karadžić 'crafted a legend of March 18 that blamed other parties while absolving himself and the Bosnian Serb nationalists of any culpability for subsequent violence. He rhetorically magnified and elevated the agreement ... to the level of an irrevocable, binding accord'.[40] Even though the Bosnian Serbs had themselves engaged proactively in the ethnic separation of police stations, Karadžić on 24 March claimed that the separation was being 'forced upon us'.[41] The aborted agreement in principle became 'the Cutileiro Plan' and became a constituent part of the Bosnian Serb narrative about an 'imposed war' (*nametnuti rat*), which saw the Bosnian Serbs tragically forced to defend their interests with armed force. Thus, a few months later, Momčilo Krajišnik would in presiding over an RS Assembly session state that 'a large number of brave sons and daughters of our nation have died on the battlefield in the Serbian Republic, giving their lives in a struggle that has been imposed upon us, a struggle against enslavement, humiliation and extinction'.[42]

As demonstrated by his speech in Sokolac at the end of March 1992 and in his suspect interview with ICTY OTP investigators, Mićo Stanišić seems to have convinced himself that he was implementing the Cutileiro 'plan'.[43] On the same days as the Sokolac speech, Stanišić attended a meeting with Croat and Muslim representatives of the SRBiH MUP aimed at effectuating the reorganization of the ministry. And as previously noted, on 1 April the Steering Council of SRBiH MUP did in a dispatch mention that an agreement had been reached regarding 'the possible future state organization of BiH'.

Both in his suspect statement and in his subsequent book, Stanišić blamed Izetbegović and the Bosnian Muslims exclusively for the chaotic collapse of the SRBiH MUP and the ensuing commencement of armed conflict.[44] According to Stanišić, Izetbegović had disingenuously played along with the internationally supervised negotiations only as a ploy to gain time until he could attain international recognition of Bosnia's independence, which occurred on 6 April 1992.[45] In Stanišić's view, the blame rests squarely on the shoulders of the SDA for allegedly abandoning international negotiations when international recognition of Bosnia and Herzegovina became imminent. 'The Serbian side was left with no other choice', so Stanišić, but to pursue the creation and implementation of the RS MUP.[46] Again, this puts Stanišić in complete alignment with the official SDS ideological presentation of the armed conflict as 'an imposed war' in which the Bosnian Serbs were merely defending themselves.[47]

Yet the fact remains that all subsequent events showed that the Bosnian Muslims did not accept the establishment of the RS MUP. There are no explicit signs in the subsequent dispatches from SRBiH MUP that Minister Delimustafić believed Mandić's dispatch of 31 March to have been a valid implementation of some kind of accord reached during the negotiations supervised by Cutileiro. On the contrary, Delimustafić on 10 April wrote of the 'forcible establishment of working units of the so-called Serb MUP' and of threats of termination of employees of 'non-Serbian nationality' if they refused to sign statements of loyalty to RS MUP.[48]

Any considerations of this matter must also take into consideration the covert arming which had been ongoing throughout 1991 and early 1992. For obvious reasons, the illegal arming and other illegal and covert activities undertaken by the Bosnian Serbs and other members of the SRBiH MUP prior to the commencement of armed conflict are difficult to analyse. However, the ICTY heard extensive testimony on this subject in various trials. Even more importantly, and from the point of view of source criticism more credibly, the Bosnian Serbs in the halcyon days of the nascent Republika Srpska found occasion to document repeatedly their illicit prewar activities.

Contemporaneously with these developments, for example, Serbs serving in the police in the Sarajevo area had begun to prepare actively for armed conflict. In a subsequent nomination for commendation written in September 1993 by SJB Ilidža, the former Commander (and later Chief) of SJB Ilidža, Tomislav Kovač, was commended for having organized 'illegal meetings' in 1991 in his capacity as Commander of SJB Ilidža.

> At those meetings which were held in Dobrinja, Ilidža and Blažuj, in addition to the obligations of gathering Serbs and their preparations for war, it was agreed to work intensively on the arming of citizens of Serb nationality. The supplying of weapons was carried out from Ravna Romanija, Pale, Sokolac, Kalinovik, Nedavići village, Trnovo[,] Tošići village, Hadžići, Jusuf Džonlagić Barracks, Lukavica and Nedjarići [sic]. On 3 March 1992, the MUP armoury at Donji Potok was blockaded and taken into control and weapons and munitions were distributed to the Serbian people.[49]

The document further described prewar preparations. 'One of the priority tasks was the strengthening of the reserve police stations Centar-Ilidža, Lužani and Blažuj, which covered the urban portion of the municipality, which had the greatest strategic importance, and also the expulsion [protjerivanje] of Muslims from the SJB. Those were the preconditions for the creation of a Serb SJB.'[50] According to an RS MUP nomination for commendation of RS MUP officers at SJB Ilidža written in 1993, this particular SJB had been in the vanguard of preparations for a Bosnian Serb MUP.[51]

War

On 6 April 1992, the independence of the Republic of Bosnia and Herzegovina was recognized internationally. However, the Bosnian Serbs refused to recognize the state's independence, and moved politically and militarily to secure and expand the territory controlled by the Serb Republic of Bosnia and Herzegovina. In doing so, the Bosnian Serbs relied upon the methodology developed in the previous months, and in particular on the 19 December 1991 Instructions. The Bosnian Serb Ministry of Internal Affairs played a key role in this process and particularly during the first weeks of the war, when the Bosnian Serb republic still did not have its own armed forces. It should be noted that the Bosnian Serb Minister of Defence, Bogdan Subotić, on 16 April declared an imminent threat of war, triggering a full mobilization.[52] It is one of the peculiarities of the Bosnian conflict that the Bosnian Serbs actually did not declare an actual state of war in 1992, though they did later declare an end to this state.[53]

As will be seen, the role and the extent of the involvement of the police varied greatly throughout Bosnia. Particularly in those municipalities of Bosnia, the Serbs' takeover of power was immediate and featured the extensive involvement of various security forces and paramilitary formations from Serbia. In some of these municipalities, the RS MUP only later established its control after having to challenge the power of paramilitaries. In some Serb-majority municipalities, the takeover took place relatively peacefully without much contestation. In still other municipalities claimed by the Serbs, the takeover was very violent but transpired weeks after the commencement of armed conflict. While it is impossible to cover events in all of Bosnia's municipalities, a few sample municipalities will serve to highlight the role of the police: Bijeljina, Bileća, Banja Luka and Pale.

Bijeljina

Located in the extreme northeast of Bosnia, Bijeljina achieved immediate notoriety at the outset of the war, not because of the Bosnian Serb police, but on account of the arrival of Željko Ražnatović Arkan's paramilitary forces. Prior to war, Bijeljina had a Serb majority population, but 29.8 per cent of the population was Muslim.[54] Because of its Serb majority, Bijeljina was a Variant A municipality and had also featured SDS control of the municipality including the police since the 1990 elections. SSUP police inspector Mićo Davidović testified that the SDS had replaced the chief of SJB Bijeljina with Predrag Ješurić, a mediocre lawyer without prior police training – indeed, his experience with the police was limited to being arrested on suspicion of criminal conduct.[55] During the regionalization process, the SDS included Bijeljina in the SAO Northern Bosnia, which was later renamed SAO Semberija. Prior to the war, Ješurić facilitated what he himself later called the 'illegal arming' of Serbs in Bijeljina, while simultaneously preventing the Muslims from obtaining weapons.[56]

Arkan's forces entered Bijeljina on 31 March 1992, ostensibly to protect the town's Serb population.[57] Together with other paramilitary forces, the JNA and the municipal TO, the Serbs had no difficulty in assuming control of the municipality. Yet already during the takeover, Arkan's forces in particular killed several dozen Muslims without any police intervention on behalf of the victims. The police in the municipality ceased all cooperation with the SRBiH MUP, heeding Mandić's order to cooperate with the newly established RS MUP instead. When SRBiH Presidency member Biljana Plavšić visited Bijeljina on 3 April, she publicly hailed Arkan and kissed him, accepting his claims that he had come to defend the Serbs. Arkan rebuffed Plavšić's request that he turn control of the town over to the JNA.[58] Following this initial takeover, a campaign of terror continued against Bijeljina's Muslims, including killings, abductions, robberies, armed assaults and the destruction of Islamic cultural heritage.[59] Countless Muslims were eventually detained at the nearby Batković detention facility run by the VRS and at other detention facilities.

Instead of initiating an enquiry into the bloody events that had just transpired in Bijeljina, Minister Mićo Stanišić implicitly rewarded SJB Chief Ješurić by making him the new chief of CSB Bijeljina, SJB Bijeljina having been upgraded to CSB Bijeljina pursuant to the new RS Law on Internal Affairs. Subsequently, the police undertook no substantive investigations into the murders or other crimes committed against the Muslims of the municipality. On the contrary, the police not only played a complicit role in facilitating the crimes of other perpetrators, but also in the coming months participated directly in these crimes. This included the systematic looting and the removal of most Muslims from the municipality.[60] One particularly egregious example of police perpetration occurred months later, in September 1992, when an RS MUP special police unit led by Duško Malović and based in Bijeljina murdered twenty-two members of several prominent Muslim families.[61] The RS MUP did not subsequently investigate these killings.

The pattern of the takeover of power in Bijeljina was later replicated elsewhere in eastern and northern Bosnia, including in Bosanski Šamac, Zvornik and Brčko.[62] In a preview of later events elsewhere, those Serbs who attempted to protect Muslims or whose loyalty to the new authorities was uncertain were also subjected to persecution and violence. As will be seen, only later, when residual violence and criminal conduct were aimed primarily at Serbs in Bijeljina did the RS authorities, including the RS MUP, finally make a concerted effort to establish law and order in the now largely ethnically homogeneous municipality.

Bileća

Like Bijeljina, the eastern Herzegovinian municipality of Bileća was a Variant A municipality, featuring a substantial majority of 80.9 per cent Serbs and SDS control since the multi-party elections.[63] Bileća hosted a considerable military and police presence, and in the period leading up to the war these forces increasingly openly aligned themselves with SDS. Since January 1992, Bileća served as the headquarters of the newly formed 13th Corps of the JNA, and was commanded by Momčilo Perišić.[64] This permitted the Bosnian Serbs to quickly seize complete control of the municipality in April 1992, with very little armed resistance from the Bosnian Muslims and Croats. Hence, unlike in Bijeljina, the takeover took place without any incidents of mass violence.

The chief of SJB Bileća at the outset of the war was Miroslav Duka, and the commander was Goran Vujović.[65] In the context of a SJB, the top two posts were that of chief and commander. The post of chief of a SJB was a managerial and administrative position. The commander, who was subordinate to the chief of the SJB, was directly involved in the day-to-day operations of the police under his command. As of June 1991, Bosnian Muslims were overrepresented in SJB Bileća compared to their proportion in the population: the SJB's employees were 23 per cent Bosnian Muslim and 69 per cent Serbian, whereas the respective proportions in the general population were 14.7 per cent and 80.3 per cent. It should be noted that prior to the war, the Bosnian Serbs in Eastern Herzegovina had expressed a strong desire to no longer be subordinate to CSB Mostar, which covered all of Herzegovina. Instead, they wanted a separate CSB to be established in Trebinje, covering Bileća, Ljubinje, Nevesinje, Gacko and Trebinje municipalities.[66] They also sought an increase in the number of reserve police officers in police stations in areas with a Serb majority, such as Bileća.[67]

As mentioned in the previous chapter, the outbreak of war in Croatia had had a very deleterious effect on Bosnia, and this was particularly the case in a municipality like Bileća located very close to the new border. In the context of the war between the JNA and the nascent Croatian army in southern Dalmatia, the nearby Eastern Herzegovina hinterland, including Trebinje and Bileća, served as a staging area for the JNA and for Serbian irregular forces. Thus, already in the autumn of 1991, a special police unit of SAO Herzegovina had been sent to the Dubrovnik battlefield.[68] In sum, a significant portion of the Bosnian Serb members of the reserve police in Eastern Herzegovina participated in combat activities and were in frontline areas in or near Croatia during the second half of 1991.

As in Bijeljina, Serbs in the SRBiH MUP in Bileća participated in arming Serbs in the municipality. Already in May 1991, the SRBiH MUP's Administration for Affairs and Tasks for the Elimination and Investigation of Crime observed the illegal transportation of weapons in Bileća municipality.[69] Among those involved was Miroslav Duka, who at that time had not yet begun working in SJB Bileća.[70] A month later, Ejup Ganić complained at a session of the SRBiH Presidency attended by Federal Secretary of People's Defence Veljko Kadijević that such smuggling was ongoing, while Nikola Koljević countered with information regarding weapons smuggling from Hungary to Croatia and Bosnia.[71] At that meeting, Kadijević observed that 'everyone was arming' in Bosnia, and asked the assembled members of the presidency to refrain from asking the JNA to perform policing for which it was not capable.[72]

During the period of regionalization enacted by the SDS, Bileća joined SAO Herzegovina, which was created on 12 September 1991. Its self-proclaimed regional government included a 'SAO Ministry of Internal Affairs' headed by a Bosnian Serb police officer, Krsto Savić, the later chief of CSB Trebinje.[73] For those municipalities such as Bileća, that were included in SAO Herzegovina, this marked the beginnings of a parallel system of command and control, exclusively controlled by Bosnian Serbs.[74]

Unfortunately, the absence of violence during the takeover did not translate into subsequent peace or an absence of atrocities. With the advent of Serbian rule in Bileća, the situation of the Bosnian Muslim population became more difficult. 'Leading up to April 1992 and onwards, Muslims in Bileća were intimidated by Serbs who increasingly carried weapons in public. Checkpoints were erected in the municipality and restrictions on the movement of Muslim residents were imposed.'[75]

In order to secure and maintain power in Eastern Herzegovina and Bileća, the Serb authorities moved to disarm the non-Serb population. According to the ICTY judgement in the Prosecutor vs Momčilo Krajišnik, the campaign to disarm the Bosnian Muslims in Bileća municipality began on 10 June 1992 and immediately resulted in a mass coordinated arrest of a large number of Muslim males by regular and reserve police forces. This coincided with the arrival of several Serb paramilitary groups in the municipality.[76] Several of these groups, such as the 'Yellow Wasps' (*Žute ose*) and Željko Ražnatović Arkan's 'Tigers' (*Tigrovi*), were already feared by Bosnian Muslims owing to their violent behaviour in other municipalities. In mid-July 1992, the War Presidency of neighbouring Gacko municipality called upon all Bosnian Muslims in the area to surrender.[77]

Bosnian Muslims were detained and mistreated in a number of facilities in Bileća municipality after April 1992. 'From June 1992 on, Muslim civilians were arrested and detained in five detention centres where they were regularly beaten by police and paramilitaries.'[78] These facilities included the Bileća barracks, the Bileća police station (i.e. the premises of SJB Bileća), the Bileća prison and the municipal youth house (*Đački dom*).[79] The use of the Bileća SJB building was also discussed in the UN Commission of Experts' report in 1994.[80] Bosnian Muslim property was looted in Bileća, and three mosques were destroyed, although this latter destruction may have occurred after 1992.

Banja Luka

As the second-largest city in Bosnia and the regional capital of Bosnian Krajina, Banja Luka held critical importance.[81] Because the town never suffered direct military assault or witnessed any combat, it also offers an interesting case in which the police in a relatively 'peaceful' context nevertheless exercised control and implemented a policy of apartheid and ethnic cleansing. Banja Luka had a Serb majority population of 55 per cent in 1991, with 15 per cent Croats and 15 per cent Muslims, and over 12 per cent self-declared Yugoslavs.[82] Hence, Banja Luka was a Variant A municipality. As will be seen in more detail later, the takeover in Banja Luka proceeded deceptively peacefully, even as a shadowy conglomeration of pro-SDS paramilitary forces signalled menacingly. Instead of the maelstrom of violence that swept eastern Bosnia, the takeover of power in Banja Luka proceeded more incrementally, and was initially characterized more by the imposition of a type of administrative or bureaucratic apartheid against non-Serbs.

Banja Luka was a very strange place in the spring and summer of 1992. As war raged in other parts of Bosnia, and as the Muslims of eastern Bosnia were systematically 'cleansed', an eerie peace remained in Bosnia's second-largest city. Yet for those residents of Banja Luka who were not of Serbian ethnicity, or even for Serbs who had relatives or spouses of other ethnicities, these were harrowing months. Because while the authorities continued to insist that the new institutions, including the police, served all citizens, it rapidly became apparent that this was not the case.[83]

The symbol of Banja Luka's slow slide into inhumanity was the so-called 'red van' (*crveni kombi*), which came to be remembered with notoriety by those who survived. It appeared at the beginning of April 1992 and continued to operate in the city until the end of the year.[84] The persons in the vehicle abducted, stole from and physically assaulted and most likely killed those whom they preyed upon. Not only did the police not intervene to stop the activities of the red van, but the individuals who operated the vehicle and perpetrated crimes were in fact employees of the RS MUP and were based on the premises of CSB Banja Luka. As the Trial Chamber in the trial of Mićo Stanišić and Stojan Župljanin observed, 'in Banja Luka, the red van was synonymous with fear', and the clear purpose of the crimes committed by the operators of the van was 'to intimidate the non-Serb population into leaving. ... The existence of the red van and what was happening to non-Serbs was common knowledge in Banja Luka in 1992'.[85]

Pale

Pale is a small settlement located approximately 20 km east of Sarajevo. Pale came to prominence in the Bosnian war because it became the de facto capital of the Bosnian Serbs. It had a considerable Serb majority (69.5 per cent) prior to the war, with Muslims constituting a little over a quarter of the population. As such, Pale was a Variant A municipality.

Although peace generally prevailed in Pale until April 1992, the year preceding the war was marked by a steady increase in inter-ethnic tensions and an atmosphere of looming conflict.[86] Malko Koroman, the chief of SJB Pale, was at the vanguard of efforts to implement the ethnic separation of the police. As the head of the police in an SDS-controlled municipality, Koroman had engaged in the arming of the population and in the removal of Bosnian Muslims in particular from the municipal police force. On 23 March, the Pale municipal crisis staff ordered the disarming of all Muslim police officers and their dismissal.[87] Koroman presented this decision as retribution for the dismissal of Serb police officers from SJB Stari Grad in Sarajevo.[88]

The removal of all Bosnian Muslims from the police coincided with an effort to remove all Muslim inhabitants from the municipality.[89] The Bosnian Serb authorities including the police employed coercion and terror to achieve this goal. As would be the case throughout Serb-controlled areas of Bosnia in the coming weeks and months, the authorities mounted a campaign of disarming non-Serbs and used various alleged violations of increasingly discriminatory measures and legislation to justify the use of violence against non-Serbs. Even legally registered weapons had to be surrendered by non-Serbs. Barricades and police intimidation increasingly restricted the movement of non-Serbs in Pale, with arrests and beatings meted out. Non-Serb residents experienced threats, harassment, burglaries and other forms of abuse without any noticeable action by the police. On the contrary, indications pointed at the involvement of some police officers and at their personally profiting from criminal acts.[90] At the same time, most non-Serbs employed in the municipality also began to be fired, implicitly or explicitly, from their places of employment. When Bosnian Muslims living in Pale remonstrated that they wished to continue residing in the municipality, they were told by Nikola Koljević that local Serbs no longer wanted to live together with Muslims. Instead of pledging to protect the worried Muslims, Police Chief Koroman told them that he could not guarantee their safety in the light of the arrival of Serb paramilitary elements.[91]

When mass detentions of non-Serbs commenced in Pale, the building of SJB Pale was among those used as an impromptu detention facility.[92] The police beat many of those who were detained, killing a number of them. In other cases, the police stood idly by and did not intervene as soldiers or others assaulted the detainees. The Pale high school (*gimnazija*), located only a few metres from SJB

Pale, also functioned as a detention facility where atrocities were committed against detainees.[93] Finally, the campaign against non-Serbs in Pale culminated in the removal of them in convoys.[94] After being submitted to months of persecution and atrocities, those who left were permitted to take little or no possessions with them, and had to forfeit their property.

Loyalty oaths

Having seen how the takeover proceeded in several municipalities, it is next worth turning to the issue of loyalty oaths or solemn declarations which the RS MUP implemented in areas under its control. During the first half of April 1992, the police of the fledgling RS MUP took shape. The RS MUP adopted new, Serbian symbols.[95] Working on the basis of the new RS Law on Internal Affairs, RS MUP CSBs were established.[96] Simultaneously, members of the police in Serbian-controlled areas were ordered to sign loyalty oaths.[97] Those refusing to do so were put on 'annual leave' from the new Bosnian Serb MUP and ordered to hand in their service weapons and other equipment.[98] (None of these employees were subsequently allowed to return to service. They were fired retroactively, effective 1 April, the day the loyalty oaths were first announced.[99]) At a press conference on 3 April in Banja Luka, Stojan Župljanin said unambiguously that CSB employees had to sign a loyalty oath by 6 April.[100]

On 9 April 1992, it was announced that the deadline for the signing of declarations of loyalty to the RS MUP would be extended until 15 April.[101] However, it remained the case that employees refusing to take the oath were dismissed from their posts.[102] According to a later report, 304 employees of CSB Banja Luka did not sign loyalty oaths.[103] SRBiH MUP Minister Delimustafić's assertions from Sarajevo that the oath – and the RS MUP as a whole – were illegitimate and illegal were in vain.[104] It should be noted that in some areas of the RS, Muslim police officers were not offered an opportunity to take a loyalty oath.[105] Moreover, in many cases even those non-Serb employees who did sign declarations of loyalty were nevertheless dismissed.[106]

As the chief of CSB Banja Luka, Stojan Župljanin announced that who did not sign the statement [of loyalty] would be without employment. Župljanin stated that he was personally a great optimist with respect to the peaceful transformation of the MUP, and that up until now a large number of employees of all nationalities had signed the solemn statement which, actually, did not differ from the statement from the old law on internal affairs.[107] Župljanin insisted that he wanted to maintain a 'national representation of employees in public security stations that is adequate to the national structure of the population of the territory of the municipalities'.[108]

By contrast, Bajazid Jahić, the chief of the public security sector of the CSB, was quoted on 9 April 1992 as saying that 'already yesterday in the Banja Luka SJB there was pressure on people to sign the statement, which is not in order, because no one needs pressure'.[109] Jahić expressed his hope that the emblem worn on the uniforms would nonetheless be the Yugoslav rather than the Serbian tricolour. He believed that far fewer employees would join the RS MUP if the latter were the case. Jahić also questioned whether, if the Serbs declared a Serbian municipality of Bihać, the Bosnian Muslims would declare a Muslim municipality of Banja Luka, and if such solutions were workable. These were precisely the types of absolutely critical details that, to the extent that they could ever have been soluble, should have been the subject of extensive further negotiations.

Župljanin asserted, meanwhile, that he would not allow the harassment of anyone within the police. Yet numerous witnesses later testified at the ICTY regarding dismissals prompted when they would not swear loyalty to the RS or wear Serbian insignia on their uniforms.[110] And in Prijedor, disgruntled Bosnian Muslim employees organized by the SDA allegedly tried but failed to take over the police station.[111] In a report filed in August 1992, CSB Banja Luka stated that 'almost all members of non-Serb nationality' left the police on the territory of CSB Banja Luka.[112] RS MUP inspectors visiting from Sarajevo discovered that in SJB Banja Luka, the few remaining Bosnian Muslim employees had been put on leave. No one knew what to do with them.[113]

It is worth pausing here to briefly mention that the issue of the loyalty oaths was often later disputed at the ICTY. From the point of view of the accused, there was nothing wrong with requiring police officers to swear loyalty to the political entities in which they were policing.[114] After all, is the swearing of such oaths not standard practice throughout the world? Yet such questions obviously ignored the crucial context of a process of ethnic segregation of policing accompanied by consciously applied coercion and armed force. These questions also assumed non-existing good faith on the part of the newly created RS Ministry of Internal Affairs, which had no desire to see non-Serbs employed in its ranks. Ample evidence introduced at the ICTY in the form of both documents and witness testimony demonstrated that Bosnian Muslims and Croats were dismissed during this period not just from the police but also from the army, government organs, and public and private companies.[115] By 22 June 1992 in the ARK region, an explicit requirement had emerged that 'important' posts only be held by Serbs – specifically Serbs who were not only loyal to Republika Srpska but also to the SDS.[116]

In addition to issuing such orders, the crisis staffs enabled the creation of Serb police forces in the municipalities, including the firing of non-Serbs from the police.[117] Once purely Serb police forces were created, crisis staffs controlled or closely coordinated with their municipal police.[118] In each municipality of Republika Srpska, the chief of the local SJB was a member of the crisis staff.[119] In Sanski Most, for example, the members of the crisis staff included the commander of 6th Krajina Brigade, the commander of the Serbian TO, the chief of Police and president of SDS Deputies' Club. The deputy president of the crisis staff was responsible for 'the realisation of the ideas of the leadership of the SDS on the level of the Republic, the region, and the municipality'.[120] In Prijedor, Simo Drljača, the chief of the SJB, sent a list of municipal and regional crisis staff decisions implemented by the police to the municipal crisis staff on 1 July 1992.[121] In Bosanski Petrovac, Dragan Gaćeša, the chief of the SJB, participated in crisis staff meetings and helped to establish a detention centre.[122] And in Ključ, the crisis staff claimed that 'no significant and important questions from the military and police domain were resolved without the Crisis Staff'.[123] At the regional level, Župljanin was a member of the ARK Crisis Staff.[124]

An emerging coalition between the RS MUP and paramilitary forces

During the first months of the war, the Bosnian Serbs drew extensively on paramilitary groups for auxiliary support. Some of these groups emerged locally in various municipalities, while others – particularly in the eastern portions of the country – stemmed from Serbia. It is important to note that the relationship between these paramilitary groups and the nascent Bosnian Serb authorities varied considerably from municipality to municipality and from group to group, but it is overall possible to draw several conclusions about the purpose and behaviour of these groups. Among these conclusions is the usefulness of plausible deniability for the activities of these groups, which inculcated terror among the civilian population and perpetrated a broad array of atrocities which were euphemistically known as 'ethnic cleansing'.[125]

An important case in point for the use of paramilitary groups and their relationship with the (Serb) police is provided by the municipality of Banja Luka, the largest and most populous municipality in which the Bosnian Serbs managed to take power in the spring of 1992, and the key to the entire Bosnian Krajina region. Like the rest of Bosnia, Banja Luka had experienced a deterioration of the security situation in the second half of 1991 and in the first months of 1992. Owing to its proximity to Croatia, the city and its surrounding municipalities had been affected by the war in Croatia, with the JNA withdrawing considerable personnel and materiel to the area from Croatia after the ceasefire in January 1992.

Approximately a month before the war's outbreak, with Banja Luka still experiencing an uneasy peace, a shadowy armed organization calling itself the Serbian Defence Forces (*Srpske odbrambene snage*, SOS) appeared on the scene. The group presented itself as autonomous, representing the interests of Serbs in the region, blockading the municipal building in an attempt to stop the Bosnian independence referendum at the end of February.[126] Unbeknownst to the public, the leader of the SOS, Nenad Stevandić, had as early as August 1991 spoken with Radovan Karadžić regarding paramilitary training – something 'like Golubić', the Serbian-supported training centre for Croatian Serbs near Knin.[127] Stevandić later became a member of the ARK Crisis Staff.[128]

Approximately one month after the referendum, on 3 April, the SOS began establishing checkpoints in Banja Luka. Conspicuously, the police did not intervene. Acting again as if they were autonomous, the SOS issued a set of demands which it expected the SDS to accept and impose, and which in fact occurred within one day.[129] 'These goals included the immediate enactment of the Law on Internal Affairs of the Serbian People of BiH, replacing the Latin script with Cyrillic in public insignia, the reinforcement of the [JNA] Banja Luka Corps ranks, and the dismissal of military officers and public utility managers who had voted "against Yugoslavia" in the referendum for independence held in BiH.'[130] Yet the so-called 'Miloš Group', which was loosely affiliated with the Serbian State Security Service, reported that the SOS was in fact an armed organization belonging to the SDS.[131] A later study by the investigative reporter Edin Omerčić argued that the SOS's actions in early April were designed to assist the SDS, which was under considerable international and domestic pressure to compromise with the representatives of the Bosnian Muslims and Bosnian Croats.[132]

Moreover, the Miloš Group opined that the SOS was contributing to an increased risk of inter-ethnic armed conflict. In actual fact, the SOS, like other paramilitary organizations established during this period in ostensible defence of national interests, included in its ranks known sociopathic and criminal elements, some of whom had already seen combat in Croatia.[133] Leading staff at CSB Banja Luka were aware that there were criminal elements within the SOS. Živko Bojić, chief of the sector for crime in CSB Banja Luka, stated that the police were working with the leadership of the SOS to 'identify and arrest those criminals who infiltrated into the ranks of the Serbian Defence Forces and committed some criminal acts'.[134] The SOS began to rob, assault and rape Muslims and Croats and attack their homes and businesses – as well as those of Serbs who resisted or protested – in the Banja Luka region; the police did nothing to stop them.[135] Those not of Serb ethnicity could no longer move freely or safely about town and, facing increasing threats to their property and physical safety, many began to flee the area.

The SOS thus operated relatively uninhibitedly for many weeks in and around Banja Luka. In the end, they were neither arrested nor disbanded but were instead absorbed – with distinction one could say – into the police. Namely, the SOS became part of a special unit of CSB Banja Luka, while a few members joined the SNB.[136] On 27 April 1992, the ARK Assembly approved a proposal that CSB Banja Luka form a 'police detachment for special purposes [*odred milicije za posebne namjene*], which would number 157 + 3 members'.[137] On 28 April *Glas* wrote that the new unit had been established in accordance with a decision of the Assembly and that Župljanin was responsible for personnel and organization.[138] On 29 April, *Glas* reported that Župljanin had announced that the requested equipment had arrived and that 'the CSB had at its disposal equipment ranging from automatic rifles to armoured combat vehicles, anti-aircraft artillery and helicopters'.[139] The same article noted that the paramilitary SOS had been placed by the ARK Assembly under the control of CSB Banja Luka.[140] On 6 May Župljanin informed members of the CSB Council and heads of SJBs in the region that 'he had established a special counter-sabotage and counter-terrorist police unit of about 150 to be deployed in the regions in the most complex security operations'.[141] The unit went on to participate in battles for the 'liberation of Serbian territory'.[142] Predrag Radulović, who headed the Miloš Group, later testified that 'no one will ever be able to convince me that was necessary for some tactical or strategic reasons because in order to bring this kind of cancer into the service you can only expect the whole service to become ill'.[143]

The CSB Banja Luka special unit was commanded by Ljubomir (aka Ljuban) Ećim, who like most of the members was formerly in the SOS. A JNA captain,

Mirko Lukić, was initially appointed, apparently with the rationale that a professional military officer would be able to steer the unit in a disciplined and positive direction. However, Captain Lukić quickly left that position, as he found it impossible to perform his job.[144] The special unit quickly gained notoriety for its callous behaviour in the field.[145] On 26 June 1992, the Kotor Varoš Crisis Staff met to discuss, inter alia, complaints about the behaviour of this unit.[146] Both the local representatives of the VRS and members of the crisis staff asserted their dissatisfaction with the conduct of members of the unit. The crisis staff members had in vain sought VRS intervention against the CSB Banja Luka special unit. Savo Tepić, the chief of SJB Kotor Varoš, stated that the unit worked with a mind of its own and that any admonitions directed towards the unit were repaid with threats. The crisis staff would discuss the matter with Župljanin. On 2 July, the Kotor Varoš Crisis Staff resolved to call Ećim and Župljanin for a consultation.[147]

For the new CSB Banja Luka special unit and for the Chief of CSB Banja Luka, Stojan Župljanin, the crowning achievement was the unveiling of the police's might on the occasion of Security Day (*Dan bezbjednosti*) in the middle of May. The celebration of Security Day was carried over from socialist Yugoslavia, where the day had marked the anniversary of the establishment of the Yugoslav State Security Service on 13 May 1944. Now, in May 1992, a virtually monoethnic and nationalist police force formed on the rubble of the multi-ethnic Ministry of Internal Affairs of socialist Yugoslavia had its opportunity to shine. Press treatment of the Security Day parade noted that this unit would 'in the future carry out the most complicated tasks, independently or in co-ordination with the Army'.[148] Notably, in the days before the parade was held, Župljanin spoke to Undersecretary for Public Security Čedo Kljajić, with Župljanin telling Kljajić that the situation in Banja Luka was 'relatively good' and that the 'Muslims have realized that they have lost'.[149]

A video recording of the event shows that, from Radovan Karadžić to regional officials such as the head of the ARK Crisis Staff Radoslav Brđanin, the top leadership of Republika Srpska gathered on balcony overlooking the parade.[150] They were of course accompanied by the leading officials of the RS MUP, including Minister Mićo Stanišić and CSB Chief Stojan Župljanin. Emphasizing the Serbian nationalist atmosphere, the Minister of Internal Affairs of the RSK Milan Martić gave a speech which received rousing applause. As will be seen, the parade took place right after the RS Assembly had met in Banja Luka and adopted a set of strategic goals, illustrating that the RS MUP stood perfectly aligned with the Bosnian Serb leadership.

The RS National Security Service

Like its predecessor, the Bosnian Ministry of Internal Affairs, the RS Ministry of Internal Affairs was divided into two main services: the Public Security Service and the National Security Service. The latter, the SNB, was the descendant of the SRBiH State Security Service (*Služba državne bezbjednosti*, or SDB). Accordingly, the SNB modelled its structure heavily on that of the SDB. It should be noted that, although the SRBiH MUP ceased to exist at the beginning of April 1992, documents indicate that Serbian employees in the SRBiH MUP SDB had stopped cooperating with SRBiH MUP as early as the end of 1991.[151]

An undersecretary for National Security headed the RS MUP SNB. Slobodan Škipina was the first undersecretary of the SNB.[152] Škipina was one of many Bosnian Serb MUP officials who had retired relatively recently, but who were reactivated when the RS MUP was being established.[153] As of 6 August 1992, the undersecretary for SNB was Dragan Kijac.[154]

The SNB was charged with the gathering of intelligence related to dangers against the RS.[155] According to a 17 July 1992 action programme sent to the RS Government and RS Presidency, the SNB would 'use its powers, means and methods' predominantly for the 'collection and documentation of the activities of the enemy'.[156] It sought to strengthen the grip of the RS on its territory while weakening the hold of the enemy over its territory. It also aimed specifically at preventing Serbs in Muslim- or Croat-controlled areas from working against the interests of the RS.

The 1992 annual report on the work of the SNB stated that the Service strove to contribute to the rapid creation of the 'legal and territorial completeness of Republika Srpska'.[157] Although the report emphasized the 'modest' personnel resources available to SNB at the outset of the war, it also noted that Serbs in the SRBiH MUP SDB had begun 'much earlier' to prepare the ground for SNB.

Generally speaking, all documents related to the SNB or produced by it had a higher level of confidentiality and more restricted circulation than those related to the Public Security Service. A separate, secret rulebook (*pravilnik*) existed for the SNB. This rulebook was drafted in the course of 1992.[158] The strict confidentiality of the work of the SNB was enforced and supported by the Minister of Internal Affairs. On at least one occasion, Minister Stanišić found it necessary to advise all employees of the Public Security Service that they had no authority to intervene in or enquire about the work of the SNB.[159] In addition, only the SNB had the right to be in direct contact with the Intelligence Service of the VRS. The SNB, for its part, had to provide the chiefs of SJBs with relevant information.

At the outset of the war, the SNB was organized into five regional sectors. Each CSB housed one 'sector' of the SNB. Beneath each of these sectors were a collection of 'detachments'. This paralleled the earlier internal organization of the SRBiH MUP SDB, which had also proceeded along a hierarchical line: administrations – sectors – departments – sections – detachments.[160] During 1992, the SNB was further organized geographically into a number of 'war departments' (*ratna odjeljenja*, or ROs).[161] According to a report produced by RS MUP at the end of June 1992, the SNB in ARK had been able to establish and operate significantly better and more easily than, for example, the SNB in the Sarajevo region.[162] This was due to disparities in equipment, personnel and the combat situation. Nevertheless, even the SNB in CSB Sarajevo succeeded in providing a regular stream of intelligence on enemy activities and plans.[163] This included the submission of numerous reports to the Sarajevo-Romanija Corps.[164]

Organizationally, the SNB was also divided into several functional lines, each of which was formally referred to as an Administration or Department. Each of these lines concentrated on specific aspects of police intelligence and had its own reporting system and hierarchy. In the SDB, there were nine lines:[165]

1. Administration for Affairs and Tasks of the Discovery and Prevention of the Activities of Foreign Intelligence Services
2. Administration for Affairs and Tasks of the Discovery and Prevention of Hostile Activities of Émigrés
3. Administration for Affairs and Tasks of the Discovery and Prevention of Activities of the Internal Enemy
4. Administration for Operational-Technical Affairs and Tasks
5. Administration for Affairs and Tasks of the Security of Certain Persons and Places
6. Administration for Affairs and Tasks of Defensive Preparations
7. Administration for Analytical-Informational Affairs and Tasks
8. Department for Affairs and Tasks of Secret Surveillance
9. Department for General, Legal and Personnel Questions and Tasks.

A document produced by the RDB Centre in Banja Luka in March 1994 provided a brief retrospective overview of SDB operations in CSB Banja Luka before and after April 1992.[166] As of 1 April 1992, twenty-eight Serbs, five Croats, nine Muslims and one Yugoslav worked for the SDB Sector in Banja Luka. Between April 1992 and March 1994, one Serb left the SNB/RDB, and one was killed. Of the Croats, one refused to sign the loyalty oath, three went to work in the Public Security Service and one left the service. Of the Muslims, six refused to sign the loyalty oath, one left the service, one went to work in the Public Security Service and one went to work for the RBiH government. After April 1992, there were 121 posts in the Banja Luka Centre SNB, which covered twenty-five municipalities.

In SNB, the number of functional lines was eventually reduced to six.[167] In practice, the lines overlapped. This was especially the case after the commencement of armed hostilities. However, it should be noted that indications exist that regional SNB Centres lacked adequate direction from the centre. In October 1992, CSB Banja Luka complained about the 'non-existence of particular programmatic orientation of the work of the National Security Service'.[168] This did not mean, though, that the SNB Sector at CSB Banja Luka had remained idle during the period since its establishment. On the contrary, SNB operatives had worked on a variety of issues, including intelligence work and anti-terrorist operations. As early as April 1992, SNB operatives in the Banja Luka area had issued reports on the security situation in various ARK municipalities.[169] In addition, 'the Sector, on the invitation of the Public Security Service, and in conjunction with its legal powers, participated together with the public and military security services in the operational processing, i.e. interrogation of persons held in collective centres about illegal arming and military organisation'. The SNB could also request to interrogate persons detained in various facilities or suggest their release.[170]

In its work, the SNB cooperated closely with Military Security. The report for Line 01 for the period from April 1992 to April 1993 revealed that the SNB in ARK had begun cooperating directly with JNA Military Security at around the same time that cooperation with the SRBiH MUP stopped – i.e. at the end of 1991.[171] In May 1992, upon the formation of the VRS, the SNB began to exchange intelligence with VRS Military Intelligence.[172] During the first full year of operation, Line 01 of the SNB Sector in Banja Luka calculated that it had participated in the interrogation of 'several thousand persons' suspected of anti-constitutional activities. This included interrogations carried out in Manjača and similar detention camps which will be discussed in the following chapter.[173]

In addition to reporting regularly on combat activity in their areas of the operation, the National Security Sectors within the CSBs prepared occasional reports on enemy forces and on the 'illegal arming' of enemy forces.[174] In its review of work in 1992, the SNB Sector at CSB Banja Luka asserted that it achieved great successes in the struggle against 'Muslim-Croat extremists'.[175] The SNB Sector estimated that 10,000 such extremists had been fully equipped and ready to fight against RS forces in the area surrounding Prijedor, Ključ, Sanski Most and Jajce.

As a part of the RS MUP, the SNB was aware that large numbers of non-Serbs were departing from the territory of the RS in the summer of 1992. In late October 1992, the SNB noted the 'massive departures' of both Muslims and Croats from Prijedor municipality. According to the estimates of the SNB Sector at CSB Banja Luka, 38,000 Muslim and Croat inhabitants had left Prijedor municipality to date.[176] It was further observed that many villages in the municipality had been partly or wholly destroyed, and that 'massive plunder' of these locations had followed. Croat and Muslim property and places of worship had also been attacked.[177] Although persons in military uniform had abused non-Serbs, the military police had taken few concrete steps to remedy this.

Like other parts of the RS MUP, SNB collected materials on war crimes. Again, as with the Public Security Service, this mainly involved the collection of information about crimes committed against Serbs.[178] (Indeed, in his later testimony at the ICTY, the first Chief of the SNB, Slobodan Škipina, claimed that he had received to have obtained not a single about crimes committed against non-Serbs.)[179] From April 1992 until the end of that year, the SNB Sector at CSB Banja Luka pressed charges against only one individual for suspected war crimes. No mention was made in the SNB Sector's 1992 annual report of the commission of any war crimes against the non-Serbian population in CSB Banja Luka's AOR.[180] In at least one municipality, the SNB in 1993 compiled lists of non-Serbs who had left the municipality.

As with the RS MUP Public Security Service, the SNB had knowledge of grave violations of humanitarian law committed in the RS. In addition to the involvement of SNB in the interrogation of non-Serbs in detention facilities, the SNB also reported on occasion on attacks on non-Serbs.[181]

This chapter has shown several examples of how the Bosnian Serbs with the RS MUP at the vanguard took control of municipalities throughout Bosnia. At the ICTY, many defendants accused of crimes in Bosnia and Herzegovina contended that they had acted conscientiously and responsibly in the spring of 1992 when planning the establishment of monoethnic police forces. According to these accounts, the tragedy that ensued was the fault of 'the others', who allegedly did not respect the agreements that had been hammered out to implement the separation. Yet the historical record reveals this account to be self-serving and wrong. At the very outset of the war – and even as early as half a year before the war – police officers and intelligence operatives in the SRBiH MUP submitted their assessments that the ethnically based dismantling of the MUP carried with it a very high risk of fratricidal warfare. On 2 April 1992, the Miloš Group wrote that the formation of the RS MUP 'could lead to the total national division' and that 'the aforementioned division could manifest itself in various ways, and above all employees of Muslim and Croatian nationality would create their own services of public and state security in all locations in BiH, which would inevitably lead to interethnic conflicts'.[182]

Finally, before moving on, it is necessary to highlight briefly a peculiar phenomenon of the police in the Bosnian war. Despite the disintegration of the SRBiH MUP and the onset of a fratricidal war, former colleagues of various ethnicities who joined opposing forces did maintain some contact and communication. One particularly noteworthy and callous example of such contact can be found in an intercepted phone conversation in which Stanišić and Mandić, located at Pale or Vraca, spoke with their two most important former Croat colleagues, Bruno Stojić and Brane Kvesić. Both Stojić and Kvesić had at the outset of the war withdrawn to Mostar, where they were instrumental in creating an ethnically Croat police force. In this long and amicable conversation, the four former colleagues exhibited profound cynicism in discussing the war and, in particular, the plight of the Bosnian Muslims in Sarajevo. The telephone conversation initiated with the Croats and the Serbs playfully calling each other Chetniks and Ustashe. While some tensions were apparent regarding the division of Mostar and Herzegovina, the overall tone was boisterous and friendly. Momčilo Mandić joked that the Bosnian Serbs would create a 'new, nice Sarajevo' without mosques or synagogues and that the Bosnian Serbs would also 'hold these Turks, keep them surrounded, we will let them starve a bit, you know'.[183]

Chapter 3

SEARCH, DETAIN, DESTROY: ETHNIC CLEANSING,
EXPULSIONS AND POLICE CONCENTRATION CAMPS
(APRIL–DECEMBER 1992)

By the middle of May 1992, the Bosnian Serbs had succeeded in taking control of a large portion of Bosnia and Herzegovina. Both politically and militarily, the leaders of the Bosnian Serb republic felt ready to assess the strategic scope of the events that they had set into motion. The forum for doing so was the sixteenth session of the Bosnian Serb Assembly on 12 May 1992. This session marked a milestone, as the formation of the Army of Republika Srpska (*Vojska Republike Srpske*, VRS) was decided, and Radovan Karadžić presented a set of six strategic goals which the Bosnian Serbs intended to pursue in the coming months and years. Until this date, the 'armed forces' within RS MUP were the only armed forces exclusively and directly controlled by the RS leadership. RS MUP officials were proud of this fact and did not hesitate to emphasize it in their later reports on operations in 1992.[1] As late as April 1995, Karadžić reminisced that the people illegally armed by the SDS were, 'together with the police', the armed forces controlled by the RS in its earliest phase.[2]

Yet even as the Bosnian Serbs strove to take on attributes of statehood, symbolized by the establishment of the VRS, they continued to rely very heavily on the police of the RS MUP. Moreover, the RS MUP in turn had – sometimes tacitly, sometimes explicitly – since the beginning of the war entered into cooperation with paramilitary forces. This insidious bargain proved brutally effective in perpetrating the vast array of crimes euphemistically known as 'ethnic cleansing' against Bosnian Muslims, Bosnian Croats and others, but also carried with it parasitic and extremely malignant elements that would by the middle of the summer pose a threat to the RS authorities in several key municipalities. In other words, the very decentralizing processes which had served the Bosnian Serbs so well in helping to destabilize Bosnia and Herzegovina and to seize power had unleashed a maelstrom of violence and disorder so considerable that it threatened to spin out of control and devour the nascent Bosnian Serb republic. This chapter will show how the police helped to reassert the control of the RS 'state' even as it worked relentlessly to persecute non-Serbs and remove them from the territory controlled by the RS.

During the summer of 1992 international organizations and intrepid reporters succeeded in identifying a number of Bosnian Serb detention facilities which upon their discovery instantaneously became infamous. Based on material from trials at the ICTY, this chapter will carefully analyse how, in conjunction with the political and military leadership, the police conducted 'disarmament' campaigns which served as a pretext for the detention of tens of thousands of civilians, including children, the elderly and women. In detention facilities such as Omarska, Keraterm, Luka, Kula and others, the police over a period of months committed crimes including murder, rape and torture against those unlawfully detained based primarily on their ethnicity. At the same time, the Bosnian Serb police paradoxically had to confront their erstwhile paramilitary allies, whose particularly extreme and often chaotic violence challenged the establishment and stability of Republika Srpska. By the end of 1992, the Bosnian Serbs controlled approximately 70 per cent of the country.

The sixteenth session of the Bosnian Serb Assembly

Since its inception in October 1991, the Bosnian Serb Assembly had been the primary forum in which the SDS – which dominated the Assembly – met to discuss and debate all relevant issues and, of course, to promulgate legislation. On 12 May 1992 in Banja Luka, Momčilo Krajišnik convened the sixteenth session of the Bosnian Serb Assembly, which came to constitute an important milestone.[3] In addition to the Assembly's deputies, the session was also attended by the highest representatives of the military.

The first highlight of the sixteenth session was the establishment of the VRS. The VRS drew upon JNA and TO officers who predominantly hailed from Bosnia, and Ratko Mladić, a Bosnian Serb colonel in the JNA, was appointed general and commanding officer. The Bosnian Serb TO components were, however, not immediately absorbed into the VRS.[4]

A few weeks earlier, on 27 April 1992, the authorities in Belgrade had proclaimed a new Federal Republic of Yugoslavia consisting of Serbia (with Vojvodina and Kosovo) and Montenegro. The army of this new political entity were known as the Army of Yugoslavia (*Vojska Jugoslavije*, VJ).[5] The establishment of both the VRS and the VJ was a product of the Milošević regime's need to distance itself publicly from the wars in Croatia and Bosnia, i.e. to establish plausible deniability regarding Belgrade's involvement. The JNA, in principle, withdrew from Bosnia on 19 and 20 May 1992, and the new Bosnian Serb army was designed to appear independent.[6] Behind the scenes, however, the VRS and the VJ remained joined at the hip. In all secrecy, the salaries of the entire officer corps of the VRS continued to be paid by the Federal Republic of Yugoslavia. The payments to the VRS flowed from a secret unit known as the 30th Personnel Centre.[7]

The second highlight of the 16th Assembly Session was the adoption of six strategic goals for the Serbian Republic. Although Radovan Karadžić proclaimed and explained these goals at the session, they remained confidential and were not disseminated to the public until November 1993.[8] However, there can be no doubt that the goals created the strategic framework for the Bosnian Serb armed forces which of course encompassed the police.[9] In his speech, Karadžić repeatedly insisted that it was not the Serbs' fault that war had erupted in Bosnia. Rather, the

Muslims and Croats had forced the war upon the Serbs, against whom they had earlier in the twentieth century already once committed genocide. The risk of a new genocide against the Serbs was hence imminent. Moving to the specific goals, Karadžić continued:

> The Serbian side in BiH, the Presidency, the Government, the National Security Council which we have formed, have adopted the strategic priorities of the Serb nation, of which the first goal is the separation from the two [other] national communities, state separation. ... The second strategic goal is, it seems to me, a corridor between Semberija and Krajina. ... The third strategic goal is the establishment of a corridor in the Drina River valley or, respectively, the elimination of the Drina as a border between two worlds [i.e., between Bosnia and Serbia]. ... The fourth strategic goal is the establishment of a border on the river Una and the river Neretva. ... The fifth strategic goal is the division of the city of Sarajevo into a Serbian and a Muslim part and the establishment of in each of these two parts of effective state authorities in those constitutive states. ... The sixth strategic goal is access to the sea for the Serbian Republic of BiH.[10]

Actions taken by the Bosnian Serb armed forces in the period between the beginning of April and the 16th Assembly session, as well as subsequent events, showed that the Bosnian Serbs took the implementation of the strategic goals very seriously. In April and May, massive combined police, military and paramilitary operations had resulted in Serbian control of almost all Drina River valley municipalities, notwithstanding that these were mostly majority Muslim municipalities per the 1991 census. And in June 1992, even more massive force was deployed in Operation Corridor in order to achieve the second strategic goal.

The special police

In Bosnia before the war, the republican MUP had included only one permanently existing special police unit. As has been seen in the previous chapter, the splitting of this unit was like the decentralization process – an important step in the dissolution of the SRBiH MUP. With the outbreak of armed conflict, a haphazard and often bizarre number of self-proclaimed special police units mushroomed forth, particularly during the first two months of the conflict. In fact, it seemed as if any person with a gun, an aggressive ego and a few friends could overnight become the head of a special police unit.[11]

The most heavily armed combat unit in the RS MUP was the Special Brigade of the Police (*Specijalna brigada policije*).[12] As noted previously, the first armed operation conducted by the RS MUP was the seizure of the SRBiH MUP Police Academy at Vraca on 6 April 1992. This action was led by Momčilo Mandić, the new deputy minister of RS MUP, and Milenko Karišik.[13] The latter, a veteran of the SRBiH MUP special police unit, became the commander of the first special police force of the RS MUP.[14]

In 1992, Karišik's unit, simply referred to initially as the 'Police Detachment' (*Odred milicije*), acted more as a combat unit than as a police unit.[15] The Detachment equipped itself with heavy weapons and specialized equipment. On 21 May 1992, an overview of the RS MUP payroll for April 1992 listed two special units.[16] One was identified as the 'special unit – Pale', with twenty-eight members. The other one was identified as the 'special unit of SMUP [Federal SUP], with 43 members'. By May 1992, the payroll for Karišik's unit had grown to include 170 members.[17] Another special police unit, known as the 'Special Platoon in the Serbian Ministry of Internal Affairs', existed in April 1992 under the command of Duško Malović.[18] At the end of June, the RS MUP noted the presence of special police units at Sokolac and Pale.[19] By September 1992, the Special Brigade of the Police had five detachments, with one based at each of the five CSBs. In addition, some SJBs such as SJB Ilidža and SJB Novo Sarajevo had their own special police units.[20]

Besides deploying them in battle, the minister of internal affairs could call upon the special units of the police to carry out a variety of tasks. On 15 June 1992, Stanišić ordered the Sokolac detachment of the special police to mobilize military conscripts in Novo Sarajevo municipality, in accordance with the 20 May order of the Bosnian Serb Presidency.[21]

As has already been seen in the case of CSB Banja Luka, the CSBs in the RS also established their own special police units. Rather than participate in mere standard policing, these units were designed and equipped as light combat units, including armoured vehicles and heavy machineguns. Stojan Župljanin, the head of CSB Banja Luka, pioneered this effort. On 15 April Župljanin announced that special units were being formed which were highly trained and equipped for anti-terrorist action.[22] The standard term used by the police in referring to 'terrorist groups' was 'sabotage-terrorist groups' (*diverzantsko-terorističke grupacije*). On 21 April, Župljanin asked commanders of subordinate SJBs to nominate candidates for a new special police unit. Candidates should have specialized expertise in martial arts, marksmanship, mountaineering and/or be members of previous special units.[23] On 23 April, Župljanin sent a request to General Milutin Kukanjac, the Commander of the 2nd Military District for equipment for a 'unit for special purposes, which is being formed at the Security Services Centre in Banja Luka'. The requested equipment included military helicopters, armoured vehicles, weapons, ammunition and uniforms.[24] Kukanjac, in turn, forwarded the request to the Federal Secretariat for National Defence (SSNO) with a recommendation that it be granted.[25]

The inappropriate behaviour of the CSB Banja Luka special police unit already received mention in the preceding chapter, but its further misdeeds deserve mention here. In July 1992, two months after the unit was with great pomp introduced at the Banja Luka Security Day parade, the unit was involved in a public debacle. When two members of the unit were arrested by regular police officers for driving a stolen vehicle in Laktaši, the unit demanded the release of its members.[26] Predrag Kojić, a commander of the detachment, claimed that the arrested individuals were 'honourable' officers who had already fought for '15 months' in Croatia and Bosnia and Herzegovina. When Vladimir Tutuš, the chief of SJB Banja Luka, refused to release the two officers from prison, the members of the detachment threatened to storm the prison. At this point, Župljanin personally guaranteed that the officers would be released. When the release did not immediately occur, approximately thirty members of the detachment surrounded the prison and threatened to storm it. The prison authorities, faced with a possible attack, decided to release the two individuals. In the aftermath of the incident, Tutuš complained that the incident damaged the rule of law in the RS. He asserted that the 'state cannot be built on violence'.[27] Considerably later, in May 1993, SJB Banja Luka produced a report on crimes allegedly committed by many members of this unit during 1992. These crimes included theft and killings of civilians, including the 'massive plundering of deserted Muslim homes'.[28]

Despite such incidents and complaints from other authorities about the conduct of the RS special police units, there is no evidence of attempts to discipline those responsible. No use was made of the provisions for disciplining officers for misconduct found in the RS Law on Internal Affairs. Although Minister Mićo Stanišić stated in several orders that his subordinates would be held responsible for carrying out his orders, and also expressed an awareness that RS MUP employees had been involved in the commission of illegal acts such as theft and plunder, no disciplinary committees or courts were established.[29] Instead, on 23 July 1992, Stanišić issued a strictly confidential order in which he wrote:

> Take legal steps to remove from our ranks and put at the disposal of the VRS all employees of the MUP who have committed criminal acts (except political and verbal misdemeanours) earlier or since the commencement of combat activities or, respectively, the formation of the MUP of the Serbian Republic of Bosnia and Herzegovina. The chiefs of administrations at the seat, the Commander of the Police Detachment and the chiefs of the CSBs are responsible for implementing the order. Provide (by 31 July 1992) information on measures taken, stating the concrete number of employees who have been dismissed, the types of criminal acts that they have committed, etc.

On 24 July, a paraphrased version of the order was sent to the chiefs of all CSBs.[30] In ARK, Župljanin forwarded the order to his subordinate SJBs on 29 July, and in Prijedor SJB Chief Drljača circulated the order the following day.[31]

Impunity for criminal behaviour

The special unit of CSB Banja Luka earned notoriety in northwestern Bosnia in the spring and summer 1992 for its criminal behaviour towards the civilian population and its confrontation with the judicial organs of the RS. Unfortunately, its behaviour, while perhaps particularly egregious, was far from unusual in the RS MUP. On the contrary, the available documentation, which is voluminous and thanks to the ICTY also includes extensive testimony from victims, eyewitnesses as well as former members of the RS MUP, paints a portrait of a culture of impunity for police officers who committed criminal acts.

Much as one would expect from a police force, the RS MUP had a positive duty to protect human life and dignity, as noted in Article 12 of the RS Law on Internal Affairs. In carrying out their duties, police officers were supposed to apply only necessary force. Even allowing for the extraordinary challenges which any police force would endure in a war, the RS MUP performed very poorly in terms of these basic principles with respect to the non-Serb portion of the population. Evidence introduced at the ICTY pointed overwhelmingly to the unwillingness of the police to investigate crimes in which Muslims or Croats were the victims and Serbs were the alleged perpetrators.[32]

The RS MUP leadership including Minister Stanišić certainly knew that police officers under their command were committing illegal acts, including acts of violence. In normal circumstances, one would have expected the RS MUP to suspend, investigate and dismiss police officers who were found to have committed such acts and for prosecutors to have pursued relevant criminal charges against them. Certainly, one would also have expected such officers to have been banned from working in the police or in any other job where they could apply armed and legal force. Yet, on the contrary, the RS MUP on those occasions when it did discipline and remove police officers from duty placed these men at the disposal of the VRS.[33] On 12 September 1992, CSB Sarajevo wrote to all subordinate SJBs reminding them that all RS MUP employees who had committed criminal acts were to be put at the disposal of the VRS.[34] On 16 December, Minister Stanišić informed all CSBs that the Ministry's Steering Council on 12 December had decided that all suspended employees of the ministry would be put at the disposal of the VRS at the time of suspension, 'not awaiting the termination of the disciplinary procedure'.[35]

Operation corridor and the resubordination of RS MUP units to the VRS

For most of the war, the corridor in Posavina represented the most vulnerable spot for the Bosnian Serbs. This thin slice of land in northern Bosnia connected the northwestern Krajina region and the major city of Banja Luka with northeastern Bosnia and eastern Herzegovina. Zooming out, the corridor functioned as a lifeline not only for the two major portions of Bosnia and Herzegovina under Serbian control, but also between Serbia and the RS, on one hand, and the RSK on the other hand.

From the very outset of the war, the RS leadership proudly regarded the police as an integral part of the RS armed forces. Indeed, already on 26 January 1992, Biljana Plavšić had stated in the Assembly of the Serb People that 'these are the times, until the referendum, when the Serb people must make a state out of its own areas. It is known what the making of a state means. First, the Ministry of Internal Affairs will do whatever necessary to have its own army'.[36] Like Karadžić and many others in the SDS, Plavšić viewed sceptically the officer corps of the JNA, imbued as it was with communist ideology and the mantra of 'brotherhood and unity'. For this reason, the RS leadership initially regarded the RS MUP as the only 'army' on which it could rely completely. With the establishment of the VRS, this of course changed, but the extent of the police's involvement in cooperation did not.

During Operation Corridor, which commenced on 24 June 1992 and concluded three weeks later, both CSB Banja Luka and CSB Doboj found themselves devoting enormous resources to combat operations.[37] Andrija Bjelošević, the chief of CSB Doboj, for example, had four police companies participating in Operation Corridor under the command of the VRS's Tactical Group 3.[38] The RSK MUP also offered assistance.[39] At the end of Operation Corridor, General Ratko Mladić proclaimed that the 'the centuries long aspiration of the Serb people from BiH and Serbian Republic of Krajina to be joined with the fatherland Serbia' had been realized.[40]

Only three days after the 16th Assembly Session, on 15 May 1992, Mićo Stanišić issued an order confirming the continued militarization of the RS MUP and clarifying issues of command and control. Stanišić ordered that all employees of the RS MUP be organized formally into 'war units' (*ratne jedinice*).[41] The order formalized the cooperation of the RS MUP with the military by explaining how RS MUP units would cooperate with the VRS.[42] Owing to the at times difficult communications situation, Stanišić authorized the heads of the CSBs to implement this organization.[43] An exception was made for Sarajevo, where the Police Commander would be in charge of implementation. These units could receive orders from the Minister of Internal Affairs, the Police Commander of the Ministry (for CSB Sarajevo) and the heads of the CSBs. The Police Commander and the heads of the CSBs had to report to the Staff of the ministry (*Štab ministarstva*) when they used their combat units. The Staff commanded the collective forces of the ministry and was composed of:

- Minister of Internal Affairs Mićo Stanišić – Commander;
- Undersecretary for Public Security Čedomir Klajić, Deputy Commander;
- Undersecretary for National Security – Slobodan Škipina;
- Assistant Ministers for
  - Criminal Affairs, Dobro Planojević;
  - Police, Vlastimir Kusmuk;
  - Communications and Data Protection, Dragan Kezunović;
  - Material-Financial Matters, Bogdan Košarac;
- Commander of Police Detachment Milenko Karišik;
- Deputy Commander of Police Detachment;
- Heads of the CSBs; and
- Chief of the Minister's Office (secretary).[44]

In the course of combat, the units were subordinate to the 'command of the armed forces', although with the caveat that 'the units of the Ministry are directly commanded by the respective employees of the Ministry'.[45] Strict obedience of the Law on Internal Affairs and other legal and military regulations was emphasized. 'Each violation of regulations and failure to implement ordered tasks will be most strictly punished, and the relevant disciplinary and criminal sanctions will be taken.' Already two days later, on 17 May, Stanišić requested that all CSBs provide reports on their implementation of the 15 May order.⁴⁶ Documentation throughout 1992 shows coordination between the military and the police.⁴⁷

It must immediately be stated that the testimony of RS MUP insiders at the ICTY leads to the conclusion that this command staff existed largely on paper in 1992.⁴⁸ And, indeed, few if any subsequent RS MUP documents make reference to this body, although a 'staff of police forces' (*štab policijskih snaga*) appeared frequently in documents in 1995. That having been said, there is no doubt that the police were heavily involved in combat until at least the end of 1992.⁴⁹ The RS MUP and the VRS met frequently at various levels to discuss joint operations, including in the municipal and regional crisis staffs.⁵⁰ According to ICTY military analyst Ewan Brown, 'for the most part, the operations involving the police and the military were carried out in co-operation with each other, there were occasions when police units were directly integrated or subordinated to the VRS'.⁵¹

Joint operations between the police and the military required considerable tactical coordination, and there were frequent bureaucratic disagreements and resentment from the side of the police at being improperly deployed and tasked. On 28 May 1992, CSB Banja Luka informed its subordinate offices that the chiefs of the SJBs were not allowed to order 'any armed police activities without the prior approval of this CSB and the respective corps commander of the Serbian armed forces'.⁵² This referred especially to the dispatching of police to the territory of SJBs other than their own. Župljanin's 28 May dispatch represented an attempt to prevent the unauthorized and unorganized use of police units in combat activities.

Several months later, in September 1992, Župljanin wrote that there had been ever-increasing demands from various VRS commands for combat engagement of both the active and reserve staff of the police, including combat outside of the AOR of CSB Banja Luka. Župljanin therefore reminded his subordinates and the military commanders in the region that there existed agreements between the police and the army at the ministerial level regarding this matter. Župljanin demanded 'from the chiefs of the SJBs and all employees of the Centre, that they devote maximum effort and within their competencies organize the word of the security services so that they will as effectively as possible' protect their areas.⁵³ At the same time, Župljanin warned the

> chiefs of the SJB that members of the active and reserve staff of the police can be engaged in combat activities on the principle of resubordination to a competent military command only in the event that combat activities spread to the territory which is covered by the respective SJBs and with the approval of the chief of the CSB. Towards the goal of achieving full cooperation and synchronization of the work of the military and the police of Republika Srpska, I ask the corps commanders to through their chains of command direct the attention of their subordinate commands and to acquaint them with the agreements which have been confirmed at the joint meetings at the highest level.

A good example of the police's involvement in combat is furnished by a report of SJB Prijedor from August 1992.

After the eruption of armed conflict, the employees of the SJB at the demand of the army and pursuant to the situation in which they found themselves participated directly in the armed conflict, such that up until now 11 employees of the active and reserve staff lost their lives, and 38 in all were wounded. Together with members of military units the police participated in operations to mop up the remaining concealed enemy groups and individuals from the territory, and through operational work arrived at useful information about the conduct of the enemy on the territory of the municipality.[54]

In 1993, SJB Prijedor reported that combat operations in the municipality had commenced on 22 May 1992: 'Employees of this Station participated in those activities, primarily members of the active and reserve staff of the police. Combat activities were most intensively conducted on the territory of Kozarac, Kozaruša, Trnopolje, Kamičani, Rizvanovići, Bišćani, Hambarine, Zecovi, Čarakovo, Kurevo, Raljaš, Ćela and the town of Prijedor itself.'[55] Regular combat reports from the VRS's 1st Krajina Corps show extensive police and military cooperation.[56]

The extensive police involvement in combat necessarily led to a severe decline in the amount of resources that could be devoted to ordinary policing, notwithstanding the considerable increase in the ranks of the police because of the massive recruitment of reserves. And the problematic and in part criminal origins of the reserve forces exacerbated this problem. In his comments at a meeting of the RS MUP held in Belgrade on 11 July 1992, Minister Stanišić noted that the RS MUP was at times entirely engaged in combat, rather than police, activities and that at least eighty police officers had already lost their lives in combat by this point in time.[57]

When people think of the police in most countries, they usually picture police officers who wear clearly identifiable uniforms and who are in most cases armed with a handgun and perhaps some non-lethal equipment such as a nightstick, a flashlight and handcuffs. In contemplating the RS MUP in 1992, this notion of policing must be drastically revised. Not only did the police often for various reasons wear a variety of uniforms and insignia, but they were equipped with fully automatic weapons and in many cases used armoured vehicles and even heavy military weaponry such as artillery. For example, at the end of June, CSB Banja Luka requested 200 automatic rifles from the VRS's 1st Krajina Corps, and in November CSB Banja Luka borrowed two 30/2 artillery pieces and ammunition from the same corps.[58]

Disarming of the non-Serb population and the establishment of detention facilities

In the course of both combat and irregular operations during the war in 1992, and in particular between April and the end of August 1992, tens of thousands of Bosnian Muslim and Croat civilians found themselves swept up by a massive dragnet. The topic of detention facilities in the war in Bosnia and Herzegovina occupies a place of particular notoriety. Even decades later, many people around the world recall the harrowing images of emaciated detainees which emerged in the summer of 1992. Toponyms like Omarska and Trnopolje became synonymous not only with contemporary atrocities but also with the failure of the 'international community' to intervene.[59] Yet outside the walls of the ICTY, relatively little has been written about the role of the police in running such facilities.[60] This section will therefore delve into this topic, showing not only that the police's role was essential, but also that it proved controversial, not only internationally, but also within the RS MUP itself and in the police's relationship with the VRS.

A significant amount of contingency was involved in the Bosnian Serbs' establishment of detention facilities after the outbreak of the war, as can be seen by the uneven size and distribution of such facilities. The most concentrated, long-lasting and 'sophisticated' set of facilities existed in the Bosnian Krajina area, particularly in Prijedor municipality. By contrast, many other regions and municipalities had much smaller, improvised detention facilities which often existed relatively briefly. That having been said, there was nothing coincidental or accidental about the establishment of these facilities, as they formed an integral part of the strategy which the Bosnian Serb leadership knowingly adopted and implemented through civilian, police and military organs in order to establish an ethnically homogeneous political entity.

The fulcrum of this strategy was the campaign to disarm the civilian population. Like the loyalty oaths seen in the previous chapter, this campaign took an ostensibly legal and reasonable premise – quelling the conflict by removing weapons and ammunition from the hands of the civilian population – and optimized it for aggressively nationalist purposes. That which seemed proper and appropriate when viewed from a Serb nationalist perspective or, later, from an abstract perspective devoid of context, was clearly a strategy aimed at removing as many Bosnian Muslims and Croats as possible from the territory of Republika Srpska.

As has been seen in the previous chapter, some disarming took place prior to the outbreak of the war, for example at Pale, where the police had already confiscated weapons from Bosnian Muslims in March 1992. These confiscations took place even when the police knew that the owners had permits for the weapons in their possession.[61] Yet the brunt of the disarming campaign started with the onset of the war.

After the Bosnian Serbs assumed power in the Bosnian Krajina region in April 1992, the new authorities rapidly introduced large amounts of decrees and legislation restricting the rights of those persons who were not of Serbian ethnicity. A two-pronged approach took shape, in which male Serbs of military age were mobilized into military and police units, while non-Serbs faced disarmament and persecution. Moreover, events would show that the persecution of non-Serbs was not restricted to those who were males of military age.[62] This policy was formulated by the central Bosnian Serb leadership for implementation by the police and the military. On 16 April, the RS Minister of National Defence, Bogdan Subotić, declared that a state of imminent danger of war existed and ordered a full mobilization. Subotić's order allowed the authorities to take 'all necessary measures appropriate to the situation'.[63] As regional and municipal authorities controlled by the Bosnian Serbs began to function, the nature of these measures became clearer.[64] On 4 May, the ARK National Defence Council, referring back to Subotić's order, decreed a general mobilization, introduced a curfew, and set 11 May as the deadline for 'all paramilitary formations and individuals' to surrender illegal weapons.[65] Some municipal crisis staffs had undertaken similar initiatives already in late April.[66] Župljanin disseminated the 4 May order to all SJBs subject to CSB Banja Luka and held the SJB chiefs personally responsible for the implementation of ARK's decision.[67] On 5 May, Župljanin was named as a member of the newly formed ARK War Staff.[68] The following day the Council of CSB Banja Luka concluded that 'in all our activities, we are obliged to observe all measures and apply all procedures ordered by the crisis staff of the Autonomous Region'.[69]

In mid-May 1992, Župljanin and the personnel of CSB Banja Luka together with the 5th Corps of the JNA assisted in implementing the confiscation of 'illegal' weapons ordered by the ARK War Staff, which had also issued a follow-up order on 14 May requiring action by CSB Banja Luka.[70] CSB Banja Luka distributed specific instructions on this on 14 May 1992.[71] According to a military report, there was a pronounced fear of 'possible interethnic conflicts' because of the expiration of the ultimatum.[72] On 18 May, the ARK Crisis Staff declared that 'the Crisis Staffs are now the highest organ of authority in the Municipality', thereby effectively declaring that the municipal crisis staffs (containing RS MUP representatives) were in a superior position with regards to the SJBs.[73] On the same day, the ARK Crisis Staff ordered CSB Banja Luka to formulate instructions for the disarming of paramilitary formations.[74] A similar situation obtained in SAO Semberija and Majevica.[75] These operations continued throughout the summer and autumn of 1992.[76] In several municipalities, the municipal crisis staffs charged the relevant SJBs with the implementation of decisions on the disarming of the non-Serbian population.[77] The police forces' own hierarchy made it clear that both the local and the regional crisis staffs could issue orders to the police.[78] Actions to implement decisions regarding disarmament frequently evolved into larger actions including the expulsion of non-Serbian civilians from Serbian-controlled municipalities. The police cited attacks on Serbs and on the JNA, TO and the VRS as factors necessitating the disarmament of non-Serbs.[79] Yet these were largely small and isolated incidents that stood in stark contrast to the military and police operations undertaken against non-Serbs in the course of the disarmament drive.

Ključ and its surrounding municipality, located approximately 65 km from Banja Luka, provide an illustration of how this process worked. Unlike other municipalities which quickly came under the jurisdiction of CSB Banja Luka and RS MUP, Ključ remained contested for some time. But by 28 May 1992, the municipal crisis staff issued an ultimatum regarding the surrender of illegal weaponry, ostensibly as a response to attacks the previous day on Serb authorities. The police, which was constituted exclusively of Serbs by the end of May, drove around the municipality in order to announce it.[80] However, in practice, according to an ICTY trial chamber, the order 'was only enforced against non-Serbs, who were required to turn in all weapons, including the ones that they legally owned'.[81] Importantly, the police were therefore doubly discriminating against non-Serbs; first, by not enforcing the order against Serbs who possessed illegal weapons, and second by treating as illegal lawfully registered weapons owned by non-Serbs. In some cases, the police justified their confiscation of illegal weapons by claiming that Muslims or Croats serving in the police had, before their dismissal, knowingly issued weapons permits to 'extremists'.[82] This accusation was undoubtedly true to some extent but certainly would also have been valid for many Serbs. Moreover, the deadline for complying with this ultimatum was nearly immediate, and even before it expired, the VRS commenced the shelling of Muslim-majority villages in the municipality.

After the shelling, the VRS together with members of the paramilitary formation known as the White Eagles searched the village of Biljani for weapons but found none. While doing so, and in the context of 'mopping up' operations in the municipality, members of the police, the military and the paramilitary began to round up and detain or arrest large numbers of non-Serb males. They were placed in six detention facilities, of which five were improvised and one was the building of SJB Ključ.[83] Those detainees who were deemed to have participated in armed resistance against Republika Srpska, who possessed weapons or held 'extremist views' were sent to the military detention facility Manjača, located between Ključ and Banja Luka.

While plenty of initiative was shown by local and regional authorities, there can be no doubt that the disarming campaign enjoyed the support of the highest RS authorities. Thus, on 10 July 1992, Krajišnik as part of a meeting of the RS Presidency demanded that Muslims be disarmed as soon as possible.[84]

In terms of the establishment and operation of detention facilities, Prijedor municipality, located approximately 55 km northwest of Banja Luka, provided the most notorious example.[85] Prior to the war, approximately equal numbers of Bosnian Muslims and Serbs resided in the municipality, alongside much smaller groups of Croats, self-declared Yugoslavs and others.[86] As in many places in Bosnia, the villages in the municipality were often identifiably monoethnic while the town of Prijedor was more mixed.

At the latest at the beginning of the war in Bosnia, the Bosnian Serbs in the police in Prijedor began to organize covertly. Police stations where Serbs were in the majority began to ensure that everything would be ready for an eventual takeover of the municipality.[87] Yet in a report on the work of SJB Prijedor prepared in June 1992, the events of the preceding months were portrayed quite differently. According to the report, it was 'extremists' from the HDZ and the SDA who were to blame for the 'bloody conflicts' that had erupted and the 'unprecedented terror against the Serb population'.[88] Hence, the Serbs were merely reacting defensively to events. The 'extremists' were responsible for seizing control of the municipality on 29 April and of dissuading their Muslim and Croat brethren from signing loyalty oaths to the RS MUP. Yet the Serbs resisted and together the military and the police thwarted their opponents and instead 'enabled the total establishment of Serb authorities on every part of the municipality's territory'.[89] However, according to an ICTY trial chamber,

> the pretext for the takeover of the municipality was the transmission on 29 April 1992 by the Belgrade television station of a facsimile to the effect that the leader of the BiH TO had instructed the local TOs to attack and obstruct the JNA during its withdrawal from BiH, although the authorities in Sarajevo immediately declared that the facsimile was false and publicly denounced it.[90]

The Serbian takeover of power in Prijedor took place on 30 April 1992.[91] Muslim commanders in the police were replaced by Serbs, and Muslims were told to sign loyalty oaths to the RS MUP.[92] A subsequent report compiled by SJB Prijedor left no doubt that the new authorities viewed the presence of large clusters of Muslims and Croats on the territory of the municipality as a problem that needed to be solved.[93]

Throughout May, the situation for non-Serbs deteriorated in Prijedor municipality. The new authorities imposed curfews and restrictions on movement, and non-Serbs were subjected to attacks on person and property.[94] On 9 May, the Prijedor municipal board met, and SJB Chief Simo Drljača informed them that there were ongoing negotiations with police stations located at Ljubija and Kozarac. According to Drljača, the deadline for those police stations to come under the control of SJB Prijedor had been extended until 14 May, whereafter it would be necessary to mobilize not only the reserve police but also the TO.[95] On 15 May, the Council for People's Defence of the Prijedor municipal assembly decided that SJB Prijedor would together with the military command put together and implement a plan for disarming unauthorized individuals and 'paramilitary formations' in the municipality.[96]

At the end of the month, the authorities in Prijedor municipality ordered all non-Serbs to identify themselves by wearing white ribbons on their clothing and by placing white flags on the windows of their homes.[97] Official reports spoke cosmetically of careful negotiations between Prijedor's new authorities and representatives of the local Muslims and Croats leading to a 'peaceful and civilized disarming of citizens and the acceptance of the establishment of the authorities accompanied by guarantees of all civil, national and religious rights and freedoms for all loyal citizens of the Serbian Republic'.[98] However, countless witnesses at the ICTY later testified about the violent and unilateral progression of events.[99]

According to the official narrative of the Prijedor crisis staff and SJB Prijedor, Muslim extremists in the hamlet of Hambarine already at the beginning of May had sabotaged the peaceful situation by attacking a military convoy.[100] The Serb authorities were therefore forced to intervene militarily to subdue the extremists, who attacked both Serb forces and 'blindly settled accounts with those members of their nation who refused to enter into battle against the Serb forces'.[101] Similar events allegedly occurred elsewhere in the municipality.

On 31 May 1992, the Chief of SJB Prijedor, Simo Drljača, acting in accordance with a decision of the crisis staff, ordered the establishment of a 'temporary collection centre' at the Omarska mines complex east of Prijedor.[102] The centre, which became the most notorious of its kind in the municipality, was designated to receive those persons who 'are taken prisoner in combat or are detained on the basis of operational intelligence of the security service'. Mixed teams consisting of representatives of the SNB, police and military security service were to interrogate the detainees. Those who had been interrogated and for whom incriminating information was obtained were to be transferred for further processing to the investigative prisons in Banja Luka or Stara Gradiška. SJB Prijedor would provide the necessary number of policemen for guard duty around the centre.[103]

Drljača's order made mention of the necessity of providing food and potable water as well as ensuring the function of electricity, hygienic facilities, etc. However, he also ordered that the centre be surrounded by barbed wire and a minefield.[104] As Chief of the SJB, Drljača, received daily reports on the 'work' being undertaken in the centre. Strict measures were implemented to ensure that unauthorized individuals did not have access to the facility and that whatever transpired there would remain confidential. Showing that the chain of command was properly functioning, Drljača sent a copy of his order to CSB Banja Luka. The order concluded that 'the implementation of this Order shall be supervised by the Chief of Police Dušan Janković in collaboration with the Banja Luka Security Services Centre and with the support of the authorised leading personnel'.

This facility subsequently became known as 'Investigative Centre for Prisoners of War Omarska', with the police primarily responsible for the facility and the VRS providing additional security.[105] SJB Prijedor operated the detention facility at Omarska from the end of May 1992 until it was closed in August. The Prijedor Crisis Staff specified that the chief of the SJB had the 'exclusive right to sign orders to release any imprisoned person'.[106] Making it very clear why the detention facility had been erected, the same order from the crisis staff decreed at the outset that 'all Serbs who had by mistake ended up among the prisoners' were to be freed immediately.

By the end of June 1992, approximately 3,000 persons had 'gone through' Omarska, according to the estimates of SJB Prijedor.[107] This included the interrogation of every person. Again, illustrating the link between the centre and the general ongoing campaign of persecution, on 2 July the Prijedor Municipal Crisis Staff ordered SJB Prijedor to implement the formal dismissal of detained persons from their places of employment.[108]

The police, acting in concert with the crisis staff, also established other detention facilities besides Omarska in Prijedor municipality. In June 1992 a report on the activities of the SJB referred to the internment of 'a large number of Muslim and Croat extremists' in Omarska, Keraterm and Trnopolje. The report stated that security at the Omarska and Keraterm reception centres was provided 'around-the-clock by police officers, who every day arrest more people of interest to security and about whose hostile activities information was obtained from investigating people arrested earlier'.[109]

On 24 July 1992, the War Presidency of the Municipal Assembly of Prijedor ordered a reduction in the number of reserve police and requested that the military take over the security operations for Keraterm, Trnopolje and Omarska by the end of the month.¹¹⁰ However, the Chief of SJB Prijedor, Simo Drljača, reported that the military refused to accept this obligation. As a result, the approximately 300 police officers involved in the guarding of these camps continued to work in this role until it was dismantled in mid-August.

Keraterm was the name of a ceramics factory in Prijedor. Approximately a week before the mine at Omarska was requisitioned as a detention facility, the authorities requisitioned Keraterm for similar purposes. According to SJB Prijedor, Keraterm was established by a decision of the Prijedor Municipal Crisis Staff. It was guarded by both the police and the military, and prisoners were interrogated by mixed teams just as in Omarska.¹¹¹ Several dozen police officers from the Prijedor Reserve Police Station received permits to enter Keraterm.¹¹² Very quickly approximately 600 individuals were brought to Keraterm, a number that continued to grow until transfers to Omarska took place on 27 May 1992.¹¹³

Simultaneously, at the village of Trnopolje several buildings were set aside. Whereas Keraterm and Omarska rapidly became detention facilities even in the eyes of the authorities who have originally used the term 'collection centre', these authorities continued in later reports to insist on that term for Trnopolje. Rather, Trnopolje was deemed an 'open collection centre', to which frightened citizens of all ethnicities had flocked for their own safety. There was 'no kind of fence in the shape of barbed wire. And in [the facility] no kind of investigations are carried out, the Centre is protected by the army externally from extremist endangerment, the number of citizens varies because those who want to can leave the Centre whenever they desire'.¹¹⁴

All in all, several thousand people passed through Omarska, Keraterm and Trnopolje, and about 6,000 'informational interviews' were conducted with them by the aforementioned mixed teams.¹¹⁵ More than 5,500 persons were fully processed. Of these, 1,502 were subsequently transferred to the prisoner-of-war camp in Manjača, which had been established and was being run by the 1st Krajina Corps of the VRS.¹¹⁶

There is no need to recount in detail the massive number of atrocities which members of the RS MUP committed in detention facilities against those civilians who were unfortunate enough to be detained. Successive trial chambers at the ICTY from *Tadić* until *Karadžić* documented the extent and nature of these atrocities in gruelling detail. In addition to the massive violations of international humanitarian law, it should also be noted that the prolonged detention of these persons constituted illegal detention under Republika Srpska's own laws, which allowed a maximum of seventy-two hours of detention without trial.¹¹⁷

In the period until 21 August 1992, several hundred police employees were involved in guard duty in the aforementioned detention centres. Except for Trnopolje, the other reception centres were dismantled on 21 August and there were no further security requirements for them.¹¹⁸ The Trnopolje reception centre remained in place until November. In addition to women and children, there was a large concentration of Muslim men fit for military service there, including persons who had spent time in Omarska and Keraterm because of their direct or indirect involvement in 'armed rebellion'. Policemen took part in escort and security details provided for prisoner convoys.[119]

The 1992 annual report produced by SNB Prijedor noted that the SNB ROs in Prijedor, Sanski Most, Novi Grad (formerly known as Bosanski Novi) and Kozarska Dubica (formerly Bosanska Dubica) had conducted a total of 8,660 'informational interviews' with a total of 5,740 persons.[120] Beginning on 25 May 1992, SNB employees had participated together with employees from SJB Prijedor and SJB Sanski – most in 'work' in the 'investigative centres such as Omarska, Keraterm and Krings', the latter of which was located in Sanski Most municipality. This situation lasted until August. 'In the course of September and October, intensive work was done to organise the documentation which was composed in the course of the investigative procedure in the cited investigative centres.' However, a total of only four criminal complaints had been filed by these ROs during the year. The same report showed that Muslim employees had 'been removed from employment' by the SNB when the war commenced.

As has been seen above, many persons detained at Keraterm, Omarska and Trnopolje were subsequently transferred to the Manjača detention facility roughly 35 km south of Banja Luka. According to the findings of the ICTY, the JNA had established this facility already in September 1991 for prisoners of war from Croatia.[121] After the war in Bosnia commenced, and after the establishment of the VRS, the military police of the 1st Krajina Corps reopened the camp, with Colonel Božidar Popović acting as the camp's commander.[122] Hence, the military had primary control over Manjača. However, the involvement of the RS MUP extended beyond the regular transfers of prisoners to Manjača. Inspectors of the RS MUP participated in the interrogation of 'prisoners of war' detained in Manjača.[123] Police officers also helped the military police to guard prisoners.[124]

On 6 June, the acting Chief of SJB Sanski Most, Mirko Vrućinić, sent a letter to the commander of Manjača.[125] Basing his letter on a previously reached agreement with the Commander of the Banja Luka Corps, Colonel Stevilović, Vrućinić stated that a group of prisoners were being sent to Manjača. The SJB was to supply accompanying documentation about the prisoners. Further prisoners would follow once their interrogation had been completed at SJB Sanski Most. Vrućinić's dispatching of prisoners to Manjača was in direct accordance with an order of the Sanski Most Crisis Staff of 6 June.[126] Similarly, on 24 June, Vinko Kondić, the chief of SJB Ključ, wrote to the Commandant of Manjača to inform him that two police inspectors would be arriving to carry out interrogations of prisoners detained in the Manjača camp.[127]

Both the quantity and quality of prisoners which the RS MUP transferred to Manjača proved contentious in the summer of 1992. On 8 July 1992, an operational team at Manjača complained that 'the great majority' of prisoners brought to Manjača possessed no weapons, 'nor did they participate actively in the organization and execution of armed rebellion'.[128] On 7 July 1992 alone, 560 detainees had arrived from Sanski Most. Twenty-four of them had died en route to Manjača, and the probable cause of death was a lack of oxygen, because they were transported in refrigerator trucks. This approach of the organs from Sanski Most is extremely inhumane [*neljudski i nehuman*] and unprofessional. The dead were not accepted [into the camp], and they are therefore not regarded as prisoners of war of LRZ Manjača. Earlier observed lapses are recurring in that prisoners of war younger than 18 years of age and older than 60 years of age are still being brought.[129]

One month later, Colonel Stevan Bogojević, the chief of Security for the 1st Krajina Corps, notified the SNB in Prijedor that many prisoners had neither participated in armed uprisings nor did they bear uniform or weapons. Hence, the rationale for detaining them and treating them as prisoners of war was unclear. Bogojević advocated the release of such persons, which would also have the salutary effect on space and resources in Manjača. Significantly, Bogojević's dissatisfaction stemmed at least in part from his concern that Republika Srpska would suffer internationally because of international media attention on 'concentration camps'.[130] In some cases, SJBs in the region dispatched personnel to Manjača to interrogate detainees in the hope of providing justification for their continued detention.[131]

On 7 August, only a day after Bogojević's letter to SNB Prijedor, Captain 1st Class Dane Lukajić of the Manjača detention facility reported to the Department for Intelligence and Security Affairs in the 1st Krajina Corps Command that Manjača had received

> prisoners of war from Omarska camp. Their reception was accomplished in an organised manner but with many difficulties given that no documentation whatsoever was provided with the prisoners of war, not even up-to-date lists. The lists were not up to date in the sense that it is unknown whether a person came from Omarska camp. During the transportation of prisoners from Omarska to Manjača 8 prisoners died, of which some (3) were probably killed because they had visible traces of force. We did not receive the deceased prisoners but rather insisted that they take them back to Omarska and bury them there in the proscribed manner. However, it is very possible that the dead were unloaded and thrown somewhere in the forest between Manjača and Banja Luka.[132]

The personnel at Manjača characterized the behaviour of those in charge of the prisoner transport from Omarska as 'very incorrect, inhumane and violent'. When one VRS member tried to prevent those carrying out the transport from killing a 'half-dead prisoner', the soldier was told that 'if you behave like that, you will end up like him'. Captain Lukajić concluded that international criticism of the situation was not without justification, 'because we ourselves provide them with arguments'. He asked that all necessary measures be undertaken to prevent a repetition of this incident.

Although Captain 1st Class Dane Lukajić was filing a daily report, he wrote that the behaviour that he had reported was part of a pattern of a 'non-deliberate approach of the organs in Prijedor and of the superficial work of the organs of the police and the SUP [i.e., the SJB]'.[133] Whereas the police inspectors from Prijedor insisted that all of the transferred detainees were 'serious extremists', their military counterparts asserted that this was baseless. 'In the course of the reception, we encountered people who were not even capable of holding a rifle in their hands, not to speak of running and shooting. We encountered minors (born in 1977) who neither had weapons nor had participated in combat, nor even [brought] water to enemies.'

Lukajić observed that there was no room for additional detainees in Manjača.[134] However, three days later, Lukajić wrote that Manjača had been notified in the preceding days of the need to bring 1,000 prisoners from Omarska.[135] The staff at Manjača took the necessary preparatory measures before the convoy arrived belatedly. Those escorting the prisoners from Manjača became angry when the staff at Manjača refused to accept the prisoners without any procedures. Lukajić personally intervened when he observed personnel in the convoy beating prisoners to death.

Approximately ten days later, in apparent recognition of the lacking documentation accompanying transfers to Manjača, Župljanin instructed all subordinate SJBs to ensure that files existed on all prisoners. Together with this information, police at Manjača would assist in making selections for further processing.[136]

By mid-July 1992 at the latest, all leading officials of the RS MUP were fully aware of the ministry's involvement in the operation of detention camps. Moreover, they had knowledge that appalling conditions existed in some camps. On 11 July, at a meeting of the leading RS MUP officials held in Belgrade, Stojan Župljanin noted that crisis staffs and the VRS in the ARK area had demanded the 'collection' of large numbers of Muslims and established 'undefined camps' which had been placed under MUP control.[137] He claimed that conditions in these camps were very bad; 'there is no food, sometimes individuals do not respect international norms, because, amongst other things, such collection centres are inadequate or other reasons exist'.[138]

Župljanin further asserted that the problem of the detention camps was but one example of the constant meddling by civilian authorities in the work of the MUP.[139] At the same time, the RS MUP on the territory of ARK was dependent on funds from the ARK authorities. Communications were difficult at times. The courts were not functioning well, and crime was widespread.

As with the involvement of the RS MUP in combat operations, the role of the police at these 'investigative or collection centres', as they were known, consumed many man-hours and detracted from the police's performance of other tasks. As seen earlier, the sheer number of people who were swept up and detained in various camps in the summer of 1992 proved overwhelming for the RS MUP. By the middle of the summer, the authorities began to devise a kind of police triage system. As with the involvement of the RS MUP in combat operations, the role of the police at these facilities consumed many man-hours and detracted from the police's performance of other tasks.

On 20 July, Župljanin wrote about this in a letter to Minister Mićo Stanišić.[140] Župljanin noted that the processing of the detainees had resulted in the emergence of three categories. The first comprised persons suspected of commission of criminal acts. The second comprised persons suspected of aiding and abetting those from the first category. The third category comprised 'adult males concerning whom the Service has not to date, gathered any security-relevant data on the basis of which these persons may be treated as hostages'. Župljanin asked the minister to consult 'with the highest authorities of the Serbian Republic' in order to develop a 'unitary stance' with regards to several important issues. Župljanin recommended that charges be pressed against detained suspects and that they be transferred to the relevant judicial organs. He asked that a decisive stance be taken regarding elderly, invalid and minor prisoners. Significantly, regarding detainees not suspected of criminal acts, Župljanin proposed the exchange of military-age males in the aforementioned third category for Serbs being held under similar circumstances by the Muslim-Croat forces. Finally, Župljanin recommended that VRS personnel should take over the operation of detention facilities until this entire issue was finally resolved. However, the military and the police would continue to cooperate in interrogating detainees.

On 22 July 1992, two days after Župljanin sent his letter to Mićo Stanišić, the issue of prisoner exchange was discussed at a government session.[141] On 23 July, Radovan Karadžić issued an order on the treatment of non-Serbs, stressing adherence to the Geneva Conventions.[142]

By August, owing to increasing international complaints, the RS authorities found it necessary to deal with the issue of the aforementioned detention centres. In late July 1992, the ICRC and foreign journalists became aware of the existence of the camps and requested the RS authorities to allow inspection of the camps.[143] Prior to allowing the ICRC and foreign journalists to inspect the camp in Omarska the police arranged for prisoners to be moved from Omarska to Manjača.[144]

On both 5 and 6 August 1992, the RS Presidency discussed the treatment of prisoners-of-war.[145] The minutes of the latter session of the presidency used language similar to that employed by Župljanin in his 20 July letter to Stanišić.[146] On 6 August, the presidency ordered the RS MUP and the RS Ministry of Justice to examine the issue and report to the presidency within ten days.[147] Two days later, Tomislav Kovač, in his new capacity as the assistant minister for the Affairs and Tasks of Police, sent a letter to the RS president and the RS president of the government regarding this matter.[148] Kovač argued that not enough had been done in the way of sorting detainees into separate categories. Unlike Župljanin, Kovač felt that persons in the aforementioned third category could 'only have the status of refugees'. Kovač did not treat them as 'hostages' or as potential subjects of an exchange with the Muslim or Croat forces.

On 8 August 1992, the RS Presidency decided that all elderly and seriously wounded prisoners should be released from detention.[149] The following day, the RS government established two commissions, consisting of representatives of the RS Ministry of Justice and the RS MUP, to look into conditions in detention centres.[150] The commission was headed by Vojin Lale, assistant minister of Justice and Administration, and Mirko Erkić, police inspector in the RS MUP.

On 17 August, the Commission filed a report on the situation regarding detainees in ARK.[151] The Commission had visited Trnopolje, Omarska, Keraterm, Manjača, Krings (Sanski Most) and the Middle School Centre in Bosanski Šamac. The report's positive description of the conditions in the camps contrasted starkly with earlier reports and internal comments made by RS MUP officials. In addition to the Commission's report, on 22 August, the RS government received a report from the RS Ministry of Justice regarding detainees on the territory of SAO Herzegovina. That report was co-authored by Goran Sarić of the RS MUP and Slobodan Avlijaš of the RS Ministry of Justice.[152]

Throughout August 1992 CSB Banja Luka and the Ministry of Internal Affairs requested and received a number of reports in relation to the operation of the camps. On 5 August 1992, Chief of SJB Prijedor, Simo Drljača, reported to the chief of CSB Banja Luka and the minister of internal affairs that the VRS and SJB Prijedor had concluded the processing of prisoners of war.[153] As many as 1,466 persons had been found to bear criminal responsibility and would be transferred under armed escort to Manjača. The remainder would be transferred to Trnopolje. On 8 August, CSB Banja Luka sought details from SJB Prijedor with respect to prisoners remaining in Omarska. On 9 August, Drljača responded that 175 prisoners of war remained at Omarska.[154] Drljača claimed that the police were fulfilling all of their legal obligations with regards to the remaining prisoners. He also noted that the same obligations were being observed at the Trnopolje centre, which was guarded by the VRS. On 17 August, Drljača sent a list of 402 prisoners to the commandant of Manjača.[155] These prisoners were in the process of being transferred to Manjača. On 19 August, Župljanin ordered the establishment of dossiers for each prisoner sent to Manjača by SJBs in his jurisdiction.[156] This was done on the request of the 'highest organs' of the RS. On 22 August, Drljača responded that a selection of prisoners had been made at Manjača and that they had been moved to Trnopolje.[157] On the same day, the authorities in Prijedor announced that they had closed Omarska and put Trnopolje under Red Cross authority.[158] On 23 August, Drljača confirmed that he had sent the necessary dossiers to the Manjača commandant.[159] On 27 and 28 August, similar information was sent by SJB Sanski Most to Manjača.[160] Already at the beginning of August, SJB Sanski Most had reported that the military was detaining Muslims and establishing detention centres without proper coordination with the police. Military and civilian judiciary organs were not operating properly. In general, coordination between the military and the police was lacking. The Chief of SJB Sanski Most, Mirko Vrućinić, accordingly recommended that steps be taken to ascertain which institution was responsible for the various detention centres. Vrućinić also recommended the establishment of a prison at the 'level of the AR Krajina'.[161]

In the meantime, on 14 August 1992, Stojan Župljanin, in his capacity as the chief of CSB Banja Luka, had established a commission that would investigate all camps, investigative centres, detention centres and other similar facilities in the municipalities of Prijedor, Bosanski Novi and Sanski Most.[162] The commission was ordered to file a report by 17 August. The president of the commission was Vojin Bera, the chief of a section of SNB in CSB Banja Luka.[163]

Citing Župljanin's decision, SJB Bosanski Novi filed a report on 15 August.[164] It described in detail the manner in which detention facilities had come about and their subsequent operation. SJB Sanski Most presented a report to the commission on 18 August.[165] The report noted that 90 per cent of the persons brought to the facilities in Sanski Most were brought by the military. The guard force was a mix of military and police personnel, but the military element was later replaced by the police after the crisis staff intervened. Of the 1,655 persons brought to the investigative centres in Sanski Most, 1528 were Muslims and 122 were Croats. SJB Prijedor also submitted a response to the commission.[166]

Bera's commission filed its report on 18 August.[167] The report collated information from the three reports filed by the Sanski Most, Bosanski Novi and Prijedor municipalities. It argued that the camps in Prijedor had been established in order to deal with the large number of persons detained in VRS operations commencing on 24 May. These persons included both those who had been detained on suspicion of criminal or terrorist activity and those who had 'left their homes and apartments to search for food and protection'. These persons were almost exclusively of Muslim or Croat ethnicity.

The commission claimed that persons housed at Trnopolje could leave when they wanted, to destinations of their own choosing. The report also claimed that the Red Cross and other organizations delivered regular assistance to the persons in Trnopolje, who were not subject to interrogation. The report also referred to large numbers of non-Serbs who had 'voluntarily' left Prijedor municipality. The report claimed that the majority of those leaving departed out of sympathy for Muslim and Croat extremist elements.

On 19 August 1992, Karadžić ordered the VRS and MUP to treat all prisoners in accordance with international norms and to cooperate with international organizations.[168] This order was issued as a reiteration of a presidential order of 6 June, suggesting that that order had not been fully implemented.

Also on 19 August 1992, Župljanin forwarded ministerial orders of 10 and 17 August mandating that good sanitary conditions be maintained in detention centres.[169] Stanišić stated that police serving at detention centres should be put at the disposition of the military. On 20 August, Župljanin forwarded a ministerial dispatch of 19 August to the chiefs of all subordinate SJBs.[170] In the dispatch, Stanišić ordered that all RS MUP personnel dealing with detainees obey the relevant domestic and international laws. The existence of any 'wild', i.e. illegal camps or detention centres, was to be reported immediately to the minister. Criminal charges would be filed against those individuals failing to comply. On 21 August, Župljanin told all subordinate SJBs to facilitate the return of detainees to their homes, and to provide security for them upon arrival.[171] On 22 August, Župljanin ordered that persons whose detention at Manjača could not 'be confirmed by any material evidence' be released.[172]

On 24 August 1992 Mićo Stanišić forwarded a request to all CSBs and to all SJBs requiring details of the location of the collection centres, information on the authorities who had ordered their establishment and those authorities who had administered them.[173] He also requested information on the number of prisoners and persons arrested. The information had to be submitted to the ministry by 30 August. The order was distributed by Župljanin to his subordinate SJBs on 27 August, with an added request for information on Serbs detained by Muslim forces.[174]

Stanišić's request for information coincided with actions aimed at reducing the number and size of detention facilities in ARK. This allowed RS MUP officials to take a narrow perspective in formulating their responses. From Prijedor, Drljača reported that there were no detention facilities except for Manjača.[175] He thus eluded any mention of the previously existing facilities. From Ključ, Vinko Kondić replied that there were no camps, prisons or detention centres in that municipality. All detainees were being sent to Manjača.[176]

On 28 August 1992, the RS MUP wrote to CSB Sarajevo, Bijeljina and Trebinje to inform them of the arrival of a CSCE delegation. The delegation was to visit prisons at Pale, Bijeljina, Bileća, Trebinje and Foča. The dispatch noted that it was necessary to cooperate with the VRS during this visit and noted that 'the prisons were under the jurisdiction of the Ministry of Justice'.[177] On 31 August, CSB Banja Luka reported that the CSCE delegation had visited Manjača and Trnopolje.[178] At the beginning of September, a delegation of the International Committee of the Red Cross also visited Banja Luka to discuss Manjača and Trnopolje. Župljanin attended the meeting in his capacity as the 'Minister of Internal Affairs of the Autonomous Region of Krajina'.[179] On 29 September 1992, the National Defence Council of the Prijedor Municipal Assembly recommended the closing of the Trnopolje centre, 'as the departure of all registered persons from this collection centre effectively makes it unnecessary'.[180] However, as late as mid-October, some police officials were still ignoring orders to cooperate with the International Committee of the Red Cross.[181]

In some cases, the police asked the civilian authorities for assistance in matters related to detention. On 17 June 1992, SJB Sanski Most asked Župljanin to consult with the ARK authorities in order to clarify the status of prisons. At issue was a large number of Muslim prisoners detained at SJB Sanski Most and other SJBs as a result of 'combat and disarming operations and other operations and activities regarding interrogation and operational processing'.[182]

In practice, the detention facilities operated by the RS MUP and by the VRS were part of a one-way road for the removal of non-Serbs from the RS. Those detained individuals who were lucky enough to survive their stay in these facilities had no chance of being permitted to return to their homes, some of which had been destroyed, while others had been confiscated and given to Serbs. Even when the international pressure to close detention facilities reached its peak, the RS authorities only released prisoners who 'voluntarily' relinquished their property and their right to reside in Republika Srpska. For example, in Bosanski Novi, the police participated in the operation of an impromptu detention centre for mostly Muslim males even though SJB Bosanski Novi disagreed with the manner in which this centre had been established.[183] Only those Muslims who were not suspected of crimes and were also willing to leave the municipality were released.

As has been seen, the RS authorities had since early April 1992 tasked the police to detain large numbers of Muslims and Croats, primarily because they were allegedly 'extremists' intent on destroying Republika Srpska and committing genocide against Serbs. Yet an in a way more pernicious justification for the mass detentions, particularly prominent in the case of Trnopolje, was the claim that Muslims and Croats had voluntarily sought shelter in RS MUP-operated detention facilities for their own safety. In the context of the dismantling of the detention facilities in northwestern Bosnia, the logical corollary to this justification was the rationale that Muslims and Croats voluntarily wanted to leave the territory of the RS – or Bosnia and Herzegovina as a whole – in order to remain safe. The police and the RS authorities were hence in a way doing non-Serbs a favour by 'permitting' them to leave. Underlining how cynical and inhumane this policy was, Župljanin, when confronted by international reporters about the use of boxcars for deportations of Muslims and Croats, responded that 'none of the refugees asked for first-class carriages'.[184] And even years at the ICTY, victims were occasionally confronted by defence lawyers who tried to claim that 'you all wanted to leave'.[185]

The RS MUP insisted in its internal documentation that they were merely carrying out rational and necessary orders. Thus, for example, on 5 July 1992 SJB Prijedor forwarded a report to CSB Banja Luka noting that they were, in accordance with a dispatch from the CSB dated 4 July 1992, 'checking all persons of Muslim and Croat nationality, as well as those of Serb nationality who do not have a registered address or place of residence'.[186] The dispatch further stated that 'a large number of Croats and Muslims wish voluntarily to leave' the region. On 18 July, SJB Prijedor forwarded a dispatch from CSB Banja Luka advising that it had been arranged that a convoy of five buses depart from Trnopolje to Skender Vakuf.[187] In addition, on 24 August, CSB Banja Luka expressed concrete concerns about violence against those released detainees who might decide to go home.[188] The employees of SJB Prijedor were asked to prevent any eventual attacks against those returning home from the detention centres.

The assertion by SJB Sanski Most on 17 August 1992 that Muslims and Croats would be allowed to make loyalty oaths if they wanted to remain must be understood in this context.[189] On 20 August, the War Presidency of Kotor Varoš Municipality discussed the topic of emigration of detainees. It was decided that SJB Kotor Varoš would be involved in deciding who would be allowed to leave the municipality.[190]

On 22 August 1992, the War Presidency of the Municipal Assembly of Ključ wrote to CSB Banja Luka about the possible return of detainees from Manjača to Ključ. According to the municipal authorities in Ključ, 'we are absolutely not able to secure the protection of eventually returned prisoners of war from the camp Manjača, nor can we set up a reception centre for the same. We do not have even the most elementary material criteria [for this]'.[191]

On 31 August 1992, Radio Ključ carried a report on the first bus of 'emigrants' from Ključ municipality.[192] The bus left Ključ for Belgrade, with Canada as the final destination. The radio announcement was carried on the behalf of SJB Ključ so that 'other interested persons' could take advantage of the same opportunity. In early September, an auditor noted that SJB Prijedor had issued several thousand permits to Muslims who wanted to leave the municipality.¹⁹³ On 29 September, SJB Prijedor reported that it had received and processed 15,280 applications for emigration from the municipality.¹⁹⁴

Chief of SJB Ključ Vinko Kondić reported in late September 1992 that the Muslim inhabitants of the municipality had been inculcated with fear and that pressure had been put on them to leave the municipality.¹⁹⁵ Although Kondić argued that the Muslims had started an armed rebellion in Ključ on 27 May, he observed that they had been the objects of a campaign of terror, including violent attacks on their lives and property. There had also been 'monstrous crimes', including the murder of four Muslims. 'Massive theft' had been observed in the homes of those Muslims who had already left the municipality. The intensity of armed conflict had meant that few perpetrators of these crimes were apprehended. In those few instances, the only punishment meted out had been the deployment of the perpetrators to the frontline. Kondić argued that the situation was such that the continued occurrence of such crimes might prompt the international community to increase the pressure on the Bosnian Serbs. He therefore requested that clear instructions be issued on how to proceed in such cases.

In August 2013, over twenty years after the events described here, the International Commission on Missing Persons in the village of Tomašica in Prijedor municipality discovered one of the largest mass graves from the Bosnian war.¹⁹⁶ At the trial of Ratko Mladić, it emerged that Drljača, the chief of SJB Prijedor, attended a meeting with the VRS in May 1993 to discuss what to do with approximately '5,000 Muslim bodies' buried in a mine Tomašica.¹⁹⁷ While Drljača attempted to get the VRS to handle the issue, Mladić wrote in his notes from the meeting that 'they [the police] killed them, so they should get rid of them'. Mladić expressed concern that the mass grave could be discovered, and ordered Colonel Bogojević of the 1st Krajina Corps to start an investigation.

Here it bears emphasizing that I have above presented only a fragment of the available information on this topic and have in fact nearly exclusively relied upon the RS MUP's own documentation. Factoring in witness and victim testimony, as was done at the ICTY, leads to an immeasurably more devastating portrait of the police's role in the disarming, detention, atrocious mistreatment and displacement and/or deportation of the non-Serb civilian population. It is hence not surprising that successive trial chambers at the ICTY concluded that the police participated as a key actor in a 'widespread campaign of violence, arrests, mistreatments, and dismissals from employment ... constitut[ing] a large scale attack against the civilian population ... both widespread and systematic'.¹⁹⁸

The RS MUP and paramilitaries

From the very outset of the armed conflict in Bosnia – indeed even before the war began – paramilitary formations were a constituent part of the conflict. All of the three primary sides in the conflict employed paramilitary formations to some degree, though it seems safe to say that their use was particularly widespread on the Serbian side. The very use of the term 'paramilitary' was often highly subjective. During the first few months, the tendency in the RS MUP documentation was to refer to armed formations of non-Serbs as paramilitaries and in a pejorative sense; only as problems mounted with Serb paramilitary formations were these referred to as such.

This section looks at how this process developed and particularly analyses the uneasy cooperation between Serb paramilitary formations and the RS MUP. In his second book, Mićo Stanišić proudly claimed that the RS MUP engaged in an 'uncompromising struggle' against paramilitary formations, but the reality was starkly different.[199] While the Serbs in Bosnia did form a number of their own paramilitary groups, the most notable ones stemmed from Serbia, a fact which, although they were initially welcomed, created a number of challenges for the RS MUP. Initially welcomed as fraternal, heroic and courageous bands of men who selflessly came from Serbia to Bosnia to save imperiled Serbs, paramilitary groups from Serbia quickly came to be seen as highly problematic and criminal formations which, because they were not fully under the control or the RS MUP and the VRS, posed a threat to the stability of the RS.

Emerging paramilitary groups had an inherently destabilizing effect on security in the period prior to the war and as such were part and parcel of the effort to destabilize the SRBiH MUP and other Bosnian republican institutions.[200] After the war began, paramilitary formations could act as force multipliers for the Bosnian Serb leadership while at the same time affording some modicum of plausible deniability as regards the commission of atrocities. Yet as the atrocities grew in scale and scope, this plausible deniability became increasingly difficult to maintain and was also undermined by the often open adulation heaped upon 'patriotic' paramilitary leaders by the leaders of the RS. Much more problematic, however, was the inherently undisciplined and aggressive nature of paramilitary units and the spillover of their aggression onto the ethnic Serb population.

As seen in Chapter 1, the problem of paramilitary formations dated back to at least the outbreak of war in Croatia. Although paramilitary units such as the one led by Željko Ražnatović 'Arkan' came from Serbia and included commanders and members initially unknown to the Bosnian Serb authorities, there were also indigenous units led by known criminals, making it even more difficult to excuse the cooperation between such units and the police. Such was the case with Veljko Milanković and his group known as the 'Wolves from Vučijak'. As early as September 1991, CSB Banja Luka reported on the negative activities of Veljko Milanković, 'who is, on his assertion, the commander of a detachment of the police of SAO Krajina'.[201] On 23 September, Župljanin also sent a detailed report about the activities of armed groups in northwestern Bosnia, including that of Milanković, to Biljana Plavšić, Momčilo Krajišnik, Miodrag Simović, Vitomir Žepinić and Lieutenant Colonel General Nikola Uzelac.[202] In the report, Župljanin noted that Milanković had hitherto already been prosecuted seven times for felonies and seventeen times for misdemeanours. Župljanin wrote a subsequent report about Milanković in

December 1991.²⁰³ Yet by the spring and summer of 1992, Župljanin as well as the RS leadership hailed Milanković and many others like him.²⁰⁴

At the very outset, the war in northeastern Bosnia featured paramilitary activity in a manner that set the stage both in terms of atrocious behaviour and for conflicts between the nascent RS authorities and the paramilitaries. On 31 March 1992, the paramilitary Serb Voluntary Guard (*Srpska dobrovoljačka garda*, SDG) led by Arkan crossed into Bijeljina municipality from Serbia. Relatively little combat took place, and by 4 April Arkan's men had seized control of the town, though not without killing several dozen people, including both women and children.²⁰⁵ Indicating that Arkan's actions had not been at odds with the Bosnian Serb leadership, member of the RS Presidency Biljana Plavšić on 3 April publicly praised Arkan. She did ask him to transfer control of the town to the JNA, but Arkan stated that his 'business' in the municipality was not yet finished.²⁰⁶

In Bijeljina, the paramilitary formations were almost single-handedly responsible for organizing the takeover of the municipality, and the police more or less voluntarily ceded the municipality to the paramilitaries. As shown by Plavšić's praise, neither she nor the RS MUP had any notable objection to the attacks on the non-Serb (predominantly Muslim and ethnic Albanian) civilian population of Bijeljina. Most Muslims who were not killed rapidly left Bijeljina. In other municipalities the paramilitary formations coordinated to some extent with the JNA and TO (later the VRS) and the RS MUP.

In a pattern that would repeat itself elsewhere in eastern Bosnia, it rapidly became clear that the de facto ceding of control in Bijeljina to paramilitary formations was not without risks for local Serbs. Although ostensibly motivated by 'patriotism', a number of paramilitary units showed themselves to be at least equally interested in looting and stripping assets from their victims. It was not coincidental that Muslim or ethnic Albanian jewellers, business owners and entrepreneurs often found themselves among the first targets of 'ethnic cleansing'. Yet at some point the supply of non-Serb victims and assets would be exhausted, either because the victims were dead or had fled the municipality. At that point – and in some cases much earlier – the predatory behaviour of the paramilitaries would focus on mixed marriages, self-declared Yugoslavs and allegedly 'disloyal' Serbs.²⁰⁷ And as was noted in a later VRS report, finally the paramilitaries would either move on to another municipality or would slake their unquenchable thirst for looting by stealing from Serbs; 'it is not a rare occurrence that paramilitary formations, after "war booty" disappears from a certain area, start also stealing the property of Serbs, moving into their apartments and houses, even murdering them'.²⁰⁸

Countless examples illustrate the complicity of the police in the commission of atrocities by paramilitary formations. Such complicity did not need to involve explicit cooperation but could also entail what are called crimes of commission by omission. One such example regards a paramilitary group in the eastern Bosnian municipality of Milići known as the 'Vukovar detachment'. On 21 May 1992, members of that group approached officers of SJB Milići asking where they could 'execute' three Bosnian Muslims.²⁰⁹ The officers told them to contact the nearest military command to clarify this matter. The paramilitaries then proceeded to kill the Muslims once they were slightly outside the range of the police officers. On the same day, members of the same paramilitary detachment again approached police officers belonging to SJB Milići. The paramilitaries asked where they could 'blow up thirty Ustaša' so as to avoid 'wasting ammunition'. The police officers told the paramilitaries that they could not do this. Nevertheless, shortly thereafter the police heard shots. The paramilitaries had proceeded to shoot twenty-five Muslims.

In filing the above report, the chief of SJB Milići stated that 'members of Public Security Station Milići could not protect the people because the "Vukovar detachment" was accompanied by an armoured assault vehicle and 10 members of said detachment'.[210] By contrast, the police officers had only 'infantry weaponry'. In a later incident, in July 1992, the police did succeed in removing another paramilitary formation from the territory of Milići. The chief of SJB Milići assessed that the police officers had acted both times to the best of their abilities. Yet in cases such as these, the complicity of the police (and the responsible prosecutors) extended to the lack of any proper investigation or prosecution of the crimes committed by the paramilitaries. And, of course, the Serb authorities had often demonstrated enthusiasm back when these formations first emerged and arrived on the territory of the respective municipality.

By late June 1992, the irregularities observed by the RS MUP in Bijeljina and in other municipalities such as Zvornik and Brčko were significant enough to require external assistance. Pursuant to a request submitted by the RS MUP to Milan Panić on 27 June, who was at that point the president of the Federal Republic of Yugoslavia, a federal SSUP inspector named Milorad (Mićo) Davidović was sent to Bijeljina along with seventeen police officers.[211] Davidović had worked in Bijeljina before the war as the commander of a police station and had already earlier been sent to Bosnia by the SSUP to assist the RS MUP.[212]

Over the next several weeks, Davidović and his associates both observed and intervened in the municipalities in which they were deployed.[213] In early August, Davidović filed a damning report detailing his observations. Davidović described the situation in the Bijeljina area as one of widespread crime, including killings, rapes and theft in an environment of 'the abuse and terrorization of the population without regard to national affiliation'. In Bijeljina, Muslims who legally possessed firearms had been forcibly taken to a 'private prison' in the new local slaughterhouse where they had been abused and tortured even as part of the same building was used as a storage facility for various looted items. In sum, an enormous array of criminal activities had occurred in Bijeljina since April, causing Muslims as well as Serbs to flee. Paradoxically, the ranks of the reserve police in the municipality had swollen enormously just as elsewhere in Bosnia, but by the time Davidović's intervention was over, only 354 of 867 reserve police officers had been found suitable for continued service.

Indeed, Davidović had essentially found it necessary to recreate the Bijeljina police from the bottom up. Davidović had spoken with police officers who cried when they told him how Arkan's men had physically assaulted them. Davidović asked them how they could permit that 'these criminals take over the police'. His opposition to Arkan's men causes some of them to threaten to kill both Davidović and the regular police in Bijeljina.[214] Yet when Davidović reported in detail about the 'chaos' in Bijelijna to Minister Stanišić and to Federal Minister of Internal Affairs Petar Gračanin, they did not react.

> Mićo Stanišić said that he knew this and that he could not undertake anything. That was how it had to be. [...] ... he said that Arkan's forces had helped to liberate territory which they regarded as belonging to Republika Srpska. He also told me that an agreement existed according to which they could take from any territory they seized anything, any war booty and that this was the price for their engagement there.[215]

Similarly, Davidović also stated that Karadžić instructed him not to arrest Serbs, because that would set Serbs against Serbs and be akin to repeating the Second World War, when Serbs were split between Chetniks and Partisans. According to Davidović, Karadžić 'meant that this should not happen again during this war ... and that this should be prevented even if it were done at the expense of not punishing perpetrators of crimes'.[216] Davidović's clear recollection was that 'the leadership of the SDS had planned, organised activities in terms of ethnically cleansing the Muslims. Whoever helped them – well, that was the entire – that was the core of the matter'.[217]

Paramilitary formations presented 'one of the most substantial problems', even though these had 'partially participated in the liberation of these areas'.[218] Davidović described their behaviour as encompassing 'abuse, terror, looting, not seldom killings of innocent people, violent and open intentions of assuming all power in Bijeljina, Brčko and Zvornik'. He criticized the 'passivity, disorganization and chaos' of the local authorities, who in some cases also provided assistance to the paramilitaries. One of these paramilitary formations, 'the Serb Voluntary Guard' had taken control of the SJB in Bijeljina, and another, affiliated with 'Captain Dragan', had taken control of the SJB in Brčko. The SSUP representatives reported that the activities of the paramilitary organizations took place at least in some cases with assistance from the local police. Upon the arrival of the team from the SSUP, they were joined by 'an expert team' from the RS MUP. Together, they worked to stabilize and normalize the situation in Bijeljina, Brčko and Zvornik. On several occasions, Davidović and Chief Inspector Dragan Andan of the RS MUP were threatened by the paramilitary formations with physical liquidation. Some of the members of these paramilitary formations purported to be employees of the MUP of Serbia.

With time the RS authorities took an increasingly negative view of Serb paramilitary organizations. As the RS began to consolidate control over its territory, the chaos and violence caused by paramilitary organizations came to be seen as a liability to the state. As a result, the VRS and RS MUP attempted to integrate these units into regular units of the VRS or the RS MUP. On 13 June 1992, Karadžić banned 'self-organised armed groups and individuals on the territory of the Serbian Republic of Bosnia and Herzegovina'. Such groups and individuals were given three days to submit to the command of either the VRS or the RS MUP.[219] As seen earlier, in northwestern Bosnia Župljanin had already earlier integrated members of the paramilitary SOS into a new special unit controlled by CSB Banja Luka.[220]

Despite Karadžić's order, a report by the VRS Main Staff in late July 1992 identified approximately sixty active paramilitary groups on the territory of the RS, numbering between 4,000 and 5,000 members.[221] The report, authored by Colonel Zdravko Tolimir, who was the chief of intelligence and security for the Main Staff of the VRS, noted that these groups were often composed of criminal and/or 'pathological' elements who had risen to prominence with the outbreak of armed hostilities. They had little military value and concentrated their efforts mainly on looting and war profiteering, 'except for a very small number of honourable exceptions who know and accept the goals of the struggle of the Serb nation'. These groups often exhibited extreme hatred against non-Serbs, 'and it can be freely assessed that they are bearers of genocidal behaviour in the Serb nation [*nosioci genocidnosti u srpskom narodu*]'. Although the report found that none of the paramilitary groups were directly affiliated with the SDS, it also noted some associations between these groups and the SDS. The number of paramilitary organizations, the scope of their activities and the lack of condemnation of these activities created the impression that the SDS supported them. In addition, the report observed a link between these groups and corruption in government institutions. The VRS therefore concluded that 'every armed Serb was to be placed under the exclusive command of the army, or else disarmed and legal measures taken'.[222]

In those cases where the integration of paramilitary formations into the police or the army proved impossible because the formations resisted, the RS MUP participated in operations to forcibly disable paramilitaries – though never in those cases in which the paramilitary forces in question were directly supported by the MUP of Serbia. At the end of July 1992, there was a crackdown against paramilitary forces. On 29 July, the RS MUP Police Detachment (Special Police), together with the VRS Military Police, imposed a complete blockade on Zvornik municipality.[223] This was done in reaction to the continued problems caused by paramilitaries in this area, and especially by members of the 'Yellow Wasps'. Remarkably, a VRS Main Staff report alleged that the Yellow Wasps had actually not only paid a Muslim paramilitary formation for a building in Zvornik municipality but had also guaranteed that paramilitary formation safe passage out of the area.[224]

Here it is worth recalling how the Yellow Wasps had first come to Bosnia. At the beginning of the war, Branko Grujić, the head of the Zvornik Municipality Crisis Staff, had personally invited the Yellow Wasps to the municipality.[225] The Yellow Wasps were led by Vojin 'Žućo' Vučković and his brother Dušan 'Repić' Vučković, and numbered approximately 100–300 men, the unit's size fluctuating frequently as was typical for many paramilitary formations.[226] Having heeded this invitation, the Wasps set up their headquarters right next to the municipal police station, known colloquially as the 'SUP'.[227] Hence, if we also recall that the chief of SJB

Zvornik was an *ex officio* member of the crisis staff, there was no way in which the police in Zvornik could have been unaware of the arrival of an aggressively violent paramilitary formation from Serbia, particularly as the Wasps immediately began to set up barricades at various places in the municipality.

Although the relationship between the Yellow Wasps and the RS MUP was not without its rough spots, it seems that both cooperation and coexistence were possible as long as the Wasps primarily directed their attention towards Muslims in eastern Bosnia. Certainly, the Wasps' mass detention of several hundred Muslim civilians at the Drina stadium and their forcible displacement in late May 1992, accompanied by killings of some of the Muslims, did not lead to any discernible concern on the part of the RS MUP.[228] In fact, an ICTY trial chamber found indications that the police were at least partially involved in the commission of these crimes.[229] Over time, however, there were fewer and fewer Muslims left, and the RS MUP gradually began to lose patience with the looting and other crimes of the Wasps. The formation also refused to heed the RS presidential order to subordinate itself to the VRS's chain of command.[230] On 20 July, CSB Bijeljina reported that paramilitary formations were contributing to a problematic security situation in Zvornik municipality.[231] Three paramilitary groups – commanded by 'Žućo' (the Yellow Wasps), 'Pivarski' and 'Niški' – were operating in the municipality. According to the report, the first group was the most powerful and included both local recruits and members from the Republic of Serbia. CSB Bijeljina recommended that the RS MUP intervene using its special unit.

In the meantime, whatever pleas and entreaties the municipal authorities or the RS MUP used to encourage the Yellow Wasps to leave Zvornik voluntarily and cross the Drina back into Serbia fell on deaf ears. Police reports from late July indicate the growing consternation of the police with the Yellow Wasps.[232] Together with other local authorities, the police had gradually placed restrictions on the Yellow Wasps, but finally Grujić, the very man who had brought the Wasps to Zvornik, went to the RS leadership and asked that action be taken against the Wasps. Ironically, this led the Wasps to arrest Grujić and another man from Zvornik.[233] It is worth noting that during this period the State Security Service in Serbia was well aware of what was transpiring in Zvornik, as it was receiving firsthand information from informants in the municipality.[234]

On 25 July 1992, Milorad Davidović added to the growing pile of reports about the unacceptable behaviour of the Yellow Wasps.[235] The RS MUP therefore saw no alternative to the use of force and dispatched the Special Brigade of the Police to the area to subdue the Wasps. Davidović was in the charge of the operation, which commenced on 27 July.[236]

As a result of the Zvornik operation, the RS MUP apprehended dozens of individuals, most of whom were either immediately or eventually expelled to Serbia. 'During this operation a large quantity of gold, jewellery, cars, weapons, ammunition, alcohol, and other goods were found at the premises of those arrested.' Although an effort was made to return these items to their owners, by this point a very large number of Muslims had of course involuntarily left the municipality.

In some cases, the RS MUP interrogated them about their activities during the preceding period.[237] A report was also filed concerning the criminal activities of the Yellow Wasps. This report noted that both military intelligence officers and the SNB had information indicating that at least one member of the Yellow Wasps had 'carried out a massacre-genocide against citizens of Muslim nationality of the Serbian Republic of Bosnia and Herzegovina'.[238] Evidence was also uncovered that the Yellow Wasps had, as recently as 11 July, received material assistance from SJB Pale and Žućo had met with member of the RS Presidency Biljana Plavšić as well as RS Defence Minister Subotić.[239] Of the sixty-five members who were arrested, criminal investigations were initiated against eleven of them. The remaining fifty-four were put at the disposal of the armed forces of the RS.

Minister Stanišić was kept abreast of the operation and thanked Davidović for its successful implementation.[240] Stanišić also indicated that appropriate steps should be taken to conduct investigations into all criminal conduct, including that of police officers in the municipality. However, rather extraordinarily given what the RS MUP must have known about the extent of the crimes committed by the Yellow Wasps against the civilian population of Zvornik, the RS MUP's investigation into the Wasps focused above all on 'looting and confiscation of multiple VW Golf vehicles from checkpoints in Zvornik'.[241] There is no evidence that these paramilitaries were actually prosecuted in the RS for committing crimes against the non-Serb population of Zvornik municipality.[242] This should perhaps not be surprising given that the police in Zvornik like in many other municipalities rather consistently referred to Muslims against whom police action was taken as 'extremists'.[243] Moreover, many of the members of the Wasps, including their leaders, expressed incredulity that they were being arrested. After all, had they not heeded the personal invitation of the highest leaders of the RS to come and assist in the defence of the Serb nation? In sum, 'proceedings were suspended, and all the men were released by August 1992; some returned to Serbia'.[244]

It therefore seems rather predictable that the July 1992 RS MUP operation against the Yellow Wasps did not succeed in permanently subduing that organization. On 5 September, Goran Žugić, the head of RO SNB Birač, reported that Vojin Vučković 'Žućo' and his Yellow Wasps had made several recent appearances in Zvornik municipality.[245] Vučković had mentioned that he was preparing to take revenge for the July 1992 humiliation. Accordingly, the police in Zvornik were planning counter-measures. Žugić asked his superior officer, SNB Undersecretary Dragan Kijac, for advice on this matter. Kijac replied on the same day, endorsing the approach taken and advising Žugić to keep in touch with Milenko Karišik, the commander of the RS MUP Special Brigade of the Police.[246] Worries about the Yellow Wasps were repeated in an SNB dispatch to the RS Presidency, government, MUP and VRS dated 22 September 1992.[247]

Sometimes the line between paramilitary groups and the police was so fine as to be barely perceptible. One such notorious case was that of a group known as the 'Miće' operating primarily in and around Teslić municipality, and which at least in part consisted of police officers.[248] On 27 July 1992, CSB Doboj reported about the operations of paramilitary formations in its AOR and sent a long list of suggested remedies to the ministry.²⁴⁹ There was, however, subsequent information indicating mutual cooperation between paramilitary forces and CSB Doboj.

Here again, a pattern emerges in which the local authorities were relatively content to tolerate or even cooperate with a paramilitary formation until its conduct became a problem for the Serb population. Hence, when Chief of CSB Banja Luka Župljanin was notified earlier, in June 1992, of violent mistreatment of Croats and Muslims at SJB Teslić, 'Župljanin's response was that a war was going on and that similar things were happening in a number of other places'.²⁵⁰ Župljanin also tried to pass the problem over to CSB Doboj; Teslić was approximately equidistant between Banja Luka and Doboj.

More problematically from the perspective of the local authorities, the Miće had begun like a number of paramilitary organizations to usurp power in the municipality and to challenge the authorities. Apparently, Župljanin took their threat to kill the president of municipality more seriously than their actual previous atrocities towards the non-Serb civilian population. Župljanin sent Predrag Radulović of the Miloš Group to take care of the problem, and sixteen members of the group were arrested at the end of June.²⁵¹ Radulović subsequently ran SJB Teslić for approximately two months, though Župljanin and others thwarted his investigations into the group's crimes, and all detained members of the group were released by the end of July. It should be noted that even in the extremely nationalist press of the time, the Miće were viewed as being particularly notorious.²⁵² As a ICTY trial chamber noted, Župljanin took action against the group

> only because the Miće Group had become a nuisance to Serb municipal authorities. Based on this evidence, the Trial Chamber finds that Župljanin's failure to protect the Muslim and Croatian population formed part of the decision to discriminate against them and force them to leave the ARK Municipalities, and was not merely the consequence of simple negligence. ... Through the formation of a feigned commission and by providing false information to the judicial authorities, he creat[ed] a climate of impunity that encouraged the perpetration of crimes against non-Serbs and made non-Serbs decide to leave the ARK Municipalities.²⁵³

As was the case with the Yellow Wasps, the Miće became a recurring headache. According to a November 1992 report compiled by the SNB Sector at CSB Banja Luka, Andrija Bjelošević, the head of CSB Doboj, had recently arrived at a battlefield in Teslić municipality along with members of a special unit of CSB Doboj.²⁵⁴ With the permission of the local VRS commander, Colonel Slavko Lisica, Bjelošević was cooperating with the Miće. This group included persons who had already been arrested, and it had been identified earlier by SJB Teslić as being involved in attacks on non-Serbian civilians.²⁵⁵ The SNB reported that such cooperation was contrary to instructions issued by the RS MUP. Given earlier violent encounters with the members of the Miće in Teslić, the local Serbian population viewed the cooperation among the VRS, CSB Doboj and the Miće with discontent and fear.

Paramilitaries also ravaged Herzegovina. On 30 July 1992, CSB Trebinje completed a report on the activities of paramilitary organizations on the territory of SAO Herzegovina. CSB Trebinje sent the report to the RS MUP on 4 August.[256] According to the report, Serbian paramilitary activity was widespread in Herzegovina. Prominent groups included followers of Arkan and Vojislav Šešelj. Rather than engage in military activity to assist the RS forces, the paramilitary groups generally harassed the local population and committed crimes. Many members of these groups had criminal backgrounds. A report filed by CSB Trebinje in September 1992 claimed that these groups had been driven out of Eastern Herzegovina.[257] Yet at the same time, a number of problematic persons, including criminals, had managed to 'infiltrate' themselves into the police force. This, and the heavy commitment of police officers at the front, allegedly made it impossible to carry out the legal tasks of the MUP, especially in places like Bileća.

Despite the assertions of the RS MUP and the RS leadership that they were confronting the issue head on, it is in fact not difficult to identify examples of paramilitary activity after July 1992. For example, paramilitaries perpetrated continuing attacks on Muslims and Croats in Sanski Most.[258] As of August 1992, there could not be said to be a unified RS MUP stance towards Bosnian Serb paramilitary organizations. Although the ministry had adopted an overtly negative and condemnatory stance towards these organizations and their activities, prominent members of the ministry continued to cooperate selectively with these organizations without suffering disciplinary consequences.[259] On 5 August, the Chief of SJB Ilidža, Tomislav Kovač, sent an angry report to Minister Mićo Stanišić personally attacking the lack of courage and commitment shown by VRS units at Ilidža.[260] Kovač noted that these extenuating circumstances had led him to rely on 'Serb volunteers', as he had indeed done since the outbreak of the war.[261] Kovač attached a list of the weaponry and ammunitions distributed to these 'volunteers'. The following day, Kovač was promoted to Assistant Minister and Chief of the Administration for the Affairs and Tasks of the Police.[262]

Nonetheless, there were also signs in the late summer and early autumn of 1992 that the tide was turning with respect to the RS MUP's relationship with paramilitary formations. On 17 August, CSB Sarajevo reported success in subduing paramilitary activity in the Centre's area of jurisdiction.[263] This was done in cooperation with the RS MUP's Police Detachment. It was noted that reserve police personnel had participated illegally in a number of these paramilitary formations. As of mid-August, CSB Trebinje reported that some paramilitary groups remained active in Bosnian Serb-controlled parts of Herzegovina.[264] The police also observed that these groups were involved in power struggles in the region. On 8 September, CSB Sarajevo stated that paramilitaries, including some from Serbia, were still active in Bratunac municipality. 'The Public Security Station is working on the dissolution of such formations using their forces and with the assistance of the military and civilian authorities in order to put them under the command of the Armed Forces of Republika Srpska.'[265]

Indications exist that leading RS officials were still concerned by paramilitary activities towards the end of 1992. In November 1992, a report from CSB Sarajevo stated that paramilitary formations had presented a 'potential danger for the complete organization and discipline in the Serbian military and police' since their initial appearance in Bosnia and Herzegovina. At the outset of the war, these formations had enjoyed 'informal legitimacy' with the regular military. With time, however, the paramilitaries 'became strong and independent and presented a hindrance and a real object of derision in the overall front of the organization of Serbian forces'.[266] At a 20 December meeting of the Supreme Command of the VRS, which Minister Mićo Stanišić also attended, he emphasized the need for all 'paragroups' to be put under unified command.[267] Obviously such repetitive emphasis would have been unnecessary had robust and systematic steps on this front been taken much earlier in the year.

In summary, RS MUP officials, and indeed the RS authorities as a whole, were generally aware of the presence of paramilitary organizations and of their activities throughout 1992, and in particular during the first part of the war.[268] However, the activities of these groups tended to lead to a deterioration of the security situation.[269] Although attempts were made by the RS MUP, particularly after July 1992, to eliminate paramilitary activity, the emphasis was put on integrating paramilitary organizations into police or military units rather than on the investigation, arrest and prosecution of these organizations. The recurring phenomenon of direct cooperation between the RS MUP and paramilitary organizations decreased in frequency during the second half of 1992 but was never wholly eliminated. In his July 1992 report, Colonel Tolimir wrote that these formations contained 'a very small number of honourable exceptions who know and accept the goals of the struggle of the Serb nation'.[270] The reality was, however, that through their aggressive participation in ethnic cleansing, these paramilitaries very much contributed to attainment of the strategic goals which Tolimir's own military and civilian leadership had adopted in May 1992.

Police participation in other atrocities

The preceding section on paramilitaries has made it abundantly clear that the RS MUP was extensively aware of the commission of atrocities by paramilitary formations. The police's responsibility and complicity in the crimes of the paramilitary formations were of course not limited to the police's unwillingness to prevent these crimes or to subsequently investigate them. As has also been seen, the police actively collaborated with many paramilitary groups and indeed absorbed a number of these into the ranks of the RS MUP.

In addition, the police through extensive participation in ethnic cleansing and in the operation of detention facilities themselves committed systematic and extensive crimes during 1992. In most cases, the RS MUP's own documentation either omitted mention of the commission of atrocities or justified the crimes as appropriate actions taken against 'extremists' who were resisting the establishment of Republika Srpska. But what of the occasions on which the police not only committed atrocities but in fact even acknowledged internally that such crimes had been committed?

In at least one case, the RS MUP became directly aware of a large-scale massacre of non-Serbian 'refugees' in northwestern Bosnia and Herzegovina, an incident that became one of the single most notorious crimes of the Bosnian war. On 31 August, Minister Stanišić ordered an investigation into the deaths of 'approximately 150 Muslims' at Korićanske stijene in Skender-Vakuf municipality on 21 August.[271] According to a VRS report, the refugee convoy carrying, among others, detainees from Trnopolje was moving from Skender Vakuf via Mount Vlašić.[272] The VRS report, which was filed already of the day that the incident took place, characterized the ensuing massacre as an act of 'genocide' and noted the participation of police officers in the 'liquidation'.[273] The following day, the command of the 1st Krajina Corps wrote to the VRS Main Staff regarding the incident.[274] Indeed, on that day Župljanin and Drljača attended a meeting with RS Defence Minister Subotić and others to discuss the incident, and President Karadžić himself also received information about it.[275]

Extensive subsequent investigations and trials at the ICTY uncovered the full extent of the massacre at Korićanske stijene.[276] As many as 154 Muslim detainees stemming predominantly from Trnopolje and identified as belonging to 'category C' were placed in a convoy by the RS MUP on 21 August. The convoy drove towards Travnik with the implicit understanding that the prisoners would be exchanged at the frontline for Serbs detained by the Bosnian authorities. En route, the police guarding the convoy stole any items of value possessed by the prisoners. After a stop near Skender Vakuf where the prisoners were reorganized and reboarded onto the vehicles in the convoy, the convoy continued briefly before reaching the ravine known as Korićanske stijene. The police ordered the prisoners out of the vehicles again, and made the prisoners kneel along the edge of the gorge. According to the trial judgement in *Stanišić and Župljanin*, 'at this point, a person said, "Here we exchange the dead for the dead and the living for the living". Then the shooting began.'[277] After approximately half an hour in which the police shot the victims and then threw grenades after them down into the ravine, approximately 150–200 bodies lay in the gorge.[278]

After the massacre occurred, the VRS suggested that CSB Banja Luka carry out an investigation immediately. Yet it was not until 11 September that Župljanin forwarded this order to Drljača.[279] In the meantime, the priority of the local police was to cover up the crimes committed. According to the ICTY, 'on 23 or 24 August 1992, members of the PIP from Prijedor, accompanied by Simo Drljača and Župljanin, returned to Korićanske Stijene and attempted to remove the bodies'.[280] Afterwards, Drljača dispatched those of his subordinates who had been involved to a combat area near Han Pijesak. The VRS continued to express concern about the incident, though the emphasis seemed to be on the image of the Bosnian Serbs rather than on the investigation and prosecution of those responsible. On 3 September, the 1st Krajina Corps wrote to the VRS Main Staff that the massacre 'had caused the indignation not only of citizens but also of 1st Krajina Corps soldiers. The dark stain which was created did not have support [among the Serbs], but it is very fortunate that the international public did not find out about it in more detail'.[281]

On 14 September, Drljača responded that an investigation could not be carried out because the officers who had participated in the convoy on 21 August were currently deployed on the battlefield.[282] Drljača had of course knowingly and deliberately removed the implicated police officers from the immediate reach of any investigation. On 7 October, Župljanin once again sought information from Drljača regarding the killings.[283] On 13 October, SJB Prijedor provided a small amount of additional information about the incident.[284]

In his second book, Stanišić claimed that every single crime committed in 1992 by Serb perpetrators was investigated and prosecuted in accordance with the law.[285] However, as shown in numerous trials at the ICTY, the available documentation in fact shows that no one in the RS was charged with participating in the massacre at Korićanske stijene. On the contrary, perpetrators of this and other atrocities were often rewarded and their crimes were covered up. According to the trial judgement in *Stanišić and Župljanin*, 'none of the policemen involved in the incident were held accountable for their involvement, even though the incident was widely known in the RS'.[286] Rather, 'in November 1993 and June 1994, members of the intervention squad, as well as high officials involved in the incident ... were promoted and awarded medals of bravery by [Radovan Karadžić]'.[287] Many years later, at the ICTY, Darko Mrđa, who was a member of a special police unit belonging to SJB Prijedor, admitted his guilt for the massacre.[288]

The absence of any real concern or due diligence exercised with respect to the investigation of allegations of atrocities committed by RS MUP personnel against Muslims or Croats contrasts starkly with the ministry's attitude towards crimes committed against Serbs. On 17 July, RS MUP Minister Mićo Stanišić ordered the chiefs of all CSBs to collect information on crimes committed by Croatian military and paramilitary forces by 30 July 1992.[289] 'This concentrated documentation can serve not only in military and operational, but also for political purposes.'

In 1992, the RS MUP on several occasions ordered investigations to be made of war crimes.[290] Already on 16 May, Minister Stanišić, in dealing with the issue of mandatory regular reporting within the ministry, noted that the CSBs had to report daily to the RS MUP. He specifically highlighted the need to collect and forward information on 'war crimes against Serbs. It is understood that in all cases of crimes against Serbs an investigation with a full team [will be carried out], and we especially emphasis to not omit the report of the physician, as well as adding photos, video documentation, witness statements, etc. in accordance with the Law on Criminal Procedure'. A copy of this material was to be sent to the SSUP in Belgrade.[291]

In early July, in order to facilitate the proper functioning of the ministry, Stanišić issued a document entitled 'Some Basic Principles of the Functioning of the MUP in Conditions of a War Regime'.[292] Stanišić stated that the 'state of war', appearance of new types of crime (including 'war crimes' and 'war profiteering'), the inability to regulate firearms and explosives, as well as numerous other factors justified the issuance of new guidelines.

The SNB collected materials on war crimes. Yet as with the Public Security Service, this mainly involved the collection of information about crimes committed against Serbs.²⁹³ From April 1992 until the end of that year, the SNB Sector at CSB Banja Luka pressed charges against only one individual for suspected war crimes. No mention was made in the SNB Sector's 1992 annual report of the commission of any war crimes against the non-Serb population in CSB Banja Luka's AOR.²⁹⁴

The 11 July 1992 meeting in Belgrade: Taking stock of three months of RS MUP

At the beginning of July 1992, RS MUP had officially existed for three months. Much had transpired since April, and Minister Stanišić apparently felt the need to assess the overall state of affairs in the ministry.²⁹⁵ Given the fact that much of Bosnia was a battlefield, the decision was made to convene the senior staff of the ministry including the chiefs of all CSBs and their immediate deputies for public and national security at a meeting at the villa *Bosanka* in Belgrade.²⁹⁶ The ministry later produced a detailed summary of the meeting, and its contents are worth analysing, as they provide the best snapshot of the challenges and problems which the RS MUP was facing in the eyes of its own leadership.²⁹⁷

Minister Stanišić began the meeting with an opening address and a moment of silence for RS MUP casualties, which were listed 'as approximately 80 dead and 210 wounded, excluding the Sarajevo region'. Notwithstanding the exigencies of the situation in which the ministry found itself operating, Stanišić emphasized the need to strictly follow laws and regulations pertaining to internal affairs, as well as the principles of legality and the rule of law generally.

As the chief of the largest CSB, Stojan Župljanin spoke immediately after the minister.²⁹⁸ Župljanin cast the work of the RS MUP completely in the light of a law enforcement agency which faced severe 'unconstitutional' challenges from groups and individuals, above all Muslim and Croat 'extremists', who wished to violently destroy 'the Republic's public law and order'. Although Župljanin did once use the term 'Serb extremists', the use of this term referred only to a group of armed Serbs who had not submitted to inclusion in the RS's armed forces. The threats and multitudinous actions of these groups and individuals had created an exceedingly complex security situation and to a 'psychosis of fear and general anxiety of citizens'. Župljanin's entire tone cloaked the actions of the RS MUP in legitimacy, implicitly treating the establishment of both the RS and the RS MUP as if they had been achieved on a consensual basis and without the use of massive armed force. Indicatively, Župljanin treated all attempts by Muslims and Croats to form any kind of armed formation, including police forces, as seditious and illegitimate.

The tone and of portions of Župljanin's speech were to some extent decidedly surrealistic given developments in northwestern Bosnia since April. Župljanin spoke about how an 'atmosphere of national exclusion, chauvinism and revanchism presents a great danger to the peace and security of citizens'. No mention was made of how the ARK Crisis Staff, of which Župljanin was a member and whose orders he and his subordinates faithfully carried out, had systematically carried out a campaign of persecution against Muslims and Croats during the preceding months. Župljanin observed that out of approximately 8,500 active and reserve police officers in the AOR of CSB Banja Luka, 142 were not Serbs.

In terms of the extensive involvement of the RS MUP in combat operations, Župljanin believed that the time had come to regulate this matter. According to Župljanin, 'the army demands the engagement of the complete staff [of the police], subordinating and pushing it onto to the most difficult frontlines, which should be made impossible'.

Having surveyed the security situation, Župljanin turned to commenting on the challenges facing the RS MUP. He complained that local governments were interfering improperly in the work of the police. As has been seen earlier in this chapter, Župljanin expressed resentment that large numbers of Muslims had been detained in camps in which conditions were very bad. Given the extensive police involvement in the detention and operation of such facilities, Župljanin's criticism smacked of a lack of introspection. The same applied to his call for the permissible legal detention period to be extended to twenty-one days instead of three, given that thousands of illegally detained persons were languishing for weeks or months in detention facilities operated by the RS MUP. Župljanin further highlighted extensive problems with the function of the judicial system, including the military courts and suggested remedies for improving the situation.

Following Župljanin, the Chief of CSB Doboj Andrija Bjelošević confirmed that the police in his region had also been extensively involved in combat, approximately 70 per cent of the police. Not all police officers were being released from military resubordination once areas had been 'liberated'. Bjelošević also drew attention to problems with financing of the RS MUP by the municipal civilian authorities. 'He who pays wants to give the orders.' This led to interference by municipal authorities in the work of the RS MUP. Later, Assistant Minister Vlato Kusmuk backed up Bjelošević, calling for the police to be financed exclusively through the RS's budget.

According to Bjelošević, the VRS had made a habit of bringing large numbers of prisoners to the RS MUP without any supporting documentation on the reasons for their arrest. Bjelošević suggested that the VRS should henceforth be exclusively responsible for prisoners of war, while the police would only detain persons based on violations relevant to the RS MUP. Bjelošević recognized that Serb military and police officials had committed crimes, especially theft and looting, though he portrayed these crimes as the misdeeds of individuals rather than any kind of systematic or officially tolerated misbehaviour.

Zoran Cvijetić, the head of CSB Sarajevo, agreed with Župljanin's comments and thought them applicable for all CSBs. Regarding the RS MUP's combat involvement, Cvijetić caustically commented that 'the army is in the streets directing traffic, but the police is in the trenches'. Cvijetić spoke about crimes being committed against those Serbs who remained in Sarajevo, including the families of Serb police officers. Aleksandar Pantić, who was the chief of SJB Bijeljina, spoke about the situation in northeastern Bosnia given that CSB Bijeljina remained without a chief.[299] Pantić explained that his region remained a transit area for paramilitary groups and that it had proven difficult to subdue this problem. Paramilitaries had also posed a great threat to the police in some municipalities, such as in Brčko where the 'Red Berets' had twice attacked the police station before being disarmed, but the situation seemed to be slowly improving.

After these comments at the meeting in Belgrade, Stanišić emphasized that the RS government was working on a new geographical and administrative distribution of power. This, he argued, would reduce the powers of the SAOs, and hence the aforementioned problems. The ministry was operating in difficult circumstances and because the Serbs were fighting both the Muslims and the Croats, there would continue to be times when the RS MUP would have to devote manpower to strengthening the frontlines where they were most vulnerable. Stanišić reminded the attendees of the 15 May order organizing the ministry into war units.

Notwithstanding continued combat involvement, both the RS MUP and the VRS had to work harder to prevent their employees from committing crimes and, in the case of the police, on establishing and maintaining law and order. At present, VRS members committing crimes were not punished at all, Stanišić said, emphasizing like several others the need for properly functioning military courts. The impact of politics on the RS MUP had to be reduced drastically: the RS MUP had to be a professional, not a political police force. Stanišić pointed out that the presidency had formally banned 'party activities' in wartime conditions. He called for multi-party rule after the war. In the meantime, cooperation with the VRS was essential. Ultimately, the survival of the RS MUP would depend on whether the RS itself survived.

The report on the 11 July meeting ended with a long list of conclusions. On 17 July a highly confidential document entitled 'Information on Some Aspects of Work to Date and on Impending Tasks' was circulated by the RS MUP.[300] It essentially represented a paraphrased version on the internal RS MUP minutes of the 11 July meeting in Belgrade. A copy of this document was sent to the president of the presidency and to the president of the government. The document emphasized the extensive involvement of RS MUP employees in combat activities.[301] Notwithstanding this fact, the RS MUP had to redouble its efforts at professional policing. The present situation, in which the military was 'on the streets directing traffic' while the police were 'in the trenches', was unsustainable. Similarly, the police could not operate in an environment in which

> the military and the crisis staffs, or respectively the war presidencies, are demanding the collection, or the military collects, or respectively imprisons, as much of the Muslim population as possible, leaving such undefined camps to the organs of internal affairs. The conditions in some of these camps are bad – there is no food, sometimes individuals do not respect international norms, etc.

The RS MUP was also concerned with the expulsions of the civilian population. 'The question of how to resolve the emigration of certain inhabitants, villages, etc. needs especially to be discussed because it is not in the competency of the MUP and they [the army and crisis staffs] wish to impute this to the MUP.' The document also stated that the RS MUP complained that the judicial organs were not functioning properly in much of the RS.

The 17 July 1992 document resolved to crack down on theft and looting, including such activities conducted by members of the RS MUP. The police should therefore be relieved from combat duty insofar as their presence at the frontline was not essential. War crimes also had to be investigated even if they were committed by Serbs. The RS MUP had to maintain a professional rather than a party function. The role of the RS MUP was to build the rule of law and open the path for a multi-party system.

Further demonstrating resolve to improve the functioning of the police, Stanišić two days later ordered the chiefs of all CSBs to implement the main conclusions of the 11 July meeting in Belgrade.[302] By 25 July, each CSB had to deliver a report including the following information:

(a) Problems regarding the activities of some paramilitary formations, especially if there have been cases in which crimes have been committed, large-scale destruction of public order and peace, problems regarding joint command and opposition to government authorities, positive or negative connotations on the psychological-propaganda plane, possibilities of confrontation and other relevant facts and information, as well as suggestions for means for the solution of problems. We ask for more detailed facts and information because a conclusion has been made to inform the presidency and the government confidentially.
(b) Facts and information regarding the inclusion of the police in combat activities when that is not necessary:
- number of police included in combat activities (given by month – April, May, June and July) as well as corresponding indications about the number of police officers who were in the same period included in regular activities from the competency of the MUP;
- problems regarding cooperation and command;
- number of police officers killed in combat engagements with the enemy.
(c) Problems regarding the prevention and discovery of illegal acts and their perpetrators, the functioning of mixed checkpoints, confiscation of vehicles which are suspected of (or facts exist regarding) being illegally acquired or registered, protection of borders (expert matters, combat security, etc.).
(d) Approach and competence related to the treatment and guarding of prisoners, persons who have left zones of combat activities, collective centres in which the Military brings the Muslim population without documents regarding the reasons and leave such undefined camps to the organs of internal affairs.
(e) Work of military judicial organs (questions under points d and e will be raised at the meeting with the judicial organs, which are also being prepared).
(f) Exchange of information – supply the number of reports given to the Military and to the organs of military security.
(g) Other questions and suggestions for the solution of problems that have emerged.[303]

All of this looked impressive on paper, and Stanišić as minister doubtless had a vested interest in improving the functioning of the RS MUP. However, the documents issued by the RS MUP omitted any strong findings or remedies regarding the very large number of crimes which RS MUP personnel had committed since the outset of the war against the Muslim and Croat civilian population. Notwithstanding the claims made in the 17 July document and the orders issued by Stanišić two days later, the RS MUP also continued during this period to operate and engage in the operation of detention centres and in the implementation of operations to expel the non-Serb population of the RS. Those actions which the RS MUP did undertake, for example against paramilitary formations, were explicitly undertaken in order to assert the control of the RS authorities over the territory of the RS.

Disciplinary measures in the RS MUP

Given that Minister Stanišić and others in the RS MUP's leadership acknowledged that there had been problems with criminal conduct in the ranks of the police, it is logical to ask what the ministry did to discipline those who had violated the law. Here it bears emphasizing that the RS MUP as the main organ of law enforcement in Republika Srpska in principle needed to lead by example. After all, if a large number of police officers could commit crimes and get away with it, what hope would there be for the rule of law?

Although Stanišić stated in several orders that his subordinates would be held responsible for carrying out his orders, and also expressed an awareness that RS MUP employees had been involved in the commission of illegal acts such as theft and plunder, no disciplinary committees or courts were established.[304] Instead, on 23 July 1992, Stanišić issued a strictly confidential order addressing this issue. Stanišić ordered his subordinates to:

1. take legal steps to remove from our ranks and put at the disposal of the VRS all employees of the MUP who have committed criminal acts (except political and verbal misdemeanours) earlier or since the commencement of combat activities or, respectively, the formation of the MUP of the Serbian Republic of Bosnia and Herzegovina;
2. the chiefs of administrations at the seat, the Commander of the Police Detachment and the chiefs of the CSBs are responsible for implementing the order;
3. provide (by 31 July 1992) information on measures taken, stating the concrete number of employees who have been dismissed, the types of criminal acts that they have committed, etc.[305]

On 24 July 1992, a paraphrased version of the order was sent to the chiefs of all CSBs.[306] In northwestern Bosnia, Župljanin forwarded the order to his subordinate

SJBs on 29 July 1992, and in Prijedor Drljača circulated the order the following day.[307] And in the Sarajevo region, indications exist that several dozen reserve police officers faced disciplinary proceedings as a result of Stanišić's order.[308]

As is implicit in Stanišić's order, the RS Law on Internal Affairs gave him the power to maintain discipline in the ministry. The main tool for doing so was to appoint internal disciplinary prosecutors pursuant to Article 113.[309] These prosecutors could, at the behest of the minister or an appropriate official authorized by him, carry out necessary investigations and gather evidence necessary for disciplinary procedures, with the list of serious violations listed in the law's following article.[310] The prosecutors could then prosecute these cases in front of a disciplinary committee. Article 118 mandated the temporary suspension of employees from duties when disciplinary or criminal proceedings have been instituted against them if there were sufficient grounds to conclude that, regarding the nature of criminal act or gross misconduct, and the circumstances under which they have been committed, it would be harmful to the interest of the service that an employee continue to perform duties or stay in the ministry.

Pursuant to the Law on Internal Affairs, CSB Banja Luka appointed disciplinary prosecutors in July 1992.[311] However, the ICTY found no evidence that Župljanin disciplined any of his subordinates in 1992 for infractions or crimes committed against non-Serbs, including those crimes committed by the special police of CSB Banja Luka.

> He created a unit, the Banja Luka CSB Special Police Detachment, which he used to assist other Serb Forces in the takeovers of the ARK Municipalities. He was fully aware of and took part in the unlawful arrest of non-Serbs and their forcible removal. He failed to launch criminal investigations and discipline his subordinates who had committed crimes against non-Serbs, thus creating a climate of impunity which only increased the commission of crimes against non-Serbs.[312]

According to the trial chamber in *Stanišić and Župljanin*, Stanišić did in the course of the second half of 1992 initiate some form of disciplinary action against some police officials such as Simo Drljača, the chief of SJB Prijedor, and Malko Koroman, the chief of SJB Pale.[313] However, the trial chamber found that although Stanišić's orders regarding disciplinary proceedings had in some cases resulted in disciplinary proceedings against members of the RS MUP, such proceedings focused on issues such as professional conduct and minor crimes – not war crimes or crimes against humanity. Overall, the trial chamber found that 'Stanišić violated his professional obligation to protect and safeguard the civilian population in the territories under their control'.[314]

RS Prime Minister Đerić on several occasions pressed Stanišić and the VRS to cooperate more efficiently.[315] This led to a meeting on 27 July where Stanišić admitted that the RS MUP had at the outset of the war accepted anyone into the ranks of the police, regardless of qualifications. And approximately a month later, Stanišić spoke of the infiltration of the RS MUP by 'individuals whose criminal and other anti-social behaviour sullies the reputation of the MUP'.[316] Although the ministry believed that it had solved the problem of discipline by transferring problematic police officers to the VRS, this clearly did not address the underlying problem by the end of 1992. There was also a certain irony regarding the transfer of bad police to VRS, given that Stanišić had himself on 11 July stated that military courts were not functioning properly and that those arrested for crimes were merely returned to their units.

Moreover, the entire policy of transferring problematic police officers to the army was also curious because the RS MUP had information that some VRS units were themselves engaged in criminal or other inappropriate behaviour.[317] The ministry's issuance of a new set of rules on disciplinary responsibility during wartime, while a useful and necessary step, also could not by itself eliminate the issues confronting the ministry.[318]

Conclusion

From August until the end of the year, the RS MUP did in some respects succeed in consolidating itself. The ministry enacted rules and regulations – such as issuing a new rulebook in September 1992 based on the 1990 SRBiH MUP rulebook. Documentation from the last quarter of the year suggests that Minister Stanišić and his immediate subordinates made their authority felt to a greater degree, helped in part by a concomitant consolidation of power by the other RS authorities over, or at the expense of, the SAOs and crisis staffs which had proved useful during the first half of the year.[319] That having been said, it is important not to succumb to a false dichotomy, where the crisis staffs and the police somehow from April 1992 had operated as separate and at times mutually antagonistic entities. It must always be remembered that the police chiefs in all Bosnian Serb municipalities were *ex officio* members of the crisis staffs. While it is possible to draw some general conclusions about the relationship between the police and the crisis staffs, it would also be accurate to state that there were almost as many different relationships between the crisis staffs and the police as there were crisis staffs.

Notwithstanding the consolidation of the ministry, tensions between the government and Stanišić continued to increase, leading eventually to his resignation at the end of the year. At the 22nd Session of the Assembly in late November the Deputy Prime Minister of the RS government, Milan Trbojević, complained about the inability or unwillingness – and even participation – of the RS police to stop what he described as the 'plundering' of the RS.[320]

In an interview given at the end of July 1992, Minister Stanišić gave perhaps his most detailed public self-evaluation of his tenure in an interview with the RS newspaper *Javnost*.[321] In the interview, Stanišić wanted 'to emphasise that I am really satisfied with the manner in which the Ministry of Internal Affairs functions now. I am satisfied with our level of organisation, and especially with the dedication and the commitment of all members of our service to, with their maximum personal contribution, create that for which the entire Serb nation is now fighting'. Stanišić stated that the service was working properly as 'one centralised organ'. To date, all meetings of the Ministry's Steering Council (*kolegij*), including assistant ministers, under-secretaries and chiefs of the CSBs, had always met in its full composition.

Speaking of his authority within the ministry, Stanišić stated:

> In addition, it has not occurred yet that anyone of the implementers on the entire territory of Republika Srpska has turned a deaf ear to any of my orders, issued of course in accordance with the law. I would also like to emphasise that we have a very responsible approach towards the behaviour of members of our services, more specifically towards eventual lapses in certain activities, or something that they are not allowed to do. I think that this is the only ministry, in this period, in which individual employees have been excluded from its ranks. And this was not because they did something against Serbian interests ... but rather precisely because they had undertaken certain activities succumbing to base instincts, which is really incompatible with membership in our service. ... Such examples are rare, but they are significant for us. We want a ministry in whose composition it is impossible to find even one person who turns a deaf ear to the legal norms of Republika Srpska.

Mićo Stanišić noted that the police had borne the burden of combat until the formation of the VRS, but that the RS MUP and the VRS had cooperated since the latter's establishment.[322] Stanišić played down any notion of conflict of responsibilities between the RS MUP and the VRS.

Asked about war profiteering, crime and looting, Stanišić admitted that such problems were present on the territory of the RS.[323] However, Stanišić argued that the rate of such incidents was exaggerated as part of a propagandistic 'special war' prosecuted by the enemy.[324] The largest and most serious cases had taken place at the outset of the war, 'when there was a legal "vacuum"'. Stanišić stated that the rate of solved crimes in the RS was 'enviable'. 'As such, I think that the per cent of criminal acts, at this moment, has been reduced to an understandable number, more precisely a number which is present in all civilised countries.' Asked to provide figures on how many war profiteers had been caught, Stanišić refused to comment, citing the ongoing nature of investigations. Referring to the case of a large number of automobiles stolen from the factory TAS at Vogošća near Sarajevo, Stanišić expressed hope that he would soon deliver a report to the RS Assembly.[325] Minister Stanišić made no mention at all of any investigations into atrocities committed against Muslim and Croat civilians.

Similarly, at the 22nd Session of the RS Assembly on 23 November 1992, Stanišić rebuffed criticism of the presence of criminal elements in the reserve police. According to Stanišić, the RS MUP had not enjoyed the luxury of being selective at the outset of its existence. The police 'took thieves and criminals, because, please, not a single doctor of science lifted a rifle to defend his country, not a single intellectual, this was our priority, we had good intentions, maybe I was mistaken in this'.[326]

Chapter 4

OF RED BERETS AND PLAUSIBLE DENIABILITY: SERBIA'S SUPPORT FOR THE RS MUP

Although there was no ethnic majority in Yugoslavia, the Serbs constituted the largest group. Political developments between November 1990 and April 1992 demonstrated that most Bosnian Serbs strongly desired to remain part of Yugoslavia and hence opposed the secession of Bosnia and Herzegovina. The shrill propagandistic exploitation of Second World War era atrocities and genocide against Serbs created and nurtured an existential fear of imminent demise if Serbs were to be relegated to the position of a minority in a new state dominated by other ethnicities. At the same time, these fears provided essential oxygen to the regime of Serbian President Slobodan Milošević, who in the midst of economic and state crisis positioned himself as the great leader who alone could save the nation from humiliation and possible extinction.[1]

Milošević could in Croatia and Bosnia to a significant extent rely upon the Yugoslav People's Army to enforce the borders of the country and combat secession. Yet though the JNA from 1990 to 1992 slowly shed its Yugoslav ideology in favour of a new Serbian nationalist mission, Milošević, like the Bosnian Serbs, did not fully trust the JNA.[2] Moreover, keen to avoid accusations of stoking warfare in neighbouring republics, Milošević's strategy relied on portraying Croatia in particular as an aggressive (and fascist) separatist, and Serbia as the defensive preserver of Yugoslav statehood and sovereignty. At the same time, Milošević needed to ensure that Serbs in Croatia and Bosnia could seize and hold large portions of – preferably contiguous – territory before Croatia and Bosnia could assert their own sovereignty. If successful, these new Serb-controlled entities could at some future point merge with Serbia (including of course both Kosovo and Vojvodina, stripped of their autonomy in 1990) and a docile Montenegro. Maintaining this poise required plausible deniability with respect to the instigation and spread of violence and atrocities in Croatia and Bosnia. For Milošević and his most trusted advisors, this was a job for the State Security Service of Serbia.

This chapter will focus on the assistance provided by Serbia to the Bosnian Serbs before and after the establishment of the RS MUP. This assistance took as its point of departure the precedent established by the Serbian State Security's role in organizing and mobilizing the Croatian Serbs in 1990 and 1991. Already in July 1990, a number of Serb police officers from Knin sent an open letter to Petar

Gračanin, the Yugoslav federal secretary for internal affairs, informing him that they did not wish to serve in the police of Croatia.[3] As part of the model of the Serb Autonomous Areas, Croatia provided the successful test case of a template subsequently deployed in Bosnia – and in the case of select elements of policing and use of paramilitary forces, also years later in Kosovo. The chapter hence starts with a brief overview of the role of the Serbian State Security Service in Croatia. Thereafter, the narrative will move to an analysis of Serbia's role with respect to policing in Bosnia from 1991 until the end of 1992. Although units affiliated with the Serbian State Security Service continued to participate in several operations until the end of the Bosnian war, their impact was felt most decisively in 1992. In addition to extensively supporting the RS MUP, the available documentation demonstrates that employees of the State Security Service of Serbia not only possessed knowledge of the commission of atrocities by the RS MUP and Serb paramilitary groups, but also themselves directly committed war crimes and crimes against humanity.

The history and structure of the special police unit(s) of the Serbian State Security Service in the 1990s are clouded in obscurity, to a significant extent the deliberate result of conspiratorial steps taken to keep the existence, identity and deployment of such units concealed.[4] The covert nature of these units was so extensive that even the Yugoslav military – the JNA, and later the VJ – appears not to have been briefed about the existence and nature of these units. However, thanks to investigations and trials at the ICTY, particularly the trial and retrial of Jovica Stanišić, the head of the Service during most of the 1990s, and his subordinate Franko 'Frenki' Simatović, much of the Serbian State Security Service's role can be recounted and analysed.

In addition to the cooperation between the MUP of Serbia and the RS MUP, this chapter also covers another important element. As has been seen in previous chapters, the leadership of the RS and the RS MUP, particularly in the first months of the conflict in northern and eastern Bosnia, permitted a rampage of paramilitary units from Serbia. These units arrived in Bosnia, sometimes directly from Serbia, sometimes through Croatia, and were often affiliated with political parties in Serbia such as Vojislav Šešelj's Serb Radical Party, and generally enjoyed if not the direct support of the Serbian state, then at least a tacit *carte blanche* to cross the border and wreak havoc in Croatia and Bosnia. But that permissiveness had its limits with respects to the conduct of these units when they crossed the Danube, Sava or Drina rivers back into Serbia. Generally speaking, these paramilitary groups could bring home the spoils of war with few if any questions asked about the atrocities that had been committed in the course of their sojourn in Croatia and Bosnia. However, the MUP of Serbia and the Serbian State Security Service made sure that these groups checked their weapons and ammunition at the border and kept them under close surveillance lest they felt tempted to engage in problematic political activities against the Milošević regime or foment violence in ethnically mixed areas of the Federal Republic of Yugoslavia.

The SDB/RDB, the training of trainers and special units in Croatia and Bosnia

As seen in Chapter 1, as Croatia moved towards secession in 1990 and 1991, the Croatian Serbs clung to Serbia and Yugoslavia. On 26 February 1991, the Serbs in eastern Croatia convened a 'Serb National Council' and passed a 'Declaration on the Sovereign Autonomy of the Serb Nation of Slavonia, Baranja and Western Syrmia'.[5] The Declaration held the Serbs of this region to be 'an inseparable part of the sovereign Serb nation which lives in Yugoslavia'. The final paragraph of the Declaration stated:

> The sovereign Serb autonomy of Slavonia, Baranja and Western Syrmia exists and acts within the current Republic of Croatia only on the condition that Yugoslavia exists as a joint state. Insofar as Yugoslavia ceases to exist or is reformed into a gathering of independent states, this autonomy will continue to exist as part of the mother state [*matična država*] of the Serb nation.

In the meantime, Milošević told local politicians in Serbia that the Serbian government was taking relevant security measures, in order that 'we can defend the interests of the republic, and indeed also the interests of the Serb nation outside Serbia'.[6]

Weeks later, on 18 March 1991, the SAO Krajina Assembly passed a decision declaring that federal regulations and regulations of the SAO Krajina would be applied on the territory of the SAO Krajina. Legal acts of the Republic of Croatia would be applied only insofar as they did not conflict with either legal acts of the federal Yugoslav state or the SAO Krajina.[7] On the same day, the Statute of the SAO Krajina was changed to reflect a cutting of ties with Croatia.[8] Two weeks later, on 1 April, the Executive Council of the Assembly of the SAO Krajina unilaterally decided to unite the SAO Krajina with the Republic of Serbia.[9] On the same day, Milan Babić, the president of the Executive Council of the SAO Krajina, demanded that the government of Serbia order the MUP of the Republic of Serbia to extend 'technical and personnel assistance' to the SUP of the SAO Krajina.[10]

At the end of April, the SAO Krajina Assembly decided to hold a referendum on joining the SAO Krajina to the Republic of Serbia, and on staying in Yugoslavia with 'Serbia, Montenegro and others who wish to preserve Yugoslavia'.[11] On that date, the Assembly also elected Milan Babić as the president of the Executive Council of the SAO Krajina.[12] Later, the Law on the Application of the Legal Regulations of the Republic of Serbia on the Territory of the Serb Autonomous District of Krajina went into effect.[13]

The referendum was held on 12 May 1991 and resulted in a large majority favouring remaining in Yugoslavia.[14] The merger was, however, not implemented because the international costs for Serbia of effectuating a merger were prohibitive. Similar later initiatives by both the Croatian and Bosnian Serbs foundered on the rocks of the same problem: while Milošević – at disastrous cost for his own economy – bankrolled and extensively supported both the RSK and the RS, he consistently remained unwilling to go through with any kind of formal annexation or merger of rump Yugoslavia and Serb-controlled entities in Croatia and Bosnia. As late as 23 February 1994, President Milan Martić of the RSK wrote to Mirko Marjanović, who had been given the mandate to form the next government in Serbia, expressing Martić's desire for a unified state.[15]

On 20 May 1991, Mihalj Kertes, an adviser of the President of Serbia, and Radovan Pankov, the deputy president of the Assembly of the Republic of Serbia, held a meeting with representatives of Serbs from Slavonia in Bačka Palanka in Vojvodina. Goran Hadžić was among the participants. At the meeting, Kertes demanded that the Slavonian Serbs should cease seeking assistance from 'self-proclaimed helpers' and stated that the purpose of the meeting was to achieve complete agreement about joint activities.[16] Hadžić stated that he was not undertaking anything on his own initiative, but was rather doing everything in consultation with people from Belgrade and Novi Sad. However, given the number of people present at the meeting, Hadžić did not wish to provide the names of these individuals.[17] Kertes recommended that a coordinating body be formed among the Serbs from Slavonia in order to avoid disputes and misunderstandings; the participants accepted this proposal.[18] Kertes further stated that he was aware that the lack of weapons was the biggest problem, and therefore asked for the participants to tell him what their respective villages needed. 'This was also done so that at the end of the meeting Kertes had lists with the necessary weapons for the villages, which he took with him to Belgrade. At the very end of his presentation, Kertes stated that the position of Serbia was unambiguous – that all Serbs should live in one state, regardless of what it is called.'[19]

While the trial of Milošević in particular laid bare the extent of Serbian financial, military and police assistance to first the Croatian Serbs and later the Bosnian Serbs, perhaps the most interesting manifestation of Serbia's assistance was the deployment of police instructors to the Krajina region of Croatia. A programme of 'training the trainers' for other police units evolved into the nucleus of what would later become the notorious Unit of Special Operations (*Jedinica za specijalne operacije*, JSO) of the RDB in Serbia. 'The Unit', as it was colloquially known, existed under several different names but saw action throughout the battlefields of Croatia and Bosnia from 1991 to 1995.[20]

The humble beginnings of the JSO were located in the isolated settlement of Golubić near Knin. Although some uncertainty surrounds the exact date when Golubić began to operate as a training facility, Franko Simatović many years later gave a speech in the presence of Milošević in which Simatović stated that the JSO was established on 4 May 1991.[21] This may well refer to the approximate period in which personnel from the SDB of Serbia began to conduct training, 'predominantly military in character', in Golubić, but the nascent SAO Krajina MUP under Milan Martić had used the facility since August 1990.[22] Indeed, according to Milan Babić, personnel from Golubić had participated in the August 1990 'Log Revolution'.

By the spring of 1991 at the latest, training at Golubić was (also) provided by a number of persons from outside the RSK, including a Serb mercenary and émigré from Australia, Danijel Snedden (aka Dragan Vasiljković, Captain Dragan) and Simatović affiliated with the State Security Service of Serbia.[23] Simatović was involved in running the training centre for the police established at Golubić, and his role there appears to have been a leading one, at least until he came into conflict with Milan Martić.[24] In a later interview, Vasiljković claimed to have been at Golubić as early as October 1990.[25]

In the personnel file of one of the graduates of the Golubić training centre, Borjan Vučković, the unit trained at Golubić was referred to as the 'Unit for Special Purposes of the RDB of MUP Serbia'.[26] The men trained at Golubić were colloquially referred to as 'knindže', an amalgam of the toponym Knin and the term 'ninja'.[27] At a press conference in August 1991, Milan Martić acknowledged the assistance of 'Captain Dragan'.[28] During the summer of 1991, the special units and State Security Service of the SAO Krajina received material assistance from the MUP of Serbia. This included weapons,[29] communications equipment as well as motor vehicles.[30] According to Milan Babić, the SDB funded Golubić.[31]

Out of the modest beginnings of Golubić and later similar training centres in Croatia and Bosnia sprouted the seeds of a number of Serb special police and paramilitary units. By training hundreds of men, many of whom would themselves become trainers and deploy to other municipalities and regions, the people behind Golubić contributed to the spread of armed conflict.[32] The key actors included a number of people who came to play particularly notorious roles in the Bosnian war: Radojica Božović, Vaso Mijović, Dragan 'Fića' Filipović, Zoran Rajić, Žika Ivanović (aka Žika Crnogorac), Dragan Pupovac, Zvezdan Jovanović and Milorad Ulemek 'Legija'.[33] Equally usefully from the point of view of the SDB, the graduates of Golubić combined plausible deniability for Belgrade with a covert network that could keep the Serbian leadership apprised of events in Croatia and Bosnia.[34] And, as has been seen with respect to Bosnia, Belgrade's thirst for intelligence applied also to the internal deliberations of the Bosnian Serb police and government, in order to ensure some modicum of control.

After Golubić closed in approximately August 1991, some of the more elite graduates affiliated with the SDB relocated to a new facility at Ležimir in the Fruška Gora area of Vojvodina. As of December 1991, MUP Serbia had a special police unit at Ležimir, encompassing a number of those who had trained at Golubić, and with Živojin Ivanović listed as their commander.[35] Others were based at a camp called Pajzoš at Ilok on the Serbian-Croatian border. The unit's existence was still conspirative, and the regular police in the vicinity were not informed about it. At the same time, these elite members no longer referred to themselves as 'knindže' or 'Martić's men', but instead designated themselves as 'red berets'.[36] This moniker came to gain extreme notoriety. Training camps subsequently emerged at Mount Ozren near Doboj in April 1992, at Skelani in eastern Bosnia in June 1992, at Mount Tara in Serbia in late 1992 and in Bratunac in early 1993.[37] Later, in the summer of 1993, the special unit(s) of MUP Serbia appear to have undergone a transformation and formalization. This development involved the establishment of a Unit for Anti-Terrorist Actions (*Jedinica za antiteroristička dejstva*, JATD). According to the available documentation on the personnel of the special units of MUP Serbia, the JATD existed at least since Minister Zoran Sokolović signed a document on the systematization of work tasks in the JATD on 4 August 1993.[38]

After completing training, a number of members of this unit participated in combat in various areas of the RSK before then transferring to Bosnia and Herzegovina, where they again engaged in combat activities in municipalities such as Doboj and Bosanski Šamac.[39] The autobiographies of members such as Davor Subotić and Dragan Oluić point to the conclusion that the Unit for Special Purposes (*Jedinica za specijalne namjene*, JPN) of the SAO Krajina or RSK MUP, respectively, either was a MUP Serbia unit since its inception or became so by February 1992, when most or all of the unit's members committed short autobiographies to paper.[40] When operating in the RSK or the RS, the unit's members used identification papers and insignia of local units in order to conceal their true affiliation.

The Serbian State Security Service in Bosnia in 1992

The Serbian State Security Service exhibited two kinds of involvement in the Bosnian war: support or tolerance of paramilitary units and the RS MUP, and direct operation of their own units, some of whom integrated locals into these units.[41] Hence, as seen in Chapter 2, particularly in the northeastern and eastern Bosnian municipalities bordering Serbia, paramilitary groups such as the Serb Voluntary Guard of Željko Ražnatović 'Arkan' freely operated and contributed to the Serbian seizure of power. This group, closely affiliated with the RDB, played a particularly key role in taking over Bijeljina and Zvornik, two municipalities linking Serbia with the nascent Republika Srpska. As the war spread across Bosnia, units sponsored or created by the RDB also expanded their reach, operating during the Bosnian war from Bihać in the northwest and in municipalities as diverse as Teslić, Doboj, Sanski Most, Sarajevo, Bosanski Šamac, Brčko, Višegrad and Skelani. And while tensions and even armed skirmishes did at times erupt between the 'red berets' and the RS MUP, there can be no doubt that total agreement existed regarding the primary goal of establishing an ethnically homogeneous Republika Srpska at the expense of a multi-ethnic Bosnia. In July 1992, for instance, a report from SJB Teslić noted that the police in the municipality had been advised to call upon the 'red berets' who had operated in nearby Doboj, 'because they are an example of how a Serb state is created'.[42] Serb paramilitary forces tolerated or operated by the Serbian State Security Service contributed to the Bosnian Serb leadership's quest to implement their strategic goals from May 1992.

As regards Ražnatović and his paramilitary unit, the origins of his association with the MUP are to be found in his role as an émigré and career criminal who at times also acted as a hired gun in the Yugoslav State Security Service's decades-long 'war' with the 'hostile emigration', in particular the Croat diaspora.[43] Despite his association with the Serbian cause, sections of federal Yugoslav military intelligence viewed Ražnatović as an essentially criminal phenomenon, whose primary interests were to increase his own popularity among Serbs and to amass large quantities of wealth through theft, smuggling and the sale of 'ranks' to politicians and businessmen.[44] The behaviour of Ražnatović and his men met with criticism by the military, and Ražnatović was involved in physical altercations with members of the military.[45] Yet Arkan's repurposing of parts of the *Delije* fan club in the Serb Volunteer Guard as a paramilitary unit that could be deployed in Croatia and Bosnia was a welcome development to the Milošević regime. After all, Milošević had with good reason feared that football hooligans could be used to topple him in 1991. Much better to have them put their aggressive energy to use outside of Serbia's border for the 'patriotic' cause. Hence, in August 1991, the USDB Belgrade reported:

> Željko Ražnatović – Arkan has organized a group of his followers, the so-called Serb Volunteer Guard with the goal to unify in Belgrade all patriotically oriented persons in order to offer help to Serbs on the threatened territories of Croatia. The aforementioned persons, allegedly, have membership cards, are armed with automatic weapons Heckler-Koch, which Arkan supplies them with and train regularly at the stadium of the football club Red Star. ... Connected to this, Arkan has several times been in the area of Osijek with his group and had several 'successful' actions.[46]

As space does not allow for an extensive examination of all the operations of the SDB/RDB in Bosnia, this chapter will use the case of the municipality of Bosanski Šamac to illustrate how the Serbian State Security Service assisted the Bosnian Serb authorities in taking over a municipality not immediately bordering Serbia.[47] Like Brčko, another municipality where paramilitary forces became directly involved in the takeover, Bosanski Šamac was located on the Sava River immediately across from Croatia. In the second week of April Blagoje Simić, a leading SDS official in the municipality announced that the municipality would be split ethnically, with the Serbs retaining control over the town of Bosanski Šamac. Around this time, members of the Serbian State Security Service who had trained at Pajzoš arrived in the municipality and linked up with JNA and RS MUP personnel in a tactical group known as TG-17. Prior to their arrival, they had received a briefing from Franko Simatović, who had been involved in creating the special operations units of the Serbian SDB.[48] Two SDB operatives known as Dragan Đorđević 'Crni' and Slobodan Miljković 'Lugar' commanded units within TG-17, with the groups taking a variety of names, including the 'Grey Wolves' (*Sivi vukovi*).[49] TG-17 also included in its ranks paramilitary members of the Serb Radical Party (SRS).[50]

In coordination with the Serb Municipal Crisis Staff, TG-17 proceeded on 16–17 April to take control of Bosanski Šamac, even though this meant the displacement of most of the municipality's thousands of Croats and Muslims.[51] While the joint police and military takeover occurred rapidly and without significant resistance from local Croats and Muslims, this did not dissuade the members of TG-17 from committing numerous atrocities during and after their operation. In addition to numerous detentions, beatings and killings of civilians, non-Serbs were forcibly displaced or deported from the municipality, resulting in the establishment of an ethnically homogeneous 'Serbian municipality'. 'Even the local Serbs and troops were afraid' of the paramilitaries from Serbia.[52]

In November 1992, Stevan Todorović, the chief of SJB (Bosanski) Šamac, was questioned by the RS MUP regarding recent events in that municipality. The report filed by the RS MUP stated that the Main Board of the SDS in Bosanski Šamac had, prior to the war, suggested that the then commander of TG-17, Stevan Nikolić, could use his SDS and other connections with MUP Serbia. This resulted in the involvement 'of Dragan Đorđević called Crni and Srećko Radovanović called Debeli with a group of about 30 people from the Federal Republic of Yugoslavia' in the conflict in the municipality.[53] Another eighteen 'volunteers' from Bosanski Šamac who had received training at Ilok joined this group. The report further indicated that several persons of Croat and Muslim nationality who were detained had been killed in the municipality during the summer of 1992, including by Slobodan Miljković 'Lugar' and two other unidentified men who were in the group commanded by 'Crni'.

Only in August was 'Crni' arrested, and his group left Bosanski Šamac for Serbia shortly thereafter. However, at that point, the War Presidency of Bosanski Šamac appealed directly to MUP Serbia, with the support of the VRS, arguing that 'Crni's' group was needed to help in combat operations in Orašje municipality. MUP Serbia thereupon allowed the group of 'volunteers' commanded by 'Crni' to return to Bosanski Šamac, a decision that was confirmed by the Bosanski Šamac War Presidency on 4 October 1992. The RS MUP's report stated that the cooperation between the War Presidency of Bosanski Šamac with volunteers provided by MUP Serbia was further condoned by the VRS, who had already in the summer of 1992 appointed 'Crni' as the head of the Posavska Brigade of the Eastern Bosnia Corps.

In July 1993, Slobodan Miljković 'Lugar' claimed that he had been trained by the RDB of MUP Serbia.[54] In December 1993, CRDB Kragujevac proposed that Miljković be placed under operational treatment, which entailed the formalization of surveillance and other measures of the RDB against Miljković.[55] The request of CRDB Kragujevac demonstrated an awareness that Miljković had a criminal past and that he had spent time as a paramilitary in Eastern Slavonia and Bosanski Šamac. Although CRDB Kragujevac credited Miljković for contributing to the 'liberation' of Bosanski Šamac, it was noted that Miljković had removed himself and his men from the command structure of the VRS and had demonstrated negative behaviour. In Kragujevac, Miljković had also provoked incidents with local inhabitants and with the police. Miljković and his group were as of December 1993 described as being under the control of the SRS, and their possible violent or terrorist intentions towards the government in Serbia were the main reason for placing him under operational treatment.[56] In September 1993, CRDB Kragujevac had also expressed concern about indications that Miljković and his group were planning to go to Kosovo to fight against 'Albanian extremists and secessionists'.[57]

Operational Action Tomson

Given the overwhelming focus on nationalism and 'Great(er) Serbia' in both the popular and research literature on the collapse of Yugoslavia, insufficient attention has hitherto been paid to fissures and disagreements within the Milošević regime in the period from approximately 1990 to 1992. It must be recalled that during this period, even as he worked successfully to consolidate his power, Milošević and his allies still had to contend with the remnants of a federal state, evident not just in the JNA but also in the Federal Secretariat for Internal Affairs (SSUP).[58]

A particularly interesting aspect of the Serbian State Security Service's role in Croatia and later Bosnia was the apprehension and caution informing the Service's relationship with volatile actors. It should be kept in mind that Milošević's hold on power was still tenuous in the spring of 1991 – the single largest anti-Milošević protests until the late summer of 2000 took place in March 1991. Prior to his arrival at Golubić near Knin, Vasiljković had been placed under electronic surveillance by a decision of Minister Bogdanović dated 3 April 1991.[59] This surveillance was carried out by the Second Department of USDB Belgrade, where Franko Simatović worked at the time. A surveillance report of 12 April, which was signed by Dragan Filipović, noted Vasiljković's contacts with, among others, Nikola Šainović of the Serbian government. The report also stated that Vasiljković was planning to return to 'Krajina', where he had earlier been, and that Šainović had facilitated a meeting between Vasiljković and the Minister of Internal Affairs Radmilo Bogdanović. Vasiljković had arrived in Yugoslavia at the end of October 1990, and the SDB of Serbia had been concerned about his contacts with the Srpski Pokret Obnove (SPO), which was allegedly planning to forcibly remove Milošević from power.[60]

This accusation of an association between Vasiljković and the SPO was important, as the SPO and its leader Vuk Drašković had been the vanguard of the March 1991 protests in Belgrade against the Milošević government. On 15 August, Minister Sokolović renewed the authorization for wiretapping of Dragan Vasiljković, citing his links to foreign intelligence services and the SPO.[61] A request for renewed wiretapping of Vasiljković was made in November 1991.[62] This proposal recalled Vasiljković's contacts with the SPO regarding among other things 'the formation and arming of paramilitary formations, with the goal of their engagement in the resolution of political conflicts in the country'.[63] The proposal demonstrated awareness of Vasiljković's involvement in armed conflict in Croatia, and suggested that the surveillance be permanent. Vasiljković during this period also operated the 'Captain Dragan Fund', an ostensibly humanitarian nongovernmental organization that assisted victims of the war in Croatia but simultaneously also recruited men to join Serb forces in Croatia.[64] To summarize, the Milošević regime through the SDB used Vasiljković to arm and train Serb insurrectionists in Croatia – or at the very least tolerated him doing so – but also used the SDB to monitor any of his activities that could potentially destabilize the regime. The SDB also expressed concern about Vasiljković's knowledge of or involvement with weapons transports and foreign intelligence services.[65]

Notwithstanding the ever-present tensions between centralism and regional or national identities within the Yugoslav State Security Service, it remained the case that the Serbian State Security Service at the outset of the 1990s as part of its mandate was still charged with monitoring Serb nationalists as one of many forms of anticonstitutional extremism. As of 1990, these nationalists continued to be counted among the 'internal enemies' of the Yugoslav state who formed the ambit for the Third Administration of the SDB. The year 1990 did not feature any armed conflicts in the SFRJ but it was also a year in which the security situation throughout the country worsened dramatically, and this is reflected in the SDB's annual report. The SDB's work on extremism included those Serbs who harboured strong affinities for the nationalist ideology of the royalist Chetnik movement from the Second World War. According to the SDB, Serb nationalists had

> abused the process of democratization and the establishment of the multiparty system in the Republic of Serbia. It is characteristic for this group of extremists in 1990 that as a constitutive part of their ideological orientation they have adopted a pro-Chetnik stance [*pročetništvo*] [...]. This mentioned form of extremism manifests itself through the advocacy of liquidating political opponents, the forcible reshaping of borders in Yugoslavia, genocide against members of other nations, settlings of accounts with communists and veterans [*borci*], the restoration of monarchy and a total rupture with all the legacies of the postwar period.[66]

Nor were such sentiments confined merely to verbal expression, as an increase in violent physical altercations showed. The SDB noted that 'social circumstances' had made it significantly more difficult to deal with Serb extremism.

The 1990 report also noted increases in 'Muslim extremism', a significant concern given the number of Muslims living in Serbia. Confronting this phenomenon had become more difficult because of changes in Bosnia and Herzegovina. Specifically, the Muslim Party of Democratic Action (SDA) was among the victors in the November 1990 elections in Bosnia and Herzegovina and was hence a part of the government in that republic.[67]

The programmatic orientation for 1991 was 'based on the security evaluation and on relations in Yugoslavia and more broadly' and was designed to enable the SDB to perform its job as effectively as possible.[68] The SDB foresaw a particular need to focus on stabilizing the situation in Kosovo.[69]

Of particular concern to the SDB was the formation of armed groups. Although no annual report is available for the entire SDB for 1991, an annual report for the USDB Belgrade, the SDB centre covering the capital, exists.[70] Given that the USDB Belgrade was the most important office of the SDB outside of headquarters, its annual report provides some insight on the work of the SDB as a whole in 1991. The report shows that the SDB worked intensively on tracking the formation of 'party armies' (*stranačke vojske*), i.e. paramilitary groups established by newly emerging political parties, especially those of Serbian nationalist orientation.[71] Vuk Drašković, the Serb Movement of Renewal (SPO) and the Serb Guard

(*Srpska garda*) were mentioned, as was the SRS. The USDB Belgrade collected information concerning the situation in Croatia both from refugees and from volunteers returning from Croatia.[72]

On 23 July 1991, the Minister of Internal Affairs of Serbia Zoran Sokolović remarked that

> the dramatic development of the situation in the country has significantly contributed to various attempts to organize and arm certain groups and has threatened the normal functioning of institutions of the legal state [*pravna država*] in the Republic of Serbia as well. Already, various forms and levels of anti-constitutional and illegal organizations of party, ethnic, and other armed groups are active semi-legally and illegally. The activities which individual parties are undertaking in opposition to the law with respect to recruiting and arming 'volunteers' are directly aimed at the undermining and destruction of the constitutional order in Serbia, the breaking up of the JNA and the weakening of the defensive ability of the Republic.[73]

Specific mention was made of 'Albanian secessionists' and 'Muslim extremists', and of indications that Croats and Hungarians were also arming themselves.[74] There were also attempts to disrupt the mobilization implemented by the JNA. 'Proceeding from the dispositions of the Law on Defence the organs of internal affairs have an obligation to prevent all activities related to the establishment and operation of any sort of armed and unarmed groups.'[75]

For the above reasons, Minister Sokolović in July 1991 initiated the Operational Action (*Operativna akcija*, OA) Tomson.[76] He established a staff consisting of the chief of the SDB (leader of the staff), the chief of the Public Security Service and the chief of the Administration of the Police. The staff was tasked with the 'disarming of all illegally armed individuals and groups and the preventing of the further illegal arming of groups and individuals and attempts to create paramilitary formations'.[77] All organizational units of both the SDB and the Public Security Service were to form special teams whose exclusive task it would be to work towards these goals. These teams were to cooperate with the JNA and the TO. Special attention was to be paid to Kosovo, Novi Pazar, Titovo Užice, Vojvodina and Belgrade, and to the movement of weapons and ammunition across the borders of the Federal Republic of Yugoslavia. In addition to putting together a plan for the implementation of OA Tomson, participants were also to compile all relevant information about extremists and their activities and plans.

OA Tomson encompassed intensive and continuous monitoring, surveillance, documentation and other activities aimed at countering and preventing 'the hostile activities of militant individuals and groups directed towards illegal paramilitary organization, including the registration of volunteers, the carrying out of some forms of training, attempts to gather weaponry, and similar activities'.[78]

The available documentation on paramilitary formations in Serbia focuses primarily on those established by nationalist political parties, including the SPO, the SRS and the Serb Chetnik Movement (*Srpski četnički pokret*, SČP). In July

1995, the RDB Centre Valjevo recalled that the first paramilitary formations had emerged in 1991 'through volunteers or their inclusion in the organs of internal affairs and the territorial defence, [these formations] armed and trained themselves in handling firearms, and all with the goal of deployment to the war areas in the Republic of Croatia'.[79] The RDB described the persons involved in these paramilitary formations as 'extremists'. Upon returning to Serbia from the battlefield, these persons often brought with them weapons and ammunition. Describing members of the SČP from Valjevo, the RDB noted that some of their members had 'upon return from the battlefield in Eastern Slavonia ... shown a particular interest in warehouses of weaponry and military materiel in Valjevo and the surroundings, reconnoitred the manner of security, the strength of the units, the number and position of guard posts, the location of stores in the warehouses, etc.'.[80]

The RDB hence viewed returning paramilitary formations as a security challenge. In terms of the RDB's primary mission to protect the constitutionally established order of the Republic of Serbia, paramilitary formations associated with political parties posed a potential threat to the official Serbian authorities. This was particularly the case for adherents of the SRS, 'who have stressed that their party has not given up on the destabilization of the political-security situation and the forcible takeover of power in the Republic of Serbia'.[81] Towns in Serbia such as Loznica, Valjevo and Šabac, which bordered or were proximate to eastern Bosnia, were of particular concern.[82] Furthermore, given the ethnic diversity of areas of Kosovo, Vojvodina and the Sandžak, the risk also existed that these paramilitary formations would threaten ethnic minorities. There was even the risk that the more unscrupulous members of these paramilitary formations would sell the weapons and ammunition that they had smuggled into Serbia to ethnic Albanians who entertained thoughts of armed uprising or secession.[83]

In addition to regular communications, the RDB reported on OA Tomson in its annual report for 1992. Here it was noted that the individuals under surveillance in this operation included 'numerous persons from criminal milieus, predisposed to physical attacks and intimidation of those with whom they disagree, disruption of public law and order, and even aggressive behaviour towards members of the organs of internal affairs'.[84] In the scope of OA Tomson, the RDB deployed its available operational means and methods. This included wiretapping and other forms of surveillance and electronic eavesdropping and the recruitment of informants.[85] In addition, the police and the public prosecutor used repressive means to confiscate illegal weapons and ammunition and punish those engaged in illegal activities on the territory of the Republic of Serbia. In the context of OA Tomson, the RDB cooperated with the Public Security Department, the security organs of the VJ, judicial organs and other relevant state institutions.[86]

The extent and intensity of efforts to prevent an influx of weaponry and ammunition from Croatia and Bosnia into Serbia and to militate against any potential oppositional political activities by Serb paramilitary groups stood in marked contrast to the disinterest the RDB displayed for monitoring any potential criminal behaviour by these groups in Croatia or Bosnia. This was particularly true with respect to atrocities which these groups perpetrated against civilians. In recounting the course of OA Tomson, CRDB Sremska Mitrovica observed that the paramilitary organizations under observation at the outset of the operational action in the summer of 1991 had 'directed their activity (combat activities) towards the territory of the then Republic of Croatia (second half of 1991), now the RSK – Eastern Slavonia. The aforementioned paramilitary formations were composed of groups of persons of extreme behaviour whose numbers varied between 200 and 300 members'.[87]

With respect to extreme Serbian nationalism, the crucial paradigmatic shift from suppressing it to endorsing and collaborating with it was codified in the 1992 rulebook of the Serbian State Security Service. Article 3 of the Rulebook specified that the RDB performed and provided the service of state security through counterintelligence, intelligence and other related work, and specifically through the prevention of extremism and terrorism.[88] On the surface, this was as before, however, Article 3 included the following formulation:

> Intelligence tasks are tasks of collecting intelligence, facts and information of interest to the Republic in the realms of politics, the economy, defence, security as well as in other realms of interest to the Republic. Intelligence tasks are also the tasks of collecting intelligence, facts and information about all forms of threats to the national and cultural-historical autonomy [*samosvojnost*] of Serbs who live outside the Republic.

The sentence regarding the protection of the autonomy of Serbs outside the Republic raised the question of how – and in cooperation with whom – the RDB would seek to fulfil this portion of its mandate. Moreover, depending on how the RDB operationalized this task, it arguably risked stepping beyond the activities permitted by the Law on Internal Affairs. After all, as long as Yugoslavia had existed, the state security services of Croatia and Bosnia had been responsible for combatting threats against Serbs in those two republics. Since both republics had now seceded from Yugoslavia, the logical implication was that the RDB would collaborate with the security agencies of Serb-controlled entities in Croatia and Bosnia. However, such collaboration carried with it not the risk of further international condemnation and potential intervention.

Like the 1990 annual report on the work of the SDB, the 1992 annual report on the work of the RDB covered a variety of 'extremisms', including 'Serb extremism'.[89] At the outset of the report, the RDB asserted that its work in 1992 had been complicated by attempts by 'international factors' to transfer armed conflict 'from the territory of BiH to the territory of the Republic of Serbia', and as such undermine the constitutionally established order of the Republic of Serbia.[90] The RDB was concerned about the spillover of the conflicts in Croatia and BiH to Serbia, especially to multi-ethnic areas such as Vojvodina, the Sandžak (Raška) and Kosovo.[91] These threats were accompanied by other negative tendencies such as 'war profiteering' and the illegal smuggling of weapons and ammunition in those regions of Serbia bordering conflict areas in Croatia and BiH. However, the RDB assessed that it had been largely successful in meeting these challenges.[92]

A good example of someone who, at least temporarily, was caught up in the net of OA Tomson was Dragoslav Bokan, the leader of the paramilitary group known as 'the White Eagles'. On 27 May 1992, Assistant Minister of Internal Affairs and Chief of the Public Security Division Radovan Stojičić answered a parliamentary question regarding the arrest of Bokan for the possession of illegal weapons.[93] In responding to the parliamentary question, Stojičić explained the police's procedures in such cases and noted that Bokan had allegedly brought the illegal weapons with him from 'battlefields' near Okučani and Zvornik, and had given these weapons to other persons. Although sentenced to prison for the illegal possession of weapons, Bokan never faced any charges related to atrocities allegedly committed by his group in Bosnia or Croatia.

In rare cases, information obtained by the RDB about Serb paramilitaries' commission of atrocities did lead to investigation and prosecution of some perpetrators. In July 1995, CRDB Belgrade noted that Vojin Vučković had in April 1992 through the SČP of the SRS founded the paramilitary formation 'Igor Mirković' more commonly known as 'the Yellow Wasps', which had been particularly active in Zvornik municipality.[94] The CRDB Belgrade expressed awareness that there existed information pointing to the commission by the 'Yellow Wasps' of 'war crimes against the civilian population' and looting. This led to the arrest in November 1993 of Vučković and his brother Dušan, who was nicknamed 'Repić'.[95] Weapons, ammunition and plastic explosives were also confiscated. The CRDB Belgrade interviewed both Vučković brothers, who confirmed that they had tortured, raped and killed Muslims in Zvornik. 'According to his own statement, Dušan had back then "liquidated" approximately 50 Muslims.'[96]

Employees of the Fourth Department of CRDB Belgrade at Obrenovac visited the RS from 20 to 22 October 1993 in order to gather information about the activities of paramilitary formations, in particular the Yellow Wasps. This information pointed to the conclusion that 'in essence almost all of these formations engage more in criminal activity than in warfare. It seems that their basic impulse was the attainment of material goods and the acquisition of money, and least of all patriotism and the desire to assist the Serb nation in Bosnia.'[97] The two Vučković brothers were indicted, but nothing was done to investigate or pursue those official actors who had permitted groups like the Yellow Wasps to organize, arm and deploy to Bosnia and Croatia.[98]

Other groups provide additional insight into how the RDB dealt with Serb paramilitary units active in Bosnia. In 1992 and 1993, paramilitary groups known as 'the White Eagles' (*Beli orlovi*) and 'the Avengers' (*Osvetnici*) – the latter led by Milan Lukić – were active on both the territory of eastern Bosnia and Herzegovina and on the territory of the SRJ.[99] The White Eagles were known to the RDB already in April 1992, and were a concern to the RDB because of the group's aggressive intentions towards Muslims and towards police officers in Priboj.[100] The White

Eagles were thought to be linked to the political party Serbian National Renewal (*Srpska narodna obnova*) and to be in favour of 'the most radical measures, including the physical liquidation of Muslims'.[101] By the beginning of June 1992, CRDB Užice had collected detailed information indicating that this group was involved in crimes including the killing – CRDB Užice used the word 'slaughter' – of Muslim civilians in the Višegrad area.[102] Moreover, the group desired to 'bring the fire of war also to parts of the SRJ where Muslims live'.[103]

Lukić was subsequently interviewed several times by the MUP in Serbia.[104] He stated that he and his group had undergone training at Ilok – at which point they were known as the 'Obrenovac group'. The training had been carried out by men known as 'Pupe and Zoran, red berets – *knindže*'. Thereafter Lukić's unit had departed for Višegrad, placing themselves under the command of SUP Višegrad and in the composition of the Višegrad TO.[105] According to Lukić,

> With my unit I participated in all the most important military operations on the territory of Višegrad. This is a real ethnic war, and I came to the battlefield with only one goal, to protect Serbs and Serbdom in those areas. Since the arrival of Vinko Pandurević, I am under his command in legal units of the RS. Through my personal example, I had quite an impression on the readiness of Serb fighters, and I personally liquidated a large number of Muslims – extremists from the territory of Višegrad, about whom it was known that they had mistreated the Serb inhabitants. In confronting the Muslim fighters I am uncompromising and unlike the Serbs from Višegrad, when I came, I came ready to kill everyone who threatens Serbdom.[106]

Although Lukić left Višegrad in September, he returned there at the invitation of the local leadership, having gathered new volunteers in Zvornik, Šabac and Belgrade. In the meantime, his paramilitary formation's atrocious violence consumed a number of Muslims from the Federal Republic of Yugoslavia. On 22 October 1992, the Avengers kidnapped sixteen Muslims from a bus in Mioče in eastern Bosnia and subsequently killed them. Lukić later denied having kidnapped Muslims from a bus in Sjeverin in October 1992 but said that he would congratulate whoever had done so.[107] However, on 2 November, CRDB Užice filed a report on an interview of two sources who claimed that Lukić had been involved in the killings.[108]

The abduction and murders created an outcry in the Federal Republic of Yugoslavia, with official demands for the perpetrators to be identified and extradited. On 26 October, the police in Priboj in the SRJ arrested Lukić, much to the dissatisfaction of his associates and family. The following day, President Karadžić flew to Višegrad to meet with representatives of several municipalities. Upon leaving this meeting, the parents of Milan Lukić confronted him and demanded the release of their son. When Karadžić stated that Lukić would receive due process, Lukić's father angrily threatened to gather 200 men and forcibly liberate his son, even if that means shooting at other Serbs. Karadžić's response was noteworthy:

Don't ever again either think that or say it. A Serb must never shoot at another Serb because of anyone. ... We are creating a state and in the future we will summarily execute [offenders] for indiscipline, we should have done that a long time ago. He has been detained in a state of law and we will offer legal assistance, if he is not guilty, he will be released, and if he is guilty, he will be held responsible. Let no one intervene on his behalf, I am informed about everything surrounding Milan Lukić.

Not heeding Karadžić, Lukić's father later that day gathered a group of armed men and went to see Vinko Pandurević. Trying to assuage them, Pandurević told them that the arrest had been 'coincidental' and that Lukić would be released soon. The RS authorities never held Lukić responsible for the Sjeverin incident, though he was subsequently tried in absentia for it in Serbia. As for the informants of CRDB Užice, they stated that Lukić was a valued warrior who may well have been involved in the killings but probably had not conceived of the kidnapping himself.

It should be noted that the RDB also suspected Lukić of killing Stanko Pecikoza, a Serb and SDS leader in Višegrad before the war. Pecikoza was murdered in July 1992. According to Lukić, Pecikoza was a war profiteer who had transported Višegrad Muslims to safety in Serbia rather than killing them, as Lukić thought should have been done.[109]

Another particularly notorious incident involving Lukić's group took place on the territory of eastern Bosnia and also involved citizens of the SRJ. On 27 February 1993 at the small railway station in the little eastern Bosnian village of Štrpci a passenger train travelling from Belgrade to Bar in Montenegro was stopped.[110] All the passengers on the train were searched and were asked to produce identification. Twenty of the passengers – eighteen Muslims, one Croat and one of unidentified ethnicity – were led away from the train. All of them were killed.

The authorities in Serbia became quickly if not immediately aware of this incident. Already on 4 March 1993, CRDB Užice reported that a group of thirty armed men had stopped the train, and had detained approximately twenty-three persons.[111] Milan Lukić was thought to be behind this operation. Of those who were detained, the Serbs from Bosnia and Herzegovina had been mobilized. Nothing was stated about the fate of the others. At the eighth session of the Supreme Defence Council held approximately one week later, the incident at Štrpci was discussed. Momir Bulatović stated that the authorities had tried to pay a ransom for those people who had been kidnapped from the train.[112] However, they had all been killed.

Bulatović then proceeded to state that the State Security Service of Montenegro had knowledge of Lukić's plans to kill someone, but Slobodan Milošević interrupted Bulatović. Milošević told the Supreme Defence Council that Lukić had been arrested, and 'we will see how to proceed'.[113] Milošević said that Lukić's arrest was being kept secret because other similar actors were to be apprehended. Milošević called Lukić 'a killer and a villain', but Bulatović expressed sympathy for Lukić, whom he called a 'tragic personality'. Bulatović then appeared to continue his earlier interrupted thought, noting that it would be a catastrophe if groups like the White Eagles would engage in violent behaviour in the Sandžak. 'This is one of the most important elements of our state strategy, even more so as ideas are coming from the highest positions in Republika Srpska that we should in an organized manner enter into ethnic cleansing, which would be catastrophic.'[114] This was the second time at this meeting that Bulatović had mentioned that RS officials, including the president of the RS government, were recommending 'that we ethnically cleanse the Sandžak and kill the Muslims there'.[115] Milošević stated that this was new to him and that 'with such people we have nothing to discuss'.[116] Later at the meeting, Milošević also stated that the thought that the SRJ was only for Serbs and Montenegrins rather than all citizens was also a kind of 'fascist ideology'.[117]

Generally speaking, the authorities seemed to be most concerned about weapons or ammunition that Lukić and his group – and similar paramilitary groups – might bring to Serbia from Bosnia and Herzegovina or Croatia. The other major point of concern was the possible threat posed to the government by these groups. It must be emphasized that Lukić in his own words told the RDB that he and his men had received training in 1992 from trainers known to be associated with the RDB and the later Unit for Special Operations. While little or nothing was done by the authorities of the RS or Serbia to investigate or prosecute Milan Lukić, he was later convicted by the ICTY and sentenced to life imprisonment for crimes against humanity and war crimes.

Owing to the extremely limited access available to the relevant Serbian archives, further information about the implementation of OA Tomson is sparse. On 8 March 1995, the Fifth Administration of the RDB requested that the CRDBs prepare reports on the 'results and further directions for operational work on OA "Tomson"'.[118] The reports submitted by the CRDBs during the summer of 1995 provide very detailed information about the nature and extent of paramilitary activity throughout Serbia during the period from 1991 to 1995.[119] Amazingly, OA Tomson, initiated in July 1991, was not formally terminated until January 2006, nearly five years after the extradition of Slobodan Milošević to stand trial at the ICTY.[120]

Conclusion

As will be seen in the next chapter, the Serbian State Security Service occasionally continued to operate units or condone the deployment of paramilitary units from Serbia to Bosnia until the end of the war in the autumn of 1995. Dispatches from the fall of Srebrenica show that several detachments of the MUP of Serbia were present with RS MUP units in a special joint unit. And in the late summer and early autumn of 1995, Arkan returned to Bosnia as part of a futile last-ditch attempt to shore up Bosnian Serb positions in northwestern Bosnia.

A year and a half later, at an awards ceremony at the JSO's base in Kula in Serbia in May 1997, Franko Simatović stood before a large metal map of the former Yugoslavia onto which were affixed metal images of wolves at those locations where 'the Unit' had been active.[121] Simatović stated that the unit had been formed on 4 May 1991 and had fought and worked since that date to defend the Serb nation. From its earliest days as the '*knindže*' to its existence as the JATD and, finally the establishment of the JSO in May 1996, the members of this unit regarded it as the latest evolution of a single unit dating back to the spring of 1991. In their minds, 'the Unit' had existed for years, even though its existence would still remain hidden from the public for several years to come.

Throughout the Bosnian war and the ebbs and flows of an at times uneasy relationship between Belgrade and Pale, the RDB's stance vis-à-vis the Bosnian Serbs and their war remained very consistent.[122] First, and most importantly, the RDB's support for the strategic goals of the Bosnian Serbs and the existence of Republika Srpska never wavered. Second, while the RDB from the outset obtained first-hand knowledge of the commission of atrocities by Bosnian Serb police, military and paramilitary forces – and of the participation in numerous instances of RDB-affiliated units as co-perpetrators – the authorities in Serbia did little to prosecute those responsible for these crimes. As the case of Milan Lukić shows, this included even those cases when the RDB had collected strong evidence of criminal activity. Finally, as a constituent part of the MUP of Serbia and hence the Milošević regime, the RDB acted to ensure that RDB-affiliated units and other Serb paramilitary units returning from the battlefields of Bosnia to Serbia could and would not engage in any activities that would be destabilizing to the security situation in Serbia. These units could 'import' their plunder and sell and distribute it as they saw fit as long as the Milošević regime in the guise of the Federal Customs Service under Kertes received their cut.[123] But any political or armed action against the regime or attempts to foment inter-ethnic violence on the territory of the Federal Republic of Yugoslavia faced harsh sanctions, as the turbulent political career of paramilitary leader Vojislav Šešelj and his Serb Radical Party demonstrated. After the end of the wars of Yugoslav succession and the fall of Milošević, bereft of new wars and new victims, the parasitic beast in the form of 'the Unit' would attempt to devour its host.

Chapter 5

THE BOSNIAN SERB POLICE, ONGOING ETHNIC CLEANSING AND GENOCIDE IN SREBRENICA, 1993–5

With the frontlines stabilized for much of the war's second and third years, the Bosnian Serb police concentrated on consolidating the gains and ethnic segregation achieved in the first year of the war. In many senses, at least as concerns the RS MUP, the most important developments of 1993 and 1994 were political, both with respect to international peace plans and negotiations and sparring between Radovan Karadžić and the VRS. The peace plans, in particular, also led to rising tensions between the Bosnian Serbs and Slobodan Milošević, whose support for the Bosnian Serbs was absolutely critical, but whose own regime faced crushing international pressure in the form of economic sanctions. This period of the war is in many ways the least understood. It includes protracted ongoing ethnic cleansing, as well as a mysterious alleged uprising against the Bosnian Serb leadership by disgruntled veterans disgusted by corruption and abuses of power. The police during this period also became even more deeply involved in smuggling and organized criminal activities, often across the ostensibly impermeable ethnic line of confrontation. Not without reason did RS Prime Minister Branko Đerić in November 1992 accuse the RS MUP of becoming a 'trading company'.[1]

Although the war continued unabated and although ethnic cleansing proceeded, particularly in areas like eastern Herzegovina, the overall level of atrocities was reduced compared to the spring and summer of 1992. Instead, the major development of 1993 and 1994 was the outbreak of a third front in the war, as the fragile coalition between the Bosnian government and the self-proclaimed forces of Herceg-Bosna grew ever more brittle. By the autumn of 1993, the Bosnian Croats were engaged in full-blown war with their former allies in the Bosnian government. This conflict lasted until the Washington Agreement was brokered in April 1994, whereafter a testy alliance survived until the end of the war.

The more conventional and static nature of the war in 1993 and 1994 meant that the war between the Bosnian Serbs and their opponents more closely resembled conventional warfare. The Bosnian Serbs had by the end of 1992 managed to secure control of approximately 70 per cent of Bosnia's territory. However, the territory in their possession was very irregularly shaped and quite vulnerable in several places, particularly in northern Bosnia around the Posavina corridor. The VRS hence tried to consolidate and secure its gains. Moreover, forces loyal to the Bosnian government continued to control several enclaves in eastern Bosnia such as Goražde, Srebrenica and Žepa. The armed forces of the VRS, including the RS MUP, overran the two latter enclaves in the summer of 1995.

The different character of the war in 1993 and 1994, with a decrease in mass atrocities perpetrated against civilians, can also be observed in the relative lack of ICTY indictments of Bosnian Serb political, military and police leaders for this period. The ICTY overwhelmingly indicted Bosnian Serbs for crimes committed between April 1992 and the end of the year, and then for the Srebrenica genocide in July 1995. The only exception to this is the indictments covering the shelling and sniping of the civilian population during the siege of Sarajevo, which lasted for virtually the entire length of the war, and which did not involve the police.[2]

To say that 1993 and 1994 were different than 1992 is not to say that they were uneventful, however. On the one hand, the RS MUP was able to stabilize and standardize its operations during this period, as the institutions of Republika Srpska continued to evolve. On the other hand, ethnic cleansing never completely ceased and the police and politicians of the RS had to deal with the question of whether the RS was the party-state of the SDS, or whether some modicum of political opposition and bureaucratic independence could exist.

By the end of 1992, Mićo Stanišić's tenure as minister in the RS MUP was running aground. The reasons for this are not entirely clear and the available sources all stem from the involved parties, so any interpretation must proceed with caution. In Stanišić's own words, his downfall as minister resulted from his ministry's decision to pursue investigations into the alleged financial misdoings of RS Assembly speaker and member of the collective presidency Momčilo Krajišnik and his brother.[3] On 20 January 1993, Stanišić was dismissed as minister.

In Stanišić's place came Ratko Adžić, a former teacher who at the outset of the war had served as the head of the crisis staff in the Sarajevo municipality of Ilijaš. The appointment was not propitious, given that Adžić lacked any of the considerable experience in policing that Stanišić had, after all, possessed. Indeed, some of the actions taken by Adžić in 1992 hinted that he might not be the wisest choice. For example, as the head of the municipal crisis staff and hence the most important figure in Ilijaš, Adžić had been supportive of and closely linked with paramilitaries in his municipality.[4]

This period also entailed some minor restructuring of the RS MUP, especially with respect to terminology. As regarded the uniformed police, the more international term '*policija*' at the outset of 1994 replaced the old communist '*milicija*'. In addition, the SNB, i.e. the National Security Service, changed its name to the State Security Division (*Resor državne bezbednosti*) bringing it into alignment with the terminology in Serbia. The CSBs were split into a Public Security Centre (CJB) and a State Security Division Centre (CRDB), and some new centres were created, for example in Prijedor and Zvornik. Many of these changes were introduced through the 1994 Law on Internal Affairs.[5]

This chapter will first cast a glance at the extensive cultural destruction and continued ethnic cleansing that took place with tacit approval as well as the participation of the police. Here special focus will be placed on Banja Luka, the second-largest city in Bosnia, which escaped from the war nearly unscathed but nonetheless underwent a thorough campaign of ethnic cleansing at the hands of the civilian authorities including the RS MUP. The chapter will then jump chronologically to the fall of the Srebrenica enclave and the ensuing genocide and conclude with the end of the Bosnian war.

The police and ongoing ethnic cleansing

Although the first eight months of the war in many ways marked the peak of the numerous crimes collectively referred to under the euphemism ethnic cleansing, the practice persisted into 1993 and beyond. In some areas of eastern Herzegovina, for example, many Bosnian Croats and Muslims departed involuntarily in large numbers in the early months of 1993.

The forced expulsion of departure of the ethnic Other was of course only the most important aspect of creating an ethnically homogeneous territory. The visible traces of the Other also had to be removed, as these served as reminders of a multicultural past. In Bosnia, religious architecture and houses of worship often served as the most visible symbols of this legacy.[6] While nationalists targeted mosques and churches from the very outset, for various reasons the destruction of these objects took place over a longer period. Already the bombardment of Sarajevo's National Library and the resultant destruction of its magnificent collections in May 1992 had caused widespread international outrage. Interestingly, while some of these structures were destroyed under the pretence of the armed conflict, many others were obliterated in areas that were either barely affected by the war or where combat activities had long since ceased. By February 1993, the Council of Europe decried 'a cultural catastrophe in the heart of Europe'.[7]

In his expert report prepared for *Karadžić*, András Riedlmayer found that

> the overwhelming majority of the mosques in the municipalities included in this survey – as in other municipalities surveyed – were either heavily damaged or destroyed; and that mosques and other Muslim religious monuments of particular historical and cultural importance appear to have been singled out for destruction. ... The damage to these monuments was, in many cases, clearly the result of attacks directed against them, rather than incidental to the fighting. ... In a number of towns, including Banja Luka, Bijeljina, Bosanska Krupa, Bosanski Novi, Bratunac, Čajniče, Donji Vakuf, Foča, Rogatica, Sanski Most, Zvornik, Kozluk and others, the destruction of mosques and other Islamic sites took place after the area had come under the control of Serb forces, at times when there was no military action in the immediate vicinity.[8]

Riedlmayer reached similar conclusions about Roman Catholic architectural heritage in Bosnia.[9]

Here again, the police played an important but unfortunately overwhelmingly negative role. It is not particularly contentious to suggest that the police should in normal circumstances be involved in helping to protect buildings of significant cultural and religious importance if credible threats exist against these buildings. And if arson of any kind is perpetrated against such structures, the police should investigate and identify the perpetrators and then provide the relevant prosecutor with the evidence. For the police to do nothing would send a very harmful signal.

Yet doing little or nothing to prevent the persecution and other atrocities committed against non-Serbs on the territory of Republika Srpska accurately described the RS MUP's stance during the war. Comparing the reports of Stojan Župljanin at CSB Banja Luka in the period following the 1990 multi-party elections with the later behaviour of the police in the AOR of CSB Banja Luka is particularly instructive. Župljanin went from filing concerned reports about violent inter-ethnic incidents in the summer of 1991 to allying himself with those who perpetrated such attacks.

Although there are indications that at least some Bosnian Serbs viewed such cultural destruction with extreme dismay, in not a single case did the work of the police and the public prosecutor's office during the war lead to indictments against specific individuals for these crimes.[10] By contrast, on at least one occasion, in the town of Mrkonjić Grad, the SNB took measures against a Bosnian Muslim who had filmed the destruction of a Catholic church and mosques.[11] As in the case of crimes committed against Muslims and Croats in the area, the police's interest in conducting investigations was at most perfunctory, and indications exist suggesting that the police engaged in collusion with the perpetrators of the destruction of religious objects.[12] It is hard to think of a better example of the callous attitude of the RS MUP towards the destruction of religious cultural heritage. And it is also difficult not to contrast the destruction of all of Banja Luka's sixteen mosques with the preservation of the Serbian Orthodox cathedral in the centre of Sarajevo. Despite the siege of Sarajevo and nearly daily shelling of the city by the VRS, at no point was significant damage done to the most important Serbian Orthodox structure in that city, the Serbian Orthodox Cathedral.

The near absence of combat from the town of Banja Luka and the surrounding municipality contrasts starkly with the maelstrom of violence that afflicted the towns of the Drina Valley in eastern Bosnia in the spring of 1992. In those municipalities, Bosnian Muslims constituted a majority before the war and therefore a major obstacle to both ethnic homogeneity and the creation of a Serb political entity in Bosnia that would be both territorially compact and contiguous with Serbia or rump Yugoslavia. Unlike them, Banja Luka municipality featured a slight majority Serb population in the 1991 census – 54.75 per cent in the municipality and 49.03 per cent in the town itself.[13] Like many other larger towns and cities in Yugoslavia, Banja Luka had a considerable number of ethnically mixed marriages, as well as a considerable proportion of self-declared Yugoslavs – nearly 16 per cent in 1991.[14] Yet by 1992, Radislav Vukić, the president of the SDS in Banja Luka, stated that such marriages had been a mistake and that children born in these marriages were only fit for making soap.[15]

As has been seen in previous chapters, the ethnic cleansing of Banja Luka commenced almost imperceptibly before the war, gathering furious speed in the spring of 1992 with the passage of draconian edicts curtailing or eliminating the human rights of non-Serb citizens, as amply illustrated in the cases against Radoslav Brđanin and Stojan Župljanin at the ICTY. As the main civilian law enforcement agency, the RS MUP acted as the main implementer of discriminatory and persecutory decrees.

Ethnic cleansing continued throughout the war in Banja Luka, and approximately 500 non-Serb civilians were killed in the area during the war.[16] UN Special Rapporteur Tadeusz Mazowiecki in February 1994 reported an

> escalation in the rate of ethnic cleansing ... in Banja Luka since late November 1993. ... Typical of current eviction practices was an incident on 13 December 1993 in Banja Luka when six armed and uniformed men entered by force the home of a non-Serb family, assaulted the occupants and, despite the family's possession of a court order assuring the tenancy, ejected them onto the street.[17]

In a letter to *The New York Times*, a Canadian diplomat seconded to the UNHCR made mention of a forcible eviction in Banja Luka on 29 December 1993 that escalated to multiple murders of the Muslim tenants and a neighbour.[18] Mazowiecki subsequently noted that the police responded very tardily to the incident and performed only a perfunctory investigation. This response was typical for crimes involving Muslim or Croat victims. The following day, assailants dressed in military uniform assaulted mourners at the funeral of the deceased. During this same period, Župljanin as chief of CSB Banja Luka declared publicly that his police served Serbdom.[19] Moreover, indications exist showing that the police not only condoned such crimes but also participated in them. The police were also known to steal from the aid packages delivered to the remaining Muslims and Croats by charities such as Merhamet and Caritas, and the police in the beginning of 1994 refused to investigate the explosion of a vehicle belonging to the International Committee of the Red Cross.[20] As a result, the organization withdrew from the area.

The toll of ethnic cleansing in territory controlled by the Bosnian Serbs can best be illustrated by demographic comparisons of the populations of municipalities in the RS before and after the war. In the case of Banja Luka, as noted above, Serbs constituted 54.75 per cent of the population in the municipality and 49.03 per cent in the town itself. Bosnian Muslims made up 14.6 per cent of the population of the municipality in 1991, but by 1997 they had been reduced to 2.1 per cent of the population, with Croats undergoing a decrease from 14.8 to 2.6 per cent.[21] This corresponded to an 85.6 per cent decrease in the percentage of Muslims. In several other municipalities in the RS, the decrease was even more extensive, such as in Bratunac (99.9 per cent), Bosanska Krupa (99.7 per cent), Prijedor (99.6 per cent) and Bijeljina (91.4 per cent). Similarly dramatic figures were observed for Croats in many RS municipalities. Notably, as well, in several municipalities the percentages of Muslims and Croats continued to decline in the years immediately after the war.

There can be no doubt that the Bosnian Serb leadership, using the RS MUP and the VRS as its armed forces, continued to pursue the creation of an ethnically homogeneous entity until the end of the war. At the forty-second session of the RS Assembly in July 1994, Karadžić stated forthrightly that 'our primary strategic aim … is to get rid of the enemies in our house, the Croats and Muslims, and not to be in the same state with them anymore'.[22]

In the meantime, even though Banja Luka's Serbs remained relatively unaffected by both the war and ethnic cleansing, raging inflation and a general economic collapse had forced most of the city's inhabitants into a hand-to-mouth existence where basic utilities such as electricity were no longer dependably delivered.[23] For example, by May 1993, the prices had risen to 114,000 per cent of their level a year earlier.[24] The entire Bosnian Krajina area was cut off from its natural markets in Croatia because of the war. According to intrepid investigative reporters, a number of competing 'gangs' engaged in racketeering of the city's inhabitants, and although Croats and Muslims were their initial and primary victims, Serbs were vulnerable once non-Serbs disappeared. In the words of Belgrade investigative journalist Miloš Vasić, 'it was permitted that robbery became a normal aspect of behaviour with respect to the property of Croats and Muslims; the robber, however, is first and above all a robber, and [once] he has robbed the neighbour of another faith, he will easily also rob his brother Serb'.[25]

In an apparent reaction to this untenable situation, several units of the VRS in September 1993 blocked all access to Banja Luka. Many journalists and a number of scholars have written about the events of September 1993.[26] A consensus exists that the events were not spontaneous and that they did not represent a popular uprising from below. Rather, the episode must be viewed as an expression of one or more ongoing power struggles, first and foremost between Radovan Karadžić and Ratko Mladić, and perhaps also between the regional power grouping representing the Bosnian Krajina, on the one hand, and the politicians of Pale and the Romanija region, on the other hand.

Significantly, the proclamations of the new crisis staff were cloaked in the same heady patriotic and nationalist language used by the SDS. The crisis staff spoke as sons of the nation who had,

> borne by the genetic impulse to defend freedom, moved spontaneously, quietly, without pomp into this war. We left behind that which was dearest to us. Because while we fought, the majority of our fellow citizens, the historical and newly composed surrogates of the Serb being, skilful manipulators, with the blessing of the existing authorities … increased their private empires and made their perverted dreams come true.

And in another proclamation, the crisis staff spoke of wanting to secure 'elementary, minimal human needs: food, heating, an apartment, with one word the right to the life of a dignified person, with all respect for all wartime circumstances'.[27]

Edin Omerčić argues that it is useful to compare the September 1993 crisis staff with the paramilitary organization SOS in March and April 1992.[28] Both the SOS and the crisis staff emerged seemingly out of nowhere with remarkably specific sets of demands which, upon closer examination, overlapped very well with the interests of the SDS. Omerčić concludes that the 'uprising' should instead be understood as a propagandistic distracting 'manoeuvre, which was strictly controlled [and] directed' by Karadžić, and which had as its primary goal the maintenance of the SDS's grip on power.[29]

The official end of the rebellion was anticlimactic. The crisis staff transformed itself into a commission that would monitor the assurances offered by Pale of a fight against corruption and war profiteering. Most importantly, in the context of the war and the countless atrocities committed by September 1993, there is no indication that those behind the 'uprising' in any way distanced themselves from those crimes or from the strategic goals which the Bosnian Serb leadership had proclaimed in May 1992. Certainly, there were those in the RS who had their doubts about the abilities of the RS leadership, and rifts between Karadžić and Mladić became particularly visible at the 34th Assembly Session and other sessions later in the war. And there may have been strong disagreements within the SDS about issues such as the ongoing international negotiations to end the war and on the nature of the relationship between the RS and the Federal Republic of Yugoslavia. Yet as regards the creation and continued existence of the RS at the expense of non-Serb inhabitants, and on the use of the armed forces including the police to achieve this goal, no dissent was voiced by any of the participants in the events of September 1993.

RS MUP and the genocide in Srebrenica

The genocide in Srebrenica in July 1995 in some senses marked the culmination of the Bosnian war, not least in terms of mass violence against the Bosnian Muslims. Although the Bosnian Serb Army led by General Ratko Mladić instigated and implemented the genocide, they as in earlier years relied to a considerable extent on the RS MUP. Police units helped to detain the men and boys of the Srebrenica enclave and to carry out some of the mass killings which took place after the surrender of the 'safe haven'. And in a flashback to the worst days of the war's first year, paramilitary forces from Serbia once again cooperated closely with the Bosnian Serb police. Later, as NATO began its bombardment of Republika Srpska, the Bosnian Serb police and paramilitaries acted as enforcers as their self-proclaimed state faced complete collapse. At the same time, the looming end of armed conflict meant that the police were suddenly competing for a much smaller set of spoils of war, exacerbating fissures in the police and its relations with the army.

The beginning of what would come to be the Bosnian war's final year found the RS MUP in a bit of disarray. The ministry was operating with a lame duck minister, Živko Rakić.[30] While combat involvement was nothing like what it had been back in 1992, the RS MUP continued to assist in combat operations, particularly in those municipalities whose territory encompassed part of the frontlines. The year 1995 was the fourth year in which the RS MUP as a constituent part of the RS armed forces engaged in combat activities. The RS MUP remain firmly fixed on the achievement of the strategic objectives from 1992 and wedded to the *Weltanschauung* which the RS leadership had conjured at the outset of the war. To quote the 1995 RS MUP annual report which was compiled in January 1996, the war was being fought 'for the right of Serbs to self-determination and equality, for the defence [of Serbs] from destruction and genocide'.[31] Consequently, the same report referred to the 'open aggression of the forces of Croatia, the HVO and the BiH Army' and NATO bombardment which put tremendous pressure on the RS throughout 1995. 'This led to the loss of significant Serbian territories, an unprecedented exodus of the Serb nation, during May, August, September and October, a large number of uncared for refugees, as well as war crimes against the Serb civilian population and other negative accompanying occurrences.'[32]

By the time the operation to 'liberate' Srebrenica came to be implemented, a familiar figure from 1992 re-emerged at the top of the RS MUP. It will be recalled that Tomislav Kovač, who had started the war as a gung-ho but relatively low-ranking SJB chief in the Sarajevo suburb of Ilidža, had risen to be assistant minister already by August 1992. In doing so, he had defended the police's cooperation with paramilitary units even after the RS Presidency as well as the VRS Main Staff and the RS MUP had demanded that all paramilitary units integrate themselves into the armed forces of the RS.

In July 1995, Kovač was deputy minister of the RS MUP and also acting minister, and as such was the commander of the staff of police forces (*komandant štab policijskih snaga*).[33] As of 19 June, Kovač formed a command staff for police units in those areas affected by the state of war. The staff's headquarters was located at Pale, the seat of the ministry remaining at Bijeljina.[34] Kovač appointed himself as the head of the staff, with Milenko Karišik (formerly commander of the RS MUP Special Brigade of the Police) and Malko Koroman (chief of SJB Pale) immediately below him.[35]

The RS MUP had since its establishment taken steps to professionalize and narrow its approach to combat activities. The November 1994 Law on the Implementation of the Law on Internal Affairs during an Imminent Threat of War regulated the resubordination of police units to the army.[36] Just as in 1992, even when a police unit was resubordinated to a VRS commander, that commander had to issue orders to the police unit through the unit's regular police commander, and the unit had to remain unified.

The Special Brigade of the Police (*Specijalna brigada policije*, SBP), now headed by Goran Sarić and his deputy Ljubomir Borovčanin, stood at the pinnacle of the ministry, directly subordinated to the minister.[37] In addition to the SBP, which had several subordinate detachments spread across the RS, there also existed special police units (*posebne jedinice policije*, PJPs) at the regional level based at the CJBs.[38] 'While the SBP was a separately established combat unit, the PJPs consisted of regular police officers who were organised in the PJPs for the purposes of combat missions.'[39] Both types of units could be resubordinated to VRS commands during combat.

Here it is again worth stressing that the SBP was equipped at a level that would make it nearly unrecognizable as a police unit in many if not most countries. The

Second Šekovići Detachment, for example, had mortars, armoured vehicles with mounted anti-aircraft guns and even two T-55 tanks in addition to standard police equipment and camouflage uniforms.[40] The PJPs had lighter weapons but still bore automatic weapons and also wore camouflage uniforms.[41]

In addition to the aforementioned units, a group known as the 'Jahorina Recruits' also came to play a role in the events in and around Srebrenica. This group consisting of approximately two companies of 100 men each trained at Jahorina near Sarajevo and was composed of police trainees as well as captured deserters. Their trainer, Duško Jevtić, nicknamed 'Stalin', was subordinate to Sarić and Borovčanin.[42] The recruits were not nearly as well equipped as the aforementioned units.

The events surrounding the genocide in Srebrenica have been examined more closely than those of any other episode of the wars of Yugoslav succession, so only the briefest of summaries is necessary. The UN Security Council had in April 1993 proclaimed the enclave of Srebrenica to be a safe area, a designation the Security Council subsequently also extended to Bihać, Goražde, Sarajevo and Tuzla. A very large number of Bosnian Muslim civilians, many of whom had fled from areas of eastern Bosnia now under Serbian control, resided in very difficult and unsanitary circumstances in the enclave. According to the ICTY, 'just before the attack on Srebrenica the total number of inhabitants of the Srebrenica enclave had increased from 36,000 at the beginning of the year to 42,000 persons, out of which approximately 85% were displaced persons'.[43]

Radovan Karadžić set the stage for the attack on the Srebrenica enclave when he issued Supreme Command Directive 7 in March 1995.[44] The order set forth the strategic objectives of the RS in the months to come and included a particularly notorious formulation in which Karadžić called for the armed forces 'to create with everyday planned and deliberate combat activities the conditions for the total insecurity, unbearableness and hopelessness for the further existence and life of the residents of Srebrenica and Žepa'.[45] It is worth remembering that the RS armed forces in times of either an imminent threat of war or a state of war included the police; the inclusion of MUP units in operations to take Srebrenica and Žepa and to place these areas under the full authority of the RS was therefore inevitable.

From the beginning of the Srebrenica operation, the VRS coordinated with the RS MUP. The actual attack on the Srebrenica enclave commenced on 6 July 1995 with several days of shelling by the VRS, which then began to advance into the enclave. On that day, Kovač sent a dispatch demonstrating his awareness of the beginning of the Srebrenica offensive as well as of the presence of forces belonging to MUP Serbia in Bosnia.[46] On 9 July, Karadžić authorized the VRS to enter Srebrenica.[47] The following day, Minister Kovač ordered MUP units at the Trnovo frontline southeast of Sarajevo to leave for the Srebrenica area.[48] The affected units were the Šekovići detachment of the SBP, the first company of the Zvornik PJP, as well as a mixture of police from the RSK MUP and the MUP of Serbia and the Jahorina Recruits. The units from MUP Serbia included the Scorpions, a paramilitary unit affiliated with the RDB of Serbia which would earn particular notoriety for filming the executions of six Bosnian Muslims.[49] Kovač designated

Ljubomir Borovčanin as the commander of the unit, which was to arrive at SJB Bratunac the following day. The unit was to be resubordinated to the Chief of staff of the VRS Drina Corps, General Radislav Krstić.

On 11 July, the VRS captured Srebrenica. The following day, pursuant to an order issued by Kovač, work was already underway on the establishment of a new SJB Srebrenica that would be subordinate to CJB Zvornik.[50] Two days later, the Chief of CJB Zvornik Dragomir Vasić reported to the ministry about a meeting with General Mladić. At this meeting, Mladić had informed the police that the VRS was continuing its offensive towards Žepa, 'and is leaving all remaining work to the MUP'.[51] Concretely, wrote Vasić, this meant that the police would be in charge of evacuating the remaining civilian population from Srebrenica to Kladanj in Bosnian government-controlled territory. Vasić estimated that there were about 15,000 civilians.[52] But the second task listed by Vasić was the 'liquidation of about 8,000 Muslim soldiers whom we have blocked in the forest around Konjević polje. Battles are taking place. This job is being handled only by units of the MUP'. Vasić asked for the special police detachment of Srbinje (Foča) or Doboj to be sent to Konjević polje and promised that he would keep the ministry abreast of further developments.[53]

Kovač appeared in videos filmed in Srebrenica immediately following the capitulation of the enclave.[54] There can therefore be no doubt that Kovač, as the most responsible and ranking RS MUP official at the time, was aware of the nature of RS MUP activities in Srebrenica and the surrounding area in the days before, during and after the massacres there. As for Borovčanin, a journalist filmed a documentary of events in and around Srebrenica while driving around with Borovčanin on 13 and 14 July 1995. 'These include shots of the happenings at Potočari and the Bratunac-Konjević Polje Road, including Sandići Meadow and the Kravica Warehouse.' The video was later used as a prosecution exhibit in several trials at the ICTY.[55]

During the Srebrenica operation, RS MUP personnel participated in disarming Dutch UNPROFOR soldiers and in taking some of them as hostages.[56] Some of the equipment confiscated from the Dutch such as the signature light blue UN helmets were subsequently used to trick Muslim men into surrendering.[57] Throughout 12 July, the police also assisted in boarding women, children and the elderly onto buses.[58] However, 'very soon after the first buses and trucks arrived, the Bosnian Serb Forces, including some Jahorina Recruits led by Mane, and the Bratunac Brigade Military Police, supervised by Momir Nikolić, started separating the Bosnian Muslim men from their families and did not allow them to board the buses. The men separated were aged between around 15 and 65 years', with Mendeljev 'Mane' Đurić of the Jahorina Recruits telling a Dutch officer that those being separated were being screened as potential war criminals.[59] The following day, Đurić 'was again leading the Bosnian Serb Forces who were directing the people to the buses and separating the men from their families'.[60] When the Dutch officer Leendert Van Duijn realized that the Bosnian Muslims were being made to surrender their identity cards and passports, he confronted Đurić, pointing out that the police could hardly screen the detained men for war criminals if they were being stripped of identifying documents. 'Mane grinned and told Van Duijn that the men would no longer need their passports. ... Most of the men separated at Potočari on 12 and 13 July 1995 have not been seen alive since.'[61]

RS MUP units were involved in blocking those columns of Muslim men which were attempting to break out of the erstwhile enclave.[62] Police stationed along the road connecting Bratunac and Konjević polje were 'engaged in blocking and capturing large numbers of men'.[63] Some of the Muslim men surrendered, while others of them were captured. After being taken prisoner, the police participated in stealing the personal valuables of these men and in their beatings at several locations in the area.[64] In the meantime, the RDB of the RS MUP also issued bulletins to various parts of the RS MUP alerting them to the Bosnian Muslims who had succeeded in breaking out of the enclave and who were moving towards Tuzla and Kladanj. The RDB referred to these individuals as 'Muslim extremists' and warned of the risk that they would carry out acts of terrorism or sabotage.[65]

As has been extensively documented, those Bosnian Muslim men and boys who were taken prisoner in the Srebrenica enclave after its fall on 11 July were in the days that followed executed by the Bosnian Serb forces. Overwhelming evidence introduced at the ICTY showed that the bulk of the killings were carried out by VRS units, but survivors also testified that the police participated at several locations in the beatings and executions of the detained Muslim men and boys.[66] Throughout the operation, according to the trial chamber in *Krstić*, 'the evidence reveals that there was close co-operation and co-ordination between the MUP and Drina Corps units'.[67] On the evening of 13 July, an intercepted conversation shows that General Krstić and Borovčanin spoke. To Krstić's query regarding how things were going, Borovčanin responded that things were going well. Borovčanin rather cryptically added that 'work is being done on that part', and that this would be finished by the next day.[68] As late as 28 July, Vasić indicated that his entire force of police officers continued to be engaged in searching the terrain and setting ambushes for Muslims from Srebrenica. Vasić observed that this ongoing operation was taking place on a 'very wide area, in villages, in Zvornik itself, as well as in Serbia'.[69]

In a later report filed by Borovčanin, his description of the RS MUP's involvement in Srebrenica focused exclusively on combat and police activities.[70] When interviewed by the ICTY OTP in 2002, Borovčanin recalled how he had on 13 July arrived at the meadow in Sandići, where he found RS MUP units guarding large numbers of Muslims who had surrendered or who had been captured. Some of his subordinates expressed consternation that it would be difficult to guard so many prisoners. While Borovčanin was still at the meadow, General Mladić arrived and told the prisoners that they would be exchanged. 'In his interview with the Prosecution, Borovčanin stated that he thought Mladić was sincere when he said that.'[71] Significantly, acting Minister Kovač visited the Srebrenica area on 14 July.[72] The following day, Borovčanin complained at a meeting with the VRS that the police did not want to keep guarding the prisoners.[73]

In the *Popović et al.* case, Borovčanin was found guilty of aiding and abetting extermination, murder, persecution and forcible transfer. He was also found guilty of murder, but was acquitted on counts of genocide, conspiracy to commit genocide and deportation.[74] While the trial chamber found that Borovčanin did not possess the intent to commit this crime when he arrived in the Srebrenica area, it found that the events he witnessed during his stay there would have had to make him acutely aware that the evacuation of the Muslim civilian population from the enclave was not voluntary. The trial chamber also found that, while Borovčanin did not prior to the events at Srebrenica possess the intent to murder the Bosnian Muslim men of Srebrenica, police under his command participated in the killings and Borovčanin had command responsibility in terms of protecting those prisoners from harm.[75] At the Kravica warehouse, one of the primary execution sites, 'Borovčanin failed in his ongoing duty to protect the prisoners who had been in his custody in the knowledge that murder would be committed and that the removal of his units and the failure to intervene would assist in the commission of that crime. ... He thus aided and abetted murder by omission.'[76] Moreover, he failed to punish his subordinates for committing murder and extermination, though the trial chamber found that he was not himself possessed of genocidal intent.[77]

Certainly, an examination of the totality of the massive documentation and witness testimony – much of it from insider witnesses – shows absolutely no indication that the units of the RS MUP and those of the VRS operated at cross-purposes during and after the fall of the Srebrenica enclave. There also exists no credible evidence which could lead to the conclusion that the RS MUP, whether at the level of the acting minister or at the local and regional levels, at any point lodged any complaints regarding the mass execution of thousands of Muslim men and boys. On the contrary, the evidence points to the participation of MUP units in the detention of many of these victims and, at several locations, in the presence and participation of the police in their executions. That of course does not necessarily mean that the RS MUP intended to commit genocide, but they coordinated their actions with the VRS and did nothing to stop the crimes being committed.

It should also be noted that both in July 1995 and later, the RS MUP was instrumental in establishing and maintaining the narrative absolving RS armed forces of any wrongdoing or criminal conduct in and around Srebrenica. Doing so also entailed collaborating with the VRS in the ambitious but ultimately unsuccessful attempt to hide the massive forensic traces of the genocide. In the official portrayal, the RS armed forces had engaged in a legitimate military operation aimed at liberating the Srebrenica enclave, thereby solidifying the grip of the RS on the eastern portion of Bosnia and contributing to the achievement of the RS leadership's strategic goals. Seen from this perspective, the Muslim casualties in July 1995 were almost exclusively legitimate military losses inflicted upon combatants. Any and all information regarding the mass executions of captured Bosnian Muslim men and boys and other non-combatants was denied. For example, the RS MUP disseminated information according to which the Bosnian Muslims had engaged in extensive killings of their own men, including those who had tried to surrender to the RS forces. These killings had allegedly caused a chain reaction 'of killings and suicides, and a number of killings resulted from earlier internal conflicts and personal vendettas'.[78]

Conclusion

For the RS MUP, as for the RS as a whole, the period from the end of 1992 and 1995 had been all about consolidating the strategic goals which had been announced in May 1992. Ethnic cleansing proceeded, albeit at a somewhat reduced pace, even as the institutions of the RS including the police underwent modest reforms. Throughout 1993 and 1994, the armed forces of the RS proved largely capable of maintaining control of the large swathes of territory seized in 1992, and the seizure of Srebrenica and Žepa seemed like crowning achievements and were heralded as such by the RS leadership.

Only weeks after the genocide at Srebrenica, the fortunes of the RS and its armed forces took a drastic turn. At the beginning of August, the Croatian Army and the MUP of Croatia carried out a successful military operation causing the collapse of the Republika Srpska Krajina and the expulsion of the vast majority of its Serb inhabitants.[79] At the same time, the genocide in Srebrenica combined with the second mass casualty incident of the war at the Markale market in Sarajevo on 28 August 1995 to propel the international community into overdue reaction. Within forty-eight hours, NATO together with a UN Rapid Reaction Force in Sarajevo began the most coordinated attacks on Bosnian Serb targets since the beginning of the war. The reestablished coalition of ABiH and HVO forces moved to capitalize on the new strategic situation.

The exigencies of the war in the late summer and autumn of 1995 in some senses propelled the RS MUP back to where it had been in 1992. Once again, policing had to take a backseat to combat activities.[80] Yet outgunned by the new coalition on the battlefield, the coalition of the VRS, the RS MUP and paramilitary forces which had proven so successful in 1992 struggled to resist the onslaught, and the RS leadership soon found itself forced into suing for peace.

EPILOGUE AND CONCLUSION
THE BOSNIAN SERB POLICE AND NEGATIVE PEACE IN DAYTON BOSNIA

In the autumn of 1995, as the ink dried on the Dayton Peace Accords, the Bosnian Serb leadership was in a foul mood. The halcyon days of July when Srebrenica and Žepa had been 'liberated', and when the realization of the strategic goals of May 1992 seemed imminent, seemed a distant memory. Instead came first the collapse of the fraternal Republika Srpska Krajina during Operation Storm in Croatia and then late summer's NATO bombardment combined with a joint Croatian-Muslim offensive. This latter push might well have succeeded in taking Banja Luka had the Western coalition not pulled the handbrake. Then came the emasculating humiliation of being dragged muzzled to the negotiating table at Wright-Patterson Air Force Base in Ohio, where Serbian President Slobodan Milošević held sole negotiating authority for the Bosnian Serbs. On top of it all, the new International Criminal Tribunal for the Former Yugoslavia had indicted Radovan Karadžić and Ratko Mladić and was moving to indict many others.

This book's brief final chapter starts by describing how the Bosnian Serb political leadership again used the police as an enforcement mechanism, but this time as the main instrument of resistance against the Dayton Peace Accords. The Bosnian Serbs despised this agreement, and they were initially determined to undermine it by further militarizing the police and by using the police to prevent Bosnian Muslims and Croats from returning to those areas whence they had been forcibly removed during the war. The early period after Dayton saw numerous incidents in which the police in Republika Srpska either stood idly or arguably even participated in threats and harassment towards returnees. The police proved extremely reluctant to investigate low-level attacks such as the blowing up of houses, which was quite worrying given that this type of violence had in 1991 and early 1992 presaged the outbreak of war. Later, with the rise to power of Milorad Dodik, a politician originally perceived and promoted by the international community as a reformer, the RS MUP transitioned into the pillar of his regime, which it remains today.

From enemies of Dayton to defenders of Dayton

For better or worse, everything in Bosnia since the war has revolved around the Dayton Peace Agreement (DPA), which was officially signed in Paris on 14 December 1995. The DPA created the now well-known state structure in which

Bosnia was given a weak central state with two strong entities – Republika Srpska and the Federation of Bosnia and Herzegovina. The DPA not only permitted both entities to maintain both their own armed forces and their own police forces, it actually enforced the principle of decentralized – and by extension ethnically segregated – policing. Notwithstanding the earlier Washington Agreement, the Croats and the Muslims in the Federation continued to maintain separate police forces. Moreover, all three groups continued to operate their own state security services. Factoring in the cantonal structure of the Federation, and adding the Brčko District, which was created in 1999, Bosnia and Herzegovina ended up with no fewer than thirteen police forces and three intelligence services. In fact, policing within the RS was highly centralized compared to the cantonal structure of the Federation.

As countless experts have noted over the years, the DPA excelled in creating a relatively stable negative peace – no mean feat after three and a half years of atrocious warfare. However, the DPA not only failed to create the groundwork for a positive peace, but instead created a structure that maintained and inexorably reproduced the divisions which had caused the conflict in the first place.[1] The DPA contained some strong echoes of Cutileiro's erstwhile plan from 1992. Indeed, in later years at the ICTY, some defendants argued that the massive bloodshed could have been avoided had the police just been peacefully divided in 1992. For example, when testifying in the trial of Radovan Karadžić, Mićo Stanišić stated that the Cutileiro 'plan' and the Dayton Accords were 'identical. There may have been some aberrations, but more or less the situation was identical'.[2] Yet that of course elided two essential points: not only had actual events in 1992 shown that a peaceful division was an illusion, but in the meantime, over 100,000 lives had been lost and now the conflict was being frozen in place.[3]

The DPA was, to put it mildly, not well received by the RS leadership or by the RS MUP when it was finalized.[4] The 1995 RS MUP annual report, which was issued in January 1996, referred to the treaty as 'unjust towards the Serb nation'.[5] As a result, the RS policy with respect to the implementation of the DPA was initially one of opposition and across the board obstruction. Moreover, the international community's decision to hold elections very soon after the war essentially cemented and ratified the power of Bosnia's wartime politicians.[6]

This chapter will not attempt to summarize the considerable research literature about the DPA and its many problems, but one key postwar development deserves highlighting. Notwithstanding the enormous and nearly unanimous initial rejection of the DPA in the RS, the RS leadership including the RS MUP eventually evolved into fervent defenders of Dayton. The shift from principled opponents to advocates came as a result of the realization that the attainment of an ethnically defined entity offered the best assurance against the development of a strongly centralized and functional Bosnian state. And just as the RS MUP had proved essential as the vanguard of the creation of Republika Srpska, so it came to be seen by successive postwar Bosnian Serbs leaders as a fundamental prerequisite for the RS's survival – and for any potential successful future secession from Bosnia and Herzegovina.

Postwar police reform after the war

By the time the war ended in Bosnia, the widespread participation of the RS MUP in the commission of wartime atrocities was hardly a secret. The vast majority of perpetrators remained in power after the DPA was signed and exerted enormous influence over events in the country.[7] And the result on the ground was apparent in the radically changed ethnic demographics, in particular the near total absence of Bosnian Muslims from many municipalities in which they had constituted either the largest group or even a majority before the war. Consider, for example, the case of Zvornik in eastern Bosnia. In 1991, Muslims were a majority – 59 per cent – of the municipality's population; in the 2013 census, even after some refugee returns, the Muslims were reduced to 33.7 per cent.[8] The head of CJB Zvornik after the war in Zvornik was Dragomir Vasić, precisely the same person who played an instrumental role in coordinating operations with the VRS in and around Srebrenica during the genocide in 1995.

Quite obviously, therefore, the Bosnian Serbs, having effected the ethnic cleansing of the country, had no intention of standing idly by and permitting the return of Bosniak and Croat displaced persons and refugees to their homes. And both the VRS and the RS MUP could as the armed and monoethnic components of the RS work to thwart these returns. In principle, Annex 7 of the DPA required the international community to facilitate returns, but particularly in the early postwar period, the RS MUP patrolled the Inter-Entity Boundary Line as if it was an international border. (And even in the Federation, the reintegration of Bosniak and Croat police took years.[9]) Gerald Toal and Carl Dahlman note that the police in the RS 'tightened checkpoints and refused to honor Dayton's guarantees for freedom of movement and the return of displaced persons. Neither would they control the riotous mobs organized by SDS leaders to stop returns; in actuality, the police worked with the mobs to prevent returns. … Controlling "security" remained the bedrock of local ethnocratic rule'.[10] In Zvornik, Vasić referred to Bosniak returnees as 'terrorists'.[11] Moreover, in practice, the NATO troops deployed as part of the IFOR/SFOR mission exhibited severe reticence regarding returns (and other portions) of their mandate, and returns were very limited. This particularly applied to so-called minority returns, i.e. the return of refugees and displaced persons to areas in which their ethnicity had become a minority because of ethnic cleansing.

The Dayton Accords placed the issue of policing and police reform in the jurisdiction of the United Nations, which formed the UN Mission in Bosnia and Herzegovina (UNMIBH) pursuant to UN Security Council resolution 1035 on 21 December 1995.[12] UNMBIH encompassed the International Police Task Force (IPTF), which had an authorized strength of 2,057 civilian police personnel and five military liaison officers, and drew on trained police officers who were seconded from various US member states.[13] Pursuant to Annex 11 of the DPA, the IPTF had a mandate to ensure that the police in Bosnia would operate in a manner compatible with international human rights standards, but the IPTF did not have enforcement powers.[14] The European Union Police Mission (EUPM) replaced the IPTF at the end of 2002.

It is not the intent of this chapter to rehash the performance of the IPTF or the European Union Police Mission (EUPM), or the structural problems inherent in the Dayton system, subjects which have received much more attention in the research literature than has the postwar evolution of the Bosnian Serb police and other Bosnian police forces.[15] However, some major developments are worth summarizing. As a result of the massive mobilization of the reserve police during the war and the extensive involvement of the police in combat activities, the conversion of police forces in Bosnia into a normal, peacetime civilian police force faced several significant challenges. 'In essence, this was a matter of transforming the police forces from instruments of war into reliable institutions in the service of the rule of law in a democratic society.'[16] The IPTF had to deal with both quantitative and qualitative issues. The swollen ranks of the police meant that there was a police officer for every seventy-five Bosnians, and the numerous police forces accounted for 9.2 per cent of the all spending by all levels of the public sector in Bosnia.[17] By comparison, the EU average in 2016–18 was one police officer per 294 people, and spending was 'about five times the European average'.[18] Salaries accounted for the lion's share – 80 per cent! – of police expenditure, which meant that it was difficult to find money for the modernization of equipment and technology. Moreover, such skewed expenditure on personnel strengthened the suspicion that the various police forces were instead being used, like many other areas of the public sector in Bosnia, for clientelistic purposes as a way of doling out jobs for politically loyal supporters.

Needless to say, so many police jurisdictions also engendered a lot of competition and rivalry, not least given the bad blood which three and a half years of warfare had left behind. Most RS MUP police officers and their Federation counterparts viewed each other with barely concealed hostility or even still as outright enemies, so non-cooperation was the norm. For criminals, by contrast, cantonal, entity and other 'borders' often proved an asset by blocking police investigations and cooperation, and indications also exist that criminals were less likely to be dissuaded from cooperating with like-minded individuals from other ethnicities.[19] As seen in the beginning of this book, many members and leaders of paramilitary units in particular had acquired criminal records prior to the war. Though they might in the course of the war have been 'standardized' as regular military or police units, the end of the war for many of them merely signified continuation of illicit activities such as smuggling and human trafficking.[20]

Qualitatively speaking, there were plenty of problems to tackle. Many of the police officers, especially in the reserve force, had not undergone proper police training. Countless members of the police had implicated themselves in the commission of atrocities. Moreover, whereas other communist police forces had at least begun to segregate state security functions of policing from ordinary, civilian policing, these functions remained united in the RS MUP and the other police forces in Bosnia. In neither of the entities in Bosnia after the war was there any tradition or even direct experience with apolitical policing. After all, as will be recalled from Chapter 1, even the brief interlude between the November 1990 elections and the outbreak of the war had been characterized by blatant political instrumentalization of the police.

Overall, the trajectory of international involvement with police reform has been aptly summarized as having 'started as a technical project improving the training and performance of police officers and organizations, it later moved towards reform aimed at strengthening the state's capacity'.[21] In April 1996, the Bonn-Petersberg Agreement between the UN Mission in Bosnia and Herzegovina (UNMBIH) and the Federation opened the door for police reform. According to Dominique Wisler, the focus here was on the vetting of the police.

> The UN Mission created a certification following a three-stage process: the first stage was the registration of all personnel with law enforcement power; the second stage was the screening of this personnel who were to fulfil a number of conditions to be provisionally authorized; provisionally authorized personnel were issued a UN Mission ID card which they were required to wear on duty; the last stage for final authorization was to meet a number of standards to qualify to serve in a democratic police force.[22]

By 2002, 'more than 16 700 police officers had been successfully vetted and nearly 800 decertified'.[23] However, the results were suboptimal, with some in the UN and the EU arguing that the decertification had violated the rights of police officers; and the structural constraints and side effects of the Dayton system, which rewarded and reproduced clientelistic and nationalist behaviour, limited and contradicted the modest achievements of the vetting process.[24] The police also remained generally poorly regarded by the public regardless of ethnicity.[25]

The Bonn-Petersberg Agreement covered only the Federation. As noted, the RS leadership for quite some time after Dayton wanted nothing to do with the international community and exhibited a strong stance of hostility towards any reform initiatives. However, in the course of 1997, a major power struggle took place between Biljana Plavšić and Momčilo Krajišnik. Although erstwhile allies and members of the 1992 RS collective presidency – both would later go on to be indicted and convicted at the ICTY of war crimes and crimes against humanity – they had come to represent differing paths for the RS. Plavšić became the second president of the RS after the international community forced Radovan Karadžić to step down from office because the ICTY indicted him.

While Plavšić exhibited some mild reform tendencies, particularly with respect to the morass of corruption and organized crime which had emerged during the war and was now parasitically devouring the RS, Krajišnik remained a stalwart ally of Karadžić and those who continued to draw benefit from the legacy of war profiteering. The assassination in June 2000 of postwar Police Chief of Bijeljina Ljubiša Savić 'Mauzer', the erstwhile leader of the paramilitary formation – and later VRS unit – known as the Panthers, served to emphasize the volatility of the security situation in the RS. Savić, who himself had profited handsomely from the war, had sided with Plavšić in her attempts at reining in organized crime.[26]

The Plavšić-Krajišnik power struggle acted as a catalyst for the emergence of a significant new actor on the Bosnian political scene, one who would come to dominate Republika Srpska in particular. Milorad Dodik was a member of the Bosnian Serb parliament representing the constituency of Laktaši, a forgettable town located on the road connecting Banja Luka and the border town of Bosanska Gradiška.[27] In the 1990 elections, Dodik, a member of the SRBiH League of Communists, had sided not with the SDS but with the reform forces of Yugoslav Prime Minister Ante Marković. During the war, Dodik served in a caucus of independent – i.e. non-SDS – members of the Bosnian Serb parliament. In 1996, Dodik transformed this caucus into a new political party, the Party of Independent Social Democrats (*Stranka nezavisnih socijaldemokrata*, SNSD), which he has headed ever since. As the head of that party, Dodik famously gave an interview to the magazine *Slobodna Bosna* calling for Radovan Karadžić and Ratko Mladić to turn themselves in and stand trial at the ICTY.[28]

When the relationship between Krajišnik and Plavšić soured, Dodik allied with Plavšić and was elected in the September 1997 elections. In January 1998, Plavšić selected him as prime minister of the RS, which caused the SDS to boycott the relevant session of parliament. By contrast, both the representatives of the international community and of both Bosniaks and Croats viewed him as a hopeful choice. Indeed, 'one year before he was elected as prime minister for the first time, Dodik was appointed as a minister in the Alternative Council of Ministers of BiH as a civic response to the then ruling coalition of nationalist parties'.[29]

Dodik remained a darling of the international community for some years. In 2000, the SDS, now led by Mirko Šarović, defeated Dodik. Only in 2006 did Dodik succeed in returning to power, but this time his stay proved to be lasting. Not coincidentally, Dodik's views of the Dayton Accords and his appetite for reform collapsed the more solid his grip on power in the RS became. Dodik began to construct a platform that claimed that the RS was, contrary to the Dayton Accords, being slowly dismantled at the expense of the Bosnian state. According to Dodik, the ultimate goal of the Bosniaks was the extinction of Republika Srpska and the reduction of the Bosnian Serbs to second-class citizens. Seen from this point of view, any strengthening of Bosnia's state institutions was an assault on not just the Serb nation – but also on Dayton itself.

After a decade of very halting reforms, the Office of the High Representative (OHR) in 2004 established the Police Restructuring Commission 'with the mission to propose "a single structure of policing for Bosnia and Herzegovina under the overall political oversight of a ministry or ministries in the Council of Ministers"'.[30] The OHR used a negative assessment of progress issued by NATO in June 2004 as a justification for the commission's work. NATO's communique stated that 'Bosnia and Herzegovina, particularly obstructionist elements in the Republika Srpska entity, has failed to live up to its obligation to cooperate fully with ICTY, including the arrest and transfer to the jurisdiction of the Tribunal of war crimes indictees'.[31] NATO called for 'systemic changes necessary to develop effective security and law enforcement structures'.

Much has been made about the fact that the EU could not point to a single European model of policing, and indeed the EU member states – even within the considerably smaller pre-2004 EU – exhibited very different police structures ranging from the highly centralized to the federalized. In that sense, it was indeed incorrect for Ashdown to state that a highly centralized model was a requirement. Yet in terms of rule of law, etc., there were certain EU standards, and, with the exception of Belgium, the police in EU states did not operate on an ethnically divided basis. 'In no other European country was the structure of policing fragmented into several autonomous police bodies working parallel to each other.'[32]

No state-level law enforcement agency in Bosnia has a clear precedence over the entity-level and cantonal police forces. A state-level law enforcement agency, the State Investigation and Protection Agency (SIPA), was created in 2002, but while it can undertake its own investigations and police actions, it cannot compel the cooperation of other law enforcement agencies.[33] According to Wisler, 'the SIPA project was the first clear sign of recognition by the OHR that policing in Bosnia could not be territorialized, or at least not entirely territorialized, and the first step of a fundamental change to the police reform.'[34] Lindvall concurs, writing that 'SIPA would, however, turn out to be a considerable disappointment and its contribution to law enforcement in BiH would be marginal.'[35]

It should be noted that statewide consolidation of policing did occur with respect to the state security service, which as seen had, historically speaking, been a constitutive component of internal affairs in Yugoslavia and its successor states. Pursuant to intense pressure from the Office of the High Representative, and in large part owing to demonstrable obstruction related to obligatory cooperation with the ICTY, the statewide Intelligence and Security Agency (*Obavještajno-sigurnosna agencija*, OSA) was created, replacing the two entity-level agencies.[36]

At the end of 2004, the commission, which was chaired by former Belgian Prime Minister Wilfred Martens, recommended

> a single structure model with two administrative levels of policing bearing close similarities with the Belgian model: services such as the SIPA, the State Border Service, and central support services were organized at the central national level while regional police forces under the supervision of a national directorate would serve associations of municipalities (regions) that would cut across the borders of former entities and cantons.[37]

All Bosnian Serb political representatives rejected the proposed inter-entity policing, and in particular the implied dissolution of the RS MUP.[38] Yet even with the expanded Bonn Powers which had been handed to the OHR in 1997, the OHR could not implement this expansive police reform without the consent of the two entities.[39]

Here it bears reminding that a parallel process of military reform was occurring, whereby the VRS, the Army of the Republic of Bosnia and Herzegovina and Croat Defence Council (HVO) were forced to merge. This reform, although not without its imperfections, successfully resulted in the creation of the unified armed forces of Bosnia and Herzegovina on 1 December 2004.[40] Had the similarly bold police reform succeeded, Bosnia would have from the point of view of state executive power had enjoyed a significantly stronger position. Indeed, Thomas Muehlmann argues that, in initiating a very ambitious and robust police reform process, Paddy Ashdown, who was dual-hatted as the High Representative and the EU Special Representative, was 'probably inspired by the successful completion of reforms in the defence area'.[41]

For precisely this reason, the reform of the police was anathema to the vast majority of Bosnian Serb politicians. Dodik could plausibly argue that, with the disappearance of the VRS, the only armed force which the Bosnian Serbs retained was the police. The continuities with the earlier policies of the SDS – including the prewar SDS – were obvious. While Dodik for personal political reasons disparaged the SDS, it suited him to style himself as the defender of the RS and to provoke both the international community and the Bosniaks. Dodik presented himself as the only real defender of the Dayton Accords and repetitive threats to hold a referendum on the independence of the RS from Bosnia became a hallmark of Dodik's rule. Simultaneously, Dodik over time began to engage in increasingly vocal denialism of crimes perpetrated by the Bosnian Serbs during the war. The same Dodik who called for Karadžić to be tried at the ICTY eventually opened a student dormitory named in honour of Karadžić even though he himself had behind the scenes allowed the RS MUP to cooperate with the ICTY in the apprehension of fugitives including Karadžić.[42]

The RS parliament did very reluctantly pass police reform legislation in October 2005, likely because doing so was a prerequisite for Bosnia to begin negotiating the critical Stabilization and Association Agreement (SAA) with the EU.[43] Yet according to Tija Memisević, Dodik after his election as prime minister in 2006 'rejected all previously reached agreements on police reform and initiated a new negotiation process, forcing the EU onto the defensive on the substance of the criteria by using the strategy of applying pressure by orchestrating (artificial) political crises'.[44]

The upper house of the Bosnian state parliament passed police reform legislation in April 2008, and the SAA was signed in June. However, the reform was effectively stillborn owing to massive resistance in the RS, and in the meantime Nikola Špirić, who was the head of the Council of Ministers in Bosnia, resigned. Špirić stated that it was unacceptable that the international community could implement its will without the consent of Bosnia's citizens.[45] Faced with such resistance, 'even though the EU officially maintained the image of unity, in private there were some disagreements and, ultimately, the international community gave up'.[46] According to the Democratization Policy Council, 'the EU accepted a "substitute" agreement from political leaders to create several powerless state-level police agencies and to sign a written commitment for future police reform – Brussels never followed up on the latter'.[47] In both the Federation and the RS, politicians pushed to roll back those police reforms which had been implemented previously, and in 2012 the EU shut down the EUPM, 'declaring the mission a success'.[48]

Analysts of the failed reform have identified ineffective conditionality and nationalist recalcitrance as the key obstacles. It has been argued that 'police reform placed high domestic political costs on Bosnian Serb elites as it threatened the very survival of Republika Srpska'.[49] Conversely, it is correct to state that 'efforts by EU officials and EUPM police experts to portray police reform as a technical question have understandably not been successful'.[50] Yet the depiction of police reform as a stark threat to the existence of the RS accepts rather than challenges the nationalist and opportunistic arguments of the RS leadership.[51] A successful police reform as conceived by the OHR and the aforementioned commission would no more have destroyed the RS than the current administration of policing in the Federal Republic of Germany has destroyed the identity of Bavaria, Saxony, Brandenburg or any of the other federal units in that country.[52]

By contrast, successful police reform along those lines would have directly thwarted any ambitions that the RS had towards statehood, or a state merger with Serbia – hence the unacceptability of police reform in postwar Bosnia for nationalists and for political opportunists like Dodik. In this sense Dodik has become a perfect example of how Dayton structurally produces new 'nationalists', and not just on the Serbian side.

The real danger is not to the Serb nation or Bosnian Serb statehood, but to their private nationalization of their ill-gotten gains from the war.[53] Without a firm control of the police and the judiciary, Dodik and his allies would risk investigations and prosecutions that could imperil their entire power base. It is worth noting that, in March 1992, in the final lead-up to the war, SRBiH Assistant Minister Momčilo Mandić faced the imminent danger of criminal prosecution for crimes including the alleged laundering of very large amounts of money. As the Bosnian press started to publish these allegations, Mandić in all likelihood accelerated the establishment of the RS MUP and hence the violent dissolution of Bosnia.[54] The Bosnian reporter Senad Avdić, who covered these matters at the time, has recently revisited the Mandić 'affair' in the context of the current crisis involving Dodik and the RS.[55]

This threat of investigations also helps to explain Dodik's stance with respect to the State Court of Bosnia and Herzegovina, which possesses a dual mandate to prosecute both war crimes, crimes against humanity and genocide and also organized crime.[56] As the International Crisis Group has noted, 'the apparent incompetence of the police is often a strategy to mask the influence of well-connected individuals and nationalist agendas'.[57] Hence, while Bosnia ranks quite well compared to many other countries as regards ordinary crime, the country suffers from ethnic stratification and an unwillingness to robustly investigate organized criminal activity and corruption when perpetrated by power elites. According to the Democratization Policy Council, 'the capacity of the judiciary and police to provide justice and security and to prosecute sensitive cases of high-level organized crime and (political) corruption in BiH today is practically non-existent'. This predicament, which exists at the expense of the Bosnian economy and the ordinary citizens of the country, suits not only Dodik but also leading Bosniak and Croat politicians in the Federation.

Conclusion

In its final trial brief in the case of Mićo Stanišić and Stojan Župljanin, the Office of the Prosecutor at the ICTY wrote that

> in peacetime, the police serve an important role in protecting the citizenry through the enforcement of law and order. In times of ethnic strife, their role becomes critical. They either continued to perform their legal duties indiscriminately and diligently ... or they side with one ethnic group thereby propagating a culture of impunity and a climate of fear among the other ethnic groups.[58]

Both this book and the trial from which the majority of the sources are drawn showed overwhelmingly that the police in Bosnia, above all the Bosnian Serb police, tragically chose not to serve and protect the population – the first duty of any proper police force – but to seek and destroy the ethnic Other.[59] Yet while the atrocities and destruction came to a close with the peace accords at Dayton, the same forces which had propelled Bosnia into the abyss of ethnic cleansing cunningly and systematically worked to secure their gains in the decades that followed. In doing so, they relied on the police.

Many and most likely most of the perpetrators of atrocity crimes in the Bosnian war remain unrepentant, including those few who have been convicted. It is telling that Mićo Stanišić chose to conclude his second book with the following words: 'To everything which our enemies sought to impose upon on, and that which they did impose upon us – and that is an unprecedentedly difficult and bloody war – we responded with a human and natural need to defend our inherent and human rights and liberties and the defence of our centuries-old ethnic territory.'[60]

How have Bosnian Serb police perpetrators fared after the end of the war in Bosnia and Herzegovina? Mićo Stanišić and Stojan Župljanin were both convicted of war crimes and crimes against humanity and sentenced by the ICTY to twenty-two years in prison.[61] Simo Drljača, the notorious chief of SJB Prijedor in 1992, was indicted by the ICTY but was killed when NATO forces tried to arrest him in July 1997. Željko Mejakić, the commander of Omarska detention camp, and several others were convicted and sentenced, as were several other low-ranking perpetrators. The Head of SJB Bosanski Šamac, Stevo Todorović, was tried at the ICTY, found guilty and sentenced to ten years in prison. He committed suicide in 2006 after obtaining provisional release. And Darko Mrđa was sentenced to seventeen years in prison for his role in the massacre at Korićanske stijene. A number of paramilitary leaders were also indicted at the ICTY, such as Milan Lukić, who was sentenced to life imprisonment, and Željko Ražnatović 'Arkan', who was killed in Belgrade in January 2000 before he was apprehended by the ICTY. Turning to 1995, Ljubomir Borovčanin was sentenced to seventeen years in prison for crimes committed in around Srebrenca in July 1995. At the State Court of Bosnia and Herzegovina, which has jurisdiction over war crimes, quite a number of lower-level police perpetrators have been prosecuted. In early

December 2021, Goran Sarić, the former head of the RS MUP Special Brigade of the Police, who had been twice acquitted on other war crimes charges, was arrested in Bosnia.[62] And far away from Bosnia and Herzegovina, United States, Canadian and other authorities have deported Bosnian Serb police perpetrators who obtained residency and citizenship on false premises by posing as refugees and hiding their criminal pasts.

Yet as with most conflicts in human history, the vast majority of police perpetrators will never face prosecution. Many victims of mass atrocities in today's Bosnia and Herzegovina encounter perpetrators on a regular basis. And several high-ranking former officials of the RS MUP have to date not faced prosecution. One particularly noteworthy example is Tomislav Kovač, who helped to remove non-Serb personnel from SJB Ilidža prior to the war, cooperated with paramilitary forces in and around Sarajevo during the summer of 1992, and who was acting minister of the RS MUP during the genocide at Srebrenica. Kovač has had a relatively successful postwar career as a manufacturer of baked goods and appears frequently on various talk shows in Serbia to discuss topics related to the war.

Even after the SDS was dislodged from power and replaced by an ostensibly pliable and pro-Western leader, Milorad Dodik, the structural framework of Dayton and Dodik's own ambitions ensured that the police remained the main obstacle to lasting peace in Bosnia. With the forced dissolution of the Bosnian Serb Army, the Bosnian Serb police once again became the only armed force in Bosnia exclusively under Bosnian Serb control. Over a quarter of a century after the end of the Bosnian war, Dodik relies on the police to secure his power base, to prevent investigations of corruption and organized crime and to 'weaponize' his repeated threats to call for a referendum on the secession of Republika Srpska from Bosnia and Herzegovina.[63] Of particular concern has been the noticeable militarization of the RS MUP in recent years, such as the purchase of weapons from Russia.[64]

The leadership of Republika Srpska contends that the dismantling of the RS MUP would have constituted a violation of the Dayton Accords and that 'the West' along with its Bosniak allies intend in the long term to dismantle the RS entirely. But if the merger of the VRS with the BiH armed forces into one unified Bosnian army did not violate the Dayton Accords, there is no clear reason why police reform would have been different. Conversely, one could in some sense argue that not clearly announcing the goal of a unified multi-ethnic police force was the original sin of the international community's postwar involvement in Bosnia, because any attempt at reforming the police later was under even the best of circumstances going to be extremely difficult. In this sense, it was akin to the acceptance of a blatantly ethnic label for Republika Srpska – a concession which Richard Holbrooke, the primary architect of Dayton, later bitterly regretted. Accepting Republika Srpska and the continued existence of the RS MUP undoubtedly made it easier to seal the peace at Dayton. This was no small feat after three and a half years of brutal warfare and atrocities. But to a significant extent the price for doing so was a dysfunctional Bosnian state in which the worst gains of ethnic cleansing were cemented in place.

A number of experts on police reform have over the years warned of the long-term dangers for Bosnia and the wider region. Tija Memisević has criticized the EU for ignoring 'the critical relationship between post-conflict policing and transitional justice', focusing instead on 'consideration of financial and organisational efficiency'.[65] She notes that the RS MUP has also been instrumental in media campaigns aimed at focusing public attention on Serb victimhood, while keeping attention away from any atrocities committed by the RS MUP. And the major ruling political parties in Bosnia in both entities 'have secured the continuation of warlike logic in holding sway of power and assets obtained through the war, often by heavy policing, securitization and even retri-bution against its most outspoken critics'.[66]

Of course, it should be noted, as Memisević indeed does, that 'leaders of each of the ethnic groups, demonstrating a high degree of political cynicism, wished that more people, preferably from their own group, had been killed during the war'.[67] That is to say, competitive collective victimhood thrives in Bosnia, and politicians on all sides engage in it, even as they use the police to consolidate their hold on power. And although the focus in this book has been on the role of the police as perpetrators in atrocities committed against other members of other ethnicities, the same police forces which commit such crimes inevitably also violate the rights of members of the in-group. When in March 2018, a young man in Banja Luka named David Dragičević disappeared and was found dead, the authorities in the RS first tried to write his death off as a suicide. Dragičević's father, Davor, insisted that his son had been killed by 'the criminal state', and his crusade to uncover the truth behind son's death involved into the civil protest movement 'Justice for David'. Certainly, the RS police have been very heavy-handed and opaque in their approach towards these protests, arresting Davor Dragičević, banning demonstrations, removing a shrine to his son and at times forcibly dispersing peaceful demonstrators. In some cases, prominent public figures associated with the protests have had to flee the RS.[68] Meanwhile, in the Federation in recent years, politicians have also used the police against demonstrators who opposed controversial building or development projects.[69]

In 2021, the ongoing liabilities of Dayton and entity-based policing remain evident. Emboldened by opportunistic support from Serbia and Russia, Dodik continues with regular frequency and increasing boldness to declare that Bosnia and Herzegovina is a failed state. Dodik has threatened to withdraw Bosnian Serbs from state-level institutions, including the Bosnian Army, and to hold a referendum on the secession of the RS. Since the outgoing High Representative Valentin Inzko in July 2021 issued by decree a law banning genocide denial, the RS has effectively boycotted participation in Bosnian institutions.[70] According to the International Crisis Group, 'armed conflict – albeit on a smaller scale than during the 1992-1995 war – is not unthinkable. Fighting could easily erupt if Republika Srpska is serious about its announced plans to break away. Should Republika Srpska police attempt to take over border posts, for instance, they could come to blows with their state-level counterparts, particularly if the central government deploys federal reinforcements'.[71] And observers have also expressed concern in recent years at the militarization of the RS MUP with assistance from Russia.[72]

The chances of Bosnia ever having an effective police force that is not ethnically based continue to be very remote. Over twenty-five years after the end of the war, it remains the case that

> the role of the police is not seen as being 'to serve and protect' everyone, but instead to serve and protect 'one's own kind', whether they be co-nationals, colleagues or political masters. … Nowhere is this more evident than in cases involving the continuation or consolidation of wartime 'achievements': 'ethnic cleansing', the appropriation of public assets and the maintenance of national-territorial divisions.[73]

As long as the current structure remains in place in Bosnia, policing – and with it the entire population of the country – will remain at the mercy of oligarchic ethnic elites who will manufacture artificial crises to thwart transparency, effective governance and accountability. Given that this consensus serves only those elites, and that the international community has in effect decided that reforms will only occur if they are adopted by Bosnia's politicians, it is highly questionable whether any positive change will happen at all.

NOTES

Introduction

1 Even a survey restricted to English-language publications stretches to hundreds of books and articles. Catherine Baker, *The Yugoslav Wars of the 1990s* (London: Palgrave, 2015).
2 Unless otherwise noted, all references to ICTY judgements in the endnotes refer to judgements of the relevant trial chambers.
3 Barry Posen, 'The Security Dilemma and Ethnic Conflict', *Survival*, Vol. 3, No. 1 (1993), 27–47; Dejan Jović, *Jugoslavija: Država koja je odumrla* (Zagreb: Prometej, 2003); Max Bergholz, *Violence as a Generative Force: Identity, Nationalism, and Memory in a Balkan Community* (Ithaca: Cornell University Press, 2016); Mila Dragojević, *Amoral Communities: Collective Crimes in Time of War* (Ithaca: Cornell University Press, 2019); Christian Gerlach, *Extremely Violent Societies: Mass Violence in the Twentieth-Century World* (Cambridge: Cambridge University Press, 2010).
4 Christian Axboe Nielsen, *Vi troede ikke det kunne ske her: Jugoslaviens sammenbrud 1991–1999* (Copenhagen: Kristeligt Dagblads Forlag, 2018).
5 Christian Axboe Nielsen, 'Surmounting the Myopic Focus on Genocide: The Case of the War in Bosnia and Herzegovina', *Journal of Genocide Research*, Vol. 15, No. 1 (2013), 21–39; Jelena Subotić, 'Stories States Tell: Identity, Narrative and Human Rights in the Balkans', *Slavic Review*, Vol. 72, No. 2 (Summer 2013), 306–26.
6 Jovo Mijatović, 20th Session of the RS Assembly, 14–15 November 1992 (0422-6267).
7 ICTY, 'Statements of Guilt', https://www.icty.org/en/features/statements-guilt. The opportunistic subsequent retraction of the content Plavšić's guilty plea is immaterial.
8 Elissa Helms, *Innocence and Victimhood: Gender, Nation, and Women's Activism in Postwar Bosnia-Herzegovina* (Madison, WI: University of Wisconsin Press, 2013); Elissa Helms, 'Rejecting Angelina: War Rape Survivors and the Ambiguities of Sex in War', *Slavic Review*, Vol. 73, No. 3 (2014), 612–34; Heleen Touquet, 'Silent or Inaudible? Male Survivor Stories in Bosnia and Herzegovina', *Social Politics: International Studies in Gender, State & Society* (2021).
9 Mićo Stanišić, *Početak rata u Bosni i Hercegovini* (Belgrade: Donat-graf, 2017), 6.
10 Martin Broszat, Hans Buchheim, Hans-Adolf Jacobsen and Helmut Krausnik, *Die Anatomie des SS-Staates* (Olten-Freiburg im Breisgau: Walter, 1965); Helmut Krausnick and Hans-Heinrich Wilhelm, *Die Truppe des Weltanschauungskrieges: die Einsatzgruppen der Sicherheitspolizei und des SD, 1938–1942* (Stuttgart: Deutsche Verlags-Anstalt, 1981); Christopher R. Browning, *Ordinary Men: Reserve Police Battalion 101 and the Final Solution in Poland* (New York: HarperPerennial, 1992); Nikolaus Wachmann, *KL: A History of the Nazi Concentration Camps* (New York: Farrar, Straus and Giroux, 2016). Ironically, given the tendency to focus on armies as perpetrators of war crimes, the German army, the *Wehrmacht*, for many years managed to retain a comparatively innocent and benign place in German (and even European) collective memory. Christine R. Nugent, 'The Voice of the Visitor: Popular

Reactions to the Exhibition *Vernichtungskrieg. Verbrechen der Wehrmacht 1941–1944*', *Journal of European Studies*, Vol. 44, No. 3 (2014), 249–62; Hannes Heer, Walter Manoschek, Alexander Pollak and Ruth Wodak, eds., *Discursive Construction of History: Remembering the Wehrmacht's War of Annihilation* (Hampshire: Palgrave Macmillan, 2008). On local police collaboration in the Holocaust, see Martin Dean, *Collaboration in the Holocaust: Crimes of the Local Police in Belorussia and Ukraine, 1941–44* (New York: St. Martin's Press, 2000).

11 Bruce B. Campbell and Arthur D. Brenner, eds., *Death Squads in Global Perspective: Murder with Deniability* (New York: Palgrave Macmillan, 2000); Kirsten Weld, *Paper Cadavers: The Archives of Dictatorship in Guatemala* (Durham, NC: Duke University Press, 2014).

12 John J. Donohue III and Steven D. Levitt, 'The Impact of Race on Policing and Arrests', *The Journal of Law & Economics*, Vol. 14, No. 2 (2001), 367–94; Cassandra Chaney and Ray V. Robertson, 'Racism and Police Brutality in America', *Journal of African American Studies*, Vol. 17 (2013), 480–505; Clarence Taylor, *Fight the Power: African Americans and the Long History of Police Brutality in New York City* (New York: New York University Press, 2019).

13 Robert Donia, *Radovan Karadžić: Architect of the Bosnian Genocide* (Cambridge: Cambridge University Press, 2014).

14 Adis Maksić, *Ethnic Mobilization, Violence, and the Politics of Affect: The Serb Democratic Party and the Bosnian War* (London: Palgrave Macmillan, 2017).

15 Marko Attila Hoare, *How Bosnia Armed* (London: Saqi Books, 2004).

16 Christian Axboe Nielsen, 'Collective and Competitive Victimhood in the Former Yugoslavia', in Nanci Adler, ed., *Understanding the Age of Transitional Justice: Crimes, Courts, Commissions, and Chronicling* (New Brunswick: Rutgers University Press, 2018), 175–93; Nielsen, 'Surmounting the Myopic Focus on Genocide'.

17 Jan Zwierzchowski and Ewa Tabeau, 'The 1992–95 War in Bosnia and Herzegovina: Census-Based Multiple System Estimation of Casualties' Undercount', Conference Paper for the International Research Workshop on 'The Global Costs of Conflict', February 2010, https://www.icty.org/x/file/About/OTP/War_Demographics/en/bih_casualty_undercount_conf_paper_100201.pdf, 18.

18 UN International Residual Mechanism for Criminal Tribunals, Unified Court Records, http://ucr.irmct.org. Although far from ideal, this relatively new website marks a significant improvement from the previous, unwieldy and user-hostile (and still active) ICTY Court Records website, https://icr.icty.org.

19 On KOS, see the highly problematic accounts of Munir Alibabić, *Bosna u kandžama KOS-a* (Sarajevo: Behar, 1996) and *Deda, Dedo i Babo Bosnu KOSili* (Sarajevo, 2010). See also Hoare, *How Bosnia Armed*.

20 Baker, *The Yugoslav Wars of the 1990s*; Rogers Brubaker, *Ethnicity without Groups* (Cambridge: Harvard University Press, 2006).

Chapter 1

1 Nijaz Duraković quoted in Neven Anđelić, *Bosnia: The End of a Legacy* (London: Routledge, 2003), 68.

2 The terminology in Yugoslavia shifted between 'ministries' and 'secretariats'. The term 'ministry' will be used here for the sake of simplicity.

3   The structure and work of the Yugoslav Security Service is presented in Christian Axboe Nielsen, *Yugoslavia and Political Assassinations: The History and Legacy of Tito's Campaign against the Émigrés* (London: I.B. Tauris, 2020).
4   For an empathetic account, see Svetko Kovač, Bojana Dimitrijević and Irena Popović Grigorov, *Slučaj Ranković* (Belgrade: Medija Centar 'Odbrana', 2014).
5   On 'brotherhood and unity' and Yugoslav nationalities policy, see Hilde Haug, *Creating a Socialist Yugoslavia: Tito, Communist Leadership and the National Question* (London: I.B. Tauris, 2012).
6   Marko Attila Hoare, 'Whose Is the Partisan Movement? Serbs, Croats and the Legacy of a Shared Resistance', *Journal of Slavic Military Studies*, Vol. 15, No. 4 (December 2002), 24–41; Anđelić, *Bosnia*, 37; Mirzad D. Abazović, *Kadrovski rat za BiH (1945–91)* (Sarajevo: Savez logoraša Bosne i Hercegovine, 1999), 351–2. For an overview of the ethnic representation of commanding tactical officers in the JNA in the period from 1977 to 1985, see Davor Marijan, *Slom Titove armije: JNA i raspad Jugoslavije* (Zagreb: Golden Marketing, 2008), 66.
7   Anđelić, *Bosnia*, 38. See also Andrew Gilbert, *International Intervention and the Problem of Legitimacy: Encounters in Postwar Bosnia-Herzegovina* (Ithaca: Cornell University Press, 2020), 73.
8   On the chronic economic crisis, see Woodward, *Socialist Unemployment*; on the particularly conservative Bosnian communists, see Anđelić, *Bosnia*, 43–7.
9   Slavoljub Đukić, *Milošević and Marković: A Lust for Power* (Montreal: McGill-Queen's University Press, 2001); Adam LeBor, *Milošević: A Biography* (London: Bloomsbury, 2003).
10 BBC, 'Yugoslavia: Death of a Nation – Enter Nationalism', Episode 1, 00:08:48.
11 Nebojša Vladisavljević, *Serbia's Antibureaucratic Revolution: Milošević, the Fall of Communism and Nationalist Mobilization* (Houndmills: Palgrave Macmillan, 2008).
12 See video from Ranković's burial, https://youtu.be/6eu1HkDyLDI. See also ICTY, Testimony of Slavenko Terzić, *Milošević*, 7 December 2004. 'Casting Rankovic as a Serbian nationalist ultimately encouraged Serbs themselves to see his fall in national terms'. ICTY, Testimony of Audrey Helfant Budding, *Milošević*, 8 February 2005, 35872.
13 Decision of SRBiH Constitutional Court, 11 June 1990, SRBiH *Službeni glasnik* No. 17, 20 June 1990 (0113-8772-0113-8776).
14 Dušan Šehovac, 'Ko je rekao i slagao "Bili smo i ostaćemo zajedno u našoj BiH, u Jugoslaviji"', undated, Frontal.ba.
15 Medina Delalić and Suzana Sačić, *Balkan bluz* (Sarajevo, 2007). The presence of Izetbegović at the founding of the party is also a problem for Mićo Stanišić's portrayal of the SDA as a malignant force. Mićo Stanišić, *Početak rata u Bosni i Hercegovini* (Belgrade: Donat-graf, 2017), 31.
16 These Bosnian Serbs also tend to forget that Izetbegović was defended by a Serb lawyer and even received moral support from Serb nationalist dissident intellectuals in Serbia. To demonstrate ethnic impartiality, the Bosnian regime in the following year pursued a similar case against the Bosnian Serb Vojislav Šešelj, who would go on to ultranationalist notoriety in the 1990s. Anđelić, *Bosnia*, 43–5.
17 Statute of the SDS, 12 July 1990 (0030-6315-0030-6323).
18 Suad Arnautović, *Izbori u Bosni i Hercegovini '90: Analiza izbornog procesa* (Sarajevo: Promocult, 1996) (0089-6646-0049-6663).
19 Armina Galijaš, *Eine bosnische Stadt im Zeichen des Krieges: Ethnopolitik und Alltag in Banja Luka (1990–1995)* (Oldenburg: Oldenbourg Wissenschaftsverlag, 2011), 90.

20 'While the ethno-nationals quarreled in dozens of municipalities over who would get what post, they quickly agreed to entirely exclude SKBiH-SDP and SRSJ whenever their combined votes reached an absolute majority of over 50 per cent.' Adis Maksić, *Ethnic Mobilization, Violence, and the Politics of Affect: The Serb Democratic Party and the Bosnian War* (London: Palgrave Macmillan, 2017), 212–13.
21 Tomo Šimić, 'Dokumenti Predsjedništva Bosne i Hercegovina, 1991–1994', *National Security and the Future*, Vol. 7, No. 1–2 (2006), 31.
22 Andjelic, *Bosnia*, 184f.
23 'The significance of the MUP in Bosnia-Herzegovina, regardless of how one might view it as a state, was enormous because the MUP was the only armed force at the time'. ICTY, Testimony of Neđo Vlaški, *Stanišić and Župljanin*, 15 February 2010, 6334. On the TO, see Tomislav Dulić and Roland Kostić, 'Yugoslavs in Arms: Guerrilla Tradition, Total Defence and the Ethnic Security Dilemma', *Europe-Asia Studies*, Vol. 62, No. 7 (2010), 1051–72. The period between 1990 and 1992 also featured attempts by republics such as Slovenia and Croatia to transform their TOs into republican armies. Marijan, *Slom Titove armije*.
24 'Criteria for the Distribution of Municipal Posts and Departments between the peoples' parties SDS SDA HDZ', 22 December 1990 (0030-6526-0030-6527). See also 'Inter-Party Agreement Connected with CSBs of the BiH MUP', n.d. (SA03-2103-SA03-2104) and list of posts in the Assembly and government, January 1991 (SA03-2086-SA03-2096).
25 This post was subsequently removed, which proved to be one of the reasons for the SDS's dissatisfaction. ICTY, Testimony of Neđo Vlaški, *Stanišić and Župljanin*, 16 February 2010, 6376.
26 Mentioned in letter of Chief of CSB Banja Luka Stojan Župljanin to President of Council for the Protection of the Constitutional Order of SRBiH Biljana Plavšić, 25 July 1991 (SA04-0284-SA04-0285).
27 ICTY, Testimony of Vitomir Žepinić, *Stanišić and Župljanin*, 28 January 2008, 5687.
28 ICTY, Testimony of Vitomir Žepinić, *Stanišić and Župljanin*, 28 January 2008, 5685.
29 ICTY, Consolidated Statement of Mićo Davidović, 22 June 2011 (0680-2869-0680-0680-2937, at 0680-2872).
30 Andjelic, *Bosnia*, 186.
31 Andjelic, *Bosnia*, 187.
32 ICTY, Testimony of Goran Mačar, *Stanišić and Župljanin*, 5 July 2011, 22806.
33 SRBiH MUP, 'Information on Activities for the Change of Leading Personnel in the Ministry of Internal Affairs and the Need for Further Alignment of the National Structure of Employees with the National Structure of the Population', 24 June 1991 (0204-8166-0204-8212). The initial results of the 1991 census were appended to this document.
34 SRBiH MUP, 'Information on Activities for the Change of Leading Personnel in the Ministry of Internal Affairs and the Need for Further Alignment of the National Structure of Employees with the National Structure of the Population', 24 June 1991 (0204-8166-0204-8212), 13. The same report devoted particular attention to the issue of what to do with the estimated 1,084 self-declared Yugoslavs who worked in the ministry.
35 ICTY, Testimony of Goran Mačar, *Stanišić and Župljanin*, 5 July 2011, 22807–22812.
36 Goran Zečević, a former employee of the SRBiH MUP, stated that he had heard rumours regarding over 1,000 police officers stemming from the Sandžak. Letter of Goran Zečević, 22 July 1991 (SA04-1011-SA04-1014).

37 Andjelic, *Bosnia*, 169.
38 ICTY, Testimony of Witness ST-27, *Stanišić and Župljanin*, 2 October 2009, 778.
39 SRBiH MUP, 'Information on Activities for the Change of Leading Personnel in the Ministry of Internal Affairs and the Need for Further Alignment of the National Structure of Employees with the National Structure of the Population', 24 June 1991 (0204-8166-0204-8212).
40 SRBiH MUP, 'Information on Activities for the Change of Leading Personnel in the Ministry of Internal Affairs and the Need for Further Alignment of the National Structure of Employees with the National Structure of the Population', 24 June 1991 (0204-8166-0204-8212), 10; ICTY, testimony of Vitomir Žepinić, *Stanišić and Župljanin*, 28 January 2010, 5744–5.
41 Letter of Serb Employees of SJB Stari Grad Sarajevo, 5 March 1992 (0084-5078-0084-5083).
42 Letter of Goran Zečević, 22 July 1991 (SA04-1011-SA04-1014).
43 Letter of Goran Zečević, 22 July 1991 (SA04-1011-SA04-1014), 2.
44 Letter of Chief of CSB Banja Luka Stojan Župljanin to President of Council for the Protection of the Constitutional Order of SRBiH Biljana Plavšić, 25 July 1991 (SA04-0284-SA04-0285).
45 Official Note taken at CSB Banja Luka by Vojislav Pećanac, 25 July 1991 (SA04-0286-SA04-0286). Conversation between Radovan Karadžić and Žika, 20 June 1991 (0322-3359-0322-3361), conversation between Radovan Karadžić and unknown male, 20 June 1991 (0322-3364-0322-3366).
46 'Public Statement of Leading Employees of Serbian Nationality of the MUP – BiH', 9 September 1991 (0216-7017-0216-7017). The article in *Oslobođenje* (0291-8677-0291-8678) was published on 7 September 1991.
47 Conversation of Radovan Karadžić and Nikola Koljević, 9 September 1991 (0212-8664-0212-8668).
48 Conversation of Radovan Karadžić and Miodrag Simović, 16 September 1991 (0323-3154-0323-3156). Karadžić also again expressed dissatisfaction regarding what he felt was the improper sidelining of Čedo Kljajić in the Public Security Service.
49 According to Neđo Vlaški, he was appointed to this position before it was abolished. ICTY, Testimony of Neđo Vlaški, *Stanišić and Župljanin*, 16 February 2010, 6376f, 6380.
50 This practice was emulated in the HDZ and SDA as well. Maksić, *Ethnic Mobilization*, 94.
51 CSB Banja Luka to SJB Prijedor, 19 September 1991 (0063-5560-0063-5560).
52 See for example the discussion on 4 August 1991 between Biljana Plavšić and Radovan Karadžić regarding a telex that Plavšić had received from Župljanin (0207-8945-0207-8946). This concerned a new vacancy in State Security at CSB Banja Luka, which Karadžić and Plavšić wanted Neđeljko Kesić to take. Karadžić complained that the existing agreement to divide the SRBiH MUP among the three nationalist parties did not cover deputies. This had to be included in the agreement as soon as possible. Karadžić promised to discuss the matter with Alija Izetbegović and Stjepan Kljuić.
53 See, for example, the report of Stojan Župljanin, dated 20 September 1991, sent to Biljana Plavšić, Miodrag Simović, Vitomir Žepinić and Nikola Uzelac on 23 September 1991 (SA02-0124-SA02-0132).
54 Report on situation and problems in the area under the jurisdiction of Prijedor SJB, 6 September 1991 (P002-3979-P002-3990); letter from Hasan Talundžić, Prijedor SJB

Chief to SRBiH MUP Minister Delimustafić and Banja Luka CSB Chief Župljanin, 23 September 1991 (0063-5837).
55 The arrest is recorded in a SRBiH MUP report dated 9 September 1991 (0323-7669-0323-7672).
56 Tape Recording of SRBiH Presidency session of 21 June 1991, cited in *National Security and the Future*, Vol. 7, No. 3 (2006), 8.
57 See also 1 October 1991 conversation of Karadžić and Slavko regarding problems with the distribution of positions in the MUP in Srebrenica (0321-9763-0321-9767). Cf. Complaint of SDA to Izetbegović, Delimustafić, Žepinić, Hebib, Selimović and Mandić, 8 October 1991 (SA00-8550-SA00-8552); complaint of Mandić to SSNO, SSUP and SRBiH MUP, 9 January 1992 (SA00-4902-SA00-4903). On the prewar deterioration of inter-ethnic relations in Srebrenica and surrounding municipalities owing to increasing nationalism among both Bosnian Serbs and Muslims, see Ger Duijzings, *Geschiedenis en herinnering in Oost-Bosnië* (Amsterdam: Boom, 2002).
58 The SRBiH MUP SDB placed a significant number of Bosnian Serb officials under electronic surveillance during the period from approximately the summer of 1991. The intercepted telephone conversations that resulted were later provided to the ICTY. It is not clear to which extent the SDB also intercepted the conversations of Bosnian Croat or Bosnian Muslim officials. In the aforementioned letter of Goran Zečević, he also complained about the lack of power held by the SDS within the SDB. In his testimony at the ICTY, Neđo Vlaški alleged that the telephone surveillance was 'fully privatised in the service of the SDA, and, in part, the HDZ as well'. ICTY, testimony of Neđo Vlaški, *Stanišić and Župljanin*, 16 February 2010, 6386.
59 Significant conversations between Vitomir Žepinić and Radovan Karadžić on SRBiH MUP personnel issues include: 21 May 1991 (0322-3402-0322-3406), 17 June 1991 (0323-6121-0323-6131), 24 June 1991 (0322-3522-0322-3528), 24 July 1991 (0322-6330-0322-6338), 27 August 1991 (0322-6021-0322-6023), 2 September 1991 (0323-2817-0323-2830), 16 September 1991 (0323-3159-0323-3165), 18 September 1991 (0323-3175-0323-3180). Significant conversations between Momčilo Mandić and Radovan Karadžić on SRBiH MUP personnel issues include: 4 June 1991 (0322-3131-0322-3136), 17 June 1991 (0322-3279-0322-3283), 24 June 1991 (0322-3522-0322-3528), 24 June 1991 (0322-3483-0322-3485), 22 July 1991 (0322-6229-0322-6235), 23 July 1991 (0322-6266-0322-6269), 23 July 1991 (0322-6347-0322-6348), 26 August 1991 (0322-5951-0322-5954), 27 August 1991 (0322-5955-0322-5957), 28 August 1991 (0322-6024-0322-6026), 17 September 1991 (0323-3121-0323-3124).
60 Conversation between Radovan Karadžić and Vojo Krunić, an SDS member from Goražde, 29 May 1991 (0322-3567-0322-3568).
61 See the three telephone conversations between Radovan Karadžić and Biljana Plavšić on 26 July 1991 (0321-9593-0321-9603). In the course of these conversations, Karadžić and Plavšić appeared to consider whether to unveil some new tactic towards the SRBiH MUP. However, they feared that it might not succeed, and did not want to try it unless they could be certain of success. Karadžić suggested inviting Delimustafić and Žepinić to come to a meeting convened by Plavšić after Sunday (28 July 1991), where they would be told that the preservation of ethnic proportionality in the SRBiH MUP was imperative.
62 Conversation between Vitomir Žepinić and Radovan Karadžić, 17 June 1991 (0323-6121-0323-6131). There is a discrepancy in the dating of this conversation; the correct date may be 13 October 1991.

63 Conversation between Momčilo Mandić and Radovan Karadžić, 17 June 1991 (0322-3279-0322-3283). Cf. conversation between Vitomir Žepinić and Radovan Karadžić, 24 July 1991 (0322-6330-0322-6338).
64 Conversation between Vitomir Žepinić and Radovan Karadžić, 24 July 1991 (0322-6330-0322-6338). A shorter version of this same conversation appears dated as 8 July 1991 (0322-4664-0322-4666).
65 Conversation between Radovan Karadžić and Dragan Devedlaka, 24 July 1991 (0322-6339-0322-6340).
66 Conversation between Vitomir Žepinić and Radovan Karadžić, 18 September 1991 (0323-3175-0323-3180).
67 On 2 September 1991, Karadžić told Žepinić that it was insignificant that five of seven leading posts in the Administration of Police were held by Serbs because a Muslim, Avdo Hebib, headed the Administration. Conversation between Karadžić and Žepinić, 2 September 1991 (0323-2817-0323-2830).
68 Conversation between Karadžić and Žepinić, 2 September 1991 (0323-2817-0323-2830).
69 ICTY, testimony of Vitomir Žepinić, *Stanišić and Župljanin*, 29 January 2010, 5793; conversation between Karadžić and Žepinić, 16 September 1991 (0323-3159-0323-3165).
70 As an example of spillover, see CSB Doboj to SRBiH MUP, 16 September 1991 (1D00-3851) and 30 September 1991 (1D05-0853-1D05-0854).
71 Draft RS MUP Annual Report for 1992, January 1993 (FI20-1276-FI20-1319); see also CSB Trebinje, 'Report on the Work of CSB Trebinje for the Period from 4 April to 31 December 1992', 13 January 1993 (0297-1649-0297-1653); Executive Board of SDA Nevesinje, 16 July 1991 (SA02-0588-SA02-0589).
72 Letter of Stojan Župljanin to SRBiH Presidency, Assembly and MUP, 27 August 1991 (2D02-0854-2D02-0855).
73 SRBiH Presidency, 'Information on the Visit to the Municipalities Banja Luka, Bosanska Gradiška, Bosanska Dubica and Bosanski Novi and Intelligence on the Security Situation in those Municipalities', July 1991 (SA04-0967-SA04-0973). In some cases, the Serbs who arrived from Croatia bore arms. Conversely, CSB Banja Luka also suspected members of the armed forces of Croatia of concealing themselves among the arrivals. Information of CSB Banja Luka, 5 December 1991 (B004-7980-B004-7985).
74 Dispatch, dated 10 July 1991, of SRBiH MUP Minister Alija Delimustafić (P003-1451-P003-1451).
75 ICTY, testimony of Vitomir Žepinić, *Stanišić and Župljanin*, 29 January 2010, 5763-4.
76 Dispatch of SRBiH MUP Deputy Minister Vitomir Žepinić, 16 September 1991 (P002-2310-P002-2310). See also dispatch of Vitomir Žepinić, 24 September 1991 (P002-2368-P002-2368).
77 ICTY, Consolidated Statement of Mićo Davidović, 22 June 2011 (0680-2869-0680-0680-2937, at 0680-2876f).
78 ICTY, Consolidated Statement of Mićo Davidović, 22 June 2011 (0680-2869-0680-0680-2937, at 0680-2879).
79 MUP RH, Academy of Internal Affairs, 31 July 1991 (1D00-4739-1D00-4741).
80 SDA Letters to Croatian MUP, 11 July 1991 (1D06-4735-1D06-4979). Vlaški, 6392, 'This goes to show that the SDA party was using this channel to create an armed force of its own. This was a way for it to create its own army, through the Ministry of the Interior, which later proved to be true', See also 1D00-4681.

81 Minutes of 10th Session of the Council for the Protection of Constitutional Order, 23 September 1991 (SA04-0469-SA04-0475).
82 At a meeting of the SRBiH MUP Presidency in December 1991, the presidency stated that the minister of the SRBiH MUP should have sole authority regarding the use of the special police unit. Transcript of SRBiH Presidency session, 11 December 1991, cited in *National Security and the Future*, Vol. 7, No. 3 (2006), 64.
83 Dispatch of Minister Alija Delimustafić, 26 September 1991 (P002-2353-P002-2355). See also dispatch of Assistant Minister Momčilo Mandić, 26 September 1991 (0063-7158-0063-7161) and dispatch of Assistant Minister Avdo Hebib, 2 October 1991 (0063-5871). Mandić disputed the authority of the SRBiH Presidency to authorize an unlimited increase of the size of the police's reserve staff.
84 Radovan Karadžić, 'Instructions to all SDS Municipal Boards', 21 September 1991 (SA03-0386).
85 Lidija Soldo, 'I Will Negotiate until Judgement Day: Interview with BiH Internal Affairs Minister Alija Delimustafić', *NIN*, 20 December 1991, as reported in FBIS-EEU-92-004, 7 January 1992 (0365-6745-0365-6746).
86 Dispatch of Minister Alija Delimustafić, 10 July 1991 (P003-1451).
87 Minister Alija Delimustafić to chiefs of all CSBs and SJBs and to the Secretary of SUP Sarajevo, 20 September 1991 (P002-2378-P002-2379).
88 'Information on activities and observed problems in the functioning of the Point 91 action', 15 November 1991 (0323-7719-0323-7722).
89 Official note of CSB Sarajevo, SDB Sector (RO SDB Pale), 21 October 1991 (0323-7827-0323-7831).
90 SRBiH President Alija Izetbegović, Transcript of SRBiH Presidency session, 15 October 1991, cited in *National Security and the Future*, Vol. 7, No. 3 (2006), 33.
91 The best scholarly treatment of this topic is Nikica Barić, *Srpska pobuna u Hrvatskoj, 1990-1995* (Zagreb: Golden marketing-Tehnička knjiga, 2005).
92 Stef Jansen, *Antinacionalizam: Etnografija otpora u Beogradu i Zagrebu* (Belgrade: Biblioteka XX vek, 2005), 27.
93 SRH Republican Secretariat for Justice and Administration, Decision, 6 March 1990 (0214-1797-0214-1798).
94 ICTY, Agreed Facts, *Martić*, Exh. 820, para. 127.
95 Republic of Croatia, Republican Bureau of Statistics, 1991 Census, published April 1992 (0344-7982-0344-8320, at 0344-7988).
96 The later head of the Croatian Serb police and President of the self-proclaimed Republika Srpska Krajina, Milan Martić, in his 1994 interview for the BBC documentary 'Death of a Nation', referred to a 'clear indication of the restoration of [N]azism from the period 1941-45'. BBC Interview with Milan Martić, 14 October 1994 (0219-5504-0219-5518, at 0219-5504).
97 Decision on the Establishment and Constitution of the Association of Municipalities of Northern Dalmatia and Lika, by Knin Municipal Assembly, 27 June 1990 (0214-1845-0214-1846). An appended justification of this decision argued that the establishment of the association in no way threatened the sovereignty of Croatia.
98 Declaration on Sovereignty and Autonomy of the Serb People, 25 July 1990. (0214-1952-0214-1953).
99 Tanjug, '"Serbian National Council" Calls for Referendum', 31 July 1990 (Foreign Broadcast Information Service, FBIS) (R028-8592-R028-8592).
100 Report on the Performed Expression of the Serb People in the Republic of Croatia on Serbian Autonomy, 30 September 1990 (0214-1960-0214-1960).

101 BBC Interview with Milan Martić, 14 October 1994 (0219-5504-0219-5518, at 0219-5509).
102 Dispatch of Public Security Station Knin, 20 August 1990 (0207-7586-0207-7586). See also dispatch of Public Security Station Knin, 21 August 1990 (0207-7587-0207-7587).
103 See also SRBiH President Alija Izetbegović, Transcript of SRBiH Presidency session, 15 October 1991, cited in *National Security and the Future*, Vol. 7, No. 3 (2006), 33.
104 Decision of the Republika Srpska Krajina Government, 28 July 1992 (0280-7891-0280-7892). See also Časlav Ocić, 'Hronika srpske Krajine, 28. februar 1989–19. decembar 1991', in *Republika Srpska Krajina* (Knin-Belgrade: Srpsko kulturno društvo, 1996), 396–9 (0683-6129-0683-6149, at 0683-6136-0683-6137).
105 See Josip Boljkovac, '*Istina mora izaći van ...* ': *Sjećanja i zapisi prvog ministra unutarnjih poslova neovisne Hrvatske* (Zagreb: Golden Marketing, 2009); Josip Manolić, *Politika i domovina: Moja borba za suverenu i socijalnu Hrvatsku* (Zagreb: Golden Marketing, 2015); Josip Manolić, *Špijuni i domovina: Moja borba za suverenu i socijalnu Hrvatsku* (Zagreb: Golden Marketing, 2016). For analogous processes in Slovenia, see Zdenko Čepič, *Prikrita modra mreža: organi za notranje zadeve Republike Slovenije v projektu MSNZ leta 1990* (Ljubljana: Institut za novejšo zgodovino, 2010).
106 Martin Špegelj, *Sjećanja vojnika*, 2nd edn. (Zagreb: Znanje, 2001), 142–4; Aleksandar Vasiljević, *«Štit» Akcija vojne bezbednosti: Dnevničke beleške operativca* (Beograd: IGAM, 2012).
107 Špegelj, *Sjećanja vojnika*, 193.
108 Špegelj, *Sjećanja vojnika*, 154–5.
109 Špegelj, *Sjećanja vojnika*, 213–15.
110 Ocić, 'Hronika srpske Krajine, 28. februar 1989–19. decembar 1991', 403–7 (0683-6129-0683-6149, at 0683-6139-0683-6141).
111 Ilija Vučur, 'Pogibija Gorana Alavanje 23. studenoga 1990.: događaj, interpretacije, manipulacije', *Časopis za suvremenu povijest*, Vol. 49, No. 3 (2017), 587n1.
112 Vučur, 'Pogibija Gorana Alavanje 23. studenoga 1990', 593.
113 Decision on the Implementation of the Statute of the Serb Autonomous District of Krajina, 20 December 1990 (0214-1852-0214-1852).
114 Statute of the SAO Krajina, December 1990 (0214-1849-0214-1851).
115 Constitution of the Republic of Croatia, 22 December 1990 (0087-3837-0087-3850, at 0087-3839).
116 Mila Dragojević, *Amoral Communities: Collective Crimes in Time of War* (Ithaca: Cornell University Press, 2019), 10. Cf. the discussion of 'constitutive nations' (*konstitutivni narodi*) in Gilbert, *International Intervention and the Problem of Legitimacy*, Ch. 2.
117 Decision on the Establishment of the Secretariat of Internal Affairs of the SAO Krajina, 4 January 1991 (0217-2055-0217-2055); Minutes of the Session of the Executive Council of the SAO Krajina, 4 January 1991 (0217-2061-0217-2061).
118 Decision on the Establishment of the Secretariat of Internal Affairs of SAO Krajina, 4 January 1991 (0217-2055-0217-2055).
119 Decision on the Appointment of the Secretary for Internal Affairs of the Serb Autonomous District of Krajina, 4 January 1991 (0217-2060-0217-2060).
120 Notice of SAO Krajina Executive Council, 5 January 1991 (0291-8682-0291-8682).
121 Notice of the SAO Krajina Executive Council, 5 January 1991 (0291-8682-0291-8682).

122 Decision on the Establishment of the Secretariat of Internal Affairs of SAO Krajina, 4 January 1991 (0217-2055-0217-2055).
123 Decree on the Internal Organization and Work of the Ministry of Internal Affairs, 19 January 1991 (0280-3846-0280-3850).
124 Croatian Sabor Resolution on the Acceptance of the Procedure for Disassociation of the SFRJ and on the Possible Association in a Federation of Sovereign Republics, *Narodne novine*, 21 January 1991 (0089-4047-0089-4049).
125 Barić, *Srpska pobuna u Hrvatskoj, 1990-1995* (0624-6455-0624-6724, at 0624-6571).
126 Ocić, 'Hronika srpske Krajine, 28. februar 1989-19. decembar 1991', 420 (0683-6129-0683-6149, at 0683-6148).
127 Decision of the Executive Council of the Assembly of the SAO Krajina, 1 April 1991 (0217-2158-0217-2159); published in *Glasnik Krajine* on 20 April 1991 (0207-7887-0207-7887).
128 SAO Krajina Assembly, Decision on the Holding of a Referendum for the Joining of the SAO Krajina to the Republic of Serbia and that Krajina Stay in Yugoslavia with Serbia, Montenegro and Others Who Wish to Preserve Yugoslavia, 30 April 1991 (0214-1880-0214-1880).
129 Decision on the Election of the president of the Executive Council of the Assembly of the SAO Krajina, 30 April 1991 (0217-2164-0217-2164).
130 SAO Krajina Assembly, Report on the Referendum Held on the Territory of the SAO Krajina, 14 May 1991 (0214-1854-0214-1859).
131 An armed clash also took place between Serbs and Croats in Pakrac in Western Slavonia in March 1991. Ilija Petrović, *Srpsko nacionalno vijeće Slavonije, Baranje i Zapadnog Srema* (Novi Sad: Galeb, 1994) (0184-6231-0184-6498, at 0184-6296-0184-6297); Ocić, 'Hronika srpske Krajine, 28. februar 1989-19. decembar 1991', 418 (0683-6129-0683-6149, at 0683-6147). See also Letter of SDS Zagreb, 2 April 1991 (0101-9525-0101-9525).
132 Note that the Croat victim, Josip Jović, was memorialized as the first victim of the war, even though he was apparently killed by friendly fire. Plus Benkovac police officer Goran Alavanja died in November 1990. Perhaps also mention LjČ-R. Vučur, 'Pogibija Gorana Alavanje 23. studenoga 1990', 587-609.
133 Barić, *Srpska pobuna u Hrvatskoj, 1990-1995* (0624-6455-0624-6724, at 0624-6568 and 0624-6570).
134 JNA(?), Analysis of Actions of MUP Croatia on the Wider Territory of Plitvica, 31 March 1991 (?) (0608-4199-0608-4207).
135 JNA(?), Analysis of Actions of MUP Croatia on the Wider Territory of Plitvica, 31 March 1991 (?) (0608-4199-0608-4207, at 0608-4205).
136 In justifying their actions, the Croatian authorities referred to acts of disturbance of 'public order and peace' and to 'terrorist violence' on the part of the Serbs at Plitvice. Press conference of MUP Croatia in *Vjesnik*, 3 April 1991 (0266-8405-0266-8407A).
137 JNA(?), Analysis of Actions of MUP Croatia on the Wider Territory of Plitvica, 31 March 1991 (?) (0608-4199-0608-4207, at 0608-4199).
138 Dispatch of Milan Martić, 31 March 1991 (0217-0655). See also comments of Milan Martić to Radio Knin, 3 April 1991 (R108-7429-R108-7432).
139 Dispatch of Milan Martić, 25 April 1991 (0217-0645).
140 Order of Milan Babić, president of the Executive Council of the SAO Krajina, 1 April 1991 (0217-2109-0217-2109).

141 Ocić, 'Hronika srpske Krajine, 28. februar 1989–19. decembar 1991', 396–9 (0683-6129-0683-6149, at 0683-6136-0683-6137); Barić, *Srpska pobuna u Hrvatskoj, 1990–1995* (0624-6455-0624-6724, at 0624-6570).
142 See interview with Goran Hadžić in *Borovo*, 2 May 1996 (0357-7805-0357-7806).
143 Josip Reihl-Kir, the chief of police in Osijek, opposed the attack on Borovo selo. He was killed in June 1991 by nationalist Croats. Laura Silber and Allan Little, *Yugoslavia: Death of a Nation*, Revised and Updated (New York: Penguin, 1997), 140, 144.
144 On the Pakrac incident, see SDB Serbia, Official Note, 3rd Department, 3 March 1991 (0632-6341-0632-6344). BARIĆ.
145 Petrović, *Srpsko nacionalno vijeće Slavonije, Baranje i Zapadnog Srema* (0184-6231-0184-6498, at 0184-6309).
146 Marijan, *Slom Titove armije*.
147 Decision on the Election of Milan Martić as Minister of Defence of the SAO Krajina, 29 May 1991 (0214-1844).
148 Plavšić touched on the issue of 'professionalism' in a phone conversation about MUP on 19 June 1991 (0212-8426-0212-8431). In a conversation with Momčilo Mandić on 8 October 1991, Radovan Karadžić said that Serbs, 'above all', had to respect the law. 'Let the Serbs and Muslims compete to see who can respect the law. And not who can break it' (0212-8909-0212-8914).
149 For a detailed treatment of decentralization, see the section on regionalization in Patrick J. Treanor, 'The Bosnian Serb Leadership 1990–1992', Expert Report in Krajišnik and Plavšić (IT-00-39 & 40), 30 July 2002, 65–92, particularly 81–92.
150 'Decision of the Assembly of the Municipalities of Eastern and Old Herzegovina [:] SAO Herzegovina Formed', *Javnost*, 14 September 1991, 3 (0089-6735-0089-6735); excerpt from the Minutes of the 7th Session of the Community of Municipalities of Bosnian Krajina, 16 September 1991 (0040-3584-0040-3585); 'Bijeljina [:] Regionalisation – Will of the People', *Javnost*, 28 September 1991, 2 (0089-6736-0089-6736); 'Bosnia and Herzegovina [:] Life as an SAO', *Javnost*, 21 September 1991, 5 (0089-6731-0089-6731); excerpt from the Minutes of the Founding Assembly of the Serb Autonomous District of Northern Bosnia, 14 November 1991 (0051-6372-0051-6374); 'Life as an SAO [:] Serbian Northern Bosnia Constituted' and 'Birač Has Chosen', *Javnost*, 9 November 1991, 2 (0089-6737-0089-6737).
151 Again following the Croatian Serb precedent, the ARK had originally been constituted in April 1991 as the Association of Municipalities of Bosnian Krajina (*Zajednica opština Bosanske Krajine*, or ZOBK), and the establishment of similar regional associations ensued. Treanor report, para. 117.
152 Conversation of Radovan Karadžić and Slobodan Milošević, 9 September 1991 (0206-6173-0206-6176).
153 Slobodan Popović, Banja Luka city assembly member for the Alliance of Yugoslav Reform Forces quoted in Galijaš, *Eine bosnische Stadt*, 60.
154 Transcript of SRBiH Presidency session of 21 June 1991, cited in *National Security and the Future*, Vol. 7, No. 3 (2006), 9.
155 Jovo Mijatović at the 20th RS Assembly Session, 14–15 September 1992 (0422-6193-0422-6338, at 0422-6267).
156 Undated SRBiH MUP SDB paper on the possibilities of decentralizing internal affairs in Bosnia and Herzegovina (0323-7660-0323-7668).
157 A document moving in this direction was circulated by SRBiH MUP Deputy Minister Vitomir Žepinić on 26 September 1991 (0063-7282-0063-7288).

158 The working papers contain precise contemplation of the type and manner of such cooperation. For this, see the section of the present report entitled 'Cooperation of the RS MUP with S(F)RJ and Serbian Authorities'.
159 'Possibilities of Organising a Serbian Ministry for Internal Affairs', 17 October 1991 (SA02-3707-SA02-3711).
160 Patrick J. Treanor, 'The Bosnian Serb Leadership 1990–1992', ICTY Expert Report, 30 July 2002, 96.
161 Treanor, 'The Bosnian Serb Leadership 1990–1992', 93.
162 Partial Transcription of Recording of V000-0270, Speech of Radovan Karadžić in SRBiH Assembly, 15 October 1991. For the development of Karadžić's thoughts, see Robert J. Donia, *Radovan Karadžić: Architect of Genocide* (Cambridge: Cambridge University Press, 2015), 115f.
163 Minutes of the 8th Joint Session of the SRBiH Assembly, 10, 11 and 14 October 1991 (0218-9560-0218-9564)
164 Donia, *Radovan Karadžić*, 119. For Izetbegović's very different interpretation of the fateful Assembly session, see his comments in Transcript of SRBiH Presidency session, 15 October 1991, cited in *National Security and the Future*, Vol. 7, No. 3 (2006), 52.
165 Stenographic Records of the Constitutive Session of the Assembly of the Serb People in Bosnia and Herzegovina (SA01-2055-SA01-2164). The cover page of the stenographic records listed the SDS as the author. For divided opinions in the SDS on how to proceed after their unilateral withdrawal from the SRBiH Assembly, see SDS Party Council Meeting Minutes, 15 October 1991 (SA02-3844-SA02-3848). Some SDS deputies continued to attend subsequent SRBiH Assembly sessions, and Krajišnik continued to act as the president of the SRBiH Assembly until January 1992.
166 Stenographic Records of the Constitutive Session of the Assembly of the Serb People in Bosnia and Herzegovina (SA01-2055-SA01-2164, at SA01-2139).
167 Stenographic Records of the Constitutive Session of the Assembly of the Serb People in Bosnia and Herzegovina (SA01-2055-SA01-2164, at SA01-2120).
168 Decision of the Serb People of Bosnia and Herzegovina on Remaining in the Joint State of Yugoslavia, 24 October 1991, *SGSNBiH*, I, No. 1, 15 January 1992 (SA01-0629-SA01-0630).
169 Decision on the Arrangement and Implementation of a Plebiscite of the Serb People in Bosnia and Herzegovina, 24 October 1991, *Službeni glasnik srpskog naroda u Bosni i Hercegovini* (henceforth *SGSNBiH*), Vol. 1, No. 1 (15 January 1992), 2 (SA02-2907-SA02-2907, SA01-0630).
170 Report of the Main Commission for the Implementation of the Plebiscite of the Serb People of Bosnia and Herzegovina, 11 November 1991 (SA02-0831-SA02-0834).
171 Decision on the territories of municipalities, local communities and populated places in BH which are considered territory of the federal state of Yugoslavia, No. 36-02/91, 21 November 1991, *SGSNBiH I*, I, No. 1 (15 January 1992), 7 (SA01-0635).
172 Bosnian Serb Assembly, Request to the Yugoslav People's Army, 11 December 1991 (0027-0674).
173 Decision on the Formation and Selection of the Council of Ministers of the Assembly of the Serb People in Bosnia and Herzegovina, 21 December 1991, *SGSNBiH*, I, No. 1 (15 January 1992), 10 (SA01-0638); Mićo Stanišić, *Početak rata*, 56*n*63.

174 Stenographic Record of the 4th Session of the Assembly of the Serb People in Bosnia and Herzegovina, 21 December 1991 (0224-1743-0224-1850).
175 ICTY, Mićo Stanišić Defence Final Trial Brief, paras. 32, 35.
176 Stanišić, *Početak rata*, 22.
177 Stanišić, *Početak rata*, 29.
178 Stanišić, *Početak rata*, 52. On outvoting, see also ICTY, Testimony of Nedo Vlaški, *Stanišić and Župljanin*, 17 February 2010, 6462-4.
179 ICTY, Mićo Stanišić Defence Final Trial Brief, para. 33.
180 Stanišić, *Početak rata*, 25-6.
181 SDS confidential position paper, 'Modus Operandi of Municipalities in the Conditions that Republican Organs Cease to Function', 23 February 1991 (SA02-8819-SA02-8822).
182 'Civilian Protection', February 1991 (SA02-9148-SA02-9152; citation at SA02-9149).
183 Dorothea Hanson, 'Bosnian Serb Crisis Staffs, War Presidencies and War Commissions, 1991-1995', ICTY Expert Report, 8 April 2009, 5.
184 SDS Main Board, 'Instructions for the Organization and Activity of Organs of the Serbian People in Bosnia and Herzegovina in Extraordinary Circumstances)', 19 December 1991 (0018-4274-0018-4283).
185 See conversation between Karadžić and a person named Zoran regarding Bosanski Novi municipality, 29 June 1991, in which Karadžić states that 'we have a crisis staff' (0322-3587-0322-3588).
186 CSB Banja Luka, 'Weekly Information (for the period 16 to 23 September 1991)' (0061-9485-0061-9491).
187 CSB Banja Luka, Informational Report, 23 September 1991 (SA02-0124-SA02-0132).
188 CSB Banja Luka, Information on the Criminal Activity and Other Illegal Activity of Veljko Milanković and Other Members of Paramilitary Formations from the Territory of Prnjavor, 2 December 1991 (0531-6068-0531-6076).
189 Main Staff of the VRS, Information on Paramilitary Formations on the Territory of the Serb Republic of BiH, 28 July 1992 (0362-9736-0362-9741).
190 SRBiH MUP, 'Information on Activities in the Country and Abroad Directed at the Violent Change or Endangerment of the Constitutionally Confirmed Order', December 1991 (0323-7723-0323-7739). This particular version of the report appears to include hand-written comments critical of the report's findings. See also CSB Banja Luka, SDB Sector, 'Information and Intelligence Connected to the Existence and Doings of Paramilitary Formations and Other Current Events of Intelligence Interest', 29 December 1991 (B004-7574-B004-7581).
191 The report identified 155 incidents of explosions in forty-five different municipalities.
192 In Sanski Most municipality, some police officers openly joined nationalist parties before the war. SJB Sanski Most, 'Report on the Work of SJB Sanski Most for the [First] Six Months of 1992', 20 July 1992 (0049-3712-0049-3729).
193 CSB Banja Luka, Monthly Information, 30 January 1992 (P005-6504-P005-6504).
194 Declaration on the Proclamation of the Republic of the Serbian People of Bosnia and Herzegovina, 9 January 1992, *SGSNBiH*, I, No. 2 (27 January 1992), 13-14 (0040-7993-0040-7994).
195 Stenographic Notes of the 5th Session of the Assembly of the Serb People in BiH, 9 January 1992 (0224-1677-0224-1741, at 0224-1685).
196 Transcript of the 50th SRBiH Presidency session, 10 January 1992, cited in *National Security and the Future*, Vol. 7, No. 3 (2006), 77.

197 Letter of Radovan Karadžić, 6 February 1992 (SA02-4201-SA02-4202).
198 Minutes of Meeting Held in Banja Luka on 11 February 1992 (SA00-6590-SA00-6597). Karadžić knew by 13 February 1992 at the latest of the meeting, and of Mandić's attendance. Župljanin came a few days later to a meeting of the SDS in Sarajevo on 14 February 1992. Telephone conversation between Radovan Karadžić and Jovan Čizmović, 13 February 1992 (0324-5475-0324-5480).
199 Kljajić had been removed from his post as police inspector in the SRBiH MUP in the summer of 1991. Kljajić's dismissal greatly aggravated Karadžić, who through Mandić pushed hard for Kljajić's reinstatement or appointment to a high-level post. Kljajić was later appointed as the head of the Public Security Service in the RS MUP. Mićo Stanišić, *Početak rata*, 285. On Kljajić, see Christian Axboe Nielsen, 'Report on the Establishment and Performance of the Ministry of Internal Affairs of Republika Srpska in Bosnia and Herzegovina, 1990–1992', Expert Report, *The Minister of Citizenship and Immigration and the Minister of Public Safety and Emergency Preparedness and Čedo Kljajić* (Canada), 2017.
200 Minutes of Meeting Held in Banja Luka on 11 February 1992 (SA00-6590-SA00-6597).
201 Minutes of a Meeting Held in Banja Luka, 11 February 1992 (SA00-6590-SA00-6597).
202 Strong evidence suggests that Mandić and other top Serbian officials had doubts about Žepinić as early as the summer of 1991. In a conversation between Radovan Karadžić and Biljana Plavšić on 17 June 1991, Plavšić expressed dissatisfaction with the performance of Žepinić (0207-8935-0207-8936). See the conversations between Radovan Karadžić and Momčilo Mandić, and between Radovan Karadžić and Vitomir Žepinić, cited in footnotes 17 and 18.
203 Assistant Minister Momčilo Mandić to Župljanin, Bjelošević, Stojanović, Savić, Cvijetić, Ješurić and Stanišić, 13 February 1992 (0063-7176-0063-7176).
204 With respect to the substance of the 14 February 1992 meeting, see the journal notes apparently taken by an SDS municipal functionary from Bosanski Petrovac, Jovo Radojko (or an associate), who attended the meeting in an unknown capacity, dated 14 February 1992 (0059-2512-0059-2646; 0059-2531, specific page). Compare with the minutes of the SDS Municipal Board in Prijedor's meetings of 13 and 17 February 1992 (P003-7444-P003-7550; P003-7530-P003-7536, specific pages), and with the minutes of a meeting of the Bratunac SDS Municipal Board, 24 February 1992 (0219-2723-0219-2725, specific pages; full range of minutes of meetings, 1991–5: 0219-2709-0219-2806).
205 Summary of Banja Luka Radio *Dnevnik*, 5 March 1992 (B002-2344).
206 Crisis Staff of the Serbian People in BiH, 'Conditions for Negotiations', 2 March 1992 (SA04-1161-SA04-1161).
207 Testimony of Neđo Vlaški, 15 February 2010, 6354.
208 SRBiH MUP SDB report, 6 March 1992 (0323-7746-0323-7757).
209 Crisis Staff of the Serb People in BiH, 'Conditions for Negotiations', 2 March 1992 (SA04-1161-SA04-1161).
210 SRBiH MUP SDB report, 6 March 1992 (0323-7746-0323-7757).
211 Letter with attached report from Undersecretary of SDB, Branko Kvesić, to Minister of Internal Affairs Delimustafić, 13 March 1992, attaching information on MUP workers (19) who took part in Sarajevo barricades, both Muslim and Serbian, including: Momčilo Mandić, Čedo Kljajić, Dragan Devedlaka and Malko Koroman. In addition, five people, including Mandić and Mićo Stanišić, were identified as

having been present at the SDS Crisis Staff meeting, giving instructions to the field (0063-7355-0063-7359). The contents of Kvesić's letter were apparently leaked to *Slobodna Bosna*, which published a summary of the report's findings on 19 March 1992 (0208-3566-0208-3567). The same article noted that 'Momčilo Mandić is once again coming to the attention of the public in Bosnia and Herzegovina after the March unrest in Sarajevo. In the course of this, he had very hefty tasks given to him *by the Crisis Staff of the Serbian Democratic Party* – from the establishment of barricades to the recruitment of seasoned criminals to go out with weapons to the barricades. Let us also state by the way that an analysis of the March events, undertaken by the MUP BiH for its own needs, established that a total of 24 employees of the Ministry of Internal Affairs participated in organising and functioning of the barricades in Sarajevo. Without even once denying his participation in the blockade around Sarajevo, Momčilo Mandić, after the situation has calmed down, continues his media activities, pointing to the need for a reconstruction of the MUP. This should be done in concord with the protection of the interests of Serbian cadres in the MUP, whose interests are, in Mandić's opinion, threatened'.

212 Conversation between Biljana Plavšić and Rajko Dukić, 2 March 1992 (0207-9054-0207-9057).
213 Undated document by the 'Crisis Staff of the Serbian People of Bosnia and Herzegovina', 'Conditions for Negotiation' (SA04-1161-SA04-1161).
214 'Plan for Work on Mixed Patrols of the MUP BiH and JNA on the Territory of BiH', signed by Colonel-General Milutin Kukanjac and Minister Alija Delimustafić, 8 March 1992 (0063-7344-0063-7345). See also the treatment of the '3 March' crisis in 'And Now Every One Goes to Sleep!' *Slobodna Bosna*, 5 March 1992 (0210-0563-0210-0566).
215 Minutes of 13th Session of the Council for the Protection of Constitutional Order, 9 March 1992 (SA02-0671-SA02-0675). The more objective use of the term 'paramilitary' is noteworthy here, as the politicians of the SDA, SDS and HDZ – and the senior police officials loyal to these parties, had a tendency to subjectively refer only to the forces of the 'others' as being paramilitary. See for example Mićo Stanišić, *Početak rata*, 60; Mićo Stanišić, *Ratni sukobi na granicama Republika Srpske* (Belgrade: Svet knjige, 2020), 5.
216 'Zašto Delimustafić štiti Žepinića' (Why Is Delimustafić protecting Žepinić?), *Slobodna Bosna*, 12 March 1992 (0210-0549-0210-0552).
217 'Boro and Ramiz' was a reference to an old Partisan story featuring partnership between a Serb (Boro) and an Albanian (Ramiz).
218 'Stanice milicije [sic] Stari Grad: Da li Srbi hoće podjelu? Ko koga ugrožava?' *Slobodna Bosna*, 12 March 1992 (0210-0551-0210-0552).
219 'Peace – [A] Strategic Goal', *Glas*, 3 March 1992 (0202-9654-0202-9654).
220 'Peace – [A] Strategic Goal', *Glas*, 5 March 1992 (0202-9664-0202-9664).
221 Delimustafić to chiefs of all CSBs and SJBs, 12 March 1992 (0063-3199-0063-3208).
222 For example, Serbian personnel serving at SJB Stari Grad in Sarajevo complained that the situation for them had deteriorated continuously since the November 1990 elections. They further accused their Muslim colleagues and their Muslim commander, Ismet Dahić, of supporting the 'Green Berets' and other Muslim paramilitary formations. Letter of Serbian Employees of SJB Stari Grad to SRBiH MUP, CSB Sarajevo and SUP Sarajevo, 5 March 1992 (0084-5078-0084-5082).
223 'Statement of Police Officers of Muslim Nationality about Their Dismissal from SJB Pale and SJB Sokolac', 24 March 1992 (0204-8150-0204-8151).

224 'Information on Abuses, Illegalities and Manipulations by SDA and HDZ Cadres in the State Security Service of the SRBiH MUP in Personnel Policies, the New Organization and Systemisation and in the One-Sided Use of Methods and Means of the Work of the Service in the Interest of the SDA-HDZ Alliance to the Damage of the Serbian Nation and the Politics of the SDS – Suggestions for the Overcoming of These Problems', March 1992 (0323-7758-0323-7764).
225 Delimustafić may not, however, have been immune to manipulation of the SRBiH MUP for personal and political gain. Unconfirmed reports in the Bosnian media allege that Delimustafić owed his rise to minister to illicit dealings. See, for example, *Slobodna Bosna,* 3 October 1998 (0065-5932-0065-5939).
226 Thus the SRBiH Presidency, at the 6th Session of the Council for the Protection of Constitutional Order, in the first half of 1991 felt it necessary to complain about a lack of information provision by the MUP. 6th Session of the Council for the Protection of Constitutional Order, n.d. (but first half of 1991) (SA04-0977-SA04-0979). In September 1991, Delimustafić reported that he was dissatisfied with the reporting of certain regional and municipal police organs. Delimustafić to all CSBs, SJBs, and SUP Sarajevo, 20 September 1991 (P002-2378-P002-2379).
227 See for example the Minutes of the 8th Session of the Council for the Protection of Constitutional Order, 24 June 1991 (SA02-0554-SA02-0559).
228 Stenographic Minutes of 10th Session of the Assembly of the Serb People in Bosnia and Herzegovina (SA02-5626-SA02-5709).
229 Stenographic Minutes of 11th Session of the Assembly of the Serb People in Bosnia and Herzegovina (SA02-5710-SA02-5780).
230 At the 6th Session of the Assembly, held on 26 January 1992, Vještica had cited the need to coordinate the drafting, promulgation and implementation of legislation both at the level of the autonomous regions and the Assembly 'so that we can both in the field and in the SDK [Service of Social Accounting] and in the SUP and the People's Defence, etc. take power'. Tape transcript of 6th Session of the Assembly of the Serb People in Bosnia and Herzegovina (SA02-5232-SA02-5305).
231 Stenographic Minutes of the 11th Session of the Assembly of the Serb People in Bosnia and Herzegovina (SA02-5710-SA02-5780).
232 Radovan Karadžić to (SDS) municipal presidents, 23 March 1992 (0018-4272-0018-4273).
233 Radovan Karadžić quoted in Stenographic Minutes of 12th Session of the Assembly of the Serb People in BiH, 24 March 1992 (0089-6856-0089-6902). Karadžić's reference to a 'unique [*jedinstven*] methodology' is likely a reference to the implementation of the 19 December 1991 Instructions. '*Jedinstven*' can also be translated as 'unified', in the sense of a single methodology.
234 Stenographic Minutes of 13th Session of Assembly of the Serb People in Bosnia and Herzegovina (SA01-1109-SA01-1120).
235 Stenographic Minutes of 13th Session of Assembly of the Serb People in Bosnia and Herzegovina (SA01-1109-SA01-1120, at SA01-1116).
236 'Transcript of 13th Session of the Council of the SRBiH Presidency for the Protection of the Constitutional Order', Sarajevo, 9 March 1992 (SA02-0671-SA02-0675).
237 Barry Posen, 'The Security Dilemma and Ethnic Conflict', *Survival*, Vol. 35, No. 1 (1993), 27–47.
238 See Anđelić, *Bosnia*; Galijaš, *Eine bosnische Stadt*, 88–9; Jansen, *Antinacionalizam*, Dragojević, *Amoral Communities*.

Chapter 2

1   Transcript of the Review of the Police, 30 March 1992 (1D05-5169).
2   'Critical in Sanski Most', *Glas*, 31 March 1992 (0202-9734-0202-9734).
3   'Žepinić Withdrawn from Bosnia and Herzegovina MUP', *Glas* (Banja Luka), 31 March 1992 (SA04-6954-SA04-6954).
4   Telex message by Momčilo Mandić, Assistant Minister of Internal Affairs, SRBiH MUP UZSK, No. 02-2482, 31 March 1992 (0049-0125-0049-0125).
5   'Žepinić Withdrawn from the BiH MUP', *Glas* (Banja Luka), 31 March 1992 (SA04-6954-SA04-6954).
6   Vitomir Žepinić to president of Bosnian Serb Assembly, 4 April 1992 (SA02-6813-SA02-6813).
7   Mićo Stanišić, *Početak rata u Bosni i Hercegovini* (Belgrade: Donat-graf, 2017), 313.
8   Stanišić, *Početak rata*, 314.
9   SRBiH MUP Dispatch, 1 April 1992 (P004-4293).
10 Statement of Vitomir Žepinić, 27 August 1992 (0323-8738-0323-8749).
11 ICTY Testimony of Vitomir Žepinić, *Stanišić and Župljanin*, 29 January 2010, 5834. During his testimony at the ICTY, Žepinić also regretted that he and like-minded individuals did not stage a coup. ICTY Testimony of Vitomir Žepinić, *Stanišić and Župljanin*, 1 February 2010, 5889. Momčilo Mandić in his testimony claimed that he and Minister Delimustafić had at the end of 1991 proposed arresting both Karadžić and Izetbegović. Given Mandić's very close cooperation with Karadžić at that time, this seems quite unlikely. ICTY Testimony of Momčilo Mandić, *Stanišić and Župljanin*, 3 May 2010, 9448.
12 It should be noted that Žepinić's memory in this statement puts his resignation a day later than his resignation letter of 4 April 1992. Cf. Stanišić, *Početak rata*, 323.
13 Delimustafić telex, 31 March 1992 (0049-0126). The statements of Mandić and Delimustafić were both published in *Večernje novine* on 1 April 1992 (0210-0212-0212-0213).
14 SRBiH MUP Dispatch, 1 April 1992 (P004-4292).
15 SJB Zvornik to SRBiH MUP, 31 March 1992 (SA04-0273).
16 Stanišić to all CSBs and SJBs, 3 April 1992 (P004-4288). Stanišić was responding to an apparent attempt by the SRBiH MUP to send out a telex in Mandić's name asking all persons to return to their regular posts.
17 'The SAOfication of the Police', *Oslobođenje*, 1 April 1992 (0210-0215-0210-0218).
18 'Clearer – Later', *Oslobođenje*, 1 April 1992 (0210-0219-0210-0220). The same article reported on rumours that the Croats would follow the Serbs in forming a separate MUP on 5 April.
19 'Clearer – Later', *Oslobođenje*, 1 April 1992 (0210-0219-0210-0220).
20 Dispatch of Delimustafić, 8 April 1992 (P004-4267-P004-4267).
21 RS MUP Announcement signed by Minister Mićo Stanišić, 5 April 1992 (0324-6514-0324-6515).
22 On the Bosnian Muslim Green Berets and the paramilitary Patriotic League (*Patriotska liga*), see Marko Attila Hoare, *How Bosnia Armed* (London: Saqi Books, 2004).; Sefer Halilović, *Lukava strategija* (Sarajevo: Maršal, 1997).
23 Dispatch of Minister Mićo Stanišić, 3 April 1992 (P004-4288).
24 See Mandić's account of this action in his April 1998 interview with *Slobodna Bosna* and in his contribution to *Rat u Bosni: Kako je počelo* (0047-7534-0047-7534), 76–8.

25 Order of Mićo Stanišić, 19 May 1992 (0324-6100-0324-6100), refers to Vraca as the seat of the RS MUP. It appears, however, that the Hotel 'Košuta' at Jahorina was used as the seat of the ministry by late June 1992. See order of Mićo Stanišić, 28 June 1992 (0324-6098-0324-6098). In October, the ministry moved partly to Bijeljina, with some parts remaining at Jahorina. CSB Banja Luka to chiefs of subordinate SJBs, 23 October 1992 (P004-3428-P004-3428).
26 Karišik's initial rank in the RS MUP was as 'Commander of the Police Detachment'. Order of Momčilo Mandić, 13 April 1992 (0324-6105-0324-6105).
27 ICTY OTP Suspect Interview of Mićo Stanišić, 16 and 17 July 2007 (V000-7306); Stanišić, *Početak rata*, 326.
28 Interview with Momčilo Mandić in *Slobodna Bosna* published on 10 April 1998 (0215-5571-0215-5576).
29 Conversation between General Milutin Kukanjac and Momčilo Mandić, 18 April 1992 (0322-0216-0322-0218); conversation between Colonel Vukota Vukotić and Momčilo Mandić, 18 April 1992 (0322-0214-0322-0215).
30 Stanišić, *Početak rata*, 333.
31 Law on Internal Affairs, *Službeni glasnik srpskog naroda u Bosni i Hercegovini*, I, No. 4 (23 March 1992), 74–88 (0018-4319-0018-4333).
32 Independent Union of Workers of the MUP of SRBiH, 'Report from the 4th Session of the Republican Board, Held on 17 March 1992', 29 (26) March 1992 (P004-4315-P004-4318).
33 ICTY, *Stanišić and Župljanin*, Judgement, Vol. 2, para. 552.
34 Stanišić, *Početak rata*, 282f.
35 'Statement of Principles for New Constitutional Arrangements for Bosnia and Herzegovina', https://www.peaceagreements.org/viewmasterdocument/547. This is the version from 18 March 1992; for previous versions see 0056-5138-0056-5140 and SA01-7151-SA01-7153. Glaurdić notes that 'the draft left the terminology of the constituent units basically undetermined but did refer to them repeatedly as "states," which was also how they were presented in the local media'. Josip Glaurdić, *The Hour of Europe: Western Powers and the Breakup of Yugoslavia* (New Haven: Yale University Press, 1995), 399*n*205.
36 Radovan Karadžić at Meeting of SDS Delegates, 28 February 1992 (SA01-1403-SA01-1404).
37 ICTY, Testimony of Herbert Okun, 23 June 2004, *Krajišnik*, 4195f.
38 Warren Zimmermann, *Origins of a Catastrophe* (New York: Times Books, 1996), 189. Izetbegović, meanwhile, told Zimmermann that he was worried that the Cutileiro negotiations were steering towards 'partition from within'. Ibid., 190.
39 Glaurdić, *The Hour of Europe*, 290; Robert Donia, *Radovan Karadžić: Architect of the Bosnian Genocide* (Cambridge: Cambridge University Press, 2014), 150–4.
40 Donia, *Radovan Karadžić*, 176.
41 Radovan Karadžić, 12th RS Assembly session, 24 March 1992 (0089-6883).
42 Transcription and Tape Recording from the 17th Session of the RS Assembly, 24 June–6 July 1992 (0214-9496-0214-9600, at 0214-9498).
43 P2301, Second Session of OTP Interview with Mićo Stanišić. The same applies to the Chief of CSB Banja Luka Stojan Župljanin; see CSB Banja Luka dispatch, 3 April 1992 (P004-4289).
44 ICTY OTP Suspect Interview of Mićo Stanišić, 16 and 17 July 2007 (V000-7306).
45 Stanišić caustically claimed later that the international community recognized 'a state that did not exist'. Mićo Stanišić, *Ratni sukobi na granicama Republika Srpske* (Belgrade: Svet knjige, 2020), 22.

46 Stanišić, *Početak rata*, 319.
47 Stanišić goes so far as to refer to the mobilization of 'defensive forces' as a synonym of 'armed forces'. Stanišić, *Ratni sukobi*, 40, 81, 311.
48 Dispatch of Minister Delimustafić, 10 April 1992 (P004-4254).
49 SJB Ilidža, 20 September 1993 (0297-0064-0297-0072).
50 SJB Ilidža, 20 September 1993 (0297-0064-0297-0072). The word '*protjerivanje*' is spelled incorrectly in the text as '*protjevanje*', but is clearly identifiable as such.
51 RS MUP nominations for commendation, 1993 (0297-0050-0297-0062).
52 Order of Minister Bogdan Subotić, RS Ministry of People's Defence, 16 April 1992 (0057-4584-0057-4585).
53 ICTY, *Krajišnik*, Judgement, para. 175.
54 ICTY, Tabeau report P1627 (*Stanišić and Župljanin*), 69, 73, 77.
55 ICTY, Consolidated statement of Mićo Davidović, 22 June 2001 (0680-2869-0680-2937, at 0680-2872).
56 Short Review of work of the RS MUP with suggestions for future work – report based on meeting of leading RS MUP officials on 11 July 1992 (0324-1848-0324-1879, at 0324-1861).
57 ICTY, *Stanišić and Župljanin*, Judgement, Vol. 1, para. 888.
58 ICTY, *Stanišić and Župljanin*, Judgement, Vol. 1, para. 889.
59 ICTY, *Stanišić and Župljanin*, Judgement, Vol. 1, para. 890f.
60 ICTY, Consolidated statement of Mićo Davidović, 22 June 2001 (0680-2869-0680-2937, at 0680-2893).
61 ICTY, *Stanišić and Župljanin*, Judgement, Vol. 1, para. 895.
62 ICTY, *Stanišić and Župljanin*, Judgement, *passim*.
63 ICTY, Tabeau report P1627 (*Stanišić and Župljanin*), 69, 73, 77, 81. For a detailed overview of events in Bileća municipality, see Christian Axboe Nielsen, 'Report on the events in Bileća municipality, Bosnia Herzegovina, from November 1990 until the end of 1992, with a focus on the role of police and reserve police in those events', Expert report prepared for the Canadian Department of Justice, May 2009.
64 ICTY, Amended Indictment of Momčilo Perišić (Case IT-04-81), 26 September 2005, http://www.un.org/icty/indictment/english/per-ai050926e.pdf.
65 Bosnia and Herzegovina Radio Report, 28 March 1993 (0001-9886). The name of Goran Vujović is incorrectly rendered as 'Goran Vuković'. He remained commander of SJB Bileća throughout the war, and was removed in September 2002 by the International Police Task Force (IPTF), as were Rade Nosović and Milorad Ilić, also of SJB, later Police Station (PS), Bileća. See transcript of international joint press conference, 19 September 2002, http://ls.kuleuven.be/cgi-bin/wa?A2=ind0209&L=natodata&P=4619.
66 'Possibilities for the Organisation of a Serbian Ministry of Internal Affairs', Sarajevo, 17 October 1991 (SA02-3707-SA02-3712).
67 Undated SRBiH MUP SDB paper on the possibilities of decentralizing internal affairs in Bosnia and Herzegovina (0323-7660-0323-7668).
68 See also CSB Trebinje, 'Report on the Work of CSB Trebinje for the Period from 4 April to 31 December 1992', 13 January 1993 (0297-1649-0297-1653); Executive Board of SDA Nevesinje, 16 July 1991 (SA02-0588-SA02-0589).
69 SRBiH MUP Administration for Affairs and Tasks for the Elimination and Investigation of Crime, 27 May 1991 (0204-9811-0204-9813); SRBiH MUP, 'Information on the Discovery of Illegally Bringing of Weapons to Bosnia and Herzegovina', undated (0204-9814-0204-9816).

70 Together with a certain Slavko Radovanović nicknamed 'Gazda', Miroslav Duka on 24 May 1991 blocked police officers of the SRBiH MUP from escorting a truck with seized illegal weapons and ammunition to CSB Mostar. SRBiH MUP, 'Information on the Discovery of Illegally Bringing of Weapons to Bosnia and Herzegovina', undated (0204-9814-0204-9816, at 0204-9815).
71 Transcript of Session of SRBiH Presidency, 21 June 1991, published in *National Security and the Future*, Vol. 7, No. 3 (2006), 8, 12.
72 Transcript of Session of SRBiH Presidency, 21 June 1991, published in *National Security and the Future*, Vol. 7, No. 3 (2006), 21f.
73 'Decision of the Assembly of the Municipalities of Eastern and Old Herzegovina [:] SAO Herzegovina Formed', *Javnost*, 14 September 1991, p. 3 (0089-6735-0089-6735).
74 On the deteriorating political and security situation in Eastern Herzegovina and its effects on the police in the region, see also the draft 1992 RS MUP Annual Report, January 1993 (fi20-1276-fi20-1319, at fi20-1283).
75 ICTY, *Krajišnik*, Judgment, 27 September 2006, para. 608.
76 ICTY, *Krajišnik*, Judgment, 27 September 2006, para. 609.
77 War Presidency of the Assembly of Gacko Municipality, 11 July 1992 (0209-6313-0209-6314).
78 ICTY, *Krajišnik*, Judgment, 27 September 2006, para. 614.
79 ICTY, *Krajišnik*, Judgment, 27 September 2006, paras. 609-14.
80 UN Commission of Experts Report Pursuant to UN Security Council Resolution 780 (1992), 1994, https://www.icty.org/x/file/About/OTP/un_commission_of_experts_report1994_en.pdf
81 Armina Galijaš has produced the most authoritative and detailed account of Banja Luka in the 1990s. Armina Galijaš, *Eine bosnische Stadt im Zeichen des Krieges: Ethnopolitik und Alltag in Banja Luka (1990–1995)* (Oldenburg: Oldenbourg Wissenschaftsverlag, 2011). See also the ICTY judgements in *Brđanin* and *Karadžić*.
82 ICTY Tabeau report P1627 (*Stanišić and Župljanin*), 69, 73.
83 The most detailed account of the takeover of Banja Luka and the subsequent commission of atrocities in that city and surrounding municipalities is provided in ICTY, *Brđanin*, Judgement.
84 Testimony of Predrag Radulović, *Stanišić and Župljanin*, 25 May 2010, 107812f.
85 Stanišić and Župljanin judgement, Vol. 1, para. 159; Galijaš, *Eine bosnische Stadt*, 201f.
86 Mladen Vuksanović, *Dnevnik s Pala 1992*, https://sarajevo.co.ba/mladen-vuksanovic-dnevnik-s-pala-1992/
87 'Statement of Police Officers of Muslim Nationality about Their Dismissal from SJB Pale and SJB Sokolac', 24 March 1992 (0204-8150-0204-8151).
88 ICTY, *Stanišić and Župljanin*, Judgement, Vol. 1, para. 1298.
89 ICTY, *Stanišić and Župljanin*, Judgement, Vol. 1, para. 1299f.
90 ICTY, *Stanišić and Župljanin*, Judgement, Vol. 1, para. 1305f.
91 ICTY, *Stanišić and Župljanin*, Judgement, Vol. 1, para. 1301.
92 ICTY, *Stanišić and Župljanin*, Judgement, Vol. 1, para. 1310f.
93 ICTY, *Stanišić and Župljanin*, Judgement, Vol. 1, para. 1317f.
94 ICTY, *Stanišić and Župljanin*, Judgement, Vol. 1, para. 1335f.
95 'From Today On – New Emblems', *Glas*, 8 April 1992 (0202-9743).
96 Banja Luka *Dnevnik*, 8 April 1992 (B005-2396).
97 For an example of such an oath, see the oath – or 'solemn declaration' (*svečana izjava*) as it was officially called, signed by Dragan Stojičić on 6 April 1992 at CSB Banja Luka (0206-1520).

98 Župljanin to RS MUP and all SJBs and SMs on the territory of CSB Banja Luka, 16 April 1992 (P004-4242-P004-4242). However, the fledgling RS MUP required all of its employees to take oaths to Republika Srpska. SRBiH Assistant Minister of Internal Affairs Momčilo Mandić to SRBiH MUP, 31 March 1992 (0049-0125). These oaths had to be taken 'without any pressure by 15 April 1992'. Chief of CSB Banja Luka Stojan Župljanin to SRBiH MUP, RS MUP and all SJBs, 10 April 1992 (P004-4255-P004-4255).

99 This was admitted in a later CSB dispatch, dated 28 May 1992 (P004-3558-P004-3558). On 5 June 1992, Simo Drljača observed that the service of those who had not taken the loyalty oath was severed effective 31 March 1992. However, these individuals had received a portion of their April 1992 salaries: Drljača to CSB Banja Luka, 5 June 1992 (P000-3455-P000-3455).

100 'Peace in the Interest of All Three Peoples', *Glas*, 4 April 1992 (0095-1932-0095-1934).

101 'Deadline for Loyalty Extended', *Glas*, 9 April 1992 (0202-9748).

102 'The Demands of SOS Are Adopted', *Glas*, 4 April 1992 (0095-1933). Župljanin contended in his letter of 3 April 1992 that everyone had the possibility to stay in their positions (P004-4289-P004-4289a). A dispatch from SJB Prijedor dated 16 April 1992, citing a 10 April 1992 dispatch of CSB Banja Luka, stated that the deadline for taking the oath was 15 April 1992: Hasan Talundžić, Chief of SJB Prijedor, 16 April 1992 (P000-3932).

103 CSB Banja Luka, 'Report on the Work of CSB Banja Luka from 4 April to 31 December 1992', January 1993 (B009-8119-B009-8147).

104 Delimustafić dispatch on RS MUP oaths, 10 April 1992 (P004-4254). On the same day, Stojan Župljanin issued a dispatch contradicting Delimustafić. Chief of CSB Banja Luka Stojan Župljanin to SRBiH MUP, RS MUP and to all SJBs, 10 April 1992 (P004-4255-P004-4255).

105 A document from SJB Nevesinje dated 4 May 1992 stated that Muslim employees in Bileća and Kalinovik were not allowed to express their loyalty to the RS (FI20-1967-FI20-1968).

106 Stanišić and Župljanin judgement, Vol. 2, para. 44.

107 'Deadline for Loyalty Extended', *Glas*, 9 April 1992 (0202-9748-0202-9748).

108 'Deadline for Loyalty Extended', *Glas*, 9 April 1992 (0202-9748). See also 'Only Cadres Loyal to the Serb BiH', *Glas*, 1 and 2 May 1992 (0095-1928).

109 'Deadline for Loyalty Extended', *Glas*, 9 April 1992 (0202-9748).

110 Stanišić and Župljanin judgement, Vol. 2, paras. 222, 295, 515, 722.

111 Report of Miloš Group, 9 April 1992 (B008-0496).

112 CSB Banja Luka, 'Information on the Formation and Performance of the Special Detachment of the Police of CSB Banja Luka', approximately 5 August 1992 (0360-5790-0360-5791).

113 'Report on Completed Inspection of the CSB and Public Security Stations on the Territory of AR Krajina', 5 August 1992 (0360-5785-0360-5789).

114 Not surprisingly, Stanišić to this continues to insist that there was nothing wrong with the oaths, and that non-Serbs were treated well in the RS MUP, whereas Serbs were terrorized in the SRBiH MUP. Stanišić, *Ratni sukobi*, 87–9.

115 ICTY, *Stanišić and Župljanin*, Judgement, Vol. 1, para. 279.

116 ARK Crisis Staff decision, signed by Brđanin, 22 June 1992 (P005-4023).

117 Examples of crisis staff ordering the creation of Serbian police and firing non-Serbs from police include:

Brčko: 'With the start of military action and the same day as the take-over of the Public Security Station the War Presidency appointed the head of the Public Security Station (Dragan Veselić) and began filling the ranks of the station with Serbs previously employed there.' 'Summary of Events and Situation in Brčko' (0074-1394-0074-1411).
Ključ: Crisis staff announced the formation of Serbian police force and change of insignia. Public Announcement of the Crisis Staff, 8 May 1992 (0091-4749-0019-4750).
Pale: Muslim policemen were 'informed of the decision by the Crisis Staff of Pale Municipality and the Government of the Romanija SAO that all policemen of Muslim nationality must hand in their weapons and equipment issued to them'. Statements by policemen of Muslim nationality, 24 March 1992. (0204-8150-0204-8151).
Prijedor: Simo Drljača, the chief of SJB Prijedor, informed CSB Banja Luka on 5 July 1992 that the SJB was carrying out disarming in accordance with a decision of the municipal crisis staff (0063-3273-0063-3274).

118 Evidence of the crisis staff control of the police includes:
Bosanska Krupa: 'Order to activate reserve police forces', 30 December 1991 (0091-4269-0091-4270). The War Presidency ordered how the police were to function in times of war. 'Decision on Organization and Manner of Work of the Serbian Municipality of Bosanska Krupa under Wartime Conditions', 7 May 1992 (0059-0289-0059-0291).
Bosanski Petrovac: Police asks for crisis staff advice on the issue of prisons. Minutes of 36th Session of Crisis Staff of Petrovac Municipality, 18 June 1992 (0094-6832-0094-6833). Police charged with implementation of curfew. Public Announcement of Petrovac Municipal Crisis Staff, 23 June 1992 (0091-6093). Crisis staff charges TO and police with arrest of militarily capable Muslim males. Minutes of 41st Session of Crisis Staff of Petrovac Municipality, 30 June 1992 (0094-6846). Crisis staff decides that all 'registered Muslim extremists' and individuals possessing illegal weapons should be detained. Decision of Crisis Staff of Petrovac Municipality, 28 October 1992 (0039-1083).
Foča: 'With the commencement of combat activities in Srbinje (i.e., Foča) on 8 April 1992, all activities and work of the Station were in agreement with the Crisis Staff of the Municipality, which gave the guidelines for particular actions'. CJB Srbinje, 'Information on the Work of SJB Srbinje for the Period April 1992 to April 1994', June 1994 (0297-2044-0297-2061).
Ključ: SJB collected weapons 'according to the decision of the Crisis Staff'. "Information on the Work and Activities of SJB Ključ during Combat Operations on the Territory of Ključ Municipality"), no. 9/92, July 1992. (0048-9819-0048-9838).
Kotor Varoš: Crisis staff requests that chief of SJB discuss matters with CSB Banja Luka. Excerpts from the Minutes of the 31st Session of the Crisis Staff, 21 June 1992 (0041-5625). Crisis staff reviewed the work of the SJB. The crisis staff requests that police and army undertake security and create conditions for full security on the municipal territory. 'Bulletin of Crisis Staff', no. I/3, 26 June 1992 (0041-6213-0041-6216). War Presidency decides that all companies are obliged to finance the police and the Army. Excerpt from Minutes of the 9th Session of the War Presidency, 11 July 1992 (0041-5546-0041-5547) War Presidency increases the size of the reserve police force and asks CSB Banja Luka for additional resources. Excerpt from Minutes of 22nd Session of the War Presidency, 18 July 1992 (0041-5544-0041-5544). War Presidency tasks police and military with the

drafting of a list of persons to be expelled from the territory of the municipality. Excerpt from Minutes of 133rd Session of War Presidency, 4 December 1992 (0041-5638).

Prijedor: See the 'Summary of Conclusions, Orders and Decisions Adopted by the Crisis Staff/War Presidency Relating to the SJB and the Regional Command from 29 May to 24 July 1992' (0063-3784-0063-3786); also Professional Service of Prijedor Municipal Assembly, 'Information on the Implementation of Conclusions of the Crisis Staff of Prijedor Municipality', 13 July 1992 (P000-7104-P000-7108). The crisis staff asks for information confirming SJB compliance with crisis staff instructions, orders, decisions and resolutions and conclusions. Technical Service of Prijedor Municipal Assembly to Simo Drljača, 23 June 1992 (0063-3804). The police reported to the crisis staff on their execution of crisis staff orders. Report of SJB Prijedor, 1 July 1992 (0063-3809-0063-3810).

Sanski Most: Crisis staff makes decisions concerning police finances and equipment. Conclusions of municipal crisis staff meeting, 21 April 1992 (0047-1864-0047-1867); police are charged with implementing a curfew and with organizing a checkpoint together with the military police. Conclusions of municipal crisis staff meeting, 24 April 1992 (0047-1860-0047-1861). Crisis staff named member of crisis staff as new chief of police. 'Conclusions', no. 11/92, 27 April 1992 (0047-1858-0047-1859). Crisis Staff takes decision concerning financing of municipal reserve police force. Conclusions of municipal crisis staff meeting, 7 May 1992 (0047-1342-0047-1344). Crisis staff orders SJB Sanski Most to undertake an analysis of the personnel structure of the police. Conclusions of municipal crisis staff meeting, 21 May 1992 (0047-1324-0047-1327). Crisis staff orders issued to police include: Crisis staff order, 6 June 1992 (0047-1232-0047-1233). Crisis staff orders TO and SJB to undertake disarming operation 'and other operations from the purview of the SJB'. Crisis staff conclusions, 8 June 1992 (0047-1270-0047-1273). Crisis staff stipulates that SJB will issue documents confirming the permanent departure of persons from the municipality. 'Decision on the Criteria for Possibilities of Departure from the Territory of the Municipality', 2 July 1992 (0047-1756-0047-1759). Crisis staff orders the formation of joint patrols of the military and police if the TO is dissolved and the 6th Brigade is reorganized. Minutes meeting of Coordination Board of the Municipal Assembly, 4 November 1992 (0049-1745-0049-1748).

Šipovo: Crisis staff ordered chief of police and TO commander to carry out disarming of Muslims. Minutes of meeting of Šipovo Crisis Staff, 19 May 1992 (0219-4132-0219-4141). Crisis staff asserted the authority to solve the problems of the local police command, and name the police commander and chief of police. Minutes of meeting of Šipovo Crisis Staff, 9 June 1992 (0219-4110-0219-4115).

119 President of the Government Branko Đerić, 'Extract from the Instructions for the Work of Crisis Staffs of the Serbian Nation in the Municipalities', 26 April 1992 (0027-0617-0027-0618). On 30 April 1992, Đerić issued an urgent order telling the recipients to ignore this version of these Instructions because they had not been fully completed (0124-6815-0124-6815). However, subsequent documents from the municipalities give no indication that the Instructions were, in fact, regarded as being invalid. Letter by the Secretary of the Executive Committee of the SDS BiH addressed to three presidents of regional crisis staffs, Number 578-02/92, 31 May 1992 (0108-8782).

120 Conclusion of Sanski Most Crisis Staff, 30 May 1992 (0047-1742-0047-1745).

121 Simo Drljača to Prijedor Municipal Crisis Staff, 1 July 1992 (P004-2965-P004-2966). Cf. Prijedor Municipal Crisis Staff, 'Instructions on the Formation, Composition and Tasks of the Local Crisis Staffs on the Territory of Prijedor Municipality', June 1992 (0063-3737-0063-3746).
122 Minutes of 35th Session of Crisis Staff of Bosanski Petrovac, 16 June 1992 (0094-6864-0094-6865).
123 In Ključ, the 'VRS commanders regularly participated in Crisis Staff sessions, and had very good cooperation and co-ordination with the Crisis Staff. No significant and important questions from the military and police domain were resolved without the Crisis Staff'. 'Report on the Work of the Crisis Staff/War Presidency/of Ključ Municipal Assembly', July 1992 (0034-9532-0034-9536).
124 List of ARK War Staff members, 6 May 1992 (0048-9901-0048-9901).
125 On ethnic cleansing, see Vladimir Petrović, *Etničko čišćenje: geneza koncepta* (Belgrade: Institut za savremenu istoriju, 2019).
126 ICTY, *Karadžić*, Judgement, para. 1373.
127 Telephone conversation of Nenad Stevandić and Radovan Karadžić, 17 or 18 August 1991 (0206-6348-0206-6351). See also telephone conversation of Nenad Stevandić and Radovan Karadžić, 31 August 1991 (0304-0910-0304-0918).
128 ICTY, *Karadžić*, Judgement, para. 2046. On the Golubić training centre, see ICTY, *Stanišić and Simatović*, Retrial, Judgement, para. 387f.
129 ICTY, *Karadžić*, Judgement, para. 1373; 'The Demands of SOS Are Adopted', *Glas*, 4 April 1992 (0095-1933).
130 ICTY, *Stanišić and Župljanin*, Judgement, Vol. 1, para. 144.
131 Report of Miloš Group, 2 April 1992 (B008-0506). On the group codenamed Miloš, which was formed in 1991, see the testimony of Predrag Radulović, *Stanišić and Župljanin*, 25 May 2010, 10720f.
132 Edin Omerčić, 'Za šta smo se borili', 7.
133 ICTY, *Stanišić and Župljanin*, Judgement, Vol. 1, 143, 145.
134 'Deadline for Loyalty Extended', *Glas*, 9 April 1992 (0202-9748-0202-9748). See also 'We Guarantee Peace', 12 May 1992 (0202-9932-0202-9932).
135 Testimony of Predrag Radulović, *Stanišić and Župljanin*, 25 May 2010, 10776; Report of Miloš Group, 17 May 1992 (0084-9896-0084-9897); ICTY *Stanišić and Župljanin*, Judgement, Vol. 1, para. 157.
136 Testimony of Predrag Radulović, *Stanišić and Župljanin*, 25 May 2010, 10783f.
137 Dispatch of 'Miloš', 27 April 1992 (B008-0474-B008-0474).
138 'Special Unit', *Glas*, 28 April 1992 (0095-1920-0095-1920).
139 'Soon a Special Detachment', *Glas*, 29 April 1992 (0095-1922-0095-1922).
140 One of the earlier demands of the SOS when they appeared in Banja Luka was the adoption of the RS Law on Internal Affairs. 'Proclamation of the Serbian Defence Forces', *Glas*, 3/4 April 1992 (0095-1932-0095-1934).
141 'Conclusions Reached at the Meeting of the Expanded Centre Council Held on 6 May 1992', 20 May 1992 (0063-3164-0063-3168).
142 SNB Sector Banja Luka to Executive Board of Municipal Assembly of Banja Luka, 18 December 1993 (B001-1271-B001-1271).
143 Testimony of Predrag Radulović, *Stanišić and Župljanin*, 25 May 2010, 10777.
144 Testimony of Predrag Radulović, *Stanišić and Župljanin*, 25 May 2010, 10785f.
145 SJB Bosanski Novi Report to CSB Banja Luka, 'Information on the Work and Behaviour of the Detachment for Special Purposes on the Territory of This SJB', 21 May 1992 (B007-8680-B007-8681). This report concerns complaints filed by

citizens of the Bosanski Novi municipality regarding the special police detachment led by Mirko Lukić and Ljuban Ećim. It was stated that members of the special unit had on 15 May 1992 stolen DM 18,000 and other items from Fadil Ometlić and had on 18 May 1992 beaten the Muslim cleric Ramiz Aljović. Dragomir Kutlija, the chief of SJB Bosanski Novi, wrote to CSB Banja Luka and Ljuban Ećim that 'we request that the conduct of this unit be reviewed because disagreement with the manner in which the unit works also exists among citizens of Serb nationality [in] Bosanska Kostajnica'. See also SJB Prijedor to Chief of CSB Banja Luka, 13 June 1992 (0063-3256). Notwithstanding complaints directed at the conduct of his unit, Ljuban Ećim advanced to positions of greater responsibility. He later began to work for the SNB Sector in Banja Luka as an inspector. SNB Sector Banja Luka to Executive Board of Municipal Assembly of Banja Luka, 18 December 1993 (B001-1271). See also CSB Special Detachment payroll, August 1992 (B007-7456-B007-7462).

146 Excerpt from Minutes of 40th Session of Kotor Varoš Crisis Staff, 26 June 1992 (0041-5614). Savo Tepić, the chief of SJB Kotor Varoš, also enquired about the status of approximately seventy-three prisoners. He was told that 'this was a police matter'. See also Excerpt from Minutes of 47th Session of Kotor Varoš Crisis Staff, 29 June 1992 (0041-5607).

147 Excerpt from Minutes of 53rd Session of Kotor Varoš Crisis Staff, 2 July 1992 (0041-5600).

148 'Review of Police Forces', *Glas*, 13 May 1992 (0202-9936); 'Decisiveness in the Defence of Peace', *Glas*, 14 May 1992 (0202-9947).

149 Conversation between Čedo Kljajić and Stojan Župljanin, 7 May 1992 (0400-7276-0400-7297, at 0400-7277).

150 Video recording of Security Day Parade in Banja Luka, 13 May 1992 (V000-8836).

151 The report of the Banja Luka SNB Sector (Line 01) for April 1992–April 1993 indicated that the break had taken place 'already at the end of 1991'. Banja Luka SNB Sector, 'Overview of Activities of the SNB Banja Luka Sector for Line 1 for the Period April 1992–April 1993', 12 April 1993 (B003-6980-B003-6988).

152 RS MUP Ministerial Payroll for May 1992 (FI20-0983-FI20-0984).

153 Testimony of Slobodan Škipina, *Stanišić and Župljanin*, 30 March 2010, 8288.

154 Appointment decision, signed by Mićo Stanišić, 6 August 1992 (fi20-0591-fi20-0591). See also RS MUP SNB to all chiefs of SNB Sectors in CSBs, 12(?) August 1992 (0296-9606).

155 On 17 August, RS MUP's Administration for Analytical-Informational Matters sent information on intelligence activities aimed against the RS to SNB. RS MUP Administration for Analytical-Informational Matters to SNB, 17 August 1992 (0324-8494-0324-8495).

156 RS MUP, 'Information on Some Aspects of Work to Date and on Impending Tasks', 17 July 1992 (0324-6855-0324-6867).

157 RS MUP SNB, 'Report on the Work of the National Security Service in the Period from 1 April to 31 December 1992', 30 April 1993 (B001-0776-B001-0789).

158 RS MUP, 'Information on Some Aspects of Work to Date and on Impending Tasks', 17 July 1992 (0324-6855-0324-6867).

159 Order of Stanišić to all CSBs and all SNB Sectors, 28 August 1992 (B003-1307).

160 SRBiH MUP Rulebook on the Internal Organisation of the State Security Service of the Republican Secretariat for Internal Affairs of the Socialist Republic of Bosnia and Herzegovina, 1 March 1990 (0113-7521-0113-7669).

161 SNB War Department Šipovo, 27 July 1992 (B006-8855-B006-8856); SNB War Department Mrkonjić Grad to Public Security Service Mrkonjić Grad, November 1992 (0087-6130-0087-6131). For an example of the organizational schematic of the SNB at the level of the CSB and below, see CSB Sarajevo – Sector SNB, 'Report on the Work of the SNB Sector Sarajevo from July to August', 18 August 1992 (0074-9701-0074-9701).
162 RS MUP, 'Report on Work for the Period from April to June 1992', 29 June 1992 (0324-6791-0324-6809).
163 CSB Sarajevo to RS MUP, 25 July 1992 (0324-7361-0324-7363).
164 Dissatisfaction was however expressed by the SNB in CSB Sarajevo because of the lack of military intelligence being passed to the SNB by the Sarajevo-Romanija Corps.
165 SRBiH MUP Rulebook on the Internal Organisation of the State Security Service of the Republican Secretariat for Internal Affairs of the Socialist Republic of Bosnia and Herzegovina, 1 March 1990 (0113-7521-0113-7669).
166 In 1994, the SNB became the State Security Division (*Resor državne bezbjednosti*). RDB Centre Banja Luka, 23 June 1994 (B003-6977).
167 RS MUP SNB, 'Report on the Work of the National Security Service in the Period from 1 April to 31 December 1992', 30 April 1993 (B001-0776-B001-0789).
168 CSB Banja Luka, 'Report on the Work of the Public Security Centre Banja Luka for the Period from 1 July to 30 September 1992', October 1992 (0074-9601-0074-9650). See also SNB Sector, CSB Banja Luka, 'Fundamental Accents of the Work of SNB Banja Luka in 1992 and Some Problems in the Work', 9 July 1992 (B003-3221-B003-3227).
169 SNB Sector, CSB Banja Luka, 'Current Security Evaluation on the Territory of RO Prijedor', 15 April 1992 (B004-8007-B004-8008); SNB Sector, CSB Banja Luka, 'Evaluation of the Current Security Situation on the Territory of RO Bosanska Dubica', 16 April 1992 (B004-8009-B004-8009); SNB Sector, CSB Banja Luka, 'Evaluation of Security Situation on the Territory of Bosanski Novi', 16 April 1992 (B004-8010-B004-8010); SNB Sector, CSB Banja Luka, 'Evaluation of the Current Security Situation on the Territory of Sanski Most', 14 April 1992 (B004-8011-B004-8011).
170 SNB RO Mrkonjić Grad, 'Plan for the Application of Operational Measures and Activities towards Persons from the Territory of Mrkonjić Grad who Deserve Operational Interest', 1 July 1992 (B006-9071-B006-9082); see also SNB RO Mrkonjić Grad, 'Plan for the Application of Operational Measures and Activities towards Persons from Mrkonji} Grad', 25 August 1992 (B006-9085-B006-9085); SNB RO Klju~, 'Suggestion for the Release of Prisoners of War from the Camp Manja~a', 9 November 1992 (B008-8566-B008-8567).
171 Banja Luka SNB Sector, 'Overview of Activities of the SNB Banja Luka Sector for Line 1 for the Period April 1992–April 1993', 12 April 1993 (B003-6980-B003-6988).
172 The report noted, however, that cooperation with the VRS was not without friction.
173 Banja Luka SNB Sector, 'Report on the Work of SNB Sector Banja Luka for 1992', January 1993 (B003-1813-B003-1821). See also Official Note of SNB Detachment Mrkonjić Grad, 14 December 1992 (B008-8114-B008-8114). The SNB's interest in persons detained at Manjača continued after their release from Manjača. On 29 September 1992, SNB RO Ključ requested a list of all former Manjača detainees from the VRS. According to SNB RO Ključ, former detainees now located outside

the former Yugoslavia were conducting activities hostile to the RS. Official note of SNB RO Ključ, 29 September 1992 (B008-8582-B008-8582).
174 See the three reports of CSB Banja Luka, 'Overview of the State of Security on the Territory of the Autonomous Region of Bosnian Krajina', June 1992, 'More Information Obtained in the Course of the Clarification of the Circumstances of the Case "Kozarac" and the Attack on Prijedor by Muslim and Croat Extremists', June 1992, and 'Newer Information Obtained in the Course of the Clarification of the Circumstances Surrounding the Attack on the Military Patrol and Surrounding the Paramilitary Organisation and Illegal Arming on the Territory of Kozarac, Prijedor and Other Nearby Places', June 1992 (B003-4287-B003-4306). See also Banja Luka SNB Sector, 'New Information on Illegal Arming on the Territory of Banja Luka', July 1992 (B003-1840-B003-1844) and Banja Luka Sector, 'Channel of Illegal Arming of Muslim Extremists in Some Villages in Bosanska Gradiška Severed', May 1992 (B003-1663-B003-1666).
175 Banja Luka SNB Sector, 'Report on the Work of SNB Sector Banja Luka for 1992', January 1993 (B003-1813-B003-1821). On reporting within the SNB, see also SNB Undersecretary Dragan Kijac to all CSB SNB Sectors, 3 October 1992 (0370-1695-0370-1698); Kijac to all SNB Sectors, 22 October 1992 (0370-1700-0370-1700); Kijac to all SNB Sectors, 23 October 1992 (0370-1701-0370-1701).
176 CSB Banja Luka, SNB Sector, 'Security Situation for the Territory of Prijedor Municipality', 23 October 1992 (0063-3340-0063-3343). See also the May 1993 SNB Sector Banja Luka overview of population changes in the area covered by CSB Banja Luka, and Official note of CSB Banja Luka SNB Sector, 19 October 1992 (B007-9266-B007-9267). CSB Banja Luka SNB Sector, 'Overview of Departing and Arriving Citizens on the Territories Covered by the Sector', May 1993 (B009-8148-B009-8154).
177 In a separate case, the SNB in Mrkonjić Grad decided to take measures against Dževad Velić, a Muslim who had filmed the destruction of a Catholic church and mosques in Mrkonjić Grad by 'Serbian fighters'. His acts of filming this destruction and distributing the video cassette were defined as being directed 'against the Serbian nation'. SNB Mrkonjić Grad, 2 November 1992 (B008-8910-B008-8910; see also 0087-6130-0087-6130).
178 CSB Trebinje, 'Information on the Work and Current Problems of CSB Trebinje', September 1992 (0074-1262-0074-1278).
179 ICTY, Testimony of Slobodan Škipina, *Stanišić and Župljanin,* 30 March 2010, 8335.
180 Banja Luka SNB Sector, 'Report on the Work of SNB Sector Banja Luka for 1992', January 1993 (B003-1813-B003-1821).
181 On 9 October 1992, SNB RO Šipovo reported that Islamic cultural objects had been destroyed. The report also noted that approximately 1,500 Muslims emigrated out of the municipality. Official note of SNB RO Šipovo, 9 October 1992 (B009-0248-B009-0248). On 9 April 1993, SNB RO Šipovo provided the results of a tally of non-Serbs who had left [Šipovo municipality in the course of 1992. Of 2,400 Muslims in the municipality at the beginning of 1992, 1,500 had left. Another 900 – the remainder – left in the first three months of 1993. SNB RO Šipovo, 'Report on the Work of RO for the Period from 1 January 1993 to 31 March 1993 and an Evaluation of the Security Situation on the Territory of Šipovo Municipality', 9 April 1993 (B008-8216-B008-8218).
182 Report of Miloš Group, 2 April 1992 (B008-0508).
183 Telephone conversation of Mićo Stanišić, Momčilo Mandić, Bruno Stojić and Brane Kvesić, 5 May 1992 (0322-0105-0322-0133, at 0322-0110 and 0322-0112).

Chapter 3

1. 'Report on the Analysis of the Work of SJBs in 1992 on the Territory of CSB Banja Luka', March 1993 (0324-6151-0324-6167); Draft RS MUP Annual Report for 1992, January 1993 (FI0-1276-FI20-1319).
2. Radovan Karadžić, Transcript of the 50th Session of the RS Assembly, 15–16 April 1995 (0422–6267).
3. Transcript of the 16th Session of the RS Assembly, 12 May 1992 (0084-7711-0084-7761).
4. ICTY, *Krajišnik*, Judgement, para. 195.
5. ICTY, *Perišić*, Judgement, para. 195–6.
6. ICTY, *Krajišnik*, Judgement, para. 196.
7. An analogous unit, the 40th Personnel Centre, existed for the Serb Army of the Krajina (*Srpska Vojska Krajine*, SVK).
8. Karadžić, Krajišnik and Mladić had, along with others, discussed the strategic goals at a meeting on 7 May 1992. ICTY, *Stanišić and Župljanin*, Judgement, para. 189.
9. Mićo Stanišić, *Ratni sukobi na granicama Republika Srpske* (Belgrade: Svet knjige, 2020), 312.
10. Transcript of the 16th Session of the Assembly of the Serb Nation in Bosnia and Herzegovina, 12 May 1992 (0084-7711-0084-7761, at 0084-7722-0084-7723).
11. The special police unit at SJB Ilidža was one of the units possessing heavy weaponry. SJB Ilidža dispatch to Minister Mićo Stanišić, 5 August 1992 (0323-8499-0323-8505).
12. See description of the brigade in RS MUP Rulebook on Internal Organization in Conditions of War and Imminent Threat of War, September 1992 (0324-3783-0324-3984).
13. See video V000-1977-V000-1977, in which Milenko Karišik discusses orders issued by Momčilo Mandić in the operation at Vraca.
14. See video V000-2435-V000-2435, in which Mićo Stanišić introduces Karišik and other members of the RS MUP special police unit.
15. The Police Detachment later became known as the Special Brigade of the Police. See discussion of the Special Brigade of the Police in Minutes of Expanded Session of Steering Council of the Ministry for Internal Affairs of the Serbian Republic, 5 November 1992 (0324-6041-0324-6051).
16. RS MUP, Overview of April 1992 Payroll, 21 May 1992 (FI20-1643-FI20-1644).
17. RS MUP, Overview of Payroll for May 1992 for 'CSB – Special Unit – Police Detachment' (FI20-1076-FI20-1079). Although the term CSB is used, this unit was responsible to the ministry, not to any CSB.
18. RS MUP Payroll for April 1992 for the Special Platoon in the Serbian Ministry of Internal Affairs (FI20-0877-FI20-0877).
19. RS MUP, 'Report on Work for the Period from April to June 1992', 29 June 1992 (0324-6791-0324-6809).
20. SJB Ilidža dispatch to Minister Mićo Stanišić, 5 August 1992 (0323-8499-0323-8505); Official note of SM Vraca, 31 May 1992 (0324-7382-0324-7383).
21. Order of Mićo Stanišić, 15 June 1992 (0324-6099-0324-6099).
22. 'Preserve Peace with Preventive Measures and Agreement', *Glas*, 15 April 1992 (0202-9780-0202-9780). In the same article, Župljanin sought the financial assistance of the Banja Luka Municipal Assembly because CSB Banja Luka no longer received funds from the MUP of the Republic of Bosnia and Herzegovina.

23 In the 29 April 1992 issue of *Glas*, Župljanin was quoted as stating that the majority of those hitherto serving in the paramilitary Serb Defence Forces (*Srpske odbrambene snage*, SOS) would probably serve in the special unit under the control of CSB Banja Luka. The same article noted that the SOS had been placed by the ARK Assembly under the control of CSB Banja Luka and would cease to exist. 'Soon a Special Detachment', *Glas*, 29 April 1992 (0095-1922-0095-1922). See also CSB Banja Luka to all subordinate SJBs, 21 April 1992 (0088-1659-0088-1659).
24 Letter from Chief of CSB Banja Luka Stojan Župljanin to General Kukanjac, Commander, 2nd Military District, 23 April 1992 (SA00-8162-SA00-8165); Memo from Kukanjac to Župljanin, 24 April 1992 (0018-3324-0018-3328). The request included a note by Božo Novaković of CSB Banja Luka. This stated that Novaković had visited General Talić, who had agreed that the requested equipment should be given to CSB Banja Luka.
25 2nd Military Command to SSNO, 24 April 1992 (0018-3524-0018-3527). It should be noted that, in a telephone conversation on 19 May 1992, the Federal Secretary for Internal Affairs, Petar Gračanin, discussed with Mićo Stanišić the delivery of equipment to Stojan Župljanin, the head of the Banja Luka CSB, as well as the delivery of equipment to Sarajevo and other places. Conversation between Mićo Stanišić and Petar Gračanin, 19 May 1992 (0203-0519-0203-0520).
26 'Who Decides on Release?' and 'Special Police vs. the Police', *Glas*, 23 July 1992 (0095-1946-0095-1947). SJB Banja Luka to CSB Banja Luka and RS MUP, 21 July 1992 (B006-0581-B006-0583); SJB Banja Luka to CSB Banja Luka and RS MUP, 21 July 1992 (B006-0575-B006-0576).
27 'New Details on the Violent Release of the Two Members of the CSB Banja Luka Special Detachment: An Unprecedented Case' and 'Vladimir Tutuš, Chief of SJB Banja Luka, on the Incident Involving the Release of the Arrested Members of the Special Detachment of the CSB: The State Cannot Be Built on Violence', *Glas*, 24 July 1992 (0211-2712-0211-2712).
28 SJB Banja Luka, 'Information on Proven Illegal Measures of Members of the Former Police Detachment for Special Purposes of CSB Banja Luka', 5 May 1993 (B004-3531-B004-3541).
29 At the 22nd Session of the Assembly, the Vice-President of the RS government, Milan Trbojević, complained about the inability or unwillingness – and even participation – of the RS police to stop what he described as the 'plundering' of the RS. Stenographic records of 22nd Session of the RS Assembly, 23–24 November 1992 (0214-9632-0214-9749).
30 RS MUP to chiefs of all CSBs, 24 July 1992 (0323-8843).
31 Župljanin to chiefs of all SJBs, 29 July 1992 (P004-3127-P004-3128); Drljača dispatch, 30 July 1992 (P004-3129-P004-3129).
32 *Stanišić and Župljanin*, Judgement, Vol. 2, para. 35.
33 ICTY, *Stanišić and Župljanin*, Judgement, Vol. 2, paras. 37–43. On prosecutorial disinterest, see ibid., paras. 90f.
34 CSB Sarajevo to all subordinate SJBS, 12 September 1992 (0360-9823-0360-9823).
35 Minister Mićo Stanišić to chiefs of all CSBs, 16 December 1992 (0360-6600).
36 See records of the 6th Assembly Session, 26 January 1992 (SA02-5232-SA02-5305, at SA02-5240).
37 Ewan Brown Expert Report, P1803 in Stanišić and Župljanin.
38 ICTY, *Stanišić and Župljanin*, Judgement, Vol. 2, para. 333.
39 ICTY, *Stanišić and Župljanin*, Judgement, Vol. 1, para. 1149.

40 VRS Main Staff, Directive, 22 July 1992 (0362-9109-0362-9112).
41 Order of Minister Mićo Stanišić, 15 May 1992 (0323-8857-0323-8858). For an example of the practical deployment rules affecting such units, see CSB Banja Luka to chief of SJB Prijedor, 25 August 1992 (P005-4230-P005-4237). Stanišić duly appointed himself as the head of the Staff. Order of Minister Mićo Stanišić, 15 May 1992 (0324-1805-0324-1086). For Stanišić's own interpretation of this order, see Stanišić, *Ratni sukobi*, 144.
42 This was the interpretation the RS MUP gave to the order in its 17 July 1992 document, 'Information on Some Aspects of Work to Date and on Impending Tasks', 17 July 1992 (0324-6855-0324-6867).
43 Overall, however, ICTY trial chambers found that the RS MUP was able to communicate effectively throughout the war. ICTY, *Karadžić*, Judgement, para. 3020.
44 Individual names are taken from the RS MUP Ministerial Payroll for May 1992 (FI20-0986).
45 Order of Minister Mićo Stanišić, 15 May 1992 (0323-8857-0323-8858).
46 Letter of Minister Mićo Stanišić to all CSBs, 17 May 1992 (0323-8854).
47 See, for example, 1st Krajina Corps Command to Chief of CSB Banja Luka Župljanin, 21 November 1992 (0084-1094-0084-1097); Command of 30th Partisan Division (re: establishment of defence command for Ključ Municipality), 31 May 1992 (0082-0684-0082-0685). On crisis staff coordination, see Kotor Varoš Crisis Staff, excerpt from Minutes of 40th Session, 26 June 1992 (0041-5614-0041-5615).
48 See for example the testimony of Goran Mačar and Radomir Njeguš.
49 In the period from July to September 1992, CSB Sarajevo described the participation of its police officers in combat operations as their main activity. Most of this was conducted in cooperation with the VRS. CSB Sarajevo, 'Report on Work for the Period from July to September 1992', October 1992 (0297-0877-0297–0883). See also the RS MUP, 'Report on Work for the Period from July to September 1992', October 1992 (0359-0674-0359-0359–0699).
50 Ewan Brown, 'Military Operations in Bosanska Krajina – 1992: A Background Study', 27 November 2002, 2.31, 2.39, 2.40, 2.41.
51 Ewan Brown, 'Military Operations', 2.49. For an example, see 1st Krajina Corps Command to CSB Banja Luka, 21 November 1992 (0084-1094-0084-1097) and the pursuant action by CSB Banja Luka in CSB Banja Luka Order, 22 November 1992 (0048-9761).
52 CSB Banja Luka dispatch, 28 May 1992 (P004-3229-P004-3229). This dispatch is quoted in dispatch of Simo Drljača, SJB Prijedor, 28 May 1992 (0063-3237-0063-3237).
53 CSB Banja Luka to all subordinate SJBs and commands of 1st and 2nd Krajina Corps, 18 September 1992 (0047-8748-0047-8749).
54 Report of SJB Prijedor, August 1992 (B003-2556-B003-2564, at B003-2563).
55 SJB Prijedor, 'Report on the Work of SJB Prijedor for the Last Nine Months of 1992', January 1993 (0063-3747-0063–3762).
56 See for example 1st Krajina Corps Command, Regular Combat Report, 14 June 1992 (0086-1629-0086-1640).
57 RS MUP, Short Review of the Work of the MUP and Some Suggestions for Future Work – Summary of the Meeting of Leading RS MUP Employees on 11 July 1992, July 1992 (0324-1848-0324-1879).
58 Report of 1st Krajina Corps, 30 June 1992 (0094-9833-0094-9833); order of 1st Krajina Corps to Tactical Group 1, 26 November 1992 (0084-1187-0084-1188).

59 Roy Gutman, *A Witness to Genocide: The First Inside Account of the Horrors of 'Ethnic Cleansing' in Bosnia* (Shaftesbury: Dorset, 1993).
60 See, however, Hikmet Karčić, *Torture, Humiliate, Kill: Inside the Bosnian Serb Camp System* (Ann Arbor: University of Michigan Press, 2022).
61 SJB Pale, Record, 8 February 1993 (0360-8317-0360-8318).
62 In addition to later examples, see list of Bosnian Muslims detained by SJB Donji Vakuf from 27 May to 12 July 1992 (0531-6524-0531-6526).
63 RS Ministry of National Defence decision, 16 April 1992 (0057-4584-0057-4585).
64 According to ICTY military expert Ewan Brown, 'it is clear that the ARK decisions relating to weapon surrender and the preparation for forceful action was part of a recognised plan, passed down to the municipal bodies and acted upon and in some areas the decision to disarm the population appeared to have been co-ordinated across municipal boundaries'. Ewan Brown, 'Military Operations', 2.14.
65 ARK Republic Secretariat for National Defence decision, 4 May 1992 (0034-9522-0034-9523).
66 Conclusions of Session of Sanski Most Crisis Staff, 28 April 1992 (0047-1852-0047-1853).
67 Župljanin to chiefs of all SJBs, 4 May 1992 (0063-3791-0063-3792). See also the Conclusions of the Meeting at CSB Banja Luka, 6 May 1992 in which Drljača states that SJB Prijedor must implement all decisions of the ARK Crisis Staff (0063-3793-0063-3794).
68 'Decision on the Establishment of the War Staff of the Autonomous Region of Krajina', 5 May 1992 (B000-0434).
69 Conclusions Reached at the Meeting of the Expanded Centre Council Held on 6 May 1992 (0063-3164-0063-3168).
70 Conclusions of Session of ARK War Staff, 9 May 1992 (B005-4695-B005-4696); Conclusions made at the ARK Crisis Staff meeting, signed by Brđanin, 11 May 1992 (0091-4682-0091-4683); Župljanin to chiefs of all SJBs, 11 May 1992 (P004-3255); JNA 5th Corps Command Combat Report, 15 May 1992 (0086-2230-0086-2233). According to the decisions of the ARK Crisis Staff, the deadline was extended to 15 April 1992 because all nationalities had asked to be able to hand in their weapons without police intervention. At the end of July 1992, Župljanin asked all subordinate SJBs to report on the number of weapons and amount of ammunition confiscated by them. SJB Prijedor dispatch, 31 July 1992 (P004-3073). SJB Prijedor responded on 2 August. SJB Prijedor to CSB Banja Luka, 2 August 1992 (P004-3051).
71 CSB Banja Luka to chiefs of all SJBs, National Security Divisions, Departments for the Affairs and Tasks of the Police, Departments for the Affairs and Tasks of Prevention and Detection of Crime, and RS MUP, 14 May 1992 (0063-3227-0063-3227). SJB Šipovo distributed these instructions on the following day. SJB Šipovo, 'Concrete Plan on the Removal of Illegally Possessed Weapons, Munitions and Explosive Means', 15 May 1992 (B006-9083-B006-9084). On 25 May, Župljanin requested information on the implementation of the 14 May instructions. Župljanin to heads of all SJBs, 25 May 1992 (0063-3225-0063-3225). On 10 July, SJB Sanski Most reported to CSB Banja Luka regarding the number of weapons confiscated. SJB Sanski Most to CSB Banja Luka, 10 July 1992 (0049-3302-0049-3304).
72 JNA 5th Corps Command Combat Report, 15 May 1992 (0086-2230-0086-2233, at 0086-2230).
73 Conclusions of Session of ARK Crisis Staff held on 18 May 1992, cited in Official Gazette of the Autonomous Region of Krajina (*Službeni glasnik ARK*), No. 2,

5 June 1992 (0038-8981-0038-8982). It should be kept in mind in considering the relationship between crisis staffs and the police that the chiefs of the SJBs and the CSBs were *ex officio* members of the municipal and regional crisis staffs, respectively.
74 ARK Crisis Staff Conclusions, 18 May 1992 (0049-7823-0049-7824).
75 Presidency of Assembly of SAO Semberija and Majevica, 'Decision on Temporary Hand-Over of Legal Weapons', 22 May 1992 (0045-6182-0045–6182).
76 Report of CSB/SJB Banja Luka to Executive Board of Municipal Assembly of Banja Luka regarding confiscation of illegal weapons from January 1992 to 21 September 1992, 30 September 1992 (0324-6140-0324-6147). Although the report cited only fifty-eight criminal charges brought against individuals on illegal weapons charges, it failed to mention that numerous individuals had been detained without charges at various detention centres operated by the RS authorities. Responses to later operations to collect 'illegal' weapons include: SJB Teslić to CSB Banja Luka, 6 November 1992 (B003-0582-B003-0583); SJB Drvar to CSB Banja Luka, 9 November 1992 (B003-8584-B003-8584); SJB Kneževo to CSB Banja Luka, 12 November 1992 (B003-8546-B003-8548); SJB Kneževo to CSB Banja Luka, 14 December 1992 (B003-8549-B003-8549); SJB Srbac to CSB Banja Luka, 19 November 1992 (B003-8577-B003-8577); SJB Prijedor to CSB Banja Luka, 20 November 1992 (B003-8601-B003-8601); SJB Gradiška to CSB Banja Luka, 23 November 1992 (B003-8675-B003-8576); SJB Bosansko Grahovo to CSB Banja Luka, 24 November 1992 (B003-8534-B003-8534); SJB Banja Luka to CSB Banja Luka, 24 November 1992 (B003-8554-B003-8554); SJB Kotor Varoš to CSB Banja Luka, 1 December 1992 (B003-8550-B003-8552); SJB Novi Grad to CSB Banja Luka, 3 December 1992 (B003-8555-B003-8573); SJB Petrovac to CSB Banja Luka, 9 December 1992 (B003-8540-B003-8545); SJB Bihać to CSB Banja Luka, 10 December 1992 (B003-8553-B003-8553); SJB Krupa na Uni to CSB Banja Luka, 11 December 1992 (B003-8578-B003-8578). SJB Kneževo noted, however, that all of the weapons confiscated were legally registered and had been confiscated in the course of confiscation of weaponry from non-Serbs. On 1 December 1992, Župljanin sent out a reminder asking for responses to his dispatch requesting this information. Dispatch of Župljanin, 1 December 1992 (B003-8511-B003-8511). See also undated summary by CSB Banja Luka of weaponry confiscated (B003-8506-B003-8509).
77 Examples of this phenomenon include:
ARK: ARK Crisis Staff orders confiscation of weapons by 14 May 1992. Conclusions of Session of ARK Crisis Staff, 11 May 1992 (0057-5138-0057-5138).
Bratunac: 'Decision on the Disarming of Citizens Who Possess Weapons on the Territory of Bratunac Municipality', 19 April 1992 (0083-5779-0083-5779).
Sanski Most: 'Report for the SJB Bosanski Novi', 15 August 1992 (B003-2565-B003-2573).
78 Evidence that the Ministry of Internal Affairs expected local police forces to carry out crisis staffs' orders includes:
Order from CSB Banja Luka indicates that local police stations had been accepting and carrying out orders issued by municipal and regional crisis staffs, 30 July 1992 (0045-1835-0045-1840); SJB Prijedor dispatch refers to ARK Crisis Staff order, 5 July 1992 (0063-3273-0063-3273).
79 SJB Prijedor dispatch of 5 July 1992 refers to attack on a vehicle with military conscripts at Hambarina on 21 May 1992 (0063-3273-0063-3273).
80 ICTY, *Stanišić and Župljanin*, Judgement, Vol. 1, paras. 301, 331.

81 ICTY, *Stanišić and Župljanin*, Judgement, Vol. 1, para. 301; on confiscation of legally possessed weapons from Muslims and Croats, see report of SJB Sanski Most, 15 June 1992 (0088-8035-0088-8036), see also conclusions of meeting of Sanski Most Crisis Staff, 22 May 1992 (0047-1824-0047-1827).
82 RS MUP, Short Review of the Work of the MUP and Some Suggestions for Future Work – Summary of the Meeting of Leading RS MUP Employees on 11 July 1992, July 1992 (0324-1848-0324-1879, at 0324-1853).
83 ICTY, *Stanišić and Župljanin*, Judgement, Vol. 1, para. 302; SJB Ključ, Report on Interrogation of Esad Bender, 21 June 1992 (0094-7397-0094-7398); dispatch of SJB Ključ, 25 September 1992 (0091-4676-0091-4677).
84 Notebook of Ratko Mladić, 27 May 1992 to 31 July 1995 (J000-3175-J000-3581), 305, 308, 313.
85 It is indicative that most of the text related to Prijedor in Mićo Stanišić's second book is about alleged 'Muslim terrorist actions in Prijedor'. Stanišić, *Ratni sukobi*, 199–202.
86 ICTY, *Stanišić and Župljanin*, Judgement, Vol. 1, para. 500; ICTY trial slide showing prewar ethnic distribution in Prijedor municipality. (0216-9347).
87 ICTY, *Stanišić and Župljanin*, Judgement, Vol. 1, para. 505.
88 SJB Prijedor, 'Report on Work for the First Half Year of 1992', June 1992 (P003-3215-P003-3226, at P003–3216).
89 SJB Prijedor, 'Report on Work for the First Half Year of 1992', June 1992 (P003-3215-P003-3226, at P003–3216).
90 ICTY, *Stanišić and Župljanin*, Judgement, Vol. 1, para. 511.
91 ICTY, *Stanišić and Župljanin*, Judgement, Vol. 1, para. 513; undated report of SJB Prijedor, referencing CSB Banja Luka decision of 14 August 1992 (B003-2556-B003-2564).
92 ICTY, *Stanišić and Župljanin*, Judgement, Vol. 1, para. 515.
93 Undated report of SJB Prijedor, referencing CSB Banja Luka decision of 14 August 1992 (B003-2556-B003-2564).
94 ICTY, *Tadić*, Trial Chamber Judgement, para. 148.
95 Abbreviated Minutes of Meeting of SDS Prijedor Municipal Board, 9 May 1992 (0063-3865-0063-3869, at 0063-3866).
96 Minutes of the 4th Session of the Council for People's Defence of the Prijedor Municipal Assembly, 15 May 1992 (0063-4041-0063-4043, at 0063-4042). For a later report on implementation, see SJB Prijedor to CSB Banja Luka, 5 July 1992 (0063-3273-0063-3274).
97 ICTY, *Stanišić and Župljanin*, Judgement, Vol. 1, para. 523.
98 Undated report of SJB Prijedor, referencing CSB Banja Luka decision of 14 August 1992 (B003-2556-B003-2564).
99 See Prijedor witness testimony in *Stakić, Tadić, Brđanin, Krajišnik, Karadžić* and *Stanišić and Župljanin*, among other cases.
100 Undated report of SJB Prijedor, referencing CSB Banja Luka decision of 14 August 1992 (B003-2556-B003-2564, at B003-2557).
101 Undated report of SJB Prijedor, referencing CSB Banja Luka decision of 14 August 1992 (B003-2556-B003-2564, at B003-2559).
102 SJB Prijedor to CSB Banja Luka, Crisis Staff, Coordinators of Security Services, Chief of Police et al., 31 May 1992 (0063-3763-0063-3766). 'Simo Drljača's official appointment was made by Stojan Župljanin on 30 July 1992, taking effect retrospectively from 29 April 1992, in accordance with a decision of the RS Minister of Interior dated 25 April 1992.' ICTY, *Stanišić and Župljanin*, Judgement, Vol. 1, para. 507.

103 The police station at Omarska, which was subordinate to SJB Prijedor, provided a large number of personnel for the Omarska 'collective centre'. The chief of the police station at Omarska was Željko Mejakić. See the list dated 21 June 1992 (P005-0758-P005-0759). This list also shows that the police station at Omarska was responsible for the issuing of entry permits to the camp.
104 SJB Prijedor to CSB Banja Luka, Crisis Staff, Coordinators of Security Services, Chief of Police et al., 31 May 1992 (0063-3763-0063-3766).
105 Undated report of SJB Prijedor, referencing CSB Banja Luka decision of 14 August 1992 (B003-2556-B003-2564, at B003-2559).
106 Decision of Prijedor Municipal Crisis Staff, 2 June 1992 (0063-3780-0063-3780).
107 SJB Prijedor, Report on Work for the First Half Year of 1992, June 1992 (P003-3215-P003-3226).
108 Order of Prijedor Municipal Crisis Staff, 2 July 1992 (0063-3805-0063-3805).
109 SJB Prijedor, Report on Work for the First Half Year of 1992, June 1992 (P003-3215-P003-3226).
110 Simo Drljača to RS MUP, VRS, and CSB Banja Luka, 1 August 1992 (0063-3812-0063-3812).
111 Undated report of SJB Prijedor, referencing CSB Banja Luka decision of 14 August 1992 (B003-2556-B003-2564, at B003-2559).
112 List of Members of the Police Who Will Receive Special Permits for Entry into the Reception Centre Keraterm, signed by Commander Živko Knežević (P005-0757-P005-0757). The document is undated, but a hand-written note confirms that fifty-four permits were issued on 25 June 1992.
113 Undated report of SJB Prijedor, referencing CSB Banja Luka decision of 14 August 1992 (B003-2556-B003-2564, at B003-2560).
114 Undated report of SJB Prijedor, referencing CSB Banja Luka decision of 14 August 1992 (B003-2556-B003-2564, at B003-2558).
115 For a description of the way in which these interrogations were conducted, see SJB Sanski Most to CSB Banja Luka, 2 July 1992 (0049-1518-0049-1518); also SJB Sanski Most, Report on the Work of SJB Sanski Most for the [First] six months of 1992, 20 July 1992 (0049-3711-0049-3729). Undated report of SJB Prijedor, referencing CSB Banja Luka decision of 14 August 1992 (B003-2556-B003-2564).
116 SJB Prijedor, Report on the work of the Prijedor Public Security Station during the last nine months of 1992, January 1993 (0063-3747-0063-3762). Although Manjača was under VRS control, the police were asked to assist in the processing of prisoners there. On 6 August 1992, the 1st Krajina Corps wrote to the chief of SNB Prijedor to ask for help in processing prisoners. The letter noted that the conclusion had been reached that large numbers of prisoners at Manjača were innocent. Urgent action had to be taken regarding these prisoners because of international media attention focused on camps in the RS. 1st Krajina Corps to Chief of SNB Prijedor, 6 August 1992 (P004-8620-P004-8620); Ewan Brown report, 2.55.
117 ICTY, Stanišić and Župljanin Judgement, Vol. 2, para. 89.
118 According to SJB Prijedor, Trnopolje was established by the military. Undated report of SJB Prijedor (B003-2556-B003-2564).
119 SJB Prijedor, Report on the work of the Prijedor Public Security Station during the Last Nine Months of 1992, Prijedor, January 1993, Chief of Public Security, Simo Drljača (0063-3747-0063-3762).

120 CSB Banja Luka, SNB Sector, 'Report on the Work of SNB Prijedor Detachment for the Period from 1 January to 31 December 1992', 20 January 1993 (B009-8095-B009–8102).
121 ICTY, *Stanišić and Župljanin*, Judgement, Vol. 1, para. 170.
122 ICTY, *Brđanin*, Judgement, para. 436.
123 SJB Ključ to Command of Manjača, 24 June 1992 (0531-6302-0531-6302).
124 On 27 July, the 1st Krajina Corps Command ordered the continued participation of police officers in securing Manjača. 1st Krajina Corps Command Order, 27 July 1992 (0102-9846-0124-9848).
125 Mirko Vrućinić, Acting Chief of SJB Sanski Most, to VRS Commandant, Manjača, 6 June 1992 (0106-1776-0106-1776).
126 Order of Sanski Most Crisis Staff, 6 June 1992 (0047-1232-0047-1232).
127 Vinko Kondić, chief of SJB Ključ, to VRS Commandant, Manjača, 24 June 1992 (0057-4811-0057-4811).
128 Operational Team, Manjača, 8 July 1992 (0531-6629-0531-6629).
129 See also SJB Sanski Most, 'List of Persons Turned Over to Military Investigative Organs from the Territory of Sanski Most Who Are Located in Manjača', August 1992 (0531-6474-0531–6496).
130 Colonel Stevan Bogojević, 1st Krajina Corps Command to Chief of SNB Prijedor, 6 August 1992 (P004-8620-P004-8620).
131 ICTY, Stanišić and Župljanin Trial Judgement, Vol. 1, para. 174.
132 Daily Report of Prisoner of War Camp Manjača to Department for Intelligence and Security Affairs, 7 August 1992 (0531-6630-0531-6631).
133 Daily Report of Prisoner of War Camp Manjača to Department for Intelligence and Security Affairs, 7 August 1992 (0531-6630-0531-6631).
134 Daily Report of Prisoner of War Camp Manjača to Department for Intelligence and Security Affairs, 7 August 1992 (0531-6630-0531-6631).
135 Captain 1st Class Dane Lukajić, 10 August 1992 (0531-6633-0531-6633).
136 Order of Stojan Župljanin, CSB Banja Luka, 19 August 1992 (0094-2274-0094-2274).
137 RS MUP, Short Review of the Work of the MUP and Some Suggestions for Future Work – Summary of the Meeting of Leading RS MUP Employees on 11 July 1992, July 1992 (0324-1848-0324-1879).
138 RS MUP, Short Review of the Work of the MUP and Some Suggestions for Future Work – Summary of the Meeting of Leading RS MUP Employees on 11 July 1992, July 1992 (0324-1848-0324-1879, at 0324-1855).
139 On a similar point, see the interview of Simo Drljača in *Kozarski vjesnik*, 9 April 1993 (0147-0203-0147-0203).
140 Župljanin to Stanišić, 20 July 1992 (0324-6719-0324-6721).
141 Minutes of RS government session, 22 July 1992 (0124-5447-0124-5454).
142 Order of President Radovan Karadžić, 23 July (0084-5369-0084-5369).
143 Roy Gutman, 'Death Camps', *Newsday*, 2 August 1992 (0063-6013-0063-6017). In his second book, Stanišić disparages Gutman and other Western journalists' accounts. Stanišić, *Ratni sukobi*, 348.
144 Chuck Sudetic, 'Conflict in the Balkans: Serbs in Bosnia Allow Red Cross to Visit Camps', *New York Times*, 9 August 1992 (0063-6057-0063-6059). The *Times* reported that the ICRC would begin visits to camps around Banja Luka on Wednesday (August 12). The article noted that Serbian leaders closed Keraterm and 'wound down' operations and improved conditions at Omarska before opening the camps to foreign reporters.

145 RS Presidency minutes, 5 August 1992 (0076-7907-0076-7909) and 6 August 1992 (0076-7904-0076-7906).
146 Župljanin to Stanišić, 20 July 1992 (0324-6719-0324-6721).
147 Conclusion of RS Presidency, 6 August 1992 (0049-5344).
148 Assistant Minister Kovač to RS president and RS prime minister, 8 August 1992 (0124-5167-0124-5168). Kovač later claimed that it had been impossible to separate combatants from non-combatants. ICTY, *Stanišić and Župljanin*, Judgement, Vol. 2, 657.
149 RS Presidency minutes, 8 August 1992 (0076-7899-0076-7900).
150 Minutes of RS government session, 9 August 1992 (0124-5481-0124-5486). Decision on Establishment of Collective Centres and Other Buildings for Prisoners in the Serbian Republic in Bosnia and Herzegovina (0124-6762-0124-6762).
151 Report of RS Government Commission for the Inspection of Collective Centres and Other Locations with Detainees in the Serbian Republic in Bosnia and Herzegovina, 17 August 1992 (0124-5060-0124-5067).
152 RS Ministry of Justice Report to RS Government, received on 22 August 1992 (0124-5058-0124-5059).
153 Simo Drljača to Minister Mićo Stanišić and Chief of CSB Banja Luka Stojan Župljanin, 5 August 1992 (0063-3298).
154 Simo Drljača to Chief of CSB Banja Luka Župljanin, 9 August 1992 (0063-3300).
155 Simo Drljača to Commandant of Manjača, 17 August 1992 (P000-2176-P000-2187).
156 Stojan Župljanin to chiefs of all CSBs, 19 August 1992 (0063-3185).
157 SJB Prijedor to CSB Banja Luka, 22 August 1992 (0063-3308).
158 Press Release, Prijedor, 22 August 1992 (0209-0032-0209-0032).
159 SJB Prijedor to CSB Banja Luka, 23 August 1992 (0063-3309-0063-3309).
160 SJB Sanski Most to Military-Investigative Organ Manjača, 27 and 28 August 1992 (0207-2642-0207-2643).
161 SJB Sanski Most to CSB Banja Luka, 5 August 1992 (0047-8745-0047-8746).
162 Decision of Župljanin, 14 August 1992 (B003-2587-B003-2587).
163 CSB Banja Luka, Conclusions Reached at the Meeting of the Expanded Centre Council Held on 6 May 1992, 20 May 1992 (0063-3164-0063-3168).
164 SJB Bosanski Novi report to CSB Banja Luka, 15 August 1992 (B003-2565-B003-2573).
165 SJB Sanski Most report to SNB Division of CSB Banja Luka, 18 August 1992 (B003-2543-B003-2546).
166 Undated report of SJB Prijedor, referencing CSB Banja Luka decision of 14 August 1992 (B003-2556-B003-2564).
167 CSB Banja Luka report, 18 August 1992 (B003-2527-B003-2542).
168 Order of President Karadžić, 19 August 1992 (0049-5341-0049-5342).
169 Župljanin to chiefs of all subordinate SJBs, 19 August 1992 (0047-8798); Mićo Stanišić to all CSBs, 17 August 1992 (0370-1693).
170 Župljanin to chiefs of all subordinate SJBs, 20 August 1992 (P004-2990-P004-2990); SJB Prijedor dispatch, 21 August 1992 (P004-2991-P004-2991).
171 Župljanin to chiefs of all SJBs, 21 August 1992 (0047-8799-0047-8799).
172 Župljanin to chiefs of all SJBs and Command of 1st Krajina Corps, 22 August 1992 (0047-8797-0047-8797).
173 Mićo Stanišić to all CSBs and all SJBs, 24 August 1992 (0063-3311-0063-3311).
174 Župljanin to chiefs of all SJBs, 27 August 1992 (0063-3312-0063-3312). See also SJB Prijedor, 28 August 1992 (0063-3313-0063-3313).

175 SJB Prijedor to CSB Banja Luka, 28 August 1992 (0063-3310-0063-3310).
176 SJB Ključ to CSB Banja Luka, 29 August 1992 (0057-4997-0057-5029).
177 RS MUP to CSB Sarajevo, Bijeljina and Trebinje, 28 August 1992 (0324-7335-0324-7335).
178 CSB Banja Luka to RS MUP and President Karadžić, 31 August 1992 (0323-8486-0323-8486).
179 Colonel Milutin Vukelić, 1st Krajina Corps, to VRS Main Staff and General Major Talić, 2 September 1992 (0102-9839-0102-9840); Župljanin to RS MUP, all subordinate SJBs, CSB Banja Luka (SNB), 4 September 1992 (B006-5584-B006-5584).
180 Minutes of Session of National Defence Council of Prijedor Municipal Assembly, 29 September 1992 (P005-2895-P005-2895).
181 Radovan Karadžić to General Colonel Ratko Mladić, Mićo Stanišić and Momčilo Mandić, 22 October 1992 (0049-5345-0049-5345).
182 Chief of SJB Sanski Most to Župljanin, 17 June 1992 (0049-3278-0049-3278).
183 SJB Bosanski Novi, Report, 15 August 1992 (B003-2565-B003-2573). The same report contains information on the collection of weapons by the police.
184 Župljanin quoted in Gutman, *A Witness to Genocide*, ix, 37.
185 See in particular the cruel and asinine cross-examination of witness Midho Alić by Defence Counsel Chriss Loukas, which concluded with presiding judge Alphons Orie – himself a former defence lawyer – acidly commenting that 'the purpose [of the cross-examination] is apparent. [The e]ffect is apparent as well', ICTY, *Krajišnik*, 23 April 2004, trial transcript, 2597.
186 SJB Prijedor to Chief of CSB Banja Luka, 5 July 1992 (0063-3274).
187 SJB Prijedor to CSB Banja Luka, 18 July 1992 (0063-3287-0063-3288). It is not clear whether the 18 and 19 July documents both refer to the same group of people as the 4 July document.
188 Dispatch of SJB Prijedor, 24 August 1992 (0063-3188).
189 SJB Sanski Most to Chief of CSB Banja Luka, 17 August 1992 (0047-8714).
190 Excerpt from Minutes of 58th Session of Kotor Varoš Municipal War Presidency, 20 August 1992 (0041-5736).
191 War Presidency of the Municipal Assembly of Ključ, 22 August 1992 (0531-6310).
192 Radio Ključ report, 31 August 1992 (0059-5227).
193 Minutes of inspection of work of SJB Prijedor, 4 September 1992 (B003-8610).
194 SJB Prijedor, 'Report on the Work of Public Security Station Prijedor for the Third Quarter', 29 September 1992 (P004-2819-P004–2826).
195 Dispatch of SJB Ključ, 28 September 1992 (0206-1515-0206-1516).
196 Penny Marshall, '21 Years after the War the Ground in Bosnia Is Giving Up Its Secrets', *ITV*, 14 October 2013. Back in 1992, Predrag Radulović of the 'Miloš' Group told colleagues in the RS MUP and the VRS that he regarded the atrocities mass graves in the Prijedor area 'as a case of genocide'. ICTY, Testimony of Predrag Radulović, *Stanišić and Župljanin*, 26 May 2010, 10845.
197 ICTY, *Mladić*, Judgement, Vol. 4, para. 4086.
198 This particular conclusion stems from ICTY, Stanišić and Župljanin, Vol. 1, para. 212.
199 Stanišić, *Ratni sukobi*, 229.
200 The SRBiH MUP SDB had reported on paramilitary activities in Bosnia and Herzegovina already in 1991. On 23 March 1992 SRBiH MUP SDB reported on the arrival of paramilitaries at Ilijaš. The SDS at Ilijaš had allegedly collected money to

pay for paramilitary assistance in the 'cleansing' of this municipality. SRBiH MUP SDB dispatch, 23 March 1992 (0323-7798-0323-7798).
201 CSB Banja Luka, 'Weekly Information (for the period 16 to 23 September 1991)' (0061-9485-0061-9491).
202 CSB Banja Luka, Informational Report, 23 September 1991 (SA02-0124-SA02-0132).
203 CSB Banja Luka, Information on the Criminal Activity and Other Illegal Activity of Veljko Milanković and Other Members of Paramilitary Formations from the Territory of Prnjavor, 2 December 1991 (0531-6068-0531-6076).
204 Milanković was subsequently wounded and died in February 1993. Karadžić posthumously bestowed a high order of the RS on Milanković.
205 ICTY, *Stanišić and Župljanin*, Judgement, Vol. 1, para. 888.
206 ICTY, *Stanišić and Župljanin*, Judgement, Vol. 1, para. 889.
207 ICTY, *Stanišić and Župljanin*, Judgement, Vol. 1, para. 890.
208 VRS Main Staff, Report on Paramilitary Formations on the Territory of the Serb Republic of BiH, 28 July 1992 (0094-9847-0094-9852, at 0094–9849).
209 SJB Milići to CSB Sarajevo, 3 August 1992 (0360-9769-0360-9770).
210 SJB Milići to CSB Sarajevo, 3 August 1992 (0360-9769-0360-9770).
211 ICTY, Testimony of Milorad Davidović, *Stanišić and Župljanin*, 23 August 2010, 13562; SSUP, Brigade of the Police, 'Report on the Engagement of a Group of Employees of the Brigade of the Police of the Federal MUP to Offer Professional Assistance to the MUP of the Serb Republic of Bosnia and Herzegovina', 8 August 1992 (Y032-0317-Y032–0325). The report also noted that police from the SSUP had provided assistance to the RS MUP in combat operations in Sarajevo in the period from 16 May 1992 to 20 July 1992.
212 ICTY, Witness Statement of Milorad Davidović, 15 March 2005 (0360-0770-0360–0827).
213 SSUP, Brigade of the Police, 'Report on the Engagement of a Group of Employees of the Brigade of the Police of the Federal MUP to Offer Professional Assistance to the MUP of the Serb Republic of Bosnia and Herzegovina', 8 August 1992 (Y032-0317-Y032–0325).
214 ICTY, Consolidated Witness Statement of Milorad Davidović, 22 June 2011 (0680-2869-0680-2937, at 0680-2891-0680–2892).
215 ICTY, Consolidated Witness Statement of Milorad Davidović, 22 June 2011 (0680-2869-0680-2937, at 0680–2892).
216 ICTY, Testimony of Milorad Davidović, *Stanišić and Župljanin*, 23 August 2010, 13536.
217 ICTY, Testimony of Milorad Davidović, *Stanišić and Župljanin*, 23 August 2010, 13590.
218 SSUP, Brigade of the Police, 'Report on the Engagement of a Group of Employees of the Brigade of the Police of the Federal MUP to Offer Professional Assistance to the MUP of the Serb Republic of Bosnia and Herzegovina', 8 August 1992 (Y032-0317-Y032–0325).
219 Minutes of 6th Session of RS Presidency, 13 June 1992 (0076-7938); SRNA announcement of presidential decision, 13 June 1992 (0084-6224). In early August, Karadžić referred back to this decision in reporting the recent arrest of 'outlaws' in Podrinje and Ključ: Announcement of Karadžić, 6 August 1992 (0048-8944).
220 'Soon a Special Detachment', *Glas*, 29 April 1992 (0095-1922-0095–1922).
221 VRS Main Staff report on the paramilitary formations in the territory of the Serbian Republic of BiH, 28 July 1992 (0094-9847-0094-9852).

222 On 30 July 1992, General Momir Talić issued an order pursuant to the 28 July Main Staff report. The order offered paramilitary groups the opportunity to join the VRS. 1st Krajina Corps order, 30 July 1992 (0089-0621-0089-0623).
223 RS MUP Daily Bulletin, 29 July 1992 (0323-8106-0323-8106). See also SJB Zvornik to RS MUP, CSB Bijeljina and CSB Sarajevo, 28 July 1992 (0296-9632).
224 VRS Main Staff report on the paramilitary formations in the territory of the Serbian Republic of BiH, 28 July 1992 (0094-9847-0094-9852, at 0094-9849).
225 ICTY, *Stanišić and Župljanin*, Judgement, Vol. 1, para. 1568; *Karadžić* Judgement, para. 1280.
226 ICTY, *Karadžić*, Judgement, para. 237, 1244n4285.
227 Prior to 1990, public security stations (SJBs) had been known as municipal secretariats for internal affairs, abbreviated as OSUP or SUP. For years after the change, 'SUP' remained the standard colloquial way of referring to the police station.
228 ICTY, *Stanišić and Župljanin*, Judgement, Vol. 1, paras. 1582, 1633, 1652, 1658. The municipal TO in Zvornik also had good relations with the Wasps and provided the group with arms. ICTY, *Karadžić*, Judgement, para. 237.
229 ICTY, *Stanišić and Župljanin*, Judgement, Vol. 1, para. 1670.
230 ICTY, *Karadžić*, Judgement, para 1287; SJB Bijeljina, Criminal Complaint against Vujin Vučković and others, 8 August 1992 (0052-4935-0052-4941).
231 CSB Bijeljina report, 20 July 1992 (0074-1342-0074-1346).
232 CSB Bijeljina to RS MUP, 23 July 1992 (0360-7278 and 0360-7288-0360-7289).
233 ICTY, *Karadžić*, Judgement, para. 1288.
234 Official Note of RDB Centre Valjevo, 2 July 1992 (0607-9028-0607-9032). See also the 1993 annual report of CRDB, which mentions the Yellow Wasps. CRDB Belgrade, Report on the Work in 1993, 10 December 1993 (Y036-7473-Y036-7493, at Y036-7483). Moreover, CRDB Belgrade interviewed both Vučković brothers, who confirmed that they had tortured, raped and killed Muslims in Zvornik. CRDB Belgrade, Fifth Department, 'Results and Further Directions for the Operational Work on OA "Tomson"', 19 July 1995 (Y034-5764-Y034-5798, at Y034-5768-Y034–5679).
235 ICTY, *Karadžić*, Judgement, para. 1289.
236 See ICTY, Statement of Milorad Davidović; ICTY, *Karadžić*, Judgement, para. 1290.
237 See official records of statements given by paramilitary members to CSB Bijeljina and SJB Bijeljina, 2 and 4 August 1992 (0076-8088-0076-8098; 0076-8344-0076-8346; 0075-8465-0075-8466; 0075-8467-0075-8470; 0076-6073-0076-6074; 0076-6079-0076-6100; 0076-8090-0076-8091; 0076-8114-0076-8120; 0076-8341-0076-8343; 0076-8116-0076-8118).
238 RS MUP, Administration for the Elimination of Crime, 'Information on Activities of the MUP in Uncovering Criminal Activities of the Paramilitary Formation "Yellow Wasps" on the Territory of the Serbian Municipality Zvornik', 4 August 1992 (0324-7392-0324–7394); RS MUP, Administration for the Elimination of Crime, 10 August 1992 (0324-2036-0324–2036).
239 ICTY, *Karadžić*, Judgement, para. 1287.
240 ICTY, *Karadžić*, Judgement, para. 1291.
241 ICTY, *Stanišić and Župljanin*, Judgement, Vol. 1, para. 1577.
242 The brothers Vučković were later prosecuted in Serbia and convicted for a small portion of the crimes they committed. Jovan Dulović, 'Tragovi "Žute ose"', *Vreme*, 23 November 2005.

243 SJB Zvornik had in a June 1992 report written that the police had searched over eighty premises belonging to 'Muslim extremists'. SJB Zvornik, Report on the Work of SJB Zvornik for the Period 1 April to 30 June 1992, 29 June 1992 (0360-9118-0360-9120).
244 ICTY, *Karadžić*, Judgement, para. 1292.
245 Goran Žugić, Chief of RO SNB Birač, 5 September 1992 (0324-7390-0324–7390).
246 Undersecretary Dragan Kijac to Goran Žugić, 5 September 1992 (0324-7391-0324-7391). See also SNB Sarajevo to VRS Main Staff and Minister of Internal Affairs, 10 September 1992 (0323-8342-0323-8342).
247 SNB Sarajevo to president of RS Presidency, president of the government, minister of internal affairs and VRS, 22 September 1992 (0323-8334-0323-8334).
248 Whereas the judgement in Brđanin treats the Miće more like a paramilitary formation, the judgement in Stanišić-Župljanin tends more towards treating the group like an offshoot of the police.
249 CSB Doboj to RS MUP, 27 July 1992 (0324-1970-0324-1972).
250 Witness ST207 quoted in Stanišić and Župljanin Judgement, para. 453.
251 ICTY, *Stanišić and Župljanin*, Judgement, Vol. 2, paras. 454–5.
252 *Glas*, 'The Notorious Miće Are Free' (RR03-9303).
253 ICTY, *Stanišić and Župljanin*, Judgement, para. 519.
254 Official note of SNB Sector, CSB Banja Luka, 16 November 1992 (B007-9607-B007-9607a). In 1993, SJB Teslić produced a retrospective history of events related to the SJB between September 1991 and September 1993. SJB Teslić, 25 September 1993 (B007-9512-B007-9515).
255 SJB Teslić, 8 July 1992 (B001-2326-B001-2327). On the same day and the following day, sixteen individuals were turned over to the Basic Court in Teslić by SJB Teslić. SJB Teslić to Investigating Magistrate, Teslić Basic Court, 8 July 1992 (0211-7007-0211-7009), 9 July 1992 (0211-7010-0211-7018). On 1 July 1992, the Command of the 1st Krajina Corps reported in detail on the formation of 'Serbian volunteers' as early as October 1991. The same report also noted problems with paramilitary organizations. 1st Krajina Corps Command report to RS President Radovan Karadžić, 1 July 1992 (0324-6748-0324-6753). On 3 July 1992, Marinko Đukić and Predrag Markočević, two employees of SJB Teslić, wrote official notes describing the gross misconduct of the 'Miće' in Teslić municipality, as well as the links between this group and CSB Doboj. Official notes of Marinko Đukić and Predrag Markočević, 3 July 1992 (0211-7039-0211-7053). See also SJB Teslić official note, 3 July 1992 (0211-7047-0211-7053).
256 CSB Trebinje to RS MUP, 4 August 1992 (0074-1280-0074-1289).
257 CSB Trebinje, 'Information on the Work and Current Problems of CSB Trebinje', September 1992 (0074-1262-0074–1278). This report was filed on 17 September 1992. CSB Trebinje to RS MUP, 17 September 1992 (0074-9783-0074-9784).
258 SJB Sanski Most to CSB Banja Luka, 5 August 1992 (0047-8745-0047-8746); CSB Banja Luka to chiefs of all CSBs, 18 August 1992 (P004-3045-P004-3045).
259 See the RS MUP's report on the attempt to disband paramilitary organizations or integrate them into the unified command of the RS armed forces. RS MUP, Administration for the Affairs and Tasks of the Police, 3 August 1992 (0296-9730-0296-9735; N.B. This is a fragment of the complete report). See also, on the same topic, RS MUP, Administration for the Affairs and Tasks of the Police to RS Minister of Internal Affairs, 10 August 1992 (0296-9622-0296-9624) and CSB Sarajevo, 'Report on Work for the Period from July to September 1992', October 1992 (0297-0877-0297–0883).

260 SJB Ilidža dispatch to Minister Mićo Stanišić, 5 August 1992 (0323-8499-0323-8505).
261 Most likely, these 'Serbian volunteers' included units led by Željko Ražnatović 'Arkan'. In an interview given in March 1996, Kovač told of inviting Arkan's forces to Ilidža in 1992. Interview with Tomislav Kovač in *Intervju*, 1 March 1996 (0216-1686-0216-1691).
262 Decision of Minister Mićo Stanišić, 6 August 1992 (FI20-0595).
263 CSB Sarajevo, 'Evaluation of Political-Security Situation and the Work of the Centre for the Period from 1 July to 15 August 1992', 17 August 1992 (0074-9687-0074-9700).
264 CSB Trebinje, 'Evaluation of Political-Security Situation on the Territory of CSB Trebinje', 19 August 1992 (0074-9651-0074-9663).
265 CSB Sarajevo, 8 September 1992 (0296-9107-0296-9110).
266 CSB Sarajevo, 'Some Political-Security Aspects on the Territory of the Romanija-Birač Centre of Security', 15 November 1992 (0297-0981-0297-0984).
267 Minutes of Meeting of Supreme Command of the VRS, 20 December 1992 (0084-5021-0084-5025).
268 On 18 May 1992, the Chief of SJB Prijedor, Simo Drljača, reported on the existence of paramilitary groups. He did not comment on the leadership or ethnic affiliation of these groups. SJB Prijedor to CSB Banja Luka, 18 May 1992 (0063-3222). On the same day, SJB Banja Luka reported that it possessed no information regarding paramilitary organizations on the territory of Banja Luka municipality. SJB Banja Luka to CSB Banja Luka SNB Sector, 18 May 1992 (B006-1563). On 3 July 1992, the RS Presidency ordered the RS MUP to carry out an investigation regarding the activities of paramilitary groups on the territory of Gacko and Nevesinje in eastern Herzegovina. Order of RS Presidency, signed by Karadžić, 3 July 1992 (0084-6246).

Instances of RS MUP awareness of paramilitary activities include:

17 June 1992: RS MUP orders CSB Banja Luka to erect a commission to investigate paramilitary activities near Drvar at Kulen-Vakuf. RS MUP to Chief of CSB Banja Luka, 17 June 1992 (0324-7398-0324-7399). Also reported in RS MUP Bulletin, 17 June 1992 (0324-6528).

23 March 1993: CSB Banja Luka observes a link between crime and paramilitary groups in 1992. CSB Banja Luka, 'Report on the Analysis of Work of the SJBs in 1992 on the Territory of CSB Banja Luka', 23 March 1993 (0324-6151-0324-6167).

July 1992: CSB Banja Luka notes activity of paramilitary groups. CSB Banja Luka, 'Report on the Work of CSB Banja Luka for the Period 1 January to 30 June 1992', July 1992 (0324-6764-0324-6790).

7–8 July 1992: SJB Bijeljina reports on meeting with Ljubiša Savić 'Mauzer', who threatened to blow up all of Bijeljina and complained about the police. Official notes of SJB Bijeljina, 7 and 8 July 1992 (0074-9580-0074-9581; 0074-1372-0074-1373).

11 July 1992: SJB Pale confirms that Voja Vučković of Zvornik received weapons from the police. SJB Pale declaration, 11 July 1992 (0324-7370-0324-7370).

13 July 1992: SJB Višegrad reports frequent arrival of 'volunteers' from Serbia proper. SJB Višegrad to RS MUP, 13 July 1992 (0324-6754-0324-6757).
269 CSB Trebinje, 'Evaluation of Political-Security Situation on the Territory of CSB Trebinje', 19 August 1992 (0074-9651-0074-9663).
270 VRS Main Staff, Administration for Intelligence and Security Affairs, Report on Paramilitary Formations on the Territory of the Serbian Republic in BiH, 28 July 1992 (0094-9847-0094-9852).

271 Order of Minister Mićo Stanišić, 31 August 1992 (0105-6505). At a press conference in November 1992, General Major Talić noted that the convoy involved persons from Trnopolje (V000-2840; transcription 0300-2802-0300-2804).
272 VRS Lieutenant Colonel Boško Peulić to Command of 1st Krajina Corps, 21 August 1992 (0105-6506-0105-6506). Video interview of General Major Talić on ABC News, 2 November 1992 (V000-2840-; transcription 0300-2802-0300-2804).
273 VRS combat reports also assigned responsibility for the massacre to RS MUP. 1st Krajina Corps regular combat reports, 21 August 1992 (0105-6506).
274 1st Krajina Corps Regular Combat Report, 22 August 1992 (0086-2880-0086-2883; 0086-2884-0086-2887).
275 ICTY, *Karadžić*, Judgement, paras. 1843, 3346.
276 This summary is based on ICTY, *Stanišić and Župljanin*, Judgement, Vol. 1, paras. 638–48.
277 ICTY, *Stanišić and Župljanin*, Judgement, Vol. 1, para. 641.
278 There are some indications that some of the bodies at the location might have stemmed from earlier killings.
279 Župljanin to Drljača, 11 September 1992 (0105-6504-0105-6504).
280 ICTY, *Stanišić and Župljanin*, Judgement, Vol. 1, para. 645.
281 1st Krajina Corps report on the state of morale for August 1992, 3 September 1992 (0124-2302-0124-2311, at 0124-2306). This report specifically mentioned Simo Drljača (although identifying him incorrectly as Stevo Drljača). It should be noted that the same VRS report characterized the persons in the convoy as wanting to voluntarily leave Republika Srpska, and did not mention their status as prisoners. The report also generally took a dim view of international efforts to investigate events in Bosnia.
282 Drljača to Župljanin, 14 September 1992 (0063-3335).
283 Župljanin to Drljača, 7 October 1992 (0208-1174).
284 SJB Prijedor to Župljanin, 13 October 1992 (0063-3338-0063-3338).
285 Stanišić, *Ratni sukobi*, 363.
286 ICTY, *Stanišić and Župljanin*, Judgement, Vol. 1, para. 648.
287 ICTY, *Karadžić*, Judgement, para. 1845.
288 ICTY, *Mrđa*, Case Information Sheet (IT-02-59); ICTY, *Mrđa*, Sentencing Judgement.
289 Minister Mićo Stanišić to all chiefs of CSB, 17 July 1992 (0360-9741-0360-9742).
290 See also the RS presidential order for CSBs to investigate war crimes committed against Serbs. Order of RS Presidency, 25 September 1992 (0047-8730-0047-8731). On 8 October 1992, Stojan Župljanin referred to a presidential order request urgent submission of data on war crimes against Serbs. Župljanin to all subordinate SJBs, 8 October 1992 (P004-3516-P004-3516). Cf. dispatch of SJB Prijedor, 9 October 1992 (P004-3518-P004-3518); CSB Banja Luka to SJB Prijedor, 16 October 1992 (0063-3339).
291 Dispatch of Minister Mićo Stanišić, 16 May 1992 (0323-8855-0323-8856). However, at the 11 July 1992 meeting in Belgrade, Simo Tuševljak, the chief of the criminal police department at CSB Sarajevo, did mention that his centre was 'also documenting war crimes if Serbs commit them'. RS MUP, Short Review of the Work of the MUP and Some Suggestions for Future Work – Summary of the Meeting of Leading RS MUP Employees on 11 July 1992, July 1992 (0324-1848-0324-1879, at 0324-1868).
292 RS MUP, 'Some Basic Principles of the Functioning of the MUP in Conditions of a War Regime', 6 July 1992 (0360-5768-0360–5770).
293 CSB Trebinje, 'Information on the Work and Current Problems of CSB Trebinje', September 1992 (0074-1262-0074–1278).

294 Banja Luka SNB Sector, 'Report on the Work of SNB Sector Banja Luka for 1992', January 1993 (B003-1813-B003–1821).
295 Invitation of Minister Stanišić to all chiefs of CSBs, 6 July 1992 (1D00-2747).
296 According to the Chief of CSB Doboj, Andrija Bjelošević, the meeting was the first of its kind since the RS MUP was established. ICTY, Testimony of Andrija Bjelošević, Stanišić and Župljanin, 15 April 2011, 19073f.
297 RS MUP, Short Review of the Work of the MUP and Some Suggestions for Future Work – Summary of the Meeting of Leading RS MUP Employees on 11 July 1992, July 1992 (0324-1848-0324-1879). Unfortunately, no example is available of the summary of the separate meeting of the SNB, which took place on the same date and location.
298 Župljanin began his remarks by referring to a previous meeting in Sarajevo, but it is not certain when that took place or who was in attendance.
299 Predrag Ješurić, who had headed CSB Bijeljina during the initial months, also attended the meeting in his new capacity as the chief of the department for foreigners, travel documents and border crossings. Although he referred to having led the CSB 'during the worst time', he did not take responsibility for the problems which had existed, but rather blamed the ministry. Ješurić claimed that he did not deserve to be treated poorly.
300 RS MUP, 'Information on Some Aspects of Work to Date and on Impending Tasks', 17 July 1992 (0324-6855-0324–6867). Unless otherwise noted, all quotes in this section refer to this summary.
301 Police participation in combat activities was particularly heavy in Herzegovina, where 'all employees' of the RS MUP regularly participated in combat.
302 Order of Mićo Stanišić to chiefs of all CSBs, 19 July 1992 (0045-1848-0045-1849). Other documents were also issued regarding an implementation of the 11 July meeting, and on 20 August, a meeting was scheduled at CSB Trebinje to discuss progress regarding this point. RS MUP to chiefs of all CSBs and to all Ministry administrations, 17 August 1992 (0324-7326-0324-7326); CSB Sarajevo, 'Report on Implementation of Conclusions from the Meeting of Leading Employees of the MUP on 11 July 1992', August 1992 (0324-1739-0324-1741). RS MUP, 'Report from Meeting of Leading Employees of the MUP Held on 20 August 1992 in Trebinje', August 1992 (0370-9564-0370-9580).
303 Responses by the CSBs and SJBs to the 19 July order of Mićo Stanišić include: CSB Sarajevo, 25 July 1992 (0324-7361-0324-7363); CSB Doboj, 27 July 1992 (0324-1970-0324-1972); SJB Prijedor, 4 August 1992 (0063-3294-0063-3296); CSB Trebinje, 4 August 1992 (0074-1280-0074-1288); SJB Sanski Most, 5 August 1992 (0047-8745-0047-8746). On 30 July 1992, CSB Banja Luka had circulated the 19 July 1992 order of STANIŠIĆ. On 3 August, Župljanin complained of not receiving timely responses to the order. Župljanin to chiefs of all SJBs, 3 August 1992 (P004-3072-P004-3072).
304 At the 22nd Session of the Assembly, the Vice-President of the RS Government, Milan Trbojević, complained about the inability or unwillingness – and even participation – of the RS police to stop what he described as the 'plundering' of the RS. Stenographic records of 22nd Session of the RS Assembly, 23–24 November 1992 (0214-9632-0214-9749).
305 Order of Mićo Stanišić, 23 July 1992 (0323-8844).
306 RS MUP to chiefs of all CSBs, 24 July 1992 (0323-8843).
307 Župljanin to chiefs of all SJBs, 29 July 1992 (P004-3127-P004-3128); Drljača dispatch, 30 July 1992 (P004-3129).

308 CSB Sarajevo to subordinate SJBs, 25 July 1992 (0639-3667); SJB Vlasnica to CSB Sarajevo, 6 August 1992 (0639-3676), and 25 September 1992 (0359-7130).
309 Law on Internal Affairs, *Službeni glasnik srpskog naroda u Bosni i Hercegovini*, I, No.4 (23 March 1992), 74-88 (0018-4319-0018-4333, at 0018-4331).
310 Clause 12 of this article of the 1990 law, which prohibits involvement in activities incompatible with official duty, is not present in the corresponding article in the 1992 law.
311 CSB Banja Luka, Decision on the Appointment of Disciplinary Prosecutors, 7 July 1992 (B008-0401).
312 ICTY, *Stanišić and Župljanin*, Judgement, Vol. 2, para. 518.
313 ICTY, *Stanišić and Župljanin*, Judgement, Vol. 2, para. 754.
314 ICTY, *Stanišić and Župljanin*, Judgement, Vol. 2, para. 754.
315 Minutes of Meeting of RS Government, 27 July 1992 (0124-5442-0124-5446); RS MUP, 'Information on Some Aspects of Work to Date and on Impending Tasks', 17 July 1992 (0324-6855-0324–6867). See also diary of Ratko Mladić, 27–31 May 1992 (P1755).
316 RS MUP, 'Report from Meeting of Leading Employees of the MUP Held on 20 August 1992 in Trebinje', August 1992 (0370-9564-0370-9580, at 0370–9574).
317 RS MUP, 'Report from Meeting of Leading Employees of the MUP Held on 20 August 1992 in Trebinje', August 1992 (0370-9564-0370-9580, at 0354–9568).
318 RS MUP, 'Rulebook on the Disciplinary Responsibility of the Employees of the Ministry of Internal Affairs of Republika Srpska in Conditions of Wartime Regime', 19 September 1992 (0324-6177-0324–6181).
319 See expert reports by Patrick J. Treanor and Dorothea Hanson.
320 Stenographic records of 22nd Session of the RS Assembly, 23–24 November 1992 (0214-9632-0214-9749).
321 Interview with Mićo Stanišić, *Javnost*, 30 July 1992 (0365-9864). The transcribed version of the interview included in Stanišić's book contains minor discrepancies. Stanišić, *Ratni sukobi*, 324f.
322 Interview with Mićo Stanišić, *Javnost*, 30 July 1992 (0365-9864).
323 Interview with Mićo Stanišić, *Javnost*, 30 July 1992 (0365-9864).
324 On the concept of 'special war', see *Vojna bezbednost* (Belgrade: Vojnoizdavački i novinski centar, 1986), 140–4, 197–200.
325 On the theft of the automobiles from the TAS factory, see *Stanišić and Župljanin*, Judgement, Vol. 2, para. 708.
326 Mićo Stanišić, Transcript of Tape Recording of 22nd RS Assembly Session, 23 November 1992 (0214-9632-0214-0214-9749, at 0214–9648).

Chapter 4

1 Adam LeBor, *Milošević: A Biography* (London: Bloomsbury, 2003).
2 James Gow, *The Serbian Project and Its Adversaries: A Strategy of War Crimes* (Montreal: McGill-Queen's University Press, 2003); Ewan Brown, 'Military Developments in the Bosanska Krajina, 1992', ICTY Expert Report, 27 November 2002; Reynaud Theunens, 'Military Aspects of the Role of Jovica Stanišić and Franko Simatović in the Conflict in Croatia and Bosnia-Herzegovina (BiH) (91–95)', ICTY Expert Report, 30 June 2007.

3 Časlav Ocić, 'Hronika srpske Krajine, 28. februar 1989 – 19. decembar 1991', in *Republika Srpska Krajina* (Knin-Belgrade, Srpsko kulturno društvo, 1996), 393 (0683-6129-0683-6149, at 0683-6134).
4 The Serbian State Security Service (*Služba državne bezbednosti*, SDB) was renamed the State Security Division (*Resor državne bezbednosti*, RDB) at the beginning of 1992.
5 'Declaration on the Sovereign Autonomy of the Serb Nation of Slavonia, Baranja and Western Syrmia', 26 February 1991, published 19 December 1991 in *Službeni Glasnik Srpske Oblasti Slavonija, Baranja i Zapadni Srem*, Year 1, No. 1 (0089-0422-0089-0457, at 0089-0422). According to Ilija Petrović, the declaration was actually issued on 25 January 1991, but the date was subsequently changed to 26 January 1991. Ilija Petrović, *Srpsko nacionalno vijeće Slavonije, Baranje i Zapadnog Srema* (Novi Sad: Galeb, 1994) (0184-6231-0184-6498, at 0184-6281-0184-6282).
6 Slobodan Milošević on 16 March 1991, quoted in *NIN*, 12 April 1991 (0214-4020-0214-4022, at 0214-4020).
7 Decision on the Application of Laws and Other Regulations on the Territory of the SAO Krajina, 18 March 1991, published in *Glasnik Krajine*, 2 April 1991 (0364-6098-0364-6098).
8 Statutory Decision on the Change of the Statue of the SAO Krajina, 18 March 1991, published in *Glasnik Krajine*, 2 April 1991 (0364-6098-0364-6098).
9 Decision of the Executive Council of the Assembly of the SAO Krajina, 1 April 1991 (0217-2158-0217-2159); published in *Glasnik Krajine* on 20 April 1991 (0207-7887-0207-7887).
10 Order of Milan Babić, president of the Executive Council of the SAO Krajina, 1 April 1991 (0217-2109-0217-2109).
11 SAO Krajina Assembly, Decision on the Holding of a Referendum for the Joining of the SAO Krajina to the Republic of Serbia and that Krajina Stay in Yugoslavia with Serbia, Montenegro and Others Who Wish to Preserve Yugoslavia, 30 April 1991 (0214-1880-0214-1880).
12 Decision on the Election of the president of the Executive Council of the Assembly of the SAO Krajina, 30 April 1991 (0217-2164-0217-2164).
13 Law on the Application of the Legal Regulations of the Republic of Serbia on the Territory of the Serb Autonomous District of Krajina, 29 May 1991 (0364-6115-0364-6116).
14 SAO Krajina Assembly, Report on the Referendum Held on the Territory of the SAO Krajina, 14 May 1991 (0214-1854-0214-1859). See also Decision on the Merger of the SAO Krajina with the Republic of Serbia and to Stay in Yugoslavia with Serbia, Montenegro and Others Who Desire to Preserve Yugoslavia, 17 May 1991 (0043-4080-0043-4081).
15 Letter of Milan Martić, 23 February 1994 (0207-7590-0207-7590).
16 Regional SUP Vojvodina, Department of the State Security Service, Informational Report, 20 May 1991 (Y037-1627-Y037-1650, at Y037-1628).
17 Regional SUP Vojvodina, Department of the State Security Service, Informational Report, 20 May 1991 (Y037-1627-Y037-1650, at Y037-1636).
18 Regional SUP Vojvodina, Department of the State Security Service, Informational Report, 20 May 1991 (Y037-1627-Y037-1650, at Y037-1638).
19 Regional SUP Vojvodina, Department of the State Security Service, Informational Report, 20 May 1991 (Y037-1627-Y037-1650, at Y037-1638).
20 Filip Švarm, 'Jedinica' (documentary film, 2006).

21 Speech of Franko Simatović, 4 May 1997 (V000-3533-V000-3533).
22 ICTY, *Stanišić and Simatović*, Judgement, Vol. 2, para. 1295, 1344; list of first cohorts who completed training at Golubić, undated (0280-4323-0280-4328); Wartime Path of the Plaški Brigade, 1995 (0203-2603-0203-2619, at 0203-2604). In his autobiography, Davor Subotić states that he arrived at Golubić in April 1991. Autobiography of Davor Subotić, 14 February 1992 (0558-8935-0558-8935); autobiography of Davor Subotić, undated (0706-5697-0706-5697). JNA intelligence report, May–June 1991 (0218-9157-0218-9169, at 0218-9157). See also statement of Neđeljko Orlić regarding training allegedly conducted by 'Frenki' and 'Fićo' from 10 April to 5 May 1990. Orlić gave the statement in 1993 and likely meant to refer to 1991 instead of 1990. SUP Knin, Statement of Neđeljko Orlić, 18 March 1993 (0400-4789-0400-4791).
23 Report of Danjiel Snedden to 'State Security Service', undated (0113-3710-0113-3712); letter from Dragan Vasiljković to the Secretary of the SUP, 27 May 1991 (0280-4583-0280-4584); order likely issued by Franko Simatović, 16 June 1991 (0113-3707-0113-3707); minutes of meeting attended by 'Frenki', 'Captain Dragan' and others regarding training at Golubić, 14 June 1991 (0113-3708-0113-3709); Informational Report on Daniel Snedden, alias 'Captain Dragan', 28 August 1991 (0340-4983-0340-4985). On Captain Dragan, see also report of War Staff of Dvor Municipality, 23 July 1991 (0207-7616-0207-7616); minutes of meeting of War Staff of Dvor Municipality, 24 July 1991 (0207-7620-0207-7624); report of Radio Knin, 31 July 1991 (0113-3911-0113-3919); letter of Serbian Minister of Defence Marko Negovanović to the National Assembly of the Republic of Serbia, 20 January 1992 (0160-2986-0160-2986); note of Dragan Vasiljković, undated (0113-3713-0113-3713). See also (probably military) report on the training centre Alfa, undated (R042-0473-R042-0479).
24 Order likely issued by Franko Simatović, 16 June 1991 (0113-3707-0113-3707); minutes of meeting attended by 'Frenki', 'Captain Dragan' and others regarding training at Golubić, 14 June 1991 (0113-3708-0113-3709); report of 'Captain Dragan' from Glina, 19 July 1991 (0280-5122-0280-5122); report of Živojin Ivanović, 26 July 1991 (0419-2677-0419-2678); informational Report on Daniel Snedden, alias 'Captain Dragan', 28 August 1991 (0340-4983-0340-4985); USDB Belgrade, Letter, 3(?) April 19?? (Y034-9260-Y034-9263); USDB Belgrade, 3 April 1991 (Y035-2352-Y035-2354). See also testimony of Milan Babić and witness JF-039 cited in ICTY, *Stanišić and Simatović*, Judgement, Vol. 2, paras. 1317, 1352.
25 Filip Švarm documentary film, 'Jedinica'.
26 Biography of Borjan Vučković, undated (0682-1876).
27 Report of Radio Knin, 31 July 1991 (0113-3911-0113-3919, at 0113-3914).
28 'The Cease Fire Is a Sham', *Borba*, 14 August 1991 (0207-7675-0207-7675).
29 Report, likely signed by Franko Simatović, approximately 28 July 1991 (0113-3706-0113-3706).
30 Statement of RSK TO Captain Milenko Sučević, 7 May 1992 (0281-1437-0281-1437). Some of this equipment was sent to the area of the SAO SBZS.
31 ICTY, *Stanišić and Simatović*, Judgement, Vol. 2, para. 1334.
32 According to the conclusions of the ICTY Trial Chamber, the total number of people trained at Golubić was between 350 and 700. ICTY, *Stanišić and Simatović*, Judgement, Vol. 2, para. 1369.
33 ICTY, *Stanišić and Simatović*, Judgement, Vol. 2, para. 1326. In the case of Jovanović and Ulemek, they were also much later directly involved as perpetrators of the 2003 assassination of Serbian Prime Minister Zoran Đinđić.

34 Note use of RSK MUP insignia, ICTY, *Stanišić and Simatović*, Judgement, Vol. 2, para. 1345.
35 Order of Commander Živojin Ivanović, 19 December 1991 (0682-1879-06820-1879). See also autobiography of Zoran Raić, October 1992 (0608-8232-0608-8232).
36 ICTY, *Stanišić and Simatović*, Judgement, Vol. 2, para. 1414.
37 ICTY, *Stanišić and Simatović*, Prosecution Final Trial Brief, 134.
38 Personnel document for Radojica Božović, citing ministerial decision DT 01-2497/93 of 4 August 1993, undated (0609-0181-0609-0181); personnel document for Zoran Raić, citing same decision, undated (0643-5232-0643-5232); personnel document for Dejan Slišković, 23 May 1994 (0675-1983-0675-1983). See also BIA, Report of the Commission for the Determination of the Circumstances Connected to the Documentation Sought with the Request of the Prosecutor of the ICTY Number 1691, February 2009 (0648-8998-0648-9036).
39 Autobiography of Davor Subotić, undated (0706-5697-0706-5697).
40 In addition to those already cited, see the autobiographies of Slobodan Majstorović, undated (0704-2163); Dragan Đorđević, 14 February 1992 (0613-1603) and 23 February 1992 (0613-1606); Dragiša Grujić, 14 February 1992 (0558-7976); Nikola Pilipović, 13 January 1992 (0706-5496), 14 February 1992 (0706-5495), 25 February 1992 (0706-5521), undated (0706-5525) and 4 December 1993 (0706-5505); Ilija Vučković, 13 February 1992 (0706-5850).
41 See also Iva Vukušić, *Serbian Paramilitaries in the Breakup of Yugoslavia* (London: Routledge, 2020).
42 SJB Teslić, Official Note on Events in SJB Teslić in the Period from 1 April to 1 July 1992 (0211-7024-0211-7038, at 0211-7026).
43 Christian Axboe Nielsen, *Yugoslavia and Political Assassinations: The History and Legacy of Tito's Campaign against the Émigrés* (London: I.B. Tauris, 2020); Mate Nikola Tokić, *For the Homeland Ready! Croat Diaspora Terrorism during the Cold War* (West Lafayette: Purdue University Press, 2020).
44 Information of First Military District Security Organ, 3 March 1992 (0340-4890-0340-4890); Information of Counter-Intelligence Operational Technical Centre, 14 September 1992 (0340-4893-0340-4896); on the earlier criminal background of Ražnatović see letter to Federal Secretariat for People's Defence, Third Administration, 19 July 1982 (0340-4926-0340-4927) and Report of Republican SUP of Serbia, Administration of the State Security Service, 7 January 1991 (0632-0999-0632-1010).
45 Information of First Military District Security Organ, 17 March 1992 (0340-4891-0340-4892).
46 USDB Belgrade, Information on the Creation of Paramilitary Formations in the Organization of the Unregistered Serb Chetnik Movement (SČP) and the Serb National Renewal (SNO), 1 August 1991 (Y034-9120-Y034-9128).
47 This account is based on the Prosecution Final Trial Brief in *Prosecutor v. Stanišić and Simatović*, para. 524f. See also the accounts of the takeover of Bosanski Šamac municipality in the judgements in *Simić et al.* and *Karadžić*; Iva Vukušić, 'Masters of Life and Death: Paramilitary Violence in Two Bosnian Towns', *Journal of Perpetrator Research*, Vol. 3, No. 2 (2021), 66–86.
48 ICTY, *Stanišić and Simatović*, Retrial, Judgement, para. 417.
49 ICTY, *Stanišić and Simatović*, Judgement, Vol. 1, para. 628; ICTY, *Stanišić and Simatović*, Retrial, Judgement, para. 209f.

50 In an important observation, the Trial Chamber in *Stanišić and Simatović* noted that 'evidence of affiliations with the SRS, membership of a special unit of the Serbian DB, and/or subordination to the JNA ... need not be mutually exclusive'. ICTY, *Stanišić and Simatović*, Judgement, Vol. 1, para. 648.
51 Report of JNA 17th Corps, 17 April 1992 (0051-6367).
52 ICTY, *Stanišić and Simatović*, Retrial, Judgement, para. 210.
53 RS MUP, 'Information on the State of Affairs in SJB Bosanski Šamac, the Arrest of the Chief of the SJB by Military Organs and the Closing of the Corridor Krajina – Federal Republic of Yugoslavia', 19 November 1992 (0358-8617-0358-8625). See also statement of Blagoje Simić, 14 December 1992 (0057-2330-0057-2332); statement of Dragan Đorđević, 25 November 1992 (0053-2862-0053-2867); Statement of Slobodan Miljković-Lugar, undated (0063-6948-0063-6950); Judgement of the Military Court in Banja Luka, 6 February 1993 (0057-2182-0057-2200).
54 CRDB Kragujevac, Third Administration, Official Note, 20 July 1993 (Y034-5415-Y034-5421, at Y034-5415). See also MUP Serbia, Decision on Surveillance, 20 December 1993 (1D02-2017-1D02-2019).
55 CRDB Kragujevac, Proposal for the Introduction of Operational Treatment, 3 December 1993 (Y035-0293-Y035-0298).
56 CRDB Kragujevac, Proposal for the Introduction of Operational Treatment, 3 December 1993 (Y035-0293-Y035-0298, at Y035-0294).
57 CRDB Kragujevac, Official Note, 12 September 1993 (Y035-0343-Y035-0345).
58 On 18 October 1992, officials of the MUP Serbia took over the headquarters of the SSUP in Belgrade, justifying this move based on an unresolved property dispute. This move permitted Milošević to further consolidate his grasp on power. On 2 November 1992, the Council for the Harmonization of Positions on State Policy convened to discuss the 'endangering of the constitutional order of the Federal Republic of Yugoslavia'. The Yugoslav President at the time, Dobrica Ćosić, protested unsuccessfully against the takeover of the SSUP, which thereafter existed only on paper. Minutes of the Meeting of the Council for the Harmonization of Positions on State Policy, 2 November 1992 (0294-3949-0294-3953).
59 USDB Belgrade, Second Department, Report on the Results of Surveillance on Daniel Snedden, 12 April 1991 (0607-6090-0607-6100); MUP Serbia, Decision of Minister Bogdanović, 3 April 1991 (Y036-1588-Y036-1589).
60 USDB Belgrade, Second Department, Report on the Results of Surveillance on Daniel Snedden, 12 April 1991 (0607-6090-0607-6100, at 0607-6099-0607-6100).
61 MUP Serbia, Decision of Minister Sokolović, 15 August 1991 (Y034-4388-Y034-4390).
62 USDB Belgrade, Second Department, Proposal for the Secret Control of Telephone Conversations, 6 November 1991 (Y034-9134-Y034-9137).
63 USDB Belgrade, Second Department, Proposal for the Secret Control of Telephone Conversations, 6 November 1991 (Y034-9134-Y034-9137, at Y034-9134).
64 For example, Mile Majstorović joined 'the unit' through the Captain Dragan Fund on 18 January 1992. By March he had learned that the unit was called the 'Unit for Special Purposes' of the MUP Serbia. Majstorović emphasized that he had joined the unit for nationalist reasons and that he would not under any circumstances participate in actions against other Serbs. He stated that he felt that he had been deceived into joining the unit. Statement of Mile Majstorović, 7 March 1992 (0558-8226-0558-8226). Likewise, Dragan Oluić, who trained at Golubić in May 1991, subsequently

entered the JPN of the RSK MUP. As a JPN member, Oluić saw combat at Ljubovo, Plitvice, Glina, Kostajnica, Northern Dalmatia, Bapska and Šarengrad (Pajzoš). Autobiography of Dragan Oluić, undated (0558-8502-0558-8502).

65   USDB Belgrade, Second Department, Official Note, 13 April 1991 (Y037-0570-Y037-0574, at Y037-0570).
66   RSUP SDB, Report on the Work in 1990, January 1991 (0684-0551-0684-0569, at 0684-0559); USDB Belgrade, Report on the Work in 1990, 12 January 1991 (Y036-7438-Y036-7442, at Y036-7439).
67   RSUP SDB, Report on the Work in 1990, January 1991 (0684-0551-0684-0569, at 0684-0560).
68   RSUP SDB, Programmatic Orientation of the State Security Service in 1991, January 1991 (0684-0708-0684-0712, at 0684-0710). See also RSUP SDB, Integral Programmatic Orientation of the SDB in 1990, January 1990 (Y034-9606-Y034-9612).
69   RSUP SDB, Programmatic Orientation of the State Security Service in 1991, January 1991 (0684-0708-0684-0712, at 0684-0712). See also fragment of same document (Y034-9614-Y034-9627).
70   USDB Belgrade, Report on the Work in 1991, 14 January 1992 (Y036-7443-Y036-7460, compare with 0684-0784-0684-0800).
71   USDB Belgrade, Report on the Work in 1991, 14 January 1992 (Y036-7443-Y036-7460, at Y036-7446).
72   USDB Belgrade, Report on the Work in 1991, 14 January 1992 (Y036-7443-Y036-7460, at Y036-7447).
73   MUP Serbia, Introduction of Operational Action 'Tomson', 23 July 1991 (Y034-5948-Y034-5955). See also Tape Recording of Fifth Session of the SRJ Supreme Defence Council, 7 August 1992 (0345-7047-0345-7088, at 0345-7061-0345-7065).
74   MUP Serbia, Introduction of Operational Action 'Tomson', 23 July 1991 (Y034-5948-Y034-5955, at Y034-5948-Y034-5949).
75   MUP Serbia, Introduction of Operational Action 'Tomson', 23 July 1991 (Y034-5948-Y034-5955, at Y034-5949).
76   In the available RDB documentation, this operational action is sometimes named 'Tomson', and sometimes 'Tompson'. In all likelihood, given the operational action's focus on illegal weaponry and ammunition, the name stems from the Thompson submachine gun.
77   MUP Serbia, Introduction of Operational Action 'Tomson', 23 July 1991 (Y034-5948-Y034-5955, at Y034-5949).
78   RSUP RDB, Report on the Work in 1992, February 1993 (0684-0570-0684-0593, at 0684-0575).
79   RDB Centre Valjevo, Third Section, 'Contribution to the Development of the Topic: 'Results and Further Directions for the Operational Work on OA "Tomson,"' 28 July 1995 (Y034-4165-Y034-4190, at Y034-4165).
80   RDB Centre Valjevo, Third Section, 'Contribution to the Development of the Topic: 'Results and Further Directions for the Operational Work on OA "Tomson"', 28 July 1995 (Y034-4165-Y034-4190, at Y034-4166).
81   RDB Centre Valjevo, Third Section, 'Contribution to the Development of the Topic: Results and Further Directions for the Operational Work on PO OA "Tomson"', 28 July 1995 (Y034-4165-Y034-4190, at Y034-4167-Y034-4168).
82   RDB Centre Valjevo, Third Section, 'Contribution to the Development of the Topic: 'Results and Further Directions for the Operational Work on PO OA "Tomson"', 28 July 1995 (Y034-4165-Y034-4190, at Y034-4168-Y034-4169).

83 RDB Centre Valjevo, Third Section, 'Contribution to the Development of the Topic: 'Results and Further Directions for the Operational Work on PO OA "Tomson"', 28 July 1995 (Y034-4165-Y034-4190, at Y034-4166-Y034–4167).
84 RSUP RDB, Report on the Work in 1992, February 1993 (0684-0570-0684-0593, at 0684-0575).
85 RDB Centre Valjevo, Third Section, 'Contribution to the Development of the Topic: Results and Further Directions for the Operational Work on PO OA "Tomson"', 28 July 1995 (Y034-4165-Y034-4190, at Y034-4177-Y034–4178).
86 CRDB Valjevo, Third Section, 'Contribution to the Development of the Topic: Results and Further Directions for the Operational Work on OA "Tomson"', 28 July 1995 (Y034-4165-Y034-4190, at Y034–4180).
87 CRDB Sremska Mitrovica, 'Contribution to the Development of the Topic: Results and Further Directions for the Operational Work on PO OA "Tomson"', 2 August 1995 (Y034-5848-Y034-5864, at Y034–5848).
88 Article 3, Rulebook on the Systematization of Posts in the RDB in the MUP, April 1992 (0606-0288-0606-0309, at 0606-0290).
89 RSUP RDB, Report on the Work in 1992, February 1993 (0684-0570-0684-0593, at 0684-0570A, compare with another version of same document at Y036-7363-Y036-7377).
90 RSUP RDB, Report on the Work in 1992, February 1993 (0684-0570-0684-0593, at 0684-0572).
91 RSUP RDB, Report on the Work in 1992, February 1993 (Y036-7363-Y036-7377, at Y036-7364; see also Y034-9639-Y034-9644).
92 RSUP RDB, Report on the Work in 1992, February 1993 (0684-0570-0684-0593, at 0684-0573).
93 MUP Serbia RJB, Letter of Assistant Minister Radovan Stojičić, 27 May 1992 (0160-2990-0160-2992).
94 CRDB Belgrade, Fifth Department, 'Results and Further Directions for the Operational Work on OA "Tomson"', 19 July 1995 (Y034-5764-Y034-5798, at Y034-5767-Y034–5768).
95 Statements of Vojin Vučković to officials of the MUP of Serbia, 4 and 5 November 1993 (0608-0985-0608-0987, Y034-9809-Y034-9810, Y034-9841-Y034-9844); Statement of Duško Vučković to officials of MUP Serbia, 4 November 1993 (Y034-5503-Y034-5513); Statement of Vojin Vučković to official of MUP Serbia, 4 November 1993 (Y036-7825-Y036-7830); CRDB Belgrade, Fourth Department, Obrenovac, Official Note Re: Activities of Vojin Vučković called Žuća, 4 November 1993 (Y034-5869-Y034-5874); CRDB Belgrade, Decision on Detention of Dušan Vučković 'Repić', 5 November 1993 (Y034-9837-Y037-9838); CRDB Belgrade, Decision on Detention of Vojin Vučković, 5 November 1993 (Y034-9839-Y037-9840); CRDB Valjevo, Criminal Complaint against Dušan Vučković and Vojin Vučković, 6 November 1993 (Y034-9925-Y034-9939); District Court in Šabac, Transcript of Interrogation of Accused, 8 November 1993 (0040-8552-0040-8558); CRDB Belgrade, Confirmation of Return of Items Temporarily Seized from Duško and Vojin Vučković, 10 November 1993 (Y034-9845-Y034-9849); District Court in Šabac, Indictment of Duško Vučković and Vojin Vučković, 28 April 1994 (0040-8511-0040-8516); District Court in Šabac, Judgement against Duško Vučković and Vojin Vučković, 8 July 1996 (0045-1331-0045-1351); Public Prosecutor's Office, Bijeljina, Indictment against Vojin Vučković and Others, 13 September 1999 (0365-8190-0365-8202). See also CRDB Valjevo, Informational Report, 17 October 1993 (Y034-9896-Y034-9904).

96 CRDB Belgrade, Fifth Department, 'Results and Further Directions for the Operational Work on OA "Tomson"', 19 July 1995 (Y034-5764-Y034-5798, at Y034-5768-Y034–5679).
97 CRDB Belgrade, Fourth Department, Obrenovac, Official Note Re: Activities of Vojin Vučković called Žuća, 4 November 1993 (Y034-5869-Y034-5874, at Y034-5869).
98 For evidence that the activities of Serb paramilitary formations in Croatia and Bosnia were known and discussed at the highest levels in Serbia and the SRJ, see the Stenographic Notes of the Seventh Session of the Supreme Defence Council, 10 February 1993 (0345-7152-0345-7183).
99 CRDB Užice, The Activity of Militant Groups from the Position of Serb Extremism – SČO, Serb Guard, White Eagles, Ravna Gora Movement and Others, 17 October 1995 (0641-4194-0641-4218, at 0641-4199-0641-4204). The relationship between Lukić and the White Eagles, and between the White Eagles and the Avengers, is not entirely clear. See ICTY, *Lukić*, Judgement, para. 71f. See also Vukušić, 'Masters of Life and Death', 66–86.
100 CRDB Užice, Official Note, 23 April 1992 (0641-4145-0641-4146).
101 CRDB Užice, Official Note, 24 April 1992 (0641-4147-0641-4148).
102 CRDB Užice, Official Notes, 4 June 1992 (0632-1460-0632-1461, 0641-4149-0641-4149 and 0641-4150-0641-4150); CRDB Užice Official Note, 11 June 1992 (0641-4151-0641-4151); CRDB Užice Official Note, 4 August 1992 (0641-4152-0641-4152); CRDB Užice Official Note, 24 August 1992 (0641-4153-0641-4154); CRDB Užice Official Notes, 27 August 1992 (0641-4155-0641-4155 and 0641-4156-0641-4158); CRDB Užice Official Notes, 5 October 1992 (0641-4159-0641-4159 and 0641-4160-0641-4161).
103 CRDB Užice, Official Note, 4 June 1992 (0641-4149-0641-4149).
104 Statement of Milan Lukić, 27 October 1992 (Y034-9863-Y034-9870).
105 CRDB Užice, Official Note, 2 November 1992 (Y034-9871-Y034-9878, at Y034-9871).
106 CRDB Užice, Official Note, 2 November 1992 (0607-9118-0607-9121, at 0607-9119). Vinko Pandurević, a lieutenant colonel in the VRS, was later convicted by the ICTY of crimes against humanity and war crimes in Srebrenica in 1995.
107 On the Sjeverin bus incident, see the B92 documentary film 'Otmica u Sjeverinu'.
108 CRDB Užice, Official Note, 2 November 1992 (0607-9114-0607-9117). See also CRDB Užice, Official Note, 29 October 1992 (0607-9112-0607-9113); CRDB Užice, Official Note, 2 November 1992 (0632-1391-0632-1394); CRDB Užice, Official Note, 18 November 1992 (0641-4164-0641-4165); CRDB Užice, Official Note, 2 December 1992 (0641-4166-0641-4166); CRDB Užice, Official Note, 14 December 1992 (0641-4167-0641-4168); CRDB Užice, Official Note, 17 December 1992 (0641-4169-0641-4171); CRDB Užice, Official Note, 8 February 1993 (0641-4172-0641-4173); CRDB Užice, Official Note, 22 February 1993 (0641-4174-0641-4175).
109 CRDB Užice, Official Note, 2 November 1992 (0632-1383-0632-1386).
110 Saida Mustajbegović, 'Štrpci – zločin koji je planirao vrh Srbije', *Al Jazeera Balkans*, 5 December 2014.
111 CRDB Užice, Official Notes, 4 March 1993 (Y034-9886-Y034-9890 and Y034-9891-Y034-9895).
112 Stenographic Record of the Eighth Session of the Supreme Defence Council, 12 March 1993 (0345-7184-0345-7240, at 0345-7221). See also CRDB Užice, Official Note, 3 March 1993 (0632-1395-0632-1395); CRDB Užice, Official Note, 5 March 1993 (0607-9122-0607-9123); CRDB Užice, Official Note, 8 April 1993 (0632-1404-0632-1405).

113 Stenographic Record of the Eighth Session of the Supreme Defence Council, 12 March 1993 (0345-7184-0345-7240, at 0345-7222).
114 Stenographic Record of the Eighth Session of the Supreme Defence Council, 12 March 1993 (0345-7184-0345-7240, at 0345-7222).
115 Stenographic Record of the Eighth Session of the Supreme Defence Council, 12 March 1993 (0345-7184-0345-7240, at 0345-7210).
116 Stenographic Record of the Eighth Session of the Supreme Defence Council, 12 March 1993 (0345-7184-0345-7240, at 0345-7222).
117 Stenographic Record of the Eighth Session of the Supreme Defence Council, 12 March 1993 (0345-7184-0345-7240, at 0345-7223).
118 RDB Fifth Administration request referenced in CRDB Belgrade, Fifth Department, 'Results and Further Directions for Operational Work on OA "Tomson"', 19 July 1995 (0608-1316-0608–1316).
119 See also CRDB Zaječar, 'Results and Further Directions of Operational Work on OA "Tomson"', July 1995 (Y035-2882-Y035–2893); CRDB Gnjilane, 'Results and Further Directions of Operational Work on OA "Tomson"', July 1995 (0608-1451-0608–1465); CRDB Leskovac, 'Results and Further Directions of Operational Work on OA "Tomson"', 10 July 1995 (0632-2102-0632–2106); CRDB Prizren, Fifth Administration, 'Contribution to the Development of the Topic: Results and Further Directions for the Operational Work on PO OA "Tomson"', 24 July 1995 (0608-1482-0608–1496); CRDB Novi Sad, 'Contribution to the Development of the Topic: 'Results and Further Directions for the Operational Work on PO OA "Tomson"', 24 July 1995 (Y035-2910-Y035–2935); CRDB Pančevo, 'Contribution to the Development of the Topic: Results and Further Directions for the Operational Work on PO OA "Tomson"', 26 July 1995 (Y035-2936-Y035–2956); CRDB Zrenjanin, 'Contribution to the Development of the Topic: Results and Further Directions for the Operational Work on PO OA "Tomson"', 26 July 1995 (Y035-2957-Y035–2965); CRDB Kraljevo, Fifth Administration, 'Results and Further Directions of Operational Work on OA "Tomson"', 31 July 1995 (Y034-5799-Y034–5809); CRDB Kragujevac, Fifth Administration, 'Contribution to the Development of the Topic: Results and Further Directions for the Operational Work on PO OA "Tomson"', 20 July 1995 (Y034-5810-Y034–5847); CRDB Smederevo, 'Contribution to the Development of the Topic: Results and Further Directions for the Operational Work on PO OA "Tomson"', 27 July 1995 (Y034-7550-Y034–7559); CRDB Sremska Mitrovica, 'Contribution to the Development of the Topic: Results and Further Directions for the Operational Work on PO OA "Tomson"', 2 August 1995 (Y034-5848-Y034–5864); CRDB Vranje, 'Results and Further Directions of Operational Work on OA "Tomson"', 4 August 1995 (Y036-7599-Y036–7603); CRDB Niš, 'Results and Further Directions for Operational Work on OA "Tomson"', 8 August 1995 (0608-1389-0608–1395); CRDB Subotica, 'Contribution to the Development of the Topic: Results and Further Directions for the Operational Work on OA "Tomson"', 30 August 1995 (Y034-9264-Y034–9278); CRDB Užice, 'Contribution to the Development of the Topic: Results and Further Directions for the Operational Work on PO OA "Tomson"', 19 September 1995 (Y034-9745-Y034–9808); CRDB Novi Sad, 'Activities of Militant Groups from the Position of Serb Extremism – SČO, Serb Guard, White Eagles, Ravna Gora Movement and Others (Contribution)', October 1995 (0632-2059-0632–2075).
120 Serbian Security Information Agency, Cabinet of the Director, Decision on the Termination of the Operational Action 'Tomson', 17 January 2006 (0632-2021-0632-2022).

121 This map appears in V000-3533 at approximately 20:42.
122 On rivalries among the Bosnian Serbs, see *Radovan Karadžić: Architect of the Bosnian Genocide* (Cambridge: Cambridge University Press, 2014); Nina Caspersen, *Contested Nationalism: Serb Elite Rivalry in Croatia and Bosnia in the 1990s* (New York: Berghahn Books, 2010).
123 Nedim Sejdinović, 'Zaostavština najslavnijeg carinika u novijoj istoriji', *Vreme*, 21 April 2021.

Chapter 5

1 Mićo Stanišić responding to accusation of Branko Đerić, Transcript of Tape Recording of 22nd RS Assembly Session, 23 November 1992 (0214-9632-0214-0214-9749, at 0214-9648). See also Jovo Mijatović, 32nd Session of the RS Assembly, 19–20 May 1993 (0215-0275-0215-0276); 3rd Extraordinary Session of the RS Assembly, 23–24 May 1995 (0410-1799); Delalić and Sačić, *Balkan bluz*, 197–203.
2 Senior RS MUP officials in 1992 seem not to have regarded the siege of Sarajevo as a problem. On the contrary, CSB Banja Luka Chief Župljanin suggested that the grip on Sarajevo should remain tight so that the inhabitants would starve and suffer from thirst. And the Head of the Public Security Service in the RS MUP, Čedo Kljajić, stated that this was already on the horizon. The two of them discussed cutting off the water supply to Sarajevo, which Kljajić did not consider a bad idea. Conversation between Čedo Kljajić and Stojan Župljanin, 7 May 1992 (0400-7276-0400-7297).
3 See ICTY, Suspect Interview of Mićo Stanišić; Testimony of Slobodan Škipina, *Stanišić and Župljanin*, 1 April 2010, 8467.
4 ICTY, *Karadžić*, Judgement, para. 1259; testimony of Dorothea Hanson, 8 December 2009, 4416-4418; Robert Donia, 'Bosnian Serb Leadership and the Siege of Sarajevo, 1990-1995', ICTY Expert Report, May 2009, 28–9.
5 1994 Law on Internal Affairs (4D03-0574). See also Mladen Bajagić diagram, 4D04-0354.
6 Paul Mojžes, *Yugoslavian Inferno: Ethnoreligious Warfare in the Balkans* (New York: Continuum Books, 1994).
7 Council of Europe Parliamentary Assembly, 2 February 1993, quoted in András Riedlmayer, 'Destruction of Cultural Heritage in Bosnia and Herzegovina', *Karadžić*, 3.
8 András J. Riedlmayer, 'Destruction of Cultural Heritage in Bosnia and Herzegovina', ICTY Expert Report, 15.
9 András J. Riedlmayer, 'Destruction of Cultural Heritage in Bosnia and Herzegovina', ICTY Expert Report, 19.
10 The top Bosnian Serb official in the Bosnian Krajina region, Radoslav Brđanin, stated that Banja Luka Serbs should stop complaining about cultural destruction, calling their complaints a 'satanization of Serbs by Serbs'. Radoslav Brđanin at 31st Session of RS Assembly, 9 May 1993 (0215-0209-0215-0211).
11 SNB Mrkonjić Grad, 2 November 1992 (B008-8910; see also 0087-6130).
12 Armina Galijaš, *Eine bosnische Stadt im Zeichen des Krieges: Ethnopolitik und Alltag in Banja Luka (1990–1995)* (Oldenburg: Oldenbourg Wissenschaftsverlag, 2011), 248, 250.
13 1991 Yugoslav census figures cited in Galijaš, *Eine bosnische Stadt*, 48.

14 Fedja Burić, 'Becoming Mixed: Mixed Marriages of Bosnia-Herzegovina during the Life and Death of Yugoslavia', unpublished PhD dissertation, University of Illinois-Champaign, 2012.
15 ICTY, *Tadić*, Opinion and Judgment, para. 147.
16 Galijaš, *Eine bosnische Stadt*, 194.
17 Mazowiecki Report of 21 February 1994, cited in Galijaš, *Eine bosnische Stadt*, 183.
18 Letter of Canadian diplomat Louis Gentile, 'In Banja Luka, Terror Seems Uncannily Normal', 14 January 1994, *The New York Times*.
19 Galijaš, *Eine bosnische Stadt*, 200–1.
20 Galijaš, *Eine bosnische Stadt*, 214f.
21 Ewa Tabeau et al., "Ethnic Composition and Displaced Persons and Refugees in 27 Municipalities of Bosnia and Herzegovina, 1991 and 1997, Addendum Prepared for the case of *Prosecutor v. Radovan Karadžić*," 3 February 2009, 23, 29.
22 Radovan Karadžić, 42nd Session of the RS Assembly, 18–19 July 1994 (0215-2810-0215-3020), 31.
23 Miloš Vasić, 'Banjalučka pobuna – država bez hleba', *Vreme*, No. 152, 15 September 1993.
24 Galijaš, *Eine bosnische Stadt*, 207.
25 Miloš Vasić, 'Banjalučka pobuna – država bez hleba', *Vreme*, No. 152, 15 September 1993.
26 For the scholarly accounts, see Edin Omerčić, 'Za što smo se borili? Vojna pobuna 1. Krajiškog korpusa Vojske Republike Srpske – Septembar '93', *Balkan Investigative Reporting Network*, September 2020; Nikica Barić, 'Akcija Septembar 93 – pobuna Vojske Republike Srpske u Banjoj Luci', *Prilozi*, Vol. 41 (2012), 185–201.
27 Banja Luka September 1993 crisis staff proclamations, quoted in Omerčić, 'Za što smo se borili', 14, 18.
28 Omerčić, 'Za što smo se borili', 7.
29 Omerčić, 'Za što smo se borili', 10.
30 On 12 May 1995, Minister Živko Rakić of the RS MUP wrote to his counterpart at the MUP Serbia congratulating him on the occasion of 'Security Day'. Rakić availed himself of the occasion to express his wish that 'our cooperation will also in the coming period be successful'. RS MUP Minister Živko Rakić to Minister of Internal Affairs of the Republic of Serbia, 12 May 1995 (0359-0882). By June 1995, Kovač was handling all important matters within the RS MUP, including communications with the RS Presidency. Deputy Minister Tomislav Kovač to Radovan Karadžić, 23 June 1995 (0359-1014).
31 RS MUP 1995 Annual Report (0357-2524-0357-2550, at 0357-2526).
32 RS MUP 1995 Annual Report (0357-2524-0357-2550, at 0357-2526).
33 In the meantime, Kovač had served as acting Minister of Internal Affairs from September 1993 until the end of 1994. ICTY, *Stanišić and Župljanin*, Judgement, Vol. 2, para. 39.
34 CJB Zvornik also had its own staff of police forces, which reported in mid-March 1995 that 80 police officers out of a total staff of 515 were currently deployed at the front line. CJB Zvornik to RS MUP, 21 March 1995 (0177-6557-0177-6559).
35 Dispatch of RS MUP Deputy Minister Tomislav Kovač (signed by Miloš Zuban), 19 June 1995 (0359-1114).
36 Article 14, Law on the Implementation of the Law on Internal Affairs during an Imminent Threat of War, *Službeni glasnik Republike Srpske*, 29 November 1994 (0049-7362-0049-7363).
37 See chart prepared by Defence Expert Witness Mladen Bajagić (4D04-0364).

38 See chart prepared by Defence Expert Witness Mladen Bajagić (4D04-0378).
39 ICTY, *Popović et al.*, Judgement, para. 175.
40 ICTY, *Popović et al.*, Judgement, para. 178.
41 ICTY, *Popović et al.*, Judgement, para. 183.
42 ICTY, *Popović et al.*, Judgement, paras. 180–1.
43 ICTY, *Popović et al.*, Judgement, para. 213.
44 RS Supreme Command Operational Directive for Further Activities No. 7, 8 March 1995 (0082-3159-0082-3181).
45 RS Supreme Command Operational Directive for Further Activities No. 7, 8 March 1995 (0082-3159-0082-3181, at 0082-3173).
46 RS MUP, Dispatch of Staff Commander Tomislav Kovač, 6 July 1995 (0211-4887).
47 ICTY, *Popović et al.*, Judgement, para. 252.
48 RS MUP, Order of Staff Commander Tomislav Kovač, 10 July 1995 (0294-1605); Report of Ljubomir Borovčanin, 5 September 1995 (4D04-0930-4D04-0934). On the units at Trnovo, see Order of Minister Rakić, 16 March 1995 (0359-0926). It should be noted that it seems likely that the dispatch of the RS MUP units to Srebrenica should be viewed in the context of a raging disagreement and competition between Radovan Karadžić and Ratko Mladić during the spring and summer of 1995. Seen from this perspective, Karadžić sought the participation of the RS MUP in 'liberating' Srebrenica in order to prevent Mladić from taking all the credit.
49 Report of Staff of Police Forces, 30 June 1995 (0359-0329-0359-0331); Iva Vukušić, '19 Minutes of Horror: Insights from the Scorpions Execution Video', *Genocide Studies and Prevention*, Vol. 12, No. 3 (2018), 35–53. ICTY, *Popović et al.*, Judgement, paras. 597f.
50 RS MUP, Order of Kovač, 12 July 1995 (0099-6594); CJB Zvornik to RS MUP, 12 July 1995 (0177-6571). In this dispatch, Vasić referred to the Bosnian Muslims as 'Turks'. Vasić had also done so earlier. CJB Zvornik to RS MUP, 12 June 1995 (0177-6593-0177-6594). See also the order of Vasić on 16 July 1995 (0117-6586) in which he appears to be reestablishing order in Srebrenica on the basis of an order from Kovač.
51 CJB Zvornik to RS MUP, Cabinet of the Minister, 13 July 1995 (0177-6580); see also MUP SBP report, 13 July 1995 (0359-2236).
52 A later report by Borovčanin included an estimate of there on 12 July 1995 being between 25,000 and 28,000 civilians at Potočari and a group of 12,000–15,000 military aged and predominantly armed males moving towards Tuzla. Report of Ljubomir Borovčanin, 5 September 1995 (4D04-0930-4D04-0934, at 4D04-0932).
53 In the annals of the investigations and prosecutions of the ICTY, it is very rare to find a document that expresses criminal intent as succinctly and explicitly as Vasić's 13 July 1995 dispatch. However, Richard Butler, the OTP military expert in the Srebrenica cases, concluded that Vasić was not actually referring to police involvement in mass executions. Likewise, the trial chamber in Popović et al. found that 'the latter issue was discussed in a military context'. I disagree with this reading of the dispatch. ICTY, *Popović et al.*, Judgement, para. 1100.
54 ICTY video (V000-0550).
55 ICTY, *Popović et al.*, Judgement, paras. 1458n4648.
56 ICTY, *Popović et al.*, Judgement, paras. 307–8.
57 ICTY, *Popović et al.*, Judgement, para. 382.
58 ICTY, *Popović et al.*, Judgement, para. 316.
59 ICTY, *Popović et al.*, Judgement, paras. 319–21.
60 ICTY, *Popović et al.*, Judgement, para. 323.

61 ICTY, *Popović et al.*, Judgement, para. 331.
62 ICTY, *Popović et al.*, Judgement, paras. 365, 377.
63 ICTY, *Krstić*, Judgement, para. 286.
64 ICTY, *Popović et al.*, Judgement, paras. 390, 406.
65 Dispatch of CRDB Sarajevo, 12 July 1995 (0359-2255); dispatches of RS MUP RDB, 14 July and 28 July 1995 (0324-3417, 0324-3391).
66 See, for example, ICTY, *Popović et al.*, Judgement, paras 421, 423. See however also P478 (no ERN) in *Krstić*, a conversation between Krstić and Beara on 15 July 1995 which seems to indicate that some members of the MUP refused to participate in executions. This likely pertained to the killings which members of the VRS's Bratunac Brigade instead carried out at the Branjevo Farm and the Pilića cultural centre the following day.
67 ICTY, *Krstić*, Judgement, para. 287.
68 Intercepted conversation of Ljubomir Borovčanin and Radislav Krstić, 13 July 1995, Exhibit P529, *Krstić* (no ERN).
69 Dispatch of CJB Zvornik, 28 July 1995 (0359-1826-0359-1826).
70 Report of Ljubomir Borovčanin, 5 September 1995 (4D04-0930-4D04-0934, at 4D04-0932).
71 ICTY, *Popović et al.,* Judgement, para. 1453.
72 ICTY, *Popović et al.,* Judgement, para. 1462.
73 ICTY, *Popović et al.,* Judgement, para. 1464.
74 ICTY, *Popović et al.,* Judgement, Disposition.
75 ICTY, *Popović et al.,* Judgement, paras. 1550, 1551.
76 ICTY, *Popović et al.,* Judgement, paras. 1550, 1562.
77 ICTY, *Popović et al.,* Judgement, paras. 1583, 1585, 1591.
78 RS MUP report to RS Minister of Justice and Administration, 23 September 1996 (0044-0017-0044-0019).
79 Central Intelligence Agency, *Balkan Battlegrounds: A Military History of the Yugoslav Conflict, 1990–1995*, Vol. 2 (Washington, DC, 2002), 561f.
80 RS MUP 1995 Annual Report (0357-2524-0357-2550, at 0357-2526).

Epilogue and Conclusion

1 Johan Galtung and Dietrich Fischer, 'Positive and Negative Peace', in Johan Galtung, ed., *SpringerBriefs on Pioneers in Science and Practice*, Vol. 5 (Berlin: Springer, 2013), 9–17.
2 ICTY, Testimony of Mićo Stanišić, *Karadžić*, 3 February 2014, 46343.
3 In his second book, Stanišić plays down the seriousness of the death toll in the war, comparing it to the proportionally greater death toll in Bosnia during the Second World War. Stanišić, *Ratni sukobi*, 350.
4 Richard Holbrooke, *To End a War* (New York: Penguin Random House, 1998); Derek Chollet, *The Road to the Dayton Accords: A Study of American Statecraft* (Houndmills: Palgrave Macmillan, 2005).
5 RS MUP 1995 Annual Report (0357-2524-0357-2550, at 0357-2526).
6 Christopher A. Riley, 'Neither Free Nor Fair: The 1996 Bosnian Elections and the Failure of the UN Election-Monitoring Mission', *Vanderbilt Journal of Transitional Law*, Vol. 30, No. 5 (November 1997), 1173–214; Carrie Manning, 'Elections and Political Change in Post-War Bosnia and Herzegovina', *Democratization*, Vol. 11,

No. 2 (2004), 60–86. For a very thorough and useful overview of major political developments in Bosnia since the war, see International Crisis Group, 'Bosnia's Future', 10 July 2014.

7   For early reports on the prevalence of perpetrators, see for example, Human Rights Watch, 'Bosnia-Hercegovina: The Continuing Influence of Bosnia's Warlords', December 1996; Human Rights Watch, 'The Unindicted: Reaping the Rewards of "Ethnic Cleansing" in Prijedor', January 1997; Human Rights Watch, 'Unfinished Business: Return of Displaced Persons and Other Human Rights Issues in Bijeljina', May 2000. Another report by the same organization shows that the problematic role of the police was not restricted to the RS. Human Rights Watch, 'Politics of Revenge: The Misuse of Authority in Bihać, Cazin, and Velika Kladuša', August 1997.

8   *Krajišnik*, Judgment, para. 359. The source for the 2013 census is Statistika.ba, which does, however, also cite a lower figure, 56.2 per cent, for Bosnian Muslims in 1991.

9   Sumantra Bose, 'Mostar as Microcosm: Power-Sharing in Post-War Bosnia', in Allison McCulloch and John McGarry, eds., *Power Sharing: Empirical and Normative Challenges* (London: Routledge, 2017), 189–210.

10 Gerald Toal and Carl T. Dahlman, *Bosnia Remade: Ethnic Cleansing and Its Reversal* (Oxford: Oxford University Press, 2011), 169–70, 181.

11 Toal and Dahlman, *Bosnia Remade*, 190.

12 UNSCR 1035; see archived site of UNMBIH, https://peacekeeping.un.org/mission/past/unmibh/.

13 https://peacekeeping.un.org/mission/past/unmibh/facts.html

14 Toal and Carl T. Dahlman, *Bosnia Remade*, 181; Gemma Collantes Celador, 'Police Reform: Peacebuilding through "Democratic Policing"?', *International Peacekeeping*, Vol. 12, No. 3 (2005), 364–76.

15 See for example, Daniel Lindvall, *The Limits of the European Vision in Bosnia and Herzegovina: An Analysis of the Police Reform Negotiations* (Doctoral Dissertation, Stockholm University, 2009).

16 Lindvall, *The Limits*, 68.

17 By 2002, this was reduced to '1 authorized officer for about 220 inhabitants or 1 officer for 150 if the police support process staff were included in the calculation. The ratio recommended by the United Nations is 1 officer for 450 inhabitants'. Dominique Wisler, 'The International Civilian Police Mission in Bosnia and Herzegovina: From Democratization to Nation-Building', *Police Practice and Research*, Vol. 8, No. 3 (July 2007), 259, 264, 265.

18 Eurostat, 'Police, Court and Prison Personnel Statistics', https://ec.europa.eu/eurostat/statistics-explained/index.php/Police,_court_and_prison_personnel_statistics.

19 Milorad Ulemek Legija and other Serb organized criminals who had participated in ethnic cleansing in Croatia and Bosnia later procured Croatian passports through Herceg-Bosna.

20 Peter Andreas, *Blue Helmets and Black Markets: The Business of Survival in the Siege of Sarajevo* (Ithaca: Cornell University Press, 2008).

21 Ana E. Juncos, 'Europeanization by Decree? The Case of Police Reform in Bosnia', *Journal of Common Market Studies*, Vol. 49, No. 2 (2011), 375.

22 Wisler, 'The International Civilian Police Mission in Bosnia and Herzegovina', 259.

23 Lindvall, *The Limits*, 68.

24 Historically speaking, many other vetting procedures have tended to be plagued by inconsistencies and shortcomings, from denazification in postwar Germany – both East and West – and Eastern Europe, to de-ba'athification in Iraq after the

2003 invasion. James F. Tent, *Mission on the Rhine: Reeducation and Denazification in American-Occupied Germany* (Chicago: University of Chicago Press, 1982); Molly Pucci, *Security Empire: The Secret Police in Communist Eastern Europe* (New Haven: Yale University Press, 2018); Miranda Sissons and Abdulrazzaq Al Saiedi, 'A Bitter Legacy: Lessons of De-Baaathification in Iraq' (International Coalition on Transitional Justice, 2013).
25 Lindvall, *The Limits*, 70.
26 Željko Cvijanović, 'Another Warlord Bites the Dust', *Institute for War & Peace Reporting*, 9 June 2000.
27 The N1 documentary series *Junaci doba zlog* (2021) offers a detailed portrait of Dodik's career.
28 Interview with Milorad Dodik, *Slobodna Bosna*, 22 March 1996, 18. By contrast, Dodik testified in 2013 as a defence witness in the trial of Radovan Karadžić at the ICTY. The Trial Chamber remarked that 'Dodik's evidence was marked by contradictions, indicators of insincerity and partisanship'. ICTY, *Karadžić*, Judgement, 1119*n*9597. Dodik has in the past two decades consistently portrayed himself as a critic and foe of the ICTY and has praised persons including Karadžić convicted by the ICTY.
29 https://www.anti.media/istrazivanja/dosije/dosije-milorad-dodik/.
30 Wisler, 'The International Civilian Police Mission in Bosnia and Herzegovina', 265.
31 NATO communique quoted in OHR Sarajevo, 'We Must Now Turn NATO's No into a Yes', 29 June 2004.
32 Lindvall, *The Limits*, 85.
33 The external borders of Bosnia came under the control of the State Border Police (*Granična policija*) in 2000.
34 Wisler, 'The International Civilian Police Mission in Bosnia and Herzegovina', 264.
35 Lindvall, *The Limits*, 75.
36 Helge Lurås, 'Democratic Oversight in Fragile States: The Case of Intelligence Reform in Bosnia and Herzegovina', *Intelligence and National Security*, Vol. 29, No. 4 (2014), 600–18; Dragan Stanimirović, 'Bosnia: Playing Spying Games', *Transitions Online*, 10 January 2005.
37 Wisler, 'The International Civilian Police Mission in Bosnia and Herzegovina', 265; Celador, 'Becoming "European" through Police Reform', 238; see also summary in Muehlmann, 'Police Restructuring', 6. Ironically, Belgium had the only ethnically divided police force in the EU.
38 Muehlmann, 'Police Restructuring', 6.
39 Juncos, 'Europeanization', 377.
40 Matthew D. Morton, 'Three Hearts in the Chest of One State: The Armed Forces of Bosnia and Herzegovina', *The Journal of Slavic Military Studies*, Vol. 25, No. 4 (2012), 512–32.
41 Muehlmann, 'Police Restructuring', 4.
42 'Milorad Dodik otvorio studentski dom "Dr. Radovan Karadžić" na Palama', 7 October 2014, https://youtu.be/VeaB8F_O_q4.
43 Juncos, 'Europeanization', 377.
44 Tija Memisević, 'EU Conditionality in Bosnia and Herzegovina: Police Reform and the Legacy of War Crimes', in Judy Batt et al., 'War Crimes, Conditionality and EU Integration in the Western Balkans', European Union Institute for Security Studies, 2009, 59.

45 Gemma Collantes Celador, 'Becoming "European" through Police Reform: A Successful Strategy in Bosnia and Herzegovina?' *Crime Law Social Change*, Vol. 51 (2009), 231–42. Celador points out that the 2007 crisis was exacerbated by the zero-sum politicking of Dodik and his Bosniak counterpart Haris Silajdžić with respect to the contemporaneous ruling by the International Court of Justice regarding Serbia's involvement in the Srebrenica genocide.
46 Juncos, 'Europeanization', 382.
47 Bodo Weber, 'Western Collusion in Undermining the Rule of Law in Bosnia and Herzegovina: An Overview', Democratization Policy Council, July 2021, 8.
48 Weber, Western Collusion, 13.
49 Juncos, 'Europeanization', 368.
50 Juncos, 'Europeanization', 381.
51 Muehlmann notes correctly that the Croats in the Federation 'could mainly hide behind Serb opposition', as was so often the case on other issues as well. Thomas Muehlmann, 'Police Restructuring in Bosnia-Herzegovina: Problems of Internationally-Led Security Sector Reform', *Journal of Intervention and Statebuilding*, Vol. 2, No. 1 (2008), 3.
52 Juncos argues that it was a liability for the EU that there was no single EU model for policing, and that none of the member states fully complied with the policing criteria that the Bosnian police forces were being required to adhere to. Yet that did not need to be a liability. Politicization of police is different when ethnically segregated – so while it is correct to state that there may not be a common European standard, it could be argued that there is at least an (implicit) European standard with respect to banning ethnic discrimination in the police – though the issue of ethnic discrimination *by* European police forces is of course a hotly debated topic, and many European police forces severely underperform with respect to the recruitment of minorities. Juncos, 'Europeanization', 385. Similarly, Celador points out that the EUPM did not live up to the gender quotas which it itself recommended for European police forces. Celador, 'Becoming "European"', 237.
53 A similar phenomenon can be observed in the four predominantly Serbian municipalities in northern Kosovo since 1999. International Crisis Group, 'North Kosovo: Dual Sovereignty in Practice', 14 March 2011; Oliver Ivanović, 'The Kosovo Serbs and Normalization', in Anton Bebler, ed., *'Frozen Conflicts' in Europe* (Leverkusen: Verlag Barbara Budrich, 2015), 179–82.
54 Numerous telephone conversations between Mandić and various interlocutors during the second half of March 1992 reveal that he reacted with fury to these allegations. Particularly noteworthy are the conversations between MANDI] and 'Samir' on 13, 17, 18, 19, 24 and 29 March (0111-3407-0111-3416, 0111-3426-0111-3435, 0111-3446-0111-3457, 0111-3458-0111-3468, 0111-3477-0111-3480). See also 'Mandić pada, koga će povući sa sobom?!', *Slobodna Bosna*, 19 March 1992, and the 1 April 1992 issue of *Oslobođenje*.
55 Senad Avdić, 'Rat je mio, ma koje vjere bio: Dodik će vjerovatno objasniti da se napadima na povratnike štiti "Aneks sedam" Daytonskog sporazuma' *Slobodna Bosna*, 11 January 2022.
56 Weber, Western Collusion'.
57 International Crisis Group, 'Policing the Police in Bosnia: A Further Reform Agenda', 10 May 2002, 2.
58 ICTY, OTP Final Trial Brief, *Stanišić and Župljanin*, 12 July 2012, para. 1.

59 In an interview in November 1992, Župljanin stated that 'it is my great desire to create a police force that is tailored to the people although the police is not particularly popular in any system, but we took the English Bobby as our model'. It should be noted that after leaving his post as chief of CSB Banja Luka, Župljanin became a security advisor to President Radovan Karadžić. Quoted by OTP Senior Trial Attorney Joanna Korner, ICTY, *Stanišić and Župljanin*, 14 September 2009, 190.
60 Stanišić, *Ratni sukobi*, 407.
61 See the respective ICTY Case Information Sheets.
62 'Zbog ratnog zločina uhapšen Goran Sarić, policijski general MUP Republike Srpske', *Danas*, 3 December 2021.
63 Reuf Bajrović, Richard Kraemer and Emir Suljagić, 'Bosnia on the Chopping Block: The Potential for Violence and Steps to Prevent It', Foreign Policy Research Institute, 16 March 2018.
64 Bajrović et al., 'Bosnia on the Chopping Block', 6.
65 Tija Memisević, 'EU Conditionality in Bosnia and Herzegovina: Police Reform and the Legacy of War Crimes', in Judy Batt et al., 'War Crimes, Conditionality and EU Integration in the Western Balkans', European Union Institute for Security Studies, 2009, 49.
66 Danijela Majstorović and Zoran Vučkovac, 'Bosnia and Herzegovina after the Transition: Forever Postwar, Postsocialist and Peripheral?', in Agnes Gagyi and Ondřej Slačálek, eds., *The Political Economy of Eastern Europe 30 Years into the 'Transition': New Left Perspectives on the Region* (Cham: Palgrave Macmillan, 2022), 84.
67 Memisević, 'EU Conditionality', 53. For a general indictment of Bosnia's ethnopolitical elites, see Jasmin Mujanović, *Hunger and Fury: The Crisis of Democracy in the Balkans* (London: Hurst, 2018).
68 These include Srđan Šušnica, Danijela Ratešić and Sofija Grmuša, Majstorović and Vučkovac, 'Bosnia and Herzegovina', 85. Interview with Srđan Šušnica, 26 December 2018, Index.ba, https://index.ba/srdjan-susnica-mup-rs-danas-prebija-i-ubija-srbe-jer-je-nesrbe-dobrano-istrijebio-iz-banja-luke/. Šušnica's father, Miodrag Šušnica, was a police officer who was killed in a café in Banja Luka on 10 April 1992. At the time of his death, Šušnica was working for the State Security Service of Serbia as a member of the 'Miloš' group. Slobodan Vasković, 'Ubistvo Miodraga Šušnice, policijskog inspektora', 26 August 2018, http://slobodanvaskovic.blogspot.com/2020/06/iz-arhivaubistvo-miodraga-susnice.html.
69 Danijela Majstorović, *Discourse and Affect in Postsocialist Bosnia and Herzegovina* (Cham: Palgrave Macmillan, 2021), 22, 25, 78.
70 On denial in the RS, see Jessie Barton-Hronešová, 'Ethnopopulist Denial and Crime Relativisation in Bosnian Republika Srpska', *East European Politics* (2021).
71 International Crisis Group, 'Grappling with Bosnia's Dual Crises', 9 November 2021.
72 Erduan Katana, 'Militarizacija policije RS kao mač i štit aktuelne vlasti', *Radio Slobodna Evropa*, 26 October 2016; Julian Borger, 'Arms Shipments to Bosnian Serbs Stoke Fears', *The Guardian*, 13 February 2018; Reuf Bajrović, Richard Kraemer and Emir Suljagić, 'Bosnia on the Chopping Block: The Potential for Violence and Steps to Prevent It', Foreign Policy Research Institute, 16 March 2018.
73 International Crisis Group, 'Policing the Police in Bosnia: A Further Reform Agenda', 10 May 2002, i.

BIBLIOGRAPHY

Archival Collections Consulted

United Nations Unified Court Records (https://ucr.irmct.org, previously known as ICTY Court Records)

List of Relevant ICTY Cases

Babić (IT-03-72)
Brđanin (IT-99-36)
Karadžić (IT-95-5/18)
Krajišnik and Plavšić (IT-00-39)
Krstić (IT-98-33)
Lukić and Lukić (IT-98-32/1)
Martić (IT-95-11)
Mejakić et al. (IT-02-65)
Mladić (IT-09-92)
Mrđa (IT-02-59)
Perišić (IT-04-81)
Popović et al. (IT-05-88)
Simić et al. (IT-95-9)
Stakić (IT-97-24)
Stanišić and Simatović (IT-03-69)
Stanišić and Župljanin (IT-08-91)
Tadić (IT-94-1)
Todorović (IT-95-9/1)

Abazović, Mirzad D., *Kadrovski rat za BiH (1945–1991)* (Sarajevo: Savez logoraša Bosne i Hercegovine, 1999).
Alibabić, Munir, *Bosna u kandžama KOS-a* (Sarajevo: Behar, 1996).
Alibabić, Munir, *Deda, Dedo i Babo Bosnu KOSili* (Sarajevo, 2010).
Anđelić, Neven, *Bosnia: The End of a Legacy* (London: Routledge, 2003).
Andreas, Peter, *Blue Helmets and Black Markets: The Business of Survival in the Siege of Sarajevo* (Ithaca: Cornell University Press, 2008).
Arnautović, Suad, *Izbori u Bosni i Hercegovini '90: Analiza izbornog procesa* (Sarajevo: Promocult, 1996).
Bajrović, Reuf, Richard Kraemer and Emir Suljagić, 'Bosnia on the Chopping Block: The Potential for Violence and Steps to Prevent It', Foreign Policy Research Institute, 16 March 2018.

Baker, Catherine, *The Yugoslav Wars of the 1990s* (London: Palgrave, 2015).
Barić, Nikica, *Srpska pobuna u Hrvatskoj, 1990–1995* (Zagreb: Golden marketing-Tehnička knjiga, 2005).
Barić, Nikica, 'Akcija *Septembar 93* – pobuna Vojske Republike Srpske u Banjoj Luci', *Prilozi*, Vol. 41 (2012), 185–201.
Barton-Hronešová, Jessie, 'Ethnopopulist Denial and Crime Relativisation in Bosnian Republika Srpska', *East European Politics* (2021).
Bergholz, Max, *Violence as a Generative Force: Identity, Nationalism, and Memory in a Balkan Community* (Ithaca: Cornell University Press, 2016).
Boljkovac, Josip, *Istina mora izaći van: sjećanja i zapisi prvog ministra unutarnjih poslova neovisne Hrvatske* (Zagreb: Golden Marketing, 2009).
Bose, Sumantra, 'Mostar as Microcosm: Power-Sharing in Post-War Bosnia', in Allison McCulloch and John McGarry, eds., *Power Sharing: Empirical and Normative Challenges* (London: Routledge, 2017), 189–210.
Broszat, Martin, Hans Buchheim, Hans-Adolf Jacobsen and Helmut Krausnik, *Die Anatomie des SS-Staates* (Olten-Freiburg im Breisgau: Walter, 1965).
Brown, Ewan, 'Military Developments in the Bosanska Krajina, 1992', ICTY Expert Report, 27 November 2002.
Browning, Christopher R., *Ordinary Men: Reserve Police Battalion 101 and the Final Solution in Poland* (New York: HarperPerennial, 1992).
Brubaker, Rogers, *Ethnicity without Groups* (Cambridge: Harvard University Press, 2006).
Burić, Fedja, *Becoming Mixed: Mixed Marriages of Bosnia-Herzegovina during the Life and Death of Yugoslavia*, Unpublished PhD Dissertation, University of Illinois-Champaign, 2012.
Campbell, Bruce B. and Arthur D. Brenner, eds., *Death Squads in Global Perspective: Murder with Deniability* (New York: Palgrave Macmillan, 2000).
Caspersen, Nina, *Contested Nationalism: Serb Elite Rivalry in Croatia and Bosnia in the 1990s* (New York: Berghahn Books, 2010).
Celador, Gemma Collantes, 'Police Reform: Peacebuilding through "Democratic Policing"?' *International Peacekeeping*, Vol. 12, No. 3 (2005), 364–76.
Celador, Gemma Collantes, 'Becoming "European" through Police Reform: A Successful Strategy in Bosnia and Herzegovina?' *Crime Law Social Change*, Vol. 51 (2009), 231–42.
Central Intelligence Agency, *Balkan Battlegrounds: A Military History of the Yugoslav Conflict, 1990–1995*, Vol. 2 (Washington, DC, 2002).
Čepič, Zdenko, *Prikrita modra mreža: organi za notranje zadeve Republike Slovenije v projektu MSNZ leta 1990* (Ljubljana: Institut za novejšo zgodovino, 2010).
Chaney, Cassandra and Ray V. Robertson, 'Racism and Police Brutality in America', *Journal of African American Studies*, Vol. 17 (2013), 480–505.
Chollet, Derek, *The Road to the Dayton Accords: A Study of American Statecraft* (Houndmills: Palgrave Macmillan, 2005).
Dean, Martin, *Collaboration in the Holocaust: Crimes of the Local Police in Belorussia and Ukraine, 1941–44* (New York: St. Martin's Press, 2000).
Delalić, Medina and Suzana Sačić, *Balkan bluz* (Sarajevo, 2007).
Donohue, John J. III and Steven D. Levitt, 'The Impact of Race on Policing and Arrests', *The Journal of Law & Economics*, Vol. 14, No. 2 (2001), 367–94.
Donia, Robert, 'Bosnian Serb Leadership and the Siege of Sarajevo, 1990–1995', ICTY Expert Report, May 2009.

Donia, Robert, *Radovan Karadžić: Architect of the Bosnian Genocide* (Cambridge: Cambridge University Press, 2014).
Dragojević, Mila, *Amoral Communities: Collective Crimes in Time of War* (Ithaca: Cornell University Press, 2019).
Đukić, Slavoljub, *Milošević and Marković: A Lust for Power* (Montreal: McGill-Queen's University Press, 2001).
Duijzings, Ger, *Geschiedenis en herinnering in Oost-Bosnië* (Amsterdam: Boom, 2002).
Dulić, Tomislav and Roland Kostić, 'Yugoslavs in Arms: Guerrilla Tradition, Total Defence and the Ethnic Security Dilemma', *Europe-Asia Studies*, Vol. 62, No. 7 (2010), 1051–72.
Galijaš, Armina, *Eine bosnische Stadt im Zeichen des Krieges: Ethnopolitik und Alltag in Banja Luka (1990–1995)* (Oldenburg: Oldenbourg Wissenschaftsverlag, 2011).
Galtung, Johan and Dietrich Fischer, 'Positive and Negative Peace', in Johan Galtung, ed., *SpringerBriefs on Pioneers in Science and Practice*, Vol. 5 (Berlin: Springer, 2013), 9–17.
Gerlach, Christian, *Extremely Violent Societies: Mass Violence in the Twentieth-Century World* (Cambridge: Cambridge University Press, 2010).
Gilbert, Andrew, *International Intervention and the Problem of Legitimacy: Encounters in Postwar Bosnia-Herzegovina* (Ithaca: Cornell University Press, 2020).
Glaurdić, Josip, *The Hour of Europe: Western Powers and the Breakup of Yugoslavia* (New Haven: Yale University Press, 1995).
Gow, James, *The Serbian Project and Its Adversaries: A Strategy of War Crimes* (Montreal: McGill-Queen's University Press, 2003).
Gutman, Roy, *A Witness to Genocide: The First Inside Account of the Horrors of 'Ethnic Cleansing' in Bosnia* (Shaftesbury: Dorset, 1993).
Halilović, Sefer, *Lukava strategija* (Sarajevo: Maršal, 1997).
Hanson, Dorothea, 'Bosnian Serb Crisis Staffs, War Presidencies and War Commissions, 1991–1995', ICTY Expert Report, 8 April 2009.
Haug, Hilde, *Creating a Socialist Yugoslavia: Tito, Communist Leadership and the National Question* (London: I.B. Tauris, 2012).
Heer, Hannes, Walter Manoschek, Alexander Pollak and Ruth Wodak, eds., *Discursive Construction of History: Remembering the Wehrmacht's War of Annihilation* (Hampshire: Palgrave Macmillan, 2008).
Helms, Elissa, *Innocence and Victimhood: Gender, Nation, and Women's Activism in Postwar Bosnia-Herzegovina* (Madison, WI: University of Wisconsin Press, 2013).
Helms, Elissa, 'Rejecting Angelina: War Rape Survivors and the Ambiguities of Sex in War', *Slavic Review*, Vol. 73, No. 3 (2014), 612–34.
Hoare, Marko Attila, 'Whose Is the Partisan Movement? Serbs, Croats and the Legacy of a Shared Resistance', *Journal of Slavic Military Studies*, Vol. 15, No. 4 (December 2002), 24–41.
Hoare, Marko Attila, *How Bosnia Armed* (London: Saqi Books, 2004).
Holbrooke, Richard, *To End a War* (New York: Penguin Random House, 1998).
Human Rights Watch, 'Bosnia-Hercegovina: The Continuing Influence of Bosnia's Warlords', December 1996.
Human Rights Watch, 'The Unindicted: Reaping the Rewards of "Ethnic Cleansing" in Prijedor', January 1997.
Human Rights Watch, 'Politics of Revenge: The Misuse of Authority in Bihać, Cazin, and Velika Kladuša', August 1997.
Human Rights Watch, 'Unfinished Business: Return of Displaced Persons and Other Human Rights Issues in Bijeljina', May 2000.

International Crisis Group, 'Policing the Police in Bosnia: A Further Reform Agenda', 10 May 2002.
International Crisis Group, 'North Kosovo: Dual Sovereignty in Practice', 14 March 2011.
International Crisis Group, 'Bosnia's Future', 10 July 2014.
Ivanović, Oliver, 'The Kosovo Serbs and Normalization', in Anton Bebler, ed., *'Frozen Conflicts' in Europe* (Leverkusen: Verlag Barbara Budrich, 2015), 179–82.
Jansen, Stef, *Antinacionalizam: Etnografija otpora u Beogradu i Zagrebu* (Belgrade: Biblioteka XX vek, 2005).
Jović, Dejan, *Jugoslavija: Država koja je odumrla* (Zagreb: Prometej, 2003).
Jović, Dejan, *Rat i mit: Politika identiteta u suvremenoj Hrvatskoj* (Zagreb: Fraktura, 2017).
Juncos, Ana E., 'Europeanization by Decree? The Case of Police Reform in Bosnia', *Journal of Common Market Studies*, Vol. 49, No. 2 (2011), 367–89.
Karčić, Hikmet, *Torture, Humiliate, Kill: Inside the Bosnian Serb Camp System* (Ann Arbor: University of Michigan Press, forthcoming).
Kovač, Svetko, Bojana Dimitrijević and Irena Popović Grigorov, *Slučaj Ranković* (Belgrade: Medija Centar 'Odbrana', 2014).
Krausnick, Helmut and Hans-Heinrich Wilhelm, *Die Truppe des Weltanschauungskrieges: die Einsatzgruppen der Sicherheitspolizei und des SD, 1938–1942* (Stuttgart: Deutsche Verlags-Anstalt, 1981).
LeBor Adam, *Milošević: A Biography* (London: Bloomsbury, 2003)
Lindvall, Daniel, *The Limits of the European Vision in Bosnia and Herzegovina: An Analysis of the Police Reform Negotiations*, Doctoral Dissertation, Stockholm University, 2009.
Lurås, Helge, 'Democratic Oversight in Fragile States: The Case of Intelligence Reform in Bosnia and Herzegovina', *Intelligence and National Security*, Vol. 29, No. 4 (2014), 600–18.
Majstorović, Danijela, *Discourse and Affect in Postsocialist Bosnia and Herzegovina* (Cham: Palgrave Macmillan, 2021).
Majstorović Danijela and Zoran Vučkovac, 'Bosnia and Herzegovina after the Transition: Forever Postwar, Postsocialist and Peripheral?' in Agnes Gagyi and Ondřej Slačálek, eds., *The Political Economy of Eastern Europe 30 Years into the 'Transition': New Left Perspectives on the Region* (Cham: Palgrave Macmillan, 2022), 81–96.
Maksić, Adis, *Ethnic Mobilization, Violence, and the Politics of Affect: The Serb Democratic Party and the Bosnian War* (London: Palgrave Macmillan, 2017).
Manning, Carrie, 'Elections and Political Change in Post-War Bosnia and Herzegovina', *Democratization*, Vol. 11, No. 2 (2004), 60–86.
Manolić, Josip, *Politika i domovina: Moja borba za suverenu i socijalnu Hrvatsku* (Zagreb: Golden Marketing, 2015).
Manolić, Josip, *Špijuni i domovina: Moja borba za suverenu i socijalnu Hrvatsku* (Zagreb: Golden Marketing, 2016).
Marijan, Davor, *Slom Titove armije: JNA i raspad Jugoslavije* (Zagreb: Golden Marketing, 2008).
Memisević, Tija, 'EU Conditionality in Bosnia and Herzegovina: Police Reform and the Legacy of War Crimes', in Judy Batt et al., eds., *War Crimes, Conditionality and EU Integration in the Western Balkans* (Paris: European Union Institute for Security Studies, 2009).
Mojžes, Paul, *Yugoslavian Inferno: Ethnoreligious Warfare in the Balkans* (New York: Continuum Books, 1994).

Muehlmann, Thomas, 'Police Restructuring in Bosnia-Herzegovina: Problems of Internationally-Led Security Sector Reform', *Journal of Intervention and Statebuilding*, Vol. 2, No. 1 (2008), 1–22.

Mujanović, Jasmin, *Hunger and Fury: The Crisis of Democracy in the Balkans* (London: Hurst, 2018).

Nielsen, Christian Axboe, 'Report on the events in Bileća municipality, Bosnia Herzegovina, from November 1990 until the end of 1992, with a focus on the role of police and reserve police in those events', Expert report prepared for the Canadian Department of Justice, May 2009.

Nielsen, Christian Axboe, 'Surmounting the Myopic Focus on Genocide: The Case of the War in Bosnia and Herzegovina', *Journal of Genocide Research*, Vol. 15, No. 1 (2013), 21–39.

Nielsen, Christian Axboe, 'Report on the Establishment and Performance of the Ministry of Internal Affairs of Republika Srpska in Bosnia and Herzegovina, 1990–1992', Expert Report, *The Minister of Citizenship and Immigration and the Minister of Public Safety and Emergency Preparedness and Čedo Kljajić* (Canada), 2017.

Nielsen, Christian Axboe, 'Collective and Competitive Victimhood in the Former Yugoslavia', in Nanci Adler, ed., *Understanding the Age of Transitional Justice: Crimes, Courts, Commissions, and Chronicling* (New Brunswick: Rutgers University Press, 2018), 175–93.

Nielsen, Christian Axboe, *Vi troede ikke det kunne ske her: Jugoslaviens sammenbrud 1991–1999* (Copenhagen: Kristeligt Dagblads Forlag, 2018).

Nielsen, Christian Axboe, *Yugoslavia and Political Assassinations: The History and Legacy of Tito's Campaign against the Émigrés* (London: I.B. Tauris, 2020).

Nugent, Christine R., 'The Voice of the Visitor: Popular Reactions to the Exhibition *Vernichtungskrieg. Verbrechen der Wehrmacht 1941–1944*', *Journal of European Studies*, Vol. 44, No. 3 (2014).

Omerčić, Edin, 'Za što smo se borili? Vojna pobuna 1. krajiškog korpusa Vojske Republike Srpske – Septembar '93', Balkan Investigative Reporting Network, September 2020.

Petrović, Ilija, *Srpsko nacionalno vijeće Slavonije, Baranje i Zapadnog Srema* (Novi Sad: Galeb, 1994).

Petrović, Vladimir, *Etničko čišćenje: geneza koncepta* (Belgrade: Institut za savremenu istoriju, 2019).

Posen, Barry, 'The Security Dilemma and Ethnic Conflict', *Survival*, Vol. 35, No. 1 (1993), 27–47.

Pucci, Molly, *Security Empire: The Secret Police in Communist Eastern Europe* (New Haven: Yale University Press, 2018).

Riedlmayer, András J., 'Destruction of Cultural Heritage in Bosnia and Herzegovina', ICTY Expert Report, undated.

Riley, Christopher A., 'Neither Free Nor Fair: The 1996 Bosnian Elections and the Failure of the UN Election-Monitoring Mission', *Vanderbilt Journal of Transitional Law*, Vol. 30, No. 5 (November 1997), 1173–214.

Silber, Laura and Allan Little, *Yugoslavia: Death of a Nation*, Revised and Updated (New York: Penguin, 1997).

Šimić, Tomo, 'Dokumenti Predsjedništva Bosne i Hercegovina, 1991–1994', *National Security and the Future*, Vol. 7, No. 1–2 (2006).

Sissons, Miranda and Abdulrazzaq Al Saiedi, 'A Bitter Legacy: Lessons of De-Baaathification in Iraq', *International Coalition on Transitional Justice* (2013).

Špegelj, Martin, *Sjećanja vojnika*, 2nd edn. (Zagreb: Znanje, 2001).

Stanišić, Mićo, *Početak rata u Bosni i Hercegovini* (Belgrade: Donat-graf, 2017).

Stanišić, Mićo, *Ratni sukobi na granicama Republika Srpske* (Belgrade: Svet knjige, 2020).
Subotić, Jelena, 'Stories States Tell: Identity, Narrative and Human Rights in the Balkans', *Slavic Review*, Vol. 72, No. 2 (Summer 2013), 306–26.
Taylor, Clarence, *Fight the Power: African Americans and the Long History of Police Brutality in New York City* (New York: New York University Press, 2019).
Tent, James F., *Mission on the Rhine: Reeducation and Denazification in American-Occupied Germany* (Chicago: University of Chicago Press, 1982).
Theunens, Reynaud, 'Military Aspects of the Role of Jovica Stanišić and Franko Simatović in the Conflict in Croatia and Bosnia-Herzegovina (BiH) (91–95)', ICTY Expert Report, 30 June 2007.
Toal, Gerald and Carl T. Dahlman, *Bosnia Remade: Ethnic Cleansing and Its Reversal* (Oxford: Oxford University Press, 2011).
Tokić, Mate Nikola, *For the Homeland Ready! Croat Diaspora Terrorism during the Cold War* (West Lafayette: Purdue University Press, 2020).
Touquet, Heleen, 'Silent or Inaudible? Male Survivor Stories in Bosnia and Herzegovina', *Social Politics: International Studies in Gender, State & Society* (2021).
Treanor, Patrick J., 'The Bosnian Serb Leadership 1990–1992', ICTY Expert Report, 30 July 2002.
Vasiljević, Aleksandar, *«Štit» Akcija vojne bezbednosti: Dnevničke beleške operativca* (Beograd: IGAM, 2012).
Vladisavljević, Nebojša, *Serbia's Antibureaucratic Revolution: Milošević, the Fall of Communism and Nationalist Mobilization* (Houndmills: Palgrave Macmillan, 2008).
Vojna bezbednost (Belgrade: Vojnoizdavački i novinski centar, 1986).
Vučur, Ilija, 'Pogibija Gorana Alavanje 23. studenoga 1990.: događaj, interpretacije, manipulacije', *Časopis za suvremenu povijest*, Vol. 49, No. 3 (2017), 587–609.
Vukušić, Iva, '19 Minutes of Horror: Insights from the Scorpions Execution Video', *Genocide Studies and Prevention*, Vol. 12, No. 3 (2018), 35–53.
Vukušić, Iva, 'Masters of Life and Death: Paramilitary Violence in Two Bosnian Towns', *Journal of Perpetrator Research*, Vol. 3, No. 2 (2021), 66–86.
Vukušić, Iva, *Serbian Paramilitaries in the Breakup of Yugoslavia* (London: Routledge, forthcoming).
Wachmann, Nikolaus, *KL: A History of the Nazi Concentration Camps* (New York: Farrar, Straus and Giroux, 2016).
Weber, Bodo, 'Western Collusion in Undermining the Rule of Law in Bosnia and Herzegovina: An Overview', Democratization Policy Council, July 2021.
Weld, Kirsten, *Paper Cadavers: The Archives of Dictatorship in Guatemala* (Durham, NC: Duke University Press, 2014).
Wisler, Dominique, 'The International Civilian Police Mission in Bosnia and Herzegovina: From Democratization to Peacebuilding', *Police Practice and Research*, Vol. 8, No. 3 (2007), 253–68.
Zimmermann, Warren, *Origins of a Catastrophe* (New York: Times Books, 1996).
Zwierzchowski, Jan and Ewa Tabeau, 'The 1992–95 War in Bosnia and Herzegovina: Census-Based Multiple System Estimation of Casualties' Undercount', Conference Paper for the International Research Workshop on 'The Global Costs of Conflict', February 2010, https://www.icty.org/x/file/About/OTP/War_Demographics/en/bih_casualty_undercount_conf_paper_100201.pdf.

INDEX

Abdić, Fikret 15
Adžić, Ratko 136
Alivanja, Goran 31
All People's Defence (ONO) 26, 40
Andan, Dragan 100
Anđelić, Neven 13, 17
antibureaucratic revolution 13–14
armed aggression 21, 32
Army of Bosnia and Herzegovina (ABiH) 1, 49, 147
Army of Republika Srpska (VRS) 4, 73–4, 77–84, 86–94, 96–8, 100–7, 110–11, 113–16, 124, 135–40, 142–7, 151, 153, 155–6
Army of Yugoslavia (VJ) 74
Ashdown, Paddy 155–6
Autonomous Region of Krajina (ARK) 30–4, 39, 42, 44, 64–70, 77, 83, 90, 92, 94, 97, 104, 109, 114, 119–22
Avdić, Senad 157
Avengers 130–1
Avlijaš, Slobodan 92

Babić, Milan 28, 30–2, 43, 119–21
Banja Luka 34, 37, 43–4, 46–7, 61–7, 69–70, 74, 76, 78, 83–4, 86, 88–9, 94, 104, 136–40, 149, 154, 160
Baranja 28, 30, 119
Belgrade 13–14, 17, 27, 33, 52, 74, 81, 85, 90, 95, 108–13, 120–1, 123, 125–7, 130–2, 134, 140, 158
Bera, Vojin 93
Bijelić, Slobodan 38
Bijeljina 44, 58–60, 98–100, 102, 110, 122, 139, 142, 153
Bileća 59–61, 105
Bjelošević, Andrija 39, 44, 79, 104, 110
Bogdanović, Radmilo 125
Bogojević, Stevan 89, 96
Bojić, Živko 66
Bonn-Petersberg Agreement 153

Boras, Franjo 15
Borovčanin, Ljubomir 142–6, 158
Borovo Selo 32
Bosanska Dubica 88
Bosanska Gradiška 154
Bosanska Krupa 48
Bosanski Novi 88, 92–4
Bosanski Petrovac 64
Bosanski Šamac 59, 92, 122–4, 158
Bosnia and Herzegovina (BiH) 40, 44, 51–2, 54, 56, 65–6, 71, 75, 79, 85, 129–30, 142, 154–5, 157, 159
Bosnian Croats 2–3, 6, 13, 15, 23, 27, 36, 38, 45, 53, 66, 73, 135, 137
Bosnian Krajina 47, 51, 61, 65, 82, 140
Bosnian Serb Assembly 34, 37, 39, 48–9, 52, 73–5
Bosnian Serb leadership 3–8, 21, 67, 82, 97–8, 122, 135, 139–41, 149
Bosnian Serb police 2–4, 6–9, 20, 24, 49, 51, 54, 58, 60, 74, 121, 134–5, 141, 152, 158–9
Bratunac 105, 121, 144–5
Brčko 59, 99–100, 110, 123, 150
Brđanin, Radoslav 67, 139
brotherhood and unity 1, 12–13, 35, 78
Bulatović, Momir 132–3

Captain Dragan. *See* Vasiljković, Dragan
Chetniks 100, 126
CJB. *See* Public Security Centre (CJB)
coalition 7, 15, 23, 39, 65–7, 135, 147, 149, 154
Communist Party of Yugoslavia (KPJ) 11
Counterintelligence Service (KOS) 10
CRDB. *See* State Security Division Centre (CRDB)
criminal
  acts 62, 66, 77–8, 91, 99, 103, 113–14, 116, 130, 134–5, 157
  behaviour 77–8, 129

conduct 58–9, 103, 113, 146
   records 17–18, 24, 152
crisis staff 40–1, 45, 47, 62, 64–5, 67, 80, 83, 85–8, 90, 93, 101–2, 111, 115, 123, 136, 140–1
Croat Democratic Union (HDZ) 15, 17, 19, 24, 27, 29–31, 38, 84
Croat Democratic Union of Bosnia and Herzegovina (HDZ BiH) 15, 23
Croatia 11
   independent 3, 30–1
   Plitvice incident 31–3
   policing in 26–33
   war in 23–6, 29, 31, 59–60, 65, 97, 125
Croatian Defence Council (HVO) 142, 147, 155
Croatian Sabor 29–31
CSB. *See* Security Services Centre (CSB)
Cutileiro, José 150
   negotiations 54–7
Cutileiro Plan 55–6
Cvijetić, Zoran 110

Davidović, Milorad (Mićo) 58, 99–100, 102–3
Dayton Peace Agreement or Accords (DPA) 4, 8, 149–54, 156–60
decentralization 12, 27, 33–42, 75
Delimustafić, Alija 16, 24–6, 46–7, 52–3, 56, 63
Democratization Policy Council 156–7
Đerić, Branko 114, 135
detention facility 8, 58, 62–3, 70, 73–4, 81–96, 106, 110
Devedlaka, Dragan 22
disciplinary action 77–9, 105, 113–15
Division of State Security (RDB) 69, 118, 120–4, 128–34, 143, 145
Dodik, Milorad 4, 8–9, 149, 154, 156–7, 159–60
Đorđević, Dragan 123–4
Dragičević, David 160
Drašković, Slavko 125–7
Drašković, Vuk 125–6
Drljača, Simo 64, 77, 85–7, 92, 94, 96, 107–8, 114, 158
Duka, Miroslav 59–60
Dukić, Rajko 46

Duraković, Nijaz 11
Đurić, Mendeljev 144

Ećim, Ljubomir (aka Ljuban) 66–7
elections 6–7, 14–18, 27, 30–1, 33, 46, 58–9, 90, 92, 126, 138, 150, 153–4, 156
Erkić, Mirko 92
ethnic cleansing 1, 4–5, 8, 61, 65, 73, 98, 106, 133, 135–41, 147, 151, 158–9, 161
ethnicity 8, 11, 13, 16, 18, 52, 61, 66, 74, 82, 93, 132, 151, 153
ethnicization 33
European Community (EC) 51, 54–5
European Union Police Mission (EUPM) 151–2, 156–7, 220
expulsion 57, 83, 111, 137, 147

Federal Republic of Yugoslavia 74, 99, 118, 124, 127, 131, 134, 141
Federal Secretariat for Internal Affairs (SSUP) 17, 25–6, 32, 36, 52, 58, 99–100, 108, 125
Federal Secretariat for People's Defence (SSNO) 32, 76
Foča 144

Gaćeša, Dragan 64
Gacko 60
Ganić, Ejup 15, 21, 34, 53, 60
genocide 1, 3–4, 6, 8, 28, 38, 43, 75, 95, 103, 107, 117, 126, 136–7, 141–7, 151, 157, 159–60
Golubić 65, 120–1, 125
Gračanin, Petar 100, 118
Grujić, Branko 101–2

Hadžić, Goran 31, 120
HDZ. *See* Croat Democratic Union (HDZ)
Hebib, Avdo 16, 19–20, 23
Herceg-Bosna 23, 135
HVO. *See* Croatian Defence Council (HVO)

ICRC 91
Independent State of Croatia (NDH) 11, 28, 30
Intelligence and Security Agency (OSA) 155

international community 2, 4, 54, 82, 96, 147, 149–51, 153–4, 156, 159, 161
International Crisis Group 157, 160
International Police Task Force (IPTF) 151–2
Inzko, Valentin 160
Izetbegović, Alija 15, 22, 26, 55–6

Jahić, Bajazid 63–4
JATD. *See* Unit for Anti-Terrorist Actions (JATD)
Ješurić, Predrag 44, 58
JPN. *See* Unit for Special Purposes (JPN)
JSO. *See* Unit for Special Operations (JSO)

Kadijević, Veljko 60
Karadžić, Radovan 3–5, 7, 20–3, 26, 34, 38, 40, 43–4, 48–9, 52, 55, 65, 67, 73–5, 78, 87, 91, 93, 100–1, 107–8, 131–2, 135, 137, 140–1, 143, 149–50, 153–4, 156
Karišik, Milenko 53–4, 75–6, 79, 103, 142
Keraterm 86–8
Kertes, Mihalj 120, 134
key system 13
Kijac, Dragan 46, 68, 103
Klajić, Čedomir 79
Kljajić, Čedo 44, 67
Ključ 64–5, 70, 83–4, 88, 94–6
Kljuić, Stjepan 15
Knin 27–8, 30, 32, 65, 117, 120–1, 125
knindže (Martić's men) 121, 131, 134
Koljević, Nikola 15, 20, 43, 55, 60, 62
Kondić, Vinko 88, 94, 96
Korićanske stijene 107–8, 158
Koroman, Malko 62, 114, 142
Kosovo 11–14, 74, 117–18, 124, 126, 129
Kotor Varoš 67, 95
Kovač, Tomislav 57, 91, 105, 142–5, 159
Kozarska Dubica. *See* Bosanska Dubica
Kragujevac 124
Krajina 28, 47, 51, 61, 65, 78, 82, 140
   SAO 30–4, 39, 42, 97, 119–22
1st Krajina Corps 81, 87–9, 96, 107
Krajišnik, Momčilo 15, 38–40, 42, 48–9, 52, 56, 60, 74, 84, 97, 136, 153–4
Krstić, Radislav 144–5
Krtelji 53
Kukanjac, Milutin 54, 76

Kula 133
Kusmuk, Vlato 110
Kvesić, Brane 71
Kvesić, Branko 16, 53

Lale, Vojin 92
Law on Internal Affairs 22, 29, 36–7, 44, 48–9, 51, 54, 58, 63, 65, 77–9, 114, 129, 136, 142
Leadership Research Team (LRT) 2
League of Communists of Bosnia and Herzegovina (SKBiH) 13
League of Communists of Yugoslavia (SKJ) 11–14
liquidation 100, 107, 131, 144
Lisica, Slavko 104
Ljubljana 14
Log Revolution 29, 32–3, 120
loyalty oaths 63–5, 69, 82, 84–5, 95
Lukajić, Dane 89–90
Lukić, Milan 130–4, 158
Lukić, Mirko 67

Macedonia 11, 14
Mandić, Momčilo 16, 21–3, 43–6, 51–4, 56, 58, 71, 75, 157
Manjača 70, 84, 87–95
Marković, Ante 154
Martens, Wilfred 155
Martić, Milan 21, 28, 30, 32–3, 67, 120–1
Mazowiecki, Tadeusz 139
Mejakić, Željko 158
Miće (group) 103–4
Mijatović, Jovo 3, 34
Milanković, Veljko 42, 97–8
Milići 98–9
milicija 54, 136
Miljković, Slobodan 123–4
Milošević, Slobodan 8, 13–14, 20, 34, 74, 117–20, 123, 125, 132–5, 149
Miloš Group 66, 71, 104
minority returns 151
Mirković, Igor 130
Mladić, Ratko 8, 74, 79, 96, 140–1, 144–5, 149, 154
mobilization 17, 24–6, 32, 41, 57, 83, 127, 152
Montenegro 11, 14, 17, 25, 31, 36, 39, 74, 117, 119, 132

Mostar 24, 59, 71
Mrđa, Darko 108, 158
Mrkonjić Grad 138
Municipal Secretariats of Internal Affairs (OSUP) 36
Muslims
 Bosnian (Bosniak) 3, 6–8, 10–11, 13–15, 17, 21, 23, 25, 27, 35–6, 38, 45, 53, 56, 59–62, 64, 66, 71, 73, 81–2, 84, 98, 138–9, 141, 143–6, 149, 151, 154, 156–7, 159
 Croats and 3, 6–8, 24, 35, 46, 59, 64, 66, 70, 75, 82, 85, 95, 104–5, 109, 123, 137–40, 149
 extremism 126–7, 145
 Green Berets 53

National Protection (NZ) 29
National Security Service (SNB) 52, 66–71, 86–9, 93, 103–4, 108–9, 136, 138
NATO 8, 141–2, 147, 149, 151, 154, 158
NDH. *See* Independent State of Croatia (NDH)
Nikolić, Momir 144
Nikolić, Stevan 124
non-Serbs 41
 disarmament of 81–96
 nationality 56, 64
 population 60, 81–96, 103–4, 109, 113
Novi Grad. *See* Bosanski Novi

Obrenovac group 131
Office of the High Representative (OHR) 154–5, 157
Office of the Prosecutor (OTP) 2, 9, 39, 158
Oluić, Dragan 122
Omarska 82, 86–92, 158
Operational Action (OA) Tomson 125–33
Operation Corridor 75, 79
Orašje 124

Pakrac 32
Pale 47, 52, 54, 62–3, 71, 76, 82, 94, 134, 140–2
Pandurević, Vinko 131–2
Pankov, Radovan 120
Pantić, Aleksandar 110

paramilitaries 1, 3, 5, 7–8, 26, 32, 35, 42, 46, 57–8, 60–2, 65–7, 73–5, 83–5, 96–106, 110, 112, 118, 121–31, 133–4, 136, 140–3
Partisans 100
party armies 126
Party of Democratic Action (SDA) 14–15, 17, 19, 23–5, 34, 38–40, 44, 53, 56, 64, 84, 126
Party of Independent Social Democrats (SNSD) 154
patriotism 98, 130
Pecikoza, Stanko 132
Pelivan, Jure 15
Perišić, Momčilo 59
PJPs. *See* special police units (PJPs)
plausible deniability 8, 65, 74, 97, 117, 121
Plavšić, Biljana 3, 15, 19, 21–2, 42–3, 46, 50, 58, 78, 97–8, 103, 153–4
Plitvice (incident) 31–3
Plitvice Bloody Easter 31
police
 detachment 66, 76–7, 101, 105, 113–14, 144
 and ethnic cleansing 137–41
 fragmentation of 26–33
 participation 106–9
 perpetrators 4–7
 reform 151–7
 special 75–7
police stations (PS) 18, 28–30, 36, 42, 55, 57, 59, 61, 64, 84–5, 87, 99, 101, 111, 145
policija 54, 136
policing
 Croatia war 31–3
 decentralization of 33–42
 in Yugoslavia 11–13
politicization 2, 16, 33
Popović, Božidar 88
Popović, Slobodan 34, 145–6
population
 Muslim 10, 17, 60, 111–12
 non-Serb 3, 60, 81–96, 103–4, 109, 113
 Serb 28, 35, 38, 41, 58, 84, 97, 103–4, 138
professional deformation 5
professionalism 33–4, 49, 53
Public Security Centre (CJB) 136, 142

Public Security Service (SJB) 18, 24, 108–9
  Banja Luka 64, 76–7
  Bijeljina 58, 110
  Bileća 59–61
  Ilidža 57, 76, 105, 142, 159
  Ilijaš 53, 136
  Ključ 84, 88, 95–6
  Kotor Varoš 67, 95
  Milići 98–9
  Novo Sarajevo 76
  Pale 26, 47, 62–3, 103, 114, 142
  Prijedor 21, 80–1, 84–8, 92–3, 95–6, 108, 114, 158
  Šamac 124
  Sanski Most 88, 92–5
  Sokolac 47
  Srebrenica 144
  Stari Grad 46–7, 62
  Teslić 104, 122
  Zvornik 53
Public Security Service – Croatia (SJS) 29
Pušina, Jusuf 53

Radio Ključ 95–6
Radovanović, Srećko 124
Radović, Nenad 44
Radulović, Predrag 66, 104
Rakić, Živko 141
Ranković, Aleksandar 12, 14
Ražnatović, Željko "Arkan" 58, 60, 97–100, 105, 122–3, 133, 158
RDB. *See* Division of State Security (RDB)
red berets 111, 121–2, 131
Red Cross 92–4, 139
red van *(crveni kombi)* 61–2
Republic of Croatia (RH) 28–30, 119, 128–9
Republic of Serbia 31, 102, 119–20, 126–9
Republic of the Serb Nation 42–50
Republika Srpska Krajina (RSK) 29, 31, 67, 78–9, 120, 122, 129, 147, 149
resubordination 80, 110, 142
Riedlmayer, András 137
rulebook *(pravilnik)* 36, 68

Šainović, Nikola 125
Sandžak 17, 19–20, 25, 128–9, 132–3
Sanski Most 64, 88–9, 92–5, 105
SAO Krajina Assembly 31, 119

SAO Romanija 34, 47, 51
Sarić, Goran 92, 142–3, 159
Šarović, Mirko 154
Savić, Krsto 60
Savić, Ljubiša 153
SDA. *See* Party of Democratic Action (SDA)
Second World War 1–3, 5, 7, 11, 13–14, 28–9, 43, 100, 117, 126
Secretariat for Internal Affairs (SUP) 18–20, 28, 30–1, 39, 90, 101, 119
Security Services Centre (CSB) 18, 24, 76, 86
  Banja Luka 21, 24, 41–2, 51, 61, 64, 66–7, 69–70, 76–7, 79–81, 83, 92–5, 107–9, 114, 138
  Bijeljina 58, 102, 110
  Doboj 44, 79, 103–4, 110, 121–2, 144
  Sarajevo 68, 78–9, 94, 105, 110
  Trebinje 60, 105
Šekovići detachment 143
Selimović, Hilmija 19–20
Serb Autonomous Districts (SAOs) 3, 26, 30, 33–43, 60, 111
  Herzegovina 24, 34, 60, 92, 105
  Krajina. *See* Autonomous Region of Krajina (ARK)
Serb Chetnik Movement (SČP) 127–8
Serb Defence Forces (SOS) 65–6, 101, 140
Serb Democratic Party (SDS) 3, 5, 7–8, 14–15, 17–22, 25–8, 33–4, 37–42, 44–9, 51–2, 55–6, 58–62, 64–6, 73–4, 101, 123–4, 141, 154, 156, 159
Serb Democratic Party (SDS BiH) 14
Serb Guard 126–7
Serbian Defence Forces (SOS) 65–6, 101, 140
Serbian municipality 49, 64, 124
Serbian Orthodox Cathedral 138
Serbian State Security Service 66, 117–18, 122–6, 129, 133
Serbian Steering Council 44
Serb Movement of Renewal (SPO) 125–7
Serb National Congress 28
Serb Radical Party (SRS) 118, 123–4, 127–8, 130, 134
Serb Voluntary Guard (SDG) 98, 100, 122–3
servile Serbs 21, 47

Šešelj, Vojislav 105, 118, 134
Šibenik 28
Simatović, Franko 118, 120–1, 123, 125, 133–4
Simić, Blagoje 123
Simović, Miodrag 20
SJB. *See* Public Security Service (SJB)
Škipina, Slobodan 68, 70, 79
SKJ. *See* League of Communists of Yugoslavia (SKJ)
Slovenia 11–12, 14, 23, 38
SNB. *See* National Security Service (SNB)
Socialist Federal Republic of Yugoslavia (SFRJ) 30–2, 126
Socialist Republic of Bosnia and Herzegovina (SRBiH) 14, 16–17, 26, 38, 53
Socialist Republic of Croatia (SRH) 27
Social Self-Protection (DSZ) 40
Sokolac 47, 51, 53, 56, 76
Sokolović, Zoran 122, 125, 127
Special Brigade of the Police (SBP) 75–6, 102–3, 142–3
special police units (PJPs) 142–3
Špegelj, Martin 29
Špirić, Nikola 156
SRBiH Presidency 19, 21, 26, 34, 43, 45, 49, 53, 58, 60
Srebrenica 4, 21, 42, 133, 136–7, 141–7, 149, 151, 159
Sremska Mitrovica 129
SSUP. *See* Federal Secretariat for Internal Affairs (SSUP)
Stabilization and Association Agreement (SAA) 156
staff of police forces 80, 142
Stanišić and Župljanin 54, 107–8, 114
Stanišić, Jovica 118
Stanišić, Mićo 2, 4, 39–40, 43–5, 49, 51–4, 56, 58, 61, 67–8, 71, 76–81, 91, 93–4, 97, 100, 103, 105–9, 111–16, 118, 136, 150, 158
State Investigation and Protection Agency (SIPA) 155
State Security Division Centre (CRDB) 124, 129–33, 136
 Kragujevac 124
 Užice 131–2

State Security Service (SDB) 7–8, 10, 12, 17, 20–2, 33, 43, 47, 66–7, 69, 102, 117–18, 122–7, 129, 133
Stevandić, Nenad 65
Stojić, Bruno 53, 71
Stojičić, Radovan 130
Subotić, Bogdan 57, 82–3, 103, 107
Subotić, Davor 122
Sušić, Boro 16
Syrmia 28, 30, 39, 119

Tadić 87
Territorial Defence (TO) 7, 16, 21, 26, 29, 32, 41, 49, 58, 64, 74, 83, 85, 98, 127, 131
Teslić 103–4, 122
TG-17 123–4
Tigers *(Tigrovi)* 60
Tito, Josip Broz 11–13
Todorović, Stevan 124, 158
Tolimir, Zdravko 101, 106
Tomašica 96
Trbojević, Milan 115
Treanor, Patrick J. 37–8
Trebinje 37, 43–4, 59–60, 94, 105
Trnopolje 82, 86–8, 92–5, 107
Tuđman, Franjo 27, 29, 31
Tutuš, Vladimir 76–7

Unit for Anti-Terrorist Actions (JATD) 121–2, 134
Unit for Special Operations (JSO) 120, 133–4
Unit for Special Purposes (JPN) 76, 121–2
UN Mission in Bosnia and Herzegovina (UNMIBH) 151, 153
Uzelac, Nikola 42, 97

Valjevo 128
Vasić, Dragomir 144–5, 151
Vasiljković, Dragan 100, 121, 125
Vikić, Dragan 53–4
violence 3, 8, 11, 30, 40, 55, 59–62, 73–4, 77–8, 95–6, 100, 117–18, 131, 134, 138, 141, 149
Višegrad 131–2
Vještica, Miroslav 48–9
Vlaški, Neđo 20

Vllasi, Azem 14
Vojvodina 12–14, 74, 117, 120–1
Vraca 53–4, 71, 75
VRS. *See* Army of Republika Srpska (VRS)
Vrućinić, Mirko 88, 92
Vučković, Dušan 101, 130
Vučković, Vojin 101–3
Vujović, Goran 59
Vukić, Radislav 138
Vukotić, Vukota 54
Vukovar 32
    detachment 98–9

war 57–8
    Banja Luka 61–2
    Bijeljina 58–9
    Bileća 59–61
    crimes 1–2, 4, 6, 70, 108–9, 112, 114, 118, 130, 133, 142, 153–4, 157–9
    in Croatia 23–6
    imposed 56
    Pale 62–3
    presidency 60, 86–7, 95, 111, 124
White Eagles (*Beli Orlovi*) 84, 130–2

Yellow Wasps (*Žute ose*) 60, 101–4, 130
Yoghurt Revolution 13–14
Yugoslavia 1, 3, 5
    communism in 13–23
    policing in 11–13
Yugoslavs 1, 3, 5, 10, 17, 61, 84, 98, 138
Yugoslav State Security Service 7, 10, 12, 33, 67, 122, 126

Zagreb 14, 29, 31
Zečević, Goran 19
Zenica 18
Žepa 143–4, 147, 149
Žepinić, Vitomir 16, 19–24, 39, 42, 44, 46–7, 50–3, 97
zero-sum approach 15, 41, 50
Zimmermann, Warren 55
Žugić, Goran 44, 103
Zulfikarpašić, Adil 22
Župljanin, Stojan 19–22, 42–7, 51, 61, 63–7, 76–7, 80, 83, 90–5, 97–8, 101, 104, 107–10, 113–14, 138–9, 158
Zvornik 49, 53, 59, 99–103, 122, 130–1, 136, 143–5, 151

www.ingramcontent.com/pod-product-compliance
Lightning Source LLC
Chambersburg PA
CBHW062143300426
44115CB00012BA/2024